MURDER IN MIAMI

An Analysis of Homicide
Patterns and Trends in
Dade County (Miami) Florida,
1917-1983

William Wilbanks, Ph.D.

Florida International University

UNIVERSITY
PRESS OF
AMERICA

LANHAM • NEW YORK • LONDON

Copyright © 1984 by

University Press of America,™ Inc.

4720 Boston Way
Lanham, MD 20706

3 Henrietta Street
London WC2E 8LU England

Printed in the United States of America

ISBN   (Cloth): 0-8191-4024-4

All University Press of America books are produced on acid-free
paper which exceeds the minimum standards set by the National
Historical Publications and Records Commission.

DEDICATION

This book is dedicated to the two men who have been most involved in Dade County homicides in the past three decades:

Dr. Joseph H. Davis has been the medical examiner in Dade County since 1956. During that time more than 6,000 homicides have been processed by his office.

Sgt. Mike Gonzalez has been in the homicide bureau of the Miami police department since 1955.

(Pictured above from left to right: Dr. Joseph H. Davis, William Wilbanks and Mike Gonzalez.)

ACKNOWLEDGEMENTS

The author would like to acknowledge several persons who made the research possible and facilitated the preparation of the manuscript for publication. Most of these persons worked in the various stages of the Criminal Justice System and allowed the author access to agency records and/or provided valuable help in collecting the basic data.

First, several people in the Dade County Medical Examiner's office aided the research. Dr. Joseph H. Davis encouraged the author in this research effort by allowing access to his files and encouraging his staff to provide assistance. Those who were especially helpful in this office were Norman Kasoff, Dorothy Washburn, Paul McCreary, Elaine Economus and Dorothy Kurtz.

Second, numerous persons facilitated the research in the four police departments where data was collected. Police officials who were especially helpful were Capt. Marshall Frank and Capt. Don Matthews of the Metro Police Department; Lt. Lane Bradford, Lt. Robert Murphy and Sgt. Mike Gonzalez of the Miami Police Department; Sgt. Anthony Angulo at the Hialeah Police Department; and Doug Reed and John Murphy at the Miami Police Department. In addition more than fifty homicide detectives in the four police departments gave willingly of their time to discuss their 1980 cases with the author. In addition Ruthe Howard of the Miami Police Department and Betty Cousins and Gertrude Katz of the Metro Police Department were helpful in providing assistance over a period of several months.

Third, Janet Reno, the Dade County State Attorney, provided assistance by providing space and access to her files so that data could be collected on the reasons for case attrition.

Fourth, Dean Adam Herbert and the School of Public Affairs of Florida International University supported the work of the research assistants through a small grant.

Fifth, several students were involved in the data collection effort. Cheryl Little, research assistant to the author over a period of several months, aided in the search of records at the office of the medical examiner, at two police departments and in the search of court records. She also clipped all Herald articles on 1980 homicides. Ira Vilinsky coded all of the 1980 Herald articles. Robert Blum searched the files in the office of the State Attorney to determine the reasons for case attrition. Eileen Chafetz searched all 269 arrest files in court and recorded data on the 40 who had psychiatric examinations. Nora Sullivan, aided in the search of the medical examiner files and coded all addresses of victims and the location of assaults into census tracts. Others who aided in the search of the medical examiner files were Brigita Parisi, Amy Sullivan and Colleen Sullivan. Linda O'Loughlin also aided in data collection at the police departments.

Finally, the author would like to acknowledge the help of the office of Academic Computer Services at Florida International University for aiding in the data analysis and preparation of the manuscript for publication. Betty Ruth Neilly, Dennis Murphy, Perin Patel, Julio Ibarra and Alice Hennessy provided assistance. The author owes a special debt of gratitude to Alice Hennessy of Academic Computer Services who patiently guided the author through the process of learning how to operate the word processing system utilized in typing the manuscript.

TABLE OF CONTENTS

LIST OF TABLES AND FIGURES

FIGURES

PREFACE

Dade County Florida and its major city, Miami, are synonomous in the minds of the American public with vacationing in the sun and relaxing on the beach or boating on the bay. And yet the city has developed a new reputation in the early 1980's as being the focus of the drug traffic from South America and the Caribbean and as being the crime and murder capitol of the United States.

The reputation of Dade County as a center of crime has been the focus of numerous stories by the local and national media. In 1980 the CBS program "60 Minutes" ran a story on the drug trade in South Florida and its impact on the crime rate. In January of 1981 the ABC program "20/20" aired a segment entitled "The Streets of Miami" in which viewers were told that the city of Miami had the highest homicide rate in the nation. The bad publicity for South Florida climaxed with a cover story in Time, November 23, 1981, entitled "Paradise Lost." This story described South Florida as the most dangerous place in the United States with three of its cities ranking in the ten most crime-ridden cities in the U.S. for 1980 (Miami, no. 1; West Palm Beach, no. 5; and Ft. Lauderdale, no. 8).

The local media also focused on the crime problem in South Florida. The local ABC television station (WPLG, channel 10) ran a series on homicide in South Florida in late 1980 under the title, "Just Another Day in Dodge City." The appellation, "Dodge City," has become increasingly popular with the local media and citizenry. It connotes a town full of gun-toting citizens who take the law into their own hands and settle their disputes with firearms. The extent of the use of this imagery can be seen in that prosecutors in the Dade County State Attorney's office have even used the "nickname" in court. In fact, one case was overturned (Miami Herald, April 29, 1982) when the appellate court ruled that it was improper for the state to remind the jury that people like the defendant were turning Dade County into a "Dodge City." The nickname even seems to have caught on with some criminals. In one incident after a shoot-out on an expressway during rush-hour the two apprehended gunmen were being taken to the police station when one commented to a police officer, "Well, they call this Dodge City, don't they?" (Miami Herald, July 11, 1982).

Cartoonists for local newspapers have depicted Dade Countians as all wearing holsters with handguns in a wild west setting. The "arming of Miami" has become a subject of concern to many citizens and the debate grows as to whether more guns are part of the solution or part of the problem.

The growing crime rate and the national and local media attention to the crime problem have had a strong impact on the citizens of Dade County. Fear to walk (or drive) the streets has greatly increased during 1980-1983 as the murder rate has risen sharply. And yet the average citizen really knows very little about the homicide problem in the area other than the impressions that have been gained from the reporting of selected homicide events by the media. To this point there has not been a concomitant focus on the homicide problem by academics. This lack of attention by researchers/academics has allowed the public to be "informed" by the media on a case by case basis without any overall examination of the aggregate nature of homicides in the county, the variation in risk by age, sex and race; the likelihood of an "average" or "good" citizen (as opposed to drug dealers and/or criminals) becoming a victim; where homicides most often occur (and which areas are safest); the extent to which murderers are arrested; the extent to which those arrested "get off" on the insanity plea; the extent to which those arrested are convicted; etc.

The purpose of this book is to present a scientific examination of homicide in Dade County so that the media, citizens and academics might become better informed about the extent of and nature of homicides and the manner in which the Criminal Justice System has dealt with this crime. Thus the intended audience includes lay citizens of South Florida as well as academics throughout the nation. The lay reader may not be interested in the statistics presented in numerous tables but the inclusion of these tables should not "turn-off" this type of reader since the major point to be made by the presentation of the table(s) will be made in the text and the tables will be confined to Appendix A. Moreover, since the lay reader generally prefers illustrations (references to particular cases) to statistics, the text will include references to the detailed case narratives found in appendix B. The 569 narratives contain considerable detail on the homicide event and are arranged by ethnicity of victim (Anglo, Black and Latin) so that the reader can get a good idea of how homicides vary by ethnicity.

The academic reader will find that the statistics presented are placed in the context of other major works on homicide with reference citations appearing in the text and a full bibliography appearing at the end of the book. Scientific studies of homicide in a particular jurisdiction are not new. This type of approach was pioneered by Marvin Wolfgang (1958) who examined all criminal homicides in Philadelphia from 1948-1952. Following this prototype were studies of homicide in Cleveland (Bensing and Schroeder, 1960; Hirsch, et. al., 1973; Rushforth, et. al., 1977); Houston (Pokorny, 1965; Lundsgaarde, 1977); Chicago (Pokorny, 1965; Voss and Hepburn, 1968; Block, 1977); San Francisco (Roberson, 1976); Philadelphia (Lane, 1979); Atlanta (Munford, et. al., 1975); Detroit (Boudouris, 1974); Allegheny County, PA (Costantino, et. al., 1977); Washington, D.C. (Count-Van Manen, 1977); and Miami (Wilbanks, 1979a). In addition several cities issue departmental homicide reports annually and, though unpublished in the academic sense, these provide figures comparable to those found in the published studies listed above. The most elaborate such report is the "Homicide Analysis" produced each year by the New York City Police Department.

This study will be similar to the academic studies in that patterns of victimization both over time and at one point in time will be presented. This study will differ from those previously listed in six major ways. First, data will be presented on the court disposition of the 569 homicides occurring in 1980 (previous studies have been generally limited to studies of the victim and the homicide event). Thus the cases described for the pivotal year of 1980 include data on the victim, the event, the offender and the disposition. Second, the study will not be simply statistical since case narratives of the 569 homicides in 1980 are provided in Appendix A and serve as illustrations of points made in the text. Third, the 1980 cases are placed in an historical and comparative perspective by looking at 1980 rates for the county from 1917 to 1983 and at rates in other jurisdictions for 1920 to 1980. Special attention is given to the 1925-26 period when Dade County's homicide rate reached an all-time high. Fourth, an analysis of case attrition will focus on why cases are "lost" and the extent to which offenders get off on incompetency proceedings and/or the insanity defense. Fifth an entire chapter will be devoted to testing for possible race and sex bias at four decision points from arrest to sentence. Sixth, some attention will be given to the role of newspapers in the coverage of homicides. An analysis of the extent and type of coverage of 1925-26 and 1980 homicides by the Miami Herald is presented.

The examination of the homicide problem in Dade County begins in Chapter One with a discussion of the definition of and law of homicide. This introductory chapter also details the sources of data that are available to study homicide and the reaction to it by the criminal justice system.

Chapter Two provides an historical background by examining homicide rates in Dade County from 1917 to 1982. Since the 1925-1926 period had a higher rate than that found for the 1980's, attention is given to the nature of homicides in that period compared to those of today. Also the Dade County homicide (and accident and suicide) rate for 1917-1982 is compared to other counties in Florida and to national figures over the same time period.

Chapter Three focuses on a comparison of Dade County homicide rates for 1980 with that of other jurisdictions in the U.S. Chapter Four examines the patterns of victimization in Dade homicides by age, sex and race/ethnicity over time but with particular attention to the 569 homicides occurring in 1980. Chapter Five examines the homicide event and includes data (by age, sex and race/ethnicity of victim) on type of weapon, motive, victim/offender relationship, location of assault, time of occurrence, etc. Chapter Six looks at the identified offenders in the 569 homicides for 1980 with attention given both to the inordinate number of justifiable homicides and to those offenders prosecuted. Offender rates are broken down by age, sex, race, ethnicity, weapon used, etc.

Chapter Seven looks at the role of the police in investigating and clearing homicides and the extent to which their efforts are successful. Chapter Eight examines the role of the prosecution and focuses on the role of plea bargaining and the attrition of cases due to incompetency proceedings, the insanity plea, witness problems, suppression of evidence, etc. Chapter Nine analyzes sentences handed down by Dade County judges for the convictions arising out of the 569 homicides occurring in 1980. Chapter Ten presents data on possible race and sex bias at four decision points (arrest, initial charge, conviction, and sentence) in the handling of the 569 Dade homicides in 1980. Chapter Eleven discusses the coverage of homicide in Dade County by the Miami Herald for two time periods, 1925-1926 and 1980. The discussion in that chapter centers on the role of the Herald in informing the public about the nature of the homicide problem in the county. Chapter Twelve summarizes the "facts" presented in earlier chapters and suggests several explanations for those facts. Appendix A provides the numerous tables alluded to throughout the text. Appendix B presents the 569 case narratives for 1980 and lists them in order of occurrence by ethnicity of victim (e.g., an Anglo victim list, Black victim list and Latin victim list). In addition a brief index lists all homicides of several types (i.e., all riot cases, all cases with female killers, all cases where offender received probation, etc.). Thus the reader who is interested more in reading case narratives than statistics to understand a particular category of homicide can simply read all case narratives of a particular type.

CHAPTER ONE:

DEFINITIONS AND DATA SOURCES

DEFINING HOMICIDE

No study of homicide should begin without a definition of terms. "Homicide" is generally the killing of one human being by another. The other forms of "violent" (as opposed to "natural") death are suicide and accident. The determination as to whether a death is a homicide rather than a suicide, accident or natural death is made by the police and/or the medical examiner according to the law of the respective state. In some cases the medical examiner and the police do not agree. For example, in case 196A two fleeing felons were being chased by the police when they ran over a pedestrian in their automobile. The medical examiner considers (and so reflects on the death certificate) that case to be an accident and yet the police would (and did) charge the driver with felony murder. Likewise, the medical examiner may list a particular case as a suicide and yet the police may decide that it was a homicide after their investigation (even though the death certificate still lists the death as a suicide).

However, in most cases the police and the medical examiner agree as to the type of death (natural, homicide, suicide, accident). A more critical issue is the possible bias in and the political nature of the defining of homicide in the criminal law. A number of scholars (Reiman, 1979; Del Olmo, 1979; Swartz, 1975; Staples, 1974) maintain that the definition of homicide by the legislature reflects a class bias in that the deaths that result from decisions and acts of the rich (e.g., air polution, unnecessary surgery, building of defective automobiles and other defective products; automobile fatalities involving drunk drivers, mine disasters due to failure to maintain safety standards, etc.) are considered to be "accidents" while the type of deaths that result from the actions of the poor (peasant shooting a peasant) are defined as "homicides". Granted that a case can be made for a class bias in the criminal law's definition of homicide (though in this author's view such a case is highly problematic---see Wilbanks, 1980), this study will not explore the various problems involved in attempting to

1

re-define homicide. The study will define homicides as those deaths so classified by the medical examiner of Dade County plus those felony murders defined by the police.

TYPES OF HOMICIDE

There are generally three types of homicide: criminal, justifiable, and excusable. Criminal homicides involve those homicides where the intent (or gross negligence) of the perpetrator is considered to be of a criminal nature. There are several degrees of criminal homicide such as first degree murder, second degree murder, third degree murder, manslaughter, and negligent homicide (Florida Statutes on homicide are discussed in Chapter Five).

Justifiable homicides are intentional killings in which the perpetrator is authorized under law to kill under the circumstances (such as in self-defense). Justifiable homicides may be committed by either police officers or citizens. Excusable homicides are unintentional killings of one human being by another under circumstances that are not viewed as criminal. (Case examples of justifiable and excusable homicides will be given in Chapter Five.)

NATIONAL HOMICIDE DATA SOURCES

There are several sources of data on homicides that might be utilized to study this problem in a particular jurisdiction. There are two national data sets that are available to homicide researchers. First, all deaths in the U.S. are recorded via death certificates by local medical officials and forwarded to state and national vital statistics offices. National figures are published by the National Center on Health Statistics (NCHS) via the Vital Statistics of the United States. Though detailed data on individual jurisdictions are not available in national publications the data tapes utilized to generate aggregate data are available to researchers. Thus one can compare homicides (or any other cause of death) in a particular jurisdiction to all comparable jurisdictions in the country for the variables included on the tape (type of weapon used, sex, race and age of victim).

Though the NCHS data is useful for cross-jurisdictional comparisons (e.g., to compare firearm homicides against women across cities or states), it does not provide enough detail for an in-depth study of one county. This data set has some additional problems. First, it has no data on the characteristics of the offender. Second, though it purports to include homicides that are justifiable as well as criminal, there is some evidence (Sherman and Langworthy, 1979) that it seriously undercounts this type of homicide.

Though homicide data via vital statistics have some severe limitations, this source will be utilized in this study for examining homicide victimization rates for Dade County in the years before (pre-1956) accurate figures are available from the local office of the medical examiner. The Florida office of Vital Statistics in Jacksonville has death certificate data available for Dade County (and other counties) beginning in 1917.

A second source of national homicide data is the Federal Bureau of Investigation (FBI) which collects crimes known to the police from all local police departments. Homicide is the only crime for which detailed information (such as age, sex and race of victim and offender) is available for each criminal incident. Though age, sex and race breakdowns of all homicide events are not published in the Uniform Crime Reports, data tapes are available from the FBI of the Supplemental Homicide Reports (SHR) collected from each police agency. This source has several problems that argue against its use as the primary data base for studying homicide in a particular county such as Dade. First, the tape includes some but not all of the justifiable homicides that occur in a jurisdiction. Since the police are primarily interested in cases in which prosecution of the offender will be pursued, little effort is spent to record homicides that are clearly justifiable. Second, since the data is reported to the FBI on a monthly basis it is likely that the offenders described are only those who were identified shortly after the incident occurred. Many offenders are identified and arrested months after such reports are forwarded to the FBI. Third, the dispositions of homicide cases are not recorded on the SHR forms and the absence of names on the forms precludes researchers from using a listing of offenders to search for dispositions in court files. Fourth, the

SHR forms include no narrative information on the homicide event and thus detailed information surrounding the homicide cannot be obtained.

OFFICE OF MEDICAL EXAMINER

Homicide files and annual counts are not available on a county-wide basis in Dade until 1956 when Dr. Joseph H. Davis was named the chief medical examiner. Upon assuming this post Dr. Davis instituted a record-keeping system that included files on all homicide cases and the compilation of annual aggregate statistics. Thus though victimization rates by age, sex, race, etc. can be computed for Dade from 1956-1983 such is not possible prior to 1956. The files in the office of the Medical Examiner include a great deal of data on the victim, the homicide event and the autopsy performed by the office. Thus these files allow a researcher to glean the following types of information: age, sex, race, ethnicity of victim, time of occurrence of assault and death, date of assault and death, place of birth of victim, address (and thus census tract) of assault and of the victim's residence, police department investigating the case, type of weapon utilized, marital status of victim, occupation of victim, presence and level of drugs (including alcohol) in the body of the victim, the number of wounds, etc. Many of these items are found on the death certificate included in each file while others are found on other forms routinely found in the files. However, a large number of cases have missing data on some of the above variables (e.g., marital status and occupation).

A decision was made by the author to study all 1980 Dade County homicides. Dr. Davis' files were used as the starting point for the collection of data since his office had a listing of all homicides occuring in the county. Thus all homicide cases were taken for 1980 in which both the assault and the death occurred in 1980 (Dr. Davis' counts include all deaths in a given year regardless of the date of the assault) in Dade County. Dr. Davis' counts also include cases in which the death occurred in Dade County though the assault occurred elsewhere (generally in Broward or Monroe Counties). These selection criteria resulted in a listing of 569 homicides for Dade County for 1980. After all relevant data were collected from the office of the Medical Examiner the researcher proceeded to collect data from other sources.

4

POLICE RECORDS

The second point of data collection was the homicide division of the four police agencies (Metro-Dade, Miami, Hialeah, Miami Beach) that investigate homicides occurring in the county. Though there were 26 separate police departments in the county in 1980 only four investigated homicides. Metro provided this service to the smaller police departments in the county. Each of the four homicide units maintained summary listings of all homicides occurring in its jurisdiction. The police records allowed the researcher to determine the results of the police investigation of each of the 569 homicides. In addition to determining if the case was cleared the names (and characteristics) of offenders were recorded for further follow-up in court records. An attempt was also made to develop a brief narrative describing the homicide event. The narrative was developed in part from the narrative found in the files of the medical examiner. However, richer detail was provided by interviews with detectives who worked each case. Though this process required a great deal of time and effort to locate and interview the detectives, it was felt that a more accurate picture could be obtained by talking directly with the police involved in the investigation. These interviews allowed the data collection process to include a determination as to motive and victim/offender relationship.

THE COURT RECORDS

The final stage of data collection involved a search of the court records to determine the final disposition of all persons arrested by the police for homicides occurring in 1980. A search of the court records (including records in Juvenile court for the six offenders referred there) resulted in disposition data as well as the nature of the original charge(s), the type of plea, the final charge, whether incompetency proceedings and/or the insanity plea occurred, and the name of the sentencing judge.

THE MIAMI HERALD

Since detailed data on the nature of homicide victims, events and offenders were not available for the years before 1956 the Miami Herald was utilized to study the pattern of homicides occurring in 1925-1926. Since it was believed that the Herald would describe most of the homicides occurring during these years a search was made by this author and Dr. Paul George, a local historian, of each issue of the Herald for 1925 and 1926. A data collection form was utilized to record the age, sex and race of victim and offender and the circumstances of the homicide (e.g., whether a "domestic", robbery, police killing of felon, etc.). The pattern of homicides occurring in 1925-26 is reported in Chapter Two. The manner in which homicides were covered by the Herald during this period was also examined with the results being reported in Chapter Eleven.

The type of coverage of homicide by the media is a subject of some controversy in that it is often said that the public is informed on a case by case basis by the press and television and that the reporting of cases is selective and emphasizes certain types of homicide. To test this point of view all issues of the Herald were searched for 1980 through 1983 for any mention of a 1980 case. All articles were clipped, arranged in a notebook and then coded to determine which cases received coverage by the Herald and the type of coverage that resulted depending upon the characteristics of the case.

CHAPTER TWO:

THE HISTORICAL PERSPECTIVE

*This chapter is based on a paper co-authored by Dr. Paul George and presented at the annual meeting of the Florida Historical Society, Daytona Beach, Florida, May 7, 1983.

INTRODUCTION

Most Americans believe that violence today is higher than it has ever been and yearn for the "good ol' days" when society was more peaceful and and less violent. However, criminologists and historians (Forbes, 1977; Given, 1977; Silberman, 1978; and Lane, 1979) have pointed out that in many jurisdictions the level of violence was higher in the past than today. In the 1980's newspapers in South Florida continually remind readers that the county is the most violent in the United States and (by presenting only the increasing rates of violence in recent years) that it is experiencing the greatest level of violence in its history. Media attention has focused on the extent to which "paradise" has been lost (meaning that a once pacific vacation paradise has become plagued by crime). The public is left with the impression that the problem of violence has become worse over time.

This chapter will examine the level of violent death in Dade County for a longer time period (66 years, 1917-1983) than commonly covered by the media so that a longer time perspective on the problem is presented. Three forms of violent death (homicide, suicide, and accidents) are examined over time for Dade County since strong correlations have been found (Lane, 1979; Wilbanks, 1982a) among the three. Also, a better understanding of the homicide trend can be obtained by examining comparable trends in suicide and accidents.

The purpose of this chapter is to place the level of homicide experienced in 1980 in historical context. This chapter will also present comparable rates for violent death for selected other counties within Florida and for the United States so that the trends seen for Dade County can be compared to other jurisdictions. This comparative perspective will also shed light on the attempt to explain the changes in the

Dade rates over time since it will be shown that the
peak homicide rates for Dade County occurred at similar
points in surrounding counties. Thus Dade County is
not viewed as having problems unique to the county. In
short, the Dade County trends are really part of South
Florida trends.

Once the peak period of violence is identified, an
attempt will be made to compare homicides occurring in
this period with those of 1980. Finally, some
explanation of the historical trends will be attempted.

TRENDS IN DADE COUNTY, 1917-1983

Table 2.1 (all Tables appear in Appendix A)
presents homicide, suicide and accident rates for Dade
County by race of victim for 1917-1983. The homicide
rate in 1917 (when the population of the county was
only around 35,000) was 19.8 per 100,000 (or in other
terms, one resident in 5,050 was the victim of a
homicide). That rate began to increase in 1922 (to
34.2) but made a dramatic jump in 1925 to 102.6 (from
the 34.6 of 1924). The peak rate of 110.1 was reached
in 1926 (i.e., one resident in 908 was a homicide
victim) but then dropped sharply by 50% the next year
(to 55.1) and continued to decline through the 1930's,
1940's and 1950's and early 1960's. The lowest rate of
9.2 was reached in 1963 and 1964. The rate began to
increase slightly in the 1970's to 22.7 for 1979.
However, the rate increased sharply in 1980 to 35.0 but
then dropped to 30.2 by 1982 and to 24.2 by 1983. Thus
1980 experienced the highest Dade County homicide rate
since the 35.2 for 1930. And yet the 1926 rate of
110.1 was 3.1 times the 1980 rate of 35.0.

The historical trends for the Dade population as a
whole are mirrored when the rates for white and black
victims are considered separately (also presented in
Table 2.1). The white rate peaked in 1925 at 38.9 and
declined to a low of 3.0 in 1945. The white rate began
to rise again in the late 1960's and experienced a
sharp increase (from 15.9 in 1979) to 24.2 in 1980.
However, the white rate in 1981 and 1982 was even
higher than in 1980.

The sharp rise in white victimization rates
beginning in 1980 can be largely accounted for by the
sharp increases in the victimization of Hispanics and
in the increasing proportion of Hispanics in the

8

population of the county. This author (Wilbanks, 1978) in a prior study of Dade County homicide found that the Hispanic victimization rate in 1974 was actually lower than the Anglo rate (9.0 to 10.7) but by 1980 the Hispanic rate was twice that of Anglos (35.8 to 17.7). In terms of percentage increase the victimization rate for Anglos increased by 65% from 1974 to 1980 while the corresponding increase for Hispanics was over 300% (the increase in the Black rate was "only" 16%) during the period 1974-1980.

The black victimization rate peaked in 1926 (to 392.4---thus one black resident in 254 was a homicide victim in 1926) and declined to a low of 30.3 in 1955. A gradual increase occurred in the 1970's with a dramatic rise from 58.8 (in 1979) to 98.0 in 1980. By 1982 the Black rate had dropped to 76.1. It is interesting to note that the Black to White rate ratio remained fairly stable over the 65 year period from 1917 to 1982. In 1926 the Black rate was 3.6 times the White rate and in 1980 the Black rate was 4.0 times the White rate. In short, it appears that the white and black rates rose and fell in a similar manner over time. This impression is confirmed by a the computation of a correlation coefficient (Pearson R) of $r = +.69$ between the homicide rates for blacks and whites over the 65 year period. Thus the same factors that were affecting (or causing) the white rate were also affecting the black rate.

THE SUICIDE RATE FROM 1917 - 1983

Table 2.1 also presents data on the trends in the suicide rate for the Dade County population as a whole and for white and black victims. The suicide rate is more stable over time though it also reaches a peak (37.0) in the mid-1920's (in 1927). The suicide rate remained high throughout the 1930's but then declined to a low of 11.6 in 1947 and 1950. The suicide rate then increased gradually until a peak of 22.7 in 1977 (a rate below that of the 37.0 figure for 1927). Thus the peak suicide period was also in the mid-1920's.

The breakdown in suicide rate by race of victim indicates that blacks have always had lower suicide rates than whites with the peak white rate of 45.2 in 1927 being 5.7 times the black rate of that year. Rates for both races have experienced slight increases in recent years. Many scholars (e.g., Henry and Short,

9

1954; Lester and Lester, 1975) have noted the tendency
of Blacks to have high homicide and low suicide rates
while Whites have high suicide and low homicide rates.
However, little literature is found on the correlation
of Black and White suicide rates over time. In Dade
County from 1917 to 1983 there was an r= +.27 for Black
and White suicide rates over this 65 year period. Thus
it would appear that the same factors affected the
suicide rates of the two races.

ACCIDENT RATES FROM 1917 - 1983

    The accident (all types including vehicular) rate
in Dade County, like that for homicides and suicides,
also peaked in the mid-1920's. Table 2.1 indicates
that the accident rate peaked in 1926 to 324.6 (partly
as a result of the great hurricane that took 162 lives
in the county in September of that year) and declined
thereafter. The rate of 39.7 in 1983 represents the
last low point in a continually declining accident
rate.

    The black accident rate is generally greater than
the white rate for corresponding years though the ratio
between the two remains fairly stable over time. In
fact, the correlation between the Black and White
accident rates over the 65 year period was +.89. The
White rate peaked at 313.6 in 1926 and reached rates in
the range of 30's and 40's in recent years. The black
rate peaked at 362.9 in 1926 to lows in the 40's to
70's in recent years.

DADE TRENDS COMPARED TO OTHER JURISDICTIONS

    Table 2.2 presents homicide rates in Dade County
from 1920 to 1980 compared to selected other Florida
counties, Florida and the U.S. First, it is obvious
that the Dade County homicide peak in the 1925-1926
period is matched by the other South Floria counties
(and to a lesser extent by other non-South Florida
counties). Broward County had a homicide peak of 123.2
in 1926 (greater than the 110.1 in Dade); Monroe a peak
of 35.4 in 1926 and Palm Beach a peak of 109.8) in
1926. In each case the decrease from 1926 to 1927 was
dramatic (e.g., a decline of 50% in Dade; 52% in
Broward; 80% in Monroe and 47% in Palm Beach) as was
the dramatic rise from 1924 to 1925 (e.g., increases of
197% in Dade; 719% in Broward; 23% in Palm Beach;---the

10

Monroe rate increased from 0.0 to 7.0). In short, each of these four counties (and to a lesser extent other non-South Florida counties) experienced inordinately high rates of homicide only in 1925-1926. It is interesting to note that the rate for the United States as a whole was quite stable over this time period (around 8.3).

Table 2.3 presents accident rates in Dade County from 1920 to 1980 compared to selected other Florida counties, Florida and the U.S. Again, the peak accident rate for Dade and the other South Florida counties is the year 1926. Dade's peak accident rate was 324.6; Broward's 661.3; Palm Beach's 282.7; and Monroe's 141.5. Also again the rates for these four counties rise dramatically from 1924 to 1925 (up 99% in Dade, up 110% in Broward, up 130% in Palm Beach, and up 152% in Monroe) and declined dramatically from 1926 to 1927 (down 61% in Dade, down 81% in Broward, down 55% in Palm Beach, and down 34% in Monroe). Thus the four South Florida counties experienced inordinately high accident rates only in 1925-26 (as was the case for homicide rates).

Lane (1979) found in a study of violent death in Philadelphia from 1839 to 1901 that there was a positive correlation between the accident and homicide rates over this 63 year period (i.e., both rates declined). He argues that both accidents and homicides are manifestations of violence since both are defined as physically reckless or destructive behavior. Lane also argues that suicides are negatively related to accident and homicide rates over time. In Philadelphia over the 62 year period studied homicide and accident rates decreased while the suicide rate increased. In Dade County over the 65 year period studied there was a positive correlation between homicide and suicide (r= +.52); a positive correlation between homicide and accidents (r= +.86); and a positive correlation between suicide and accidents (r= + .30). Thus in Dade County all three forms of violent death were positively related to each other. This result does not fit well with the view of Lane (in explaining the pattern found in Philadelphia) who hypothesized that declining homicide and accident rates accompanied by increasing suicide rates were an indication of the fact that people were becoming "more careful, more sober, perhaps more rational in their everyday habits and activities." Lane further asserts that the decline in homicide and accident rates and the increase in suicide rates was a

11

"product of the discipline demanded by the industrial revolution and taught in the classrooms, on the railroads, and in the factories and offices of the nineteenth century America." However, this view is not confirmed by the trends evident in Dade County since there is a positive correlation among the three rates of violent death.

Thus in Dade County over a 65 year period all forms of violent death tend to rise and fall together. Evidently whatever factors influence the rate of one form of violent death seem to also affect the other two to some extent.

HISTORICAL BACKGROUND FOR DADE COUNTY, 1925-26

Since the peak period for Dade County homicides and accidents was 1925-26 some background data on that period will be given. These years marked the apex of the great Florida land and construction boom and the beginning of the bust, a watershed in the history of Miami and Dade County. As the area of greatest speculative activity, Dade underwent, within a short period, a wrenching, often violent transformation. Its population, which included a huge transient element drawn by the prospect of amassing instant fortunes in the wildly speculative real estate market, soared in 1925 and 1926.

Other growth figures for 1925 were equally striking. Land that sold on Flagler Street, the city's major artery, for $30 an acre in 1910 now went for $75,000 an acre (Tindall, 1965). The financial ledger of Coral Gables, Miami's "master suburb," revealed $94 million in property sales for 1925 while the new development of Miami Shores showed sales of $75 for the same period (Tindall, 1965). The success of these enterprises inspired the creation of 971 other developments the same year (Miami Herald, July 26, 1942:1). Work commenced on nearly 500 hotels and apartments (Kofoed, 1960). On a single day in June, 1925, $2 million in building permits were issued (Miami Herald, June 30, 1925:2).

Municipal governments, in attempting to cope with this growth, were pushed to their limits. The city of Miami's payroll increased by 2,500 percent from 1921 to 1925 (Tebeau, 1971:384). Every department exhibited growing pains similar to those of the Miami Police

Department whose ranks increased from 40 in 1921 to more than 350 in 1925 ("Miami's Police..., 1927:18). The homicide squad of the Miami Police Department was not formed until July of 1926 (Miami Herald, July 18, 1926:2) even though the homicide rate for the previous 18 months was greater than that of today. The city also requested a second criminal court judge in August of 1926 since the single judge at that point in time disposed of over 800 criminal cases in February-March of 1926 (Miami Herald, August 2, 1926:2). Also, there was a 6,000 case backlog in civil court that resulted in a three year delay in the processing of cases (Miami Herald, October 22, 1926).

The city had the highest per capita ownership of automobiles in the U.S. as 105,000 automobiles were on county streets in February of 1926 (Miami Herald, February 4, 1926:2). The newly created street system was totally inadequate. The streets were under construction for the new trolley car tracks and the installation of gas and water lines (George, 1975:246ff). Not surprisingly, traffic accidents, including many fatalaties were plentiful.

Adding to the color---and lawlessness---of the area was the failure of prohibition for nowhere did the "Noble Experiment" fail more spectacularly than in Miami and south Florida (George, 1975:269ff). Miami's proximity to the liquor supplying Bahama Islands, a lengthy coastline whose coves and inlets delighted liquor smugglers, a large transit population which demanded (and received) alcoholic beverages, thriving moonshine activity in the county's outlying sectors and public opposition to prohibition made the area a haven for bootleg liquor and contributed signifiantly to its crime problem.

The boom was over by 1926, as land buyers were no longer plentiful and paper profits were lost when people began to default on their payments. By the middle of the year, tens of thousands of speculators had left the area.

Dade's problem grew more acute when a hurricane with winds of 135 miles per hour smashed the coast on September 17, 1926. More than 162 persons lost their lives in Dade County (plus 58 in Broward) and thousands of homes were destroyed (Miami Herald, Sept. 20, 1926:1). Many unfinished subdivisions were leveled. Land that sold for $60,000 in 1925 could be purchased for $600 in late 1926. The heady days of the boom were now but a distant memory as the area slipped into a severe economic depression three years before the rest of the nation.

EXPLANATIONS FOR 1925-26 PEAK

Any explanation for the inordinate level of violence in 1925-26 must take into account four facts. First, the same sharp rise in 1925 and decline in 1927 characterized all South Florida counties. Second, the increase in Dade homicides in 1925-26 was not significantly different for subgroups of the population or for certain types of homicide (with the exception of police homicides which are discussed in Chapter Seven). The analysis of the homicides reported in the Herald (see Tables 4.4 and 4.5) indicated that victimization was inordinately high for males and females and blacks and whites. Likewise stranger as well as acquaintance homicides were high. In short, homicides of every type were at least three to four times greater in terms of rate than in 1980 and thus the inordinate level of homicides was "across the board". This fact is important in that one cannot simply say that the rise was due to males (or females), Blacks (or whites), or robberies. All types of homicide were high.

Third, the equally high levels of accidents in 1925 and 1926 require an explanation that accounts for high accident as well as high homicide rates. The large number of deaths in the hurricane do partly explain the high accident level in 1926 but do not explain the high rate of 1925 (in all South Florida counties). Fourth, the high level of homicides did not diminish after large numbers of transients left the county in the middle of 1926. In fact, the number of homicides for the last six months was higher than it had been in the first six months of the year (or for either half of 1925). Furthermore, the "abnormal" level of homicides in 1925-26 was greater for Blacks than Whites though the latter were more likely to be transients.

It would appear that there was a (temporary) culture that promoted violence in Dade and (to a lesser extent) other South Florida counties in 1925-26. This culture was fueled by the stress created by the boom and the bust and by large numbers of transients who had no permanent roots in the community. The temporary

14

violent culture may have consisted of a broadening of the rationalizations to kill ("its wrong to kill but in these circumstances its OK"). In short not only was stress higher but the restraints (beliefs that killing is wrong) against killing had also been weakened. Granted this explanation is speculative it is not without precedent. Archer and Gartner (1976) found that homicides went up in countries that had experienced a war (and especially for those countries that won the war) and suggested that this phenomena was most likely due to war propaganda that reduced the restraints (i.e., broadened the rationalizations that it is OK to kill) to violence. They also pointed out that homicides in countries after a war are "across the board" and not the result of violent veterans returning home. It may be that Dade County underwent the equivalent of a domestic war with the boom, the bust, the hurricane and the prohibition "war" all making contributions. And just as after most wars this culture of broadened rationalizations evaporated over time.

Unfortunately the evidence for this temporary violent culture is tautological. We are attempting to explain high rates of violence and thus we infer a state of mind (greater willingness to kill) to explain that violence. But the only evidence we have of the state of mind is the rate of violence that we are trying to explain. Thus the explanation is circular (tautological) as there is no independent (of the high rates of violence) evidence of the state of mind that is inferred. And yet this explanation does appear to fit the facts already enumerated. Since no other obvious explanation is at hand we will have to live with the flawed (and circular) one.

CHAPTER THREE:

THE COMPARATIVE PERSPECTIVE

INTRODUCTION

Chapter Two has already compared Dade County's homicide rate to Florida and selected counties in Florida from 1920 to 1980. The 1980 Dade County rate of 35.0 was found to be approximately twice that of the state (15.6) and the county (Broward) with the second highest rate (17.7). Though the magnitude of Dade's rate has generally been higher than that for other urban counties in Florida over time, there is similarity in the trend in that the rate for all urban counties peaked in 1925-26 and then declined until the late 1960's. However, the sharp rise from 1979 to 1980 was not experienced by the other urban counties.

This chapter will look beyond Florida to examine Dade County's rate in the context of all urban areas in the United States for the 20 year period from 1960 to 1980. The claim that Miami is (or has always been) the urban area with the highest murder rate (the "Murder Capitol of the U.S.") in the U.S. will thus be examined.

THE CITY OF MIAMI RATE

A good deal of national media attention has been given to Dade's murder and crime problems in 1980 with many stories calling Miami the murder capitol of the U.S. The 1980 Uniform Crime Report from the FBI provides murder and non-negligent homicide rates for all major American cities but does not rank the cities. The FBI cautions that police statistics do not necessarily reflect the level of real (reported plus unreported) crime since any ranking would assume that reporting levels are stable across jurisdictions. Reporting levels vary tremendously across jurisdictions as indicated by victimization surveys (e.g., in one city one crime was reported for every 5.4 that occurred while in another one was reported for every 1.4 that occurred---see Glaser, 1978). However, one can argue that reporting levels for homicide are fairly stable since comparable (see Hindelang, 1974) figures for various jurisdictions have been found by the FBI (in the UCR) and the N.C.H.S. (in Vital Statistics of the

U.S.). Thus a ranking of murder rates from figures provided by the UCR is not as problematic as a ranking of jurisdictions on other crimes.

The rates in the 1980 UCR do indicate that the city of Miami had the highest murder rate in the U.S. in 1980 (see Table 3.1). The rate for Miami was 65.5 per 100,000 compared to a rate of 49.9 for St. Louis, the second ranking city. The cities with the next highest rates were Newark (49.4), Atlanta (47.6), Cleveland (46.3), Detroit (45.7), New Orleans (39.1), Houston (39.1), Dallas (35.1) and Los Angeles (34.1).

However, the calculation of the rates and the subsequent ranking of rates are problematic for several reasons. First, the population base upon which the rates are based is the permanent population of the city though non-permanent resident victims are counted in the calculation. The city victim count for 1980 was inflated by at least 43 victims (25 Cuban refugees, 3 Haitian refugees, 4 Columbians and 11 "other aliens") who were not permanent residents of the city. And the figure of 43 is a very conservative estimate since it is difficult to tell in many cases which victims were really permanent residents (but even a reduction of 43 victims from the 220 reported to the FBI would reduce the city rate to 52.7).

This problem is even more pronounced when rates for a particular city within a metropolitan area are calculated. If a resident of the suburbs/county is killed in Miami that murder "counts" as a city of Miami murder since the city of Miami police handled the case. However, the population pool (the suburbs/county) from which that victim was drawn does not count in the computation of the rate for the city of Miami. Thus cities with great numbers of metro (but non-city) residents who travel and work within the city (and thus subject themselves to victimization within the city) will appear more "dangerous" (as reflected in murder rates) than cities which have relatively less mobility from suburbs to central city. Several county residents were among the city homicide victims (e.g., some of the riot victims). Furthermore, as many as 75,000 of the Mariel Refugees who arrived in South Florida in 1980 may have settled in the city though they were not counted in the population base upon which the city murder rate was calculated (e.g., the census was completed shortly before their arrival).

If the murder rate for the city of Miami is
calculated after removal of all of the non-resident
victims (surburbanites, aliens, tourists, etc.) the
rate would likely be less than that of some other U.S.
cities. Unfortunately data on residence of victim is
not available to compute such a true "Miami" (permanent
residents only) homicide victimization rate. And even
if such a calculation indicated a rate below that of
some other U.S. cities one could not assume that
Miami's homicide rate is lower than those cities
without making comparable calculations (removal of
non-residents) in the other cities. In short, the
ranking of the rates from the UCR does not necessarily
mean that the city of Miami is the "murder capitol of
the U.S." There are problems in the calculations of the
rates which make it impossible to compare rates across
cities. It is safe to say, however, that the city of
Miami has one of the highest murder rates in the U.S.

THE DADE COUNTY RATE

Murder rates available in the 1980 UCR are listed
for each of 259 Standard Metropolitan Statistical Areas
(SMSA's) in the U.S. The SMSA with the highest rate is
Dade County (see Table 3.2) with a rate of 32.7.
However, since the total number of murders and the
population are given for Miami and Dade minus Miami one
can easily calculate rates for both. The Dade County
rate of 32.7 is a weighted mean of two rates, the 65.5
for the city of Miami and the 23.8 for Dade minus Miami
(thus the city rate is almost three times that of the
County minus the city rate). (Chapter Five presents
rates for Metro, Miami, Miami Beach, and Hialeah as
well as for the 237 census tracts within the
county---these figures illustrate the great variation
in rates within the county.)

Though again it appears that Dade County was the
murder capitol of the U.S. in 1980, the same criticisms
that applied to the city rate are applicable for the
SMSA ranking. For example a conservative total of 138
victims in the county (24% of the total) were
non-residents (42 were Mariel refugees; 30 were
Columbians; 3 were Haitian; 30 were "other aliens"; 26
were from outside of Dade County and 19 had unknown
residence status). The Dade County rate minus the 138
non-resident victims would compute to a rate of 26.5
(rather than the 35.0 listed by the FBI). Granted
other counties also have non-residents, it is unlikely

that many have more than 24%. One criminologist (Glaser, 1978:66) found that for 1973 Miami had the highest violent crime index of 26 cities according to the UCR but had the lowest victimization rate for personal crimes for the same 26 cities when victimization surveys were utilized. The fact that Miami was either the most dangerous or least dangerous city of the 26 (depending upon whether the UCR or victim surveys were considered) is largely a function of victim surveys counting (e.g., interviewing) only permanent residents. This disparity in rankings for Dade should point out the importance of the problem of whether or not non-resident victims should be counted.

The top five SMSA's according to rates found in the 1980 UCR were Miami-Dade (32.7), Houston (27.6), Las Vegas (23.4), Los Angeles (23.3) and New Orleans (22.3). It is interesting to note that four of the five top SMSA's are also heaving impacted by tourism and large numbers of non-residents in the area.

DADE RATE COMPARED OVER TIME

If one takes the murder rates in the UCR at face value then Dade County did have the highest rate in the U.S. in 1980. However, the distinction of having the highest murder rate has not always characterized Dade County. An examination of several jurisdictions (see Table 3.3) indicates that Dade County has not even been the murder capitol of Florida every year. In 1960 both the Ft. Lauderdale (16.2) and Jacksonville (11.2) SMSA's ranked ahead of Miami-Dade (9.6). In fact, the highest rate (of those selected for inclusion in Table 3.3) was "achieved" by different cities in different years. In 1960, 1965, 1975 Birmingham was the leader while Atlanta led in 1970, Detroit in 1976, Mobile in 1977 and Houston in 1978 and 1979. The 1981 UCR did indicate that Dade County had the highest murder rate of any SMSA in the U.S. However, the 1982 UCR indicated that the Odessa, TX SMSA had edged Dade County as the murder capitol (rate of 29.8 to 29.7 for Dade) of the U.S.

Also much has been made of the tremendous increase (up approximately 60%) in Dade's murder rate from 1979 to 1980. However, if one examines increases (see Table 3.3) for selected cities over time it is evident that the increase for Dade is far below that of other cities for the past twenty years. While the Dade rate did

20

increase by 241% from 1960 to 1980 the increases were greater in Los Angeles (up 430%) and New York City (up 425%). However, over the ten year period from 1970 to 1980 Miami-Dade did have the greatest percentage increase (up 54%---see Table 3.3) of the SMSA's examined.

It also appears that the gap between Southern and non-Southern SMSA's is narrowing. Numerous scholars have commented upon and tried to explain the disparity between Southern and non-Southern homicide rates (see Jacobson, 1975) but it appears that the need for such an explanation is vanishing since the gap is rapidly closing. Over the twenty years from 1960 to 1980 (see Table 3.3) the Southern SMSA's experienced relatively small increases (e.g., Nashville, up 17%) or decreases (Birmingham, down 6%) while non-Southern cities experienced tremendous increases (e.g., New York City, up 425% and Los Angeles, up 430%). While the top murder SMSA's were all Southern in 1960, the top SMSA's in 1980 represented more a cross-section of U.S. urban areas. One example of the "merging" trend for Southern and non-Southern murder rates is the comparison over the period 1960 to 1980 for Ft. Lauderdale and New York City. In 1960 the murder rate in Ft. Lauderdale was four times (16.2/4.0) that of NYC while by 1980 the rate in NYC was 21% greater (21.0 to 17.4) than that of Ft. Lauderdale.

CHAPTER FOUR:

PATTERNS OF VICTIMIZATION

Homicide victimization is not a random event. Some persons by virtue of their age, sex, race and lifestyle are more likely, in a statistical sense, to be killed than are others. The media generally reports the number of murders occurring in a given year in the county (sometimes with the murder rate per 100,000) without indicating to the reader/listener/viewer the wide variation in risk of victimization that exists within that overall rate for the county. This chapter will examine the variation in victimization by age, sex and race/ethnicity.

AGE VARIATION

The risk of homicide victimization varies sharply by age of victim. While the overall rate of victimization in Dade County for 1980 was 35.0 per 100,000, that figure ranged from a rate of 3.4 for county residents under 15 to a rate of 68.6 for residents 25-44 years old (see Table 4.1). Thus in simpler terms a resident 25-44 was 20 times as likely to be killed as a resident under 15 (68.6/3.4=20). Or in other terms a resident under 15 had odds of 1:29,411 (100,000/3.4) of being a victim in 1980 while a resident 25-44 had odds of 1:1,458 (100,000/68.6).

It also appears (see Table 4.2) that as the overall homicide rate in Dade County increases over time, the risk of all age groups increases. When the age group victimization rates are calculated for Dade County from the 20-year period from 1959-61 to 1980 it appears that while the overall (all ages) rate increased from 11.1 to 35.0 (up 215%), the increase in rates for the individual age categories was similar. For example, the increases for the individual age groups was up 113% for those under 15 (1.6 to 3.4); up 283% for those 15-24 (15.7 to 60.1); up 221% for those 25-44 (21.4 to 68.6); up 195% for those 45-64 (11.1 to 32.7); and up 361% for those 65 and over (2.8 to 12.9). Thus no age group was immune from the increasing trend in homicide victimization. It is interesting to note that the group with the greatest percentage increase (up 361%) was the elderly. This alarming increase in victimization of the elderly has also been found in

23

other cities (e.g., in Cleveland---see Rushforth, et.
al., 1977) though there does not appear to be a
national trend for the rate for the elderly to rise
faster than that for other age groups (Klebba, 1975).
Homicide victimization of the elderly has increased by
100% nationwide for the period of 1960 to 1975 though
that increase has been more than offset by decreases in
suicide and accident rates (Wilbanks, 1981-82).

SEX VARIATION

Homicide victimization also varies by sex. While
the overall rate of victimization in 1980 was 35.0 the
rate for males was 61.1 compared to 11.7 for females
(see Table 4.1). Thus males were five times
(61.1/11.7=5) as likely to be killed as were females.
This range of variation for sex (5:1) is thus less than
the range of variation for age groups (20:1 for those
under 15 compared to those 65 & over). The male rate
increased much more rapidly over the 20 year period
from 1959-61 to 1980 than did the female rate (see
Table 4.2). The male victimization rate increased by
280% (from 16.1 to 61.1) while the female rate
increased by "only" 86% (from 6.3 to 11.7). This
result is consistent with the national pattern of a
more rapid increase over time in male versus female
victimization (Wilbanks, 1982b, 1983a). This result
would seem to lend some evidence to the "dynamic law of
sex and homicide" formulated by Veli Verkko (Verkko,
1967) which stated that the female rate would remain
stable over time in a jurisdiction since she lives "in
a somewhat different and more peaceful atmosphere than
the man, and that the factors influencing her, also,
are not nearly so subject to changes as those affecting
a man." However, there is little evidence to support
the dynamic law as a recent review (Wilbanks, 1981b)
indicates. It should also be noted that Table 4.2 also
found a dramatic increase over the 20 year period in
homicide victimization for white women (up 194%) but
only a slight increase for black women (up 11%).
Surely one could not argue that black women are more
protected from the "causes" of homicide victimization
than are white women.

RACE VARIATION

The risk of homicide also varies sharply by race.
While the overall victimization rate for Dade County in

1980 was 35.0, the white rate was 25.8 compared to 79.2
for blacks. Thus black residents of the county were
three times (79.2/25.8=3) as likely to be killed as
were white residents. Thus the variation in
victimization for white versus black is less than the
variation for male versus female and elderly versus
young. In short, age is a better predictor of
victimization than sex and sex is a better predictor
than race.

Over the 20 year period from 1959-61 to 1980 the
victimization rate for whites has increased much more
rapidly than that for blacks. White victimization (see
Table 4.2) is up 416% (5.0 to 25.8) over that period
while black victimization is up "only" 69%. Thus while
the risk for blacks is still greater than that for
whites, the gap is narrowing (e.g., the rate ratio in
1959-61 was 9.4:1 but only 3.1:1 in 1980). This
narrowing of the black versus white victimization gap
can also be seen over the longer time span of 1917 to
1982 (see Table 2.1). At several points in the history
of Dade County that gap was much greater than that seen
in the 1980's (e.g., the gap--rate ratio--was 13:1 in
1926 and 25:1 in 1945).

ETHNICITY VARIATION

Dade County is a tri-ethnic community comprised of
Hispanics, Anglos, and Blacks. The 1980 census found
that 48% of the county population was non-Hispanic
white (or "Anglo"), 36% was Hispanic and 17% was black.
In mid-1980 the arrival of approximately 100,000 Cuban
refugees from the Mariel boatlift changed the ethnic
structure of the community to 44% Anglo and 39%
Hispanic. There is considerable variation in homicide
victimization rates by ethnicity of victim. Hispanics
have a rate approximately twice that of Anglos (36.1 to
17.9).

This higher rate for Hispanics (than Anglos) is a
new phenomena. In a prior study this author (Wilbanks,
1979a) found that in 1974 the Hispanic rate was
actually lower than the Anglo rate (9.0 to 10.7). Over
the seven year period from 1974 to 1980 the Hispanic
victimization rate increased by over 300% compared to
"only" 65% for Anglos. Thus it appears that the
dramatic rise in recent years in victimization of
whites is largely due to the increasing rate for
Hispanic whites and their growing proportion of the

25

white population.

Another factor that must be considered in the rapid increase in the Hispanic victimization rate is the changing nature of the Hispanic population. The Latin population in the early 1970's was largely the Cuban middle-class. However, during the 1970's large numbers of Hispanics from other Latin-American countries began to arrive in South Florida. Thus Dade County now has an Hispanic population that is comprised of large numbers from Columbia (30 homicide victims in 1980 were Columbians), Nicaragua, Venezuela, etc.

A great deal of attention has been given in the media to the involvement in homicide (as victims and offenders) of the Cuban Mariel refugees who arrived in April and May of 1980. Approximately 100,000 arrived during that period. At least 42 homicide victims (this number is debatable and probably conservative since the identity of "Marielitos" is difficult) in 1980 were from the Mariel boatlift. Since the refugees were only in Dade County half of 1980 their victimization rate would be approximately 84 per 100,000, a rate approximately equal to that for blacks in the county. And if one controlled for the disproportionate number of males and young adults (two groups with high homicide rates) in the boatlift population, the Mariel victimization rate would be below that of blacks in Dade County. Though the Herald has contributed to the media protrayal of the Mariel refugees as being disproportionately involved in crime, that newspaper did point out in an investigative piece (April 23, 1982) that the Mariels were not as criminal as the public perceived. Calculations by this author also indicate that the Mariel victims were responsible for only 25% of the 60% increase in homicide victimization from 1979 to 1980. In other words, even if the boatlift had not occurred the homicide rate for the county would have risen 45% from 1979 to 1980.

AGE, SEX, RACE/ETHNICITY VARIATION

Since age, sex and race/ethnicity when taken alone are all good predictors of homicide victimization, it should not be surprising that these factors when combined provide even greater predictive ability. This chapter has already pointed out the wide range in victimization rates by age (20:1 for those 25-44 to those 65 & up); sex (5:1 for males to females); and

26

race (3:1 for blacks to whites). If these three predictors are combined a far greater range in rates occurs. The lowest victimization rate (see Table 4.1) is the 0.9 for white females who are under 15 years old. The highest victimization rate was the 343.6 for black males, 25-44. Thus when age, sex and race are combined as predictors the range of variation in rates is on the order of 382:1 (343.6/0.9) in that black males 25-44 were 382 times more likely to be homicide victims in 1980 than were white females under 15. This fact makes the Dade County (overall) rate of 35.0 rather meaningless since the variation across age, sex, and race subgroups is so great.

It also appears that the overall increase (up 215%) in Dade County's homicide rate from 1959-61 to 1980 varies sharply by subgroups based on age, sex and race. The increase over this time period (see Tables 4.1 and 4.2) was much greater for white males (up 612%); white males 25-44 (up 678%); white males 65 & up (up 1,307%); white females 15-24 (up 534%); and non-white males under 15 (up 327%). On the other hand there was actually a decrease over this 20 year period for white females under 15 (down 10%); and non-white females under 15 (down 49%), 25-44 (down 12%), 45-64 (down 24%) and 65 & up (down 25%). Thus the alarming increase in Dade homicide victimization from 1959-61 to 1980 was not across the board. The probability of being killed of some subgroups (by age, sex and race) has actually declined while that for other subgroups has gone up as much as 1,300%.

The breakdowns in victimization rates by age, sex and race also helps explain some of the variation in rates based on only one of these factors. For example, whereas (see Table 4.2) it appears that female victimization has increased by 86% from 1959-61 to 1980, that figure is largely due to the increase in white female victimization (up 139%) and, more particularly, to the tremendous increase in 15-24 white female victimization (up 534%). Likewise, the large increase (up 361%) in victimization of those 65 & up is seen to be largely due to the tremendous increase in victimization rates for 65 & up white males (up 1,307%).

27

CHAPTER FIVE:

CHARACTERISTICS OF THE HOMICIDE EVENT

The previous chapter looked at variation in risk of homicide victimization by age, sex and race/ethnicity of victim. This chapter will examine several aspects of the homicide event by subgroups based on age, sex and race/ethnicity. This examination will largely be limited to the 569 cases occurring in 1980 amd will focus on the type of legal category of each homicide (whether criminal, justifiable, or excusable); the type of weapon used; the motive/circumstance; the victim/offender relationship; the degree of victim participation/precipitation; the level of alcohol in the victim's blood; the type of place of occurrence; the census tract of the victim's residence and the census tract of the location of the assault; and the time of day, day of week and month of the assault. Each of these characteristics will be examined for variation by subgroups based on age, sex and race/ethnicity of victim.

TYPE OF LEGAL CATEGORY

The 569 homicides in 1980 can be divided into four legal categories (see Table 5.1): 81.2% (N=462) were criminal; 15.1% (N=86) were justifiable; 0.9% (N=5) were excusable; and 2.9% (N=16) were cases of felony murder (a special category of criminal homicide). By comparison in 1974 Dade had 12.5% (33 of 265) homicides that were ruled as justifiable or excusable (Wilbanks, 1979a). person killing the victim is considered to be criminally liable. Florida Statutes (782.01 to 782.11) define two types of crimes, murder and manslaughter, that are included among the 462 criminal homicides occuring in 1980 (the actual charge will be discussed in Chapter Eight). Justifiable homicides include victims killed in a legal manner (i.e., self-defense) by either police or citizens (the Case Index in Appendix B lists the ID numbers of all cases of justifiable homicide). Excusable homicides according to the Florida Statutes (782.03) are homicides committed "by accident and misfortune in doing any lawful act by lawful means with usual ordinary caution, and without any unlawful intent" or homicides "by accident and misfortune in the heat of passion, upon any sudden and sufficient provocation, or upon a sudden combat, without any dangerous weapon being used and not done in a cruel or unusual manner. The five cases of excusable homicide include two mutual fights which resulted in death (048A and 448B) and three accidental shootings (114A, 175A and 521A).

The 16 cases of felony murder are listed in the Case Index preceding Appendix B. Each of these is also a criminal homicide but differs from the 462 cases described earlier in that the "killer" is not generally the person charged with criminal homicide. In 11 of the 16 cases of felony murder a citizen or a police officer justifiably shot a robber or burglar and the companion robber(s) or burglar(s) was charged with felony murder. In two cases (056L and 231A) the victim died in a fire set by an arsonist and thus this death involves a felony murder. In two other cases (136B and 196A) the victim was killed in a traffic "accident" that resulted from the driver being involved in a felonious act (in one case drug dealers were in vehicles and chasing and shooting at each other when a pedestrian was run down while in the other a burglar was fleeing from police when he ran over a pedestrian). The final case of felony murder (404L) involved a robber accidently killing his fellow robber when a bullet he fired at a store owner exited that body and struck and killed his fellow robber.

The classification of the 569 homicides into criminal, justifiable, excusable and felony murder varies somewhat by age, sex and race/ethnicity of victim. The subgroups most likely to be killed under circumstances judged to be criminal are those under 15 (90.0%), those 65 & over (96.9%) and female victims (95.0%). It is obvious that these subgroups represent those who are both relatively weak and least likely to provoke an "offender" to kill in self-defense. Likewise, the groups that are most likely to be killed under conditions of self-defense (from viewpoint of offender) are blacks (25.2%), those 15-24 (18.5%), and males (17.9%). From data available in the office of the Medical Examiner (see Table 5.3) it appears that justifiable homicides (by both police and citizens) have decreased in both rate and percentage of all homicides since 1956. However, in 1925-26 it appears that justifiable homicides by the police were 18 times as likely to occur than in 1980 (see Chapter Seven for a full discussion of police homicides).

TYPE OF WEAPON

A total of 72.1% (see Table 5.2) of all victims in 1980 were killed by guns of some type (60.1% by handguns, 7.6% by a rifle or shotgun, and 4.4% by a gun of unknown type). (The comparable total figure for the U.S. as a whole in 1980 was 62% (U.C.R., 1980:13). This figure did vary by age of victim in that only 30% of those under 15 were killed by guns whereas 79.4% of those 25-44 were gun victims. Likewise variation was found by sex in that 74.0% of male victims and 63% of female victims were killed by guns. Gun homicides also varied by ethnicity of victim in that 84.3% of Hispanic victims died by this type weapon versus 51.8% of Anglos.

Handgun death rates varied more dramatically than total gun death rates. Only 20.0% of those under 15 versus 66.4% of those 15-24 died from handguns. Males were only slightly more likely than females (61.8% to 52.0%) to die by handguns. However, Latins (72.4%) and Blacks (58.6%) were far more likely to be killed by handguns than were Anglos (43.8%).

There appears (see Table 5.3) to be a growing trend toward reliance upon firearms in homicides in Dade County. In 1956 only 57% (rate of 5.4/rate of 9.4) of all homicides were committed with firearms but by 1980 the figure was 72% (25.4/35.0) and in 1981 the figure increased to 76% (27.2/35.6). From another point of view it appears (from Table 5.3) that the increase in the homicide rate from 1956 to 1982 was 21.3 while the increase in the gun rate alone was 18.7 (24.1-5.4). Thus 88% of the increase in Dade County's homicide rate from 1956 to 1982 was due to the increase in the firearm homicide rate. (As will be demonstrated below, the knife and "other method" rate remained stable over this period.)

And yet it should be added that the firearm rate in the period 1925-26 was probably even higher than it is in the 1980's. Calculations of the firearm rate based on the Herald's coverage of 1925-26 homicides (see Tables 4.4 and 4.5) indicates that the firearm rate during that period was 82.3 compared to 25.4 in 1980 (see Wilbanks and George, 1983).

A relatively small percentage (7.6%) of the 569 victims in 1980 were killed by a rifle or shotgun. This figure ranged from 0.0% for those 65 & over to

13.1% for black victims. Blunt objects (see Table 5.2) were most likely to be used against those 65 & over (21.9%) and those under 15 (20%) and least likely against Hispanics (1.9%). Hands or feet were most likely to be used against those under 15 (40%) and those 65 & over (25.0%) and least likely against Hispanics (2.9%). Thus it appears that blunt objects and hands/feet are most likely to be used against those who are relatively weak.

Knives were used against 14.4% of the 569 victims in 1980 with those 65 & over being most likely (21.9%) and Hispanics the least likely (9.5%) to be knifing victims. As indicated earlier, the knife rate (see Table 5.3) has remained stable over time (it was 2.6 in 1956 and 3.5 in 1981). However, it appears that the knife rate has been much greater in the distant past in that calculations based on Herald coverage of 1925-26 homicides (see Table 4.4) indicates that the knife rate during those two years was 17.3 (Wilbanks and George, 1983).

MOTIVE/CIRCUMSTANCE

Other researchers (e.g., Wolfgang, 1958:185) have pointed out the difficulty of determining the true motive of an offender since this would require that we know exactly what the offender was thinking (consciously and subconsciously) at the time of the homicide. One can, however, examine the nature of the circumstances surrounding the homicide and infer the motive with some degree of accuracy. The FBI collects data on "circumstance" for each homicide reported via the SHR and several researchers have reported on the motive/circumstance of homicides in selected jurisdictions (e.g., Wolfgang, 1958; Curtis, 1975).

In Dade County in 1980 the classification of motives from the perspective of the 569 victims in 1980 (for motive classification for the arrested offenders see Table 6.5) with percentages as to frequency of occurrence (see Table 5.4) are: Other (not domestic) arguments, 29.0%; drug rip-offs, 20.4%; self-defense (justifiable), 12.8%; domestic arguments, 11.6%; robbery, 11.4%; rape, burglary or other felony, 3.5%; and other (7.0%) or unknown (4.2%). This result differs significantly from the nation as a whole as the Uniform Crime Reports (1980:13) indicate that less than 2% of homicides in the U.S. (compared to the 20% in

Dade County) are the result of disputes over narcotics. However, Dade's percentage of robbery homicides (11.4%) is similar to the national figure (10.8%) as is the percentage for domestic and other types of arguments (Dade, 40.6% to U.S. 44.6%).

But with respect to motives, Dade's homicides are different from the nation in two important respects. First, the Dade rates for various types of motives are greater even though the percentage figures might be similar. For example, though Dade's percentage of robbery-murders is similar (11.4% to 10.8%) to that of the U.S., Dade's robbery/homicide rate is 4.0 compared to a national robbery/homicide rate of 1.0. (Thus a Dade citizen is four times more likely than the average U.S. resident to be killed in a robbery.) Likewise, though the percentages of arguments are the same for Dade and the U.S. a Dade resident is 3.3 times as likely (rate of 14.2 in Dade divided by rate of 4.3 for the U.S.) to be killed in an argument as the average U.S. resident.

Second, Dade's homicide problem is greatly impacted by the drug traffic. The large percentage of drug rip-off homicides is a relatively new phenomena as a study of 1974 homicides (Wilbanks, 1979a) found an insignificant number of this type of motive. Furthermore, the number of "drug-related homicides" (a term commonly used by the media and the police) may be even higher than the 116 (or 20.4%) indicated by Table 5.4. This figure applies only to drug rip-offs but does not include the homicides that result indirectly from illegal drug activity. The only published study (Heffernan, Martin and Romano, 1982) of "drug related" homicides also restricted that term to direct drug involvement. For example, many of the 65 robbery homicides may have involved offenders seeking money to support a drug habit. Likewise, case 196A that resulted in two drug dealers hitting and killing a pedestrian as they fled is indirectly drug related.

Drug rip-offs in Dade County (see Table 5.4) almost always involve young adults 15-44 (99 of 116 cases) and males (98 of 116 cases). Hispanic victims accounted for almost half (65 of 116) of the drug rip-off victims with blacks accounting for 32 and Anglos, 19.

Some very sharp differences are seen (in Table 5.4) with respect to motives when males versus female victims are considered. Female victims were five times as likely (in percentage terms of all homicides against each sex) to be killed in a domestic dispute as were males while males were more likely to be killed as a result of other arguments, robberies and self-defense. Similar differences are also seen at the national level (see Wilbanks, 1983a).

Some very sharp differences in motive by age of victim are also apparent (from Table 5.4). Fifty percent of those 65 & up were killed in robberies (34.4%) and burglaries (15.6%) as compared to a figure of 14.9% for the Dade County population as a whole. The relative lack of criminal involvement by the elderly (for data on elderly offenders in Dade County see Wilbanks, 1982c), is reflected in the total absence of victims 65 & up in drug disputes and only one case (188B) where the elderly victim was killed by an offender in self-defense during a drunken brawl.

Motive also varies significantly by ethnicity of victim (see Table 5.4). The most frequent category of motive/circumstance for Anglos is robbery (23.4%). If the "rape, burglary, other felony" category is added (9.5%), it appears that 32.9% of Anglo victims are killed during robberies, burglaries, etc. The comparable figure for blacks was 10.8%; for Hispanics, 7.6% and for the population as a whole, 11.4%. However, this "fact" must not be confused with rates as Blacks are still more likely to be killed in a robbery, rape, burglary or other felony than Anglos or Hispanics (the rates are: Blacks, 8.6; Hispanics 2.8; and Anglos, 5.6). Thus though Blacks are more likely to be killed (as measured by rates of victimization) in a robbery, rape, burglary or other felony than Anglos or Hispanics, it still remains true that when an Anglo is killed that homicide is more likely to involve those felonious circumstances.

The rates for robbery/homicide appear to have been much higher in 1925-26 (see Table 4.4) as the estimated rate then was double (8.4 to 4.0) that of 1980. Also, the estimated argument homicide rate was almost three times as great (40.4 to 14.2) in 1925-26 as in 1980.

VICTIM/OFFENDER RELATIONSHIP

Though the Uniform Crime Reports have annually indicated that the majority of homicides involve victims and offenders who know each other (e.g., in 1980 50.9% of all U.S. murders involved family members/acquaintances with 13.3% being victimized by strangers and 35.8% having an unknown relationship---UCR, 1980:12), it is true that the proportion of all homicides in the nation that are committed by strangers is growing.

The distribution of victim/offender relationships in Dade County is not markedly different from that reported for other jurisdictions. In Dade (see Table 5.5) 6.7% of all homicides involve husbands and wives; 2.8% involve "other family" (for a total of 9.5% for all family); 9.1% involve sex partners or rivals; 28.5% involve acquaintances; 20.4 involve crime partners; 11.2% involve strangers; 8.3% involve citizens killed by citizens (5.3%) or the police (3.0%); and 8.8% involve citizens killed by felons (8.4%) or police by felons (0.4%). Since the felons killed by police and citizens killing felons categories also involved strangers, the total killings by strangers in Dade was 28.3%. In terms of rates a Dade resident was less likely to be killed by a family member (rate of 3.3) or stranger (9.9) than by someone (whether sex partner, acquaintance, or crime partner) he/she knew (20.3).

The various victim/offender categories did vary sharply by age, sex and race/ethnicity (see Table 5.5). For example, the majority (56.3%) of those 65 & over were killed by strangers as opposed to 22.4% of those 25-44. Males were more likely than females (30.2% to 19.0%) to be killed by strangers as were Anglos (48.1%) than Blacks (26.7%) or Hispanics (17.2%). Likewise, of the felons killed by citizens or police, 46 of the 47 were male. Also, 39 of the 48 citizens killed by felons were males. The most common victim/offender relationship for Hispanics was crime partners (32.9%); for Blacks, acquaintances (32.9%); and for Anglos, citizens killed by felons (22.6%). The percentages (but not the rates) for different victim/offender relationship categories appear to be little different in 1925-26 to 1980 (see Table 4.5). The stranger and relative percentages are almost identical for these two time periods.

INTER-RACIAL VS. INTRA-RACIAL

Another aspect of victim/offender relationship is the extent to which homicides are intra-racial/ethnic versus inter-racial/ethnic (Curtis, 1974). The literature of homicide unanimously reports that homicide is an intra-racial event. For example, the UCR (1980:9) presents figures that indicate over 90% of U.S. homicides are either white (offender) on white (victim) or black on black. Though Dade figures for 1980 (81.2% of the 569 homicides were intra-racial) are comparable to national figures a somewhat different picture emerges when race/ethnicity is considered. When all victims are broken down into three race/ethnic categories (Anglos, Blacks and Hispanics) it appears (see table 5.6) that only 64.9% (N=369) of all homicides are either Anglo on Anglo (N=45), Black on Black (N=169) or Hispanic on Hispanic (N=155). The remaining 35.1% (N=200) of the cases involve one of the three ethnic groups being victimized by another ethnic group (21.0%) or an unknown relationship (80 cases or 14.1%). Both Blacks and Hispanics are predominantly victimized by members of their own ethnic group (i.e., 76.1% of Black victims were killed by Black offenders and 73.8% of Hispanic victims were killed by Hispanic offenders) while Anglo on Anglo homicides (N=45) comprise only 32.8% of the 137 Anglo victims. A total of 46.0% were killed by Blacks (31.4%) or Hispanics (14.6%) and an additional 21.2% of the cases had an unknown relationship). Thus homicides are only intra-ethnic in Dade County when Black and Hispanic victims are considered. When Anglo victims are considered separately homicide is found to be inter-ethnic. This surprising result is not reported in the published literature for any other jurisdiction.

The tendency for killings of Anglo victims to be inter-ethnic is even more pronounced (see Table 5.6) when male Anglo victims are considered separately. Whereas the inter-ethnic percentage for all Anglos was 46.0%, the comparable figures for male Anglos were 50.1% and for female Anglos, 30.3% (and these percentages do not count the cases where the relationship was unknown). By contrast the inter-ethnic percentages for the other sex/ethnic groups of victims were 16.5% for Black males; 5.8% for Black females; 13.0% for Hispanic males; and 3% for Hispanic females. Thus it appears that the inter-racial nature of Anglo victim homicides was largely the result of Anglo males being killed by members of other ethnic groups. More than half (34 of 63) of the inter-ethnic homicides with Anglo victims involved a robbery or burglary.

SEX OF VICTIM VS. SEX OF OFFENDER

One of the most unusual aspects of homicide in Dade County is the virtual non-existence of female on female homicide. Nationally only 10% of all homicides (Wilbanks. 1982:169) are female on female and yet in Dade County in 1980 there occurred only one such incident in 569 (0.1%). And in this case a mother killed her female infant (see case 514A). In Dade County (see Table 5.6) when the victim is male the offender is male in 78.7% of the cases (in 9.6% the offender was female and in 11.7% the sex of offender was unknown). By contrast when females were the victims the offender was male in 81.0% of the cases (with 18 of the remaining 19 cases involving an unknown offender). Thus males are killed by males and females are killed by males. Likewise, when women kill they kill males and when men kill they generally kill males. A similar pattern of sex of victim and offender was found for homicide in Dade County in 1925-26 (see Table 4.5).

DEGREE OF VICTIM INVOLVEMENT

Marvin Wolfgang (1958) coined the term "victim precipitation" to describe those homicides in which the victim was the first to use deadly force. The term suggests that the victim, by being the first to use deadly force, precipitates or invites his/her own death. Wolfgang (1959) also suggested that the victim might even be subconsciously attempting to commit suicide by provoking the offender with the display of a weapon. Wolfgang (1958) found that 26% of the criminal homicides (obviously the figure would have been higher if justifiable homicides were included) in Philadelphia from 1948-1952 were victim precipitated. Others have found differing figures for other cities (see Curtis, 1974; Wilbanks, 1979) with a high of 38% being found for Chicago (Voss & Hepburn, 1968:506). The use of the term victim precipitated has been criticized (e.g., Silverman, 1974) for the lack of reliability in classifying homicides given the failure of the written records to always indicate who first displayed a weapon.

Others (see Davis and Wright, 1977) have criticized the term victim precipitated as being too restrictive and suggest the addition of another term, "victim participation". The latter term indicates when victims willingly participate in "risky" events that may lead to violent confrontations and even death. Thus they suggest that victim participated homicides be classified as those in which the victim and the offender were engaged together in drinking, arguing, or engaging in a criminal act. The use of this term is intended to separate those homicides in which the victim was totally innocent (did not relate to the offender in any way prior to the assault) versus those in which the victim was involved in some "risky" way with the offender prior to the assault.

Of the 569 Dade homicides in 1980, 56.9% of the victims (see Table 5.7) participated in the events leading up to the assault. Only 14.9% clearly precipitated their own death by being the first to use force or display a weapon (see case index in Appendix B for list of all victim precipitated cases). The victim was "innocent" in 23.6% of the cases in that the victim did not participate in any risky events leading to the assault or precipitate the assault. Most of the totally innocent victims were killed during robberies, burglaries or other felonies. Most of the victim precipitated homicides involved self-defense on part of the offender. Most of the victim participated cases involved drug rip-offs or arguments.

The percentage of victim precipitated and victim participated homicides varied markedly by age, sex and race/ethnicity (see Table 5.7). Those most likely to precipitate their own death were those 15-24 (18.5%); males (17.3%); Blacks (22.1%); and young Black males (24.1%). Those most likely to have participated in risky events that led to a fatal confrontation were those 25-44 (64.4%) and Hispanics (67.6%). On the other hand, those victims most likely to be totally innocent were those under 15 (68.8%) and females (34.0%).

Victim participation is also associated with high levels of alcohol consumption. Those victims who died with high levels of alcohol (above .10) were six times more likely to have precipitated the homicide and were also far more likely to have been involved in a homicide that was the result of a domestic or other argument.

ALCOHOL LEVEL OF VICTIM

In an exhaustive review of prior literature on the prevalence of alcohol in the criminal event, Greenberg (1981:95) found that there was general agreement that more than half of the homicide victims had been drinking at the time of the fatal assault (as measured by blood alcohol level) and that half or more of those who had any trace of alcohol had consumed a sufficient amount to be defined as under the influence. Greenberg concluded that this result indicates that when homicide participants drink, "they do so to the point of drunkenness"(1981:95).

Data on alcohol level of homicide victims in Dade County for 1980 (see Table 5.8) appears to confirm the conclusions of Greenberg. A total of 217 Dade victims (38% of all victims) had traces of alcohol while 287 (50.4%) were tested and found to have no trace and 65 (11.5%) were not tested. Thus 43% (217 of 504) of those tested had traces of alcohol. More than half (55.8%) of those with a trace had a level at or above .10 (the point of legal intoxication). Thus 21.3% of the 569 victims (or 24.0% of the 504 tested) were legally drunk at the time of their death. It also appears (see Table 5.3) that the 1980 percentage of tested victims that had traces of alcohol (43%) is comparable to that found in earlier years in Dade.

The groups (see Table 5.8) that were most likely to have been legally drunk at the time of their death were those 25-44 (25.1%); males (22.6%); and Blacks (25.7%) though the combination of these three characteristics (i.e., young black males) had a drunk rate of only 20.4%. Those least likely to have been legally drunk were those under 15 (0.0%); those 65 & over (15.7%); females (15.0%) and Anglos (12.4%).

The reader should not draw the conclusion that simply because the victim is usually drinking and often drunk, he/she has in some way "caused" the homicide (for review of alcohol as a cause of homicide see Wilbanks, 1981a). No measurement of the alcohol level of offenders was available from police records and thus no overall "drinking picture" of the homicide event is available. However, prior research does indicate (see Greenberg, 1981:96) that an equal proportion of victims and offenders drank at the event when alcohol was present at all. Furthermore, alcohol was present in both parties in the vast majority of cases where it was

present in either. This is not to say that alcohol was
the sole determinant of the homicide but it does appear
from prior research that alcohol is part of the complex
interpersonal dynamic involved in the interaction
between victim and offender.

There are several ways that alcohol might
conribute to the likelihood of a criminal event.
First, there is some evidence in the Dade data that
those victims who were intoxicated were more likely to
be involved in "argument homicides" than other victims.
For example, victims who were heavily intoxicated (.20
or above) or drunk but not heavily intoxicated (.10 to
.19) were six times as likely (61% and 44%,
respectively) to be involved in "other argument"
homicides than was the case (29%) for the 569 victims
as a whole. Second, as mentioned earlier, those who
were legally drunk were far more likely to have
precipitated their own demise. Thus victims who were
legally drunk often were the first to display or use a
weapon and yet their intoxicated condition made them
more susceptible to a successful counter-attack by the
offender.

Since the group most likely to be drunk at the
time of their demise was Black males, 15-24 and 25-44,
it is interesting to note the conditions under which
the drinking took place. Roizen (1981) has suggested
that the bar/tavern setting in the Black community may
contribute to many homicides in that the norms
surrounding drinking behavior in a group context
facilitate the expression of aggression. However, in
Dade the bar killing rate for Blacks (5.3 per 100,000)
was only slightly greater than that for Hispanics (4.6)
though it was significantly greater than the Anglo rate
(0.7). Perhaps taverns frequented by Blacks and
Hispanics should be studied to determine if norms that
are present in that setting (but absent in Anglo bars)
promote the expression of violence.

OTHER DRUG USE BY VICTIMS

The case files in the office of the Medical
Examiner often include a record of a drug test for
drugs other than alcohol. A total of 266 of the 569
homicide files searched had data on a drug screen for
the victim. Almost three-fourths (73.7%) had no
evidence of drugs in their bodies while 26.3% (N=70)
did have a positive result. The most common drugs

found were Valium, Quaaludes, cocaine and amphetamines. The first two are depressants or "downers" while the latter two are "uppers" and are more dangerous in that they can produce psychosis and aggression. Drugs in the body of the victim was closely associated with drug rip-offs in that 44% (31 of 70) of those type of cases in which a drug screen was conducted tested positive. Thus those who deal in drugs are also often users and one sign of a drug-related homicide is evidence of drugs in the body of the victim. Also 31% (5 of 16) of robbers killed by citizens and 50% (2 of 4) of burglars killed by citizens tested positive for drugs (of those cases in which a test was conducted). Thus it would appear that a significant proportion of robbers and burglars either are on drugs and steal to support their habit or take drugs to get the "nerve" to commit the crime. The young also seem to have been more involved in drug use as 28% of victims tested for drugs had a positive result compared to 14% for victims under 15 or 45 and over. Surprisingly, a greater percentage of female than male victims (43% to 22%) who were tested had evidence of drugs in their bodies. Also the percentages of drugs in victims by ethnic group of victim were Anglos, 37%; Hispanics, 28%; and Blacks, 19%. However, there was no relationship between alcohol and other drug use as those victims who had alcohol in their blood were no more likely than those who did not to test positive for the presence of other drugs.

TYPE OF PLACE OF OCCURRENCE

Several studies (e.g., Curtis, 1974) have reported on the place of occurrence of homicide and most have found that a home is the most likely location of the fatal assault. Figures for Dade County in 1980 (see Table 5.9) indicate that the location of the assault in order of frequency was as follows: 26.2% in the home of the victim; 15.1% in a public building; 14.6% in the street or sidewalk; 11.1% in "other" (than victim's) home; 9.8% in a motor vehicle; 9.7% in a field or canal; 8.3% in or near a bar; 4.9% in a parking lot; and 0.4% unknown location. Thus if both home locations are added, a total of 37.3% of Dade homicides in 1980 occurred in a home. This figure is down slightly from the 42.6% found for Dade in 1974 (Wilbanks, 1979a:62).

The common image of dangerous streets finds little support in these figures since a small percentage

41

occurs there. The most surprising figure is the 9.8% that occurred in motor vehicles, a result not found in studies of other jurisdictions. In percentage terms, bar killings were down slightly from the 10.0% found for Dade for 1974 (Wilbanks, 1979:62).

There was some variation in type of location by age, sex and ethnicity of victim. Those subgroups most likely to be killed at their own home were those under 15 (60.0%); those 65 & over (53.1%); females (48.0%) and Anglos (35.0%). Males were far more likely than females to be killed in bars (9.8% to 1.0%); in public buildings (17.1 to 6.0%); and on the street (16.8% to 4.0%). Also Hispanics (12.9%) were more likely to be killed in bars than were Anglos (3.6%) or Blacks (6.8%).

CENSUS TRACT OF VICTIM

It is interesting to note that numerous studies can be found in the literature that compute victimization rates by city, county or state of residence but few (e.g., Wolfgang, 1958) provide a breakdown of victimization by areas within a city or county. When victimization rates or figures are given only for a city or county as a whole, no indication is given to the residents in a particular city as to which areas of the city are safest. The absence of such data can only implicitly suggest that variation in victimization across areas of a city is not significant. However, tremendous variation exists in Dade county with respect to risk of homicide victimization depending on the area (as measured by census tract) of residence.

Of the 237 census tracts in Dade County, 57 had no residents that were homicide victims in 1980 (see Table 5.10). A total of 180 of the 237 census tracts thus had one or more residents killed. One tract (19.02) in Liberty City located around I-95 and N.W. 60th Street had 13 residents killed in 1980. With respect to rates per 100,000 residents, the victimization rates ranged from 0.0 for the 57 tracts with no victims to 925.0 for tract 37.02---meaning that on the average one resident in 108 was a homicide victim in 1980 (this tract was around Bayfront Park in downtown Miami---but of course this is an area with few residents but many "visitors").

42

The high risk census tracts also varied somewhat by sex of victim and greatly by ethnicity of victim. In one tract (19.02) a total of 12 male residents were killed (a rate of 275) while in another (37.02) the victimization rate was 1,276 for males---meaning that one male in 78 was the victim of a homicide in 1980. Female victimization rates ranged from 0.0 for 163 tracts to 94.3 for one tract (101.12). Anglo victimization rates ranged from 0.0 for 155 tracts to 762.2 for one tract (37.01). Black victimization rates ranged from 0.0 for 173 tracts to 213 for one tract (31.00). Hispanic victimization rates ranged from 0.0 for 137 tracts to 919.5 for one tract (37.02). Thus it is clear that the relative risk for males and females and the three ethnic groups varied markedly. Keeping in mind that the overall victimization rate for Dade County was 35.0, this range of variation means that in one tract (37.02) the victimization rate (925.0) was 26 times the county-wide rate.

Similar variation in risk of victimization is found for Dade County in 1980 when one examines (see Table 5.11) the census tract of the actual assault incident (versus the census tract of the resident discussed above). Though no rates were calculated for census tract of assault (the fact that a homicide occurred in an area/tract has little relationship to the number of residents of the tract), there was wide variation in the number of homicides occurring across the 237 tracts. A total of 172 tracts had one or more homicides while 65 had none. One tract, 34.00 (in the center of Overtown) had 21 homicides in 1980. Tract 34.00 was also the most dangerous location for males (20 homicides) and Blacks (15 homicides). The two most dangerous tracts for Anglos (15.01 in Liberty City and 39.04 in N. Bay Village) "achieved" this distinction due to the riot deaths in one case and a quadruple murder of two elderly couples by a burglar in the other. The most dangerous tract for Hispanics was 49.00 which is located north of Flagler Street around LeJeune.

Thus it appears (from Table 5.11) that predominantly black census tracts are the most dangerous location for Blacks and Anglos while Hispanics are more often victimized in predominantly Hispanic tracts. This result makes sense when one remembers that most Black victims are killed by other blacks (and thus in Black census tracts); most Anglo victims are killed by Blacks and Hispanics (and thus in

43

non-Anglo census tracts); and most Hispanics by other Hispanics (and thus in Hispanic census tracts).

The homicide rate of the cities in Dade County also differs significantly (the city and Metro rates given in Chapter One were from UCR figures and were for murder while these are for all 569 homicides occurring in the county in 1980). The city of Miami had a homicide rate of 68.3, Miami Beach, 19.8, Hialeah, 11.0, and all other cities and unincorporated areas (i.e., the jurisdiction of the Metro Police Department), 28.6. However, the reader should refer to Chapter One for criticisms of rates that do not take into account non-residents of the jurisdiction.

TIME OF DAY

It is a well-known fact that homicides tend to occur disproportionately at night. In Dade County in 1980 (see Table 5.12), 31.3% of the 569 homicides occurred from 8:00 PM to 2:00 AM. The second most homicide-prone time of day was in the afternoon from 2:00 PM to 8:00 PM (23.7%). A surprising 16.3% (N=93) occurred from 2:00 AM to 8:00 AM. However, there was no significant relationship between motive and time of day of occurrence (i.e., robberies and drug rip-offs were slightly more likely to occur during this time period but overall there was no difference in motive pattern by time of day).

Little variation occured in time of day of occurrence by sex or ethnicity of victim. The only significant variation by age was the tendency of those under 15 to be killed during the day (60% were killed between 8:00 AM and 8:00 PM compared to 41.8% overall).

DAY OF WEEK OF ASSAULT/HOMICIDE

Numerous studies of homicides in other jurisdictions (e.g., have found that homicides tend to occur disporportionately on the weekend when relatives and acquaintances are more likely to get together and when drinking is more prevalent. The weekend pattern found for other jurisdictions does not appear to be as pronounced for Dade County for 1980 (see Table 5.13). Though 36.7% of the homicides did occur on Saturday and Sunday one would expect 28.6% by chance alone (2 of 7 days). Likewise there was little meaningful variation in weekend assaults by age, sex or ethnicity of victim.

MONTH OF ASSAULT

It is commonly believed that violence is most likely to occur in the summer months when the weather and temperatures are hot. However, the Uniform Crime Reports have consistently failed to indicate higher numbers of homicides for the summer months or for any other month. This is not the case for other crimes (see Crime and Seasonality, 1980).

Dade County, like the nation as a whole does not appear to have a "season of homicide" (see Table 5.14). For the years 1975 to 1982 there appears to be no pattern by month. However, beginning in May of 1980 an unusual pattern began that continued for 24 months (through April of 1982). Dade County averaged only 27.0 homicides per month (see Table 5.14) for the 24 months prior to May of 1980 and then the monthly average jumped 94% to 52.5 for May 1980 to April 1982. This "plateau" dropped rather sharply in May of 1982 to a lower pleateau of 37.8 per month which contined for 20 months to the end of 1983 (when data collection ended). Though this second and current plateau is down 28% from the May 1980 to April 1982 pleateau, it is still up 40% from the monthly average for the 24 months before the riots and the Mariel boatlift of May 1980. The 1983 monthly average was 35.0.

The homicide plateau (52.5 per month) which existed for 24 months began with the riots and the arrival of the refugees but neither can account for the magnitude of the increase (up 25.5 homicides per month) for a 24 month period. Granted the 17 victims of the riot and the three cases involving either Mariel victims or offenders made up most of the increase for May, these two factors do not explain the continuance of this trend/plateau for 24 months. The riot lasted only one month and the numbers of cases involving Mariel victims or offenders cannot account for the level of homicide remaining at such a high rate. Others have suggested that the drug traffic or drug rip-off homicides increased but there is no evidence that either changed abruptly in May of 1980 and certainly neither can account for the 24 month plateau at 52.5 per month.

CHAPTER SIX:

OFFENDER CHARACTERISTICS

INTRODUCTION:

Studies of homicide victimization in a particular
jurisdiction or for the nation as a whole are much more
common in the published literature than studies of
offender characteristics. The literature focus on
victims is not because researchers do not view
offenders as being as important but because data on
offenders is less readily available. Victim data for a
particular city or county is generally available at a
single office---the medical examiner or coroner. The
records in the offices of medical examiners are
generally quite systematic and complete and are
accessible to researchers.

By contrast data on offenders is much more
difficult to obtain. First, data on offenders must be
obtained from the police and most counties (or even
"cities") have several police departments that
investigate homicides. In Dade County there are 26
departments, but only four that investigated homicides
in 1980. Second, the homicide files maintained by the
police are not as systematic or complete as that of the
medical examiner for the purposes of researchers. The
researcher is interested primarily in the
characteristics of the offender, his motive and the
disposition of the case. It is quite difficult to
obtain this kind of limited information from police
files since their purpose is quite different.
Fortunately, most police departments (including the
four in Dade County that investigate homicides) do
maintain a listing of all homicides for a given year
along with the name of suspects and the status (whether
cleared) of the case. Though such a listing does not
provide a researcher with all the information needed,
more information can be obtained orally from the
detectives assigned to the case (generally the name of
the detectives assigned is also part of the listing of
cases).

An effort was made to interview detectives so that
more information could be obtained on the circumstances
surrounding the case, the characteristics of the
offender and his/her relationship to the victim, and
the disposition.

47

ATTRITION OF OFFENDERS

A total of 269 offenders (see Table 6.1) were arrested by the four police departments in the 569 cases occurring in 1980. However, the arrest figure is only the end result of an investigative process that begins when an offender(s) is identified (by name or by sex and/or race) by the police. A total of 677 offenders (see Table 6.1) were identified by police of which 454 were identified by name (the 223 who were not identified by name involved cases where the police know only the sex and/or race of the offender but not the name). Though the majority (269 or 59.3%) of those identified by name (N=454) were arrested, many were not. A total of 92 offenders (20.3% of the 454 identified by name) were not charged since a decision was made by the police and/or prosecutor that no criminal liability existed. These were largely cases of justifiable homicide committed by citizens or police. An additional 54 offenders (11.9% of the 454) were not charged since there was insufficient evidence for arrest. The police often voiced the view that there was often probable cause that would justify an arrest but that they could not get a warrant from the prosecutor since the standard of evidence for such a warrant was greater than simple probable cause. The police expressed the view that the prosecution did not want to proceed with cases that did not stand a good chance of conviction and thus refused to issue warrants unless the evidence was stronger than probable cause.

A number of offenders (21 or 4.6% of the 454) that had been identified by name by the police were still at large (as of July, 1982, when data collection at the police level ceased). The case index preceding the case narratives in Appendix B lists all 21 cases in which the offender was still at large.

Finally, 18 offenders (4.0% of the 454) died before prosecution could be initiated. Thirteen of these were murder-suicides in that the offender killed himself shortly after the murder. All of the 13 murder/suicide cases involved male offenders and 11 killed their wife/ex-wife/lover. One (239L) shot himself after killing a man in the street and after first pointing his gun at a policeman (and then turning the gun on himself). The other (145A) shot his mother and then himself. It is interesting to note that 11 males shot their wife/lover and then committed suicide while not a single female shot a husband/lover and then herself. Evidently female offenders did not experience extreme remorse after killing a spouse/lover (perhaps because they viewed the victim as being "deserving". The phenomena of homicide followed by suicide is rare in the U.S. but in England approximately 1/3 of all homicides are followed by the suicide of the offender (West, 1966).

It is interesting to note (see Table 6.1) the variation (by age, sex, and ethnicity of offenders) in the attrition of cases from identification of offender to arrest. For example, only two females were identified by sex but not name while 160 males were so identified. Thus though males were far more likely to be arrested than females (241 to 28), this disproportionality in arrests would have been even greater if all the males and females known to have been involved in 1980 homicides had been identified by name and arrested. In short, there is strong evidence that the investigative process does not distort arrest statistics by (falsely) indicating greater involvement of males (versus females) than is warranted.

The same point can be made when ethnicity of offenders is considered. The arrest figures (in Table 6.2) by ethnicity of offender would indicate an arrest rate of 53.1 for Blacks; 14.1 for Hispanics and 4.7 for Anglos. Some might attempt to explain this disporportionality in arrest rates by asserting that the investigative process discriminates (is more likely to result in an arrest) against Black and Hispanic offenders. However, no evidence to support that claim was found in the analysis of Dade County data. For example, of the 75 identified (by name or ethnicity) Anglo offenders, only 7 (9%) were not identified by name while the comparable figures for Black and Hispanic offenders were 21% and 38%, respectively. Also while the Black to White arrest rate ratio was 11.3:1 (53.1/4.7), the comparable rate ratios for insufficient evidence cases (and thus no charge) was 8.9:1; not charged, 5.2:1; and identity unknown, 23.3:1. These figures suggest that the 11.2 rate ratio (i.e., Blacks were 11.2 times as likely to be arrested for homicide as were Whites) is not due to Anglos being more likely to be known by ethnicity but simply not identified, not charged (since self-defense), or not charged due to insufficient evidence.

Also if one wants to argue that the higher percentage of Anglo offenders for justifiable homicides indicates a bias in favor of Anglos the breakdown by race/sex (see Table 6.1) presents data difficult to explain. The race/sex subgroup that was most likely to be viewed as committing a justifiable homicide was Black females (36.7%) while the subgroup with the lowest probability was White females (5.9%). This result is opposite of what one would expect if the charging pattern indicates discrimination.

It is also interesting to note that far more Black (20 or 9.2% of those identified by name) and Hispanic (26 or 17.2%) than Anglo (6 or 8.8%) offenders were not charged due to insufficient evidence. Furthermore, while 14 Hispanic (9.3%) and 7 Black (3.2%) offenders were still at large, there were no Anglo offenders in this category. In short, there is certainly no evidence that the police are focusing more on catching and gathering evidence against Black and Hispanic than Anglo offenders.

VARIATION IN OFFENDER RATES

The 269 offenders arrested in 1980 Dade County homicides represents a rate of 16.4 per 100,000 (meaning there was one arrest for homicide for every 6,098 residents in the population----see Table 6.2). The offender rate of 16.4 varies even more sharply by age, sex and ethnicity than did the victimization rate (Table 6.3 compares the victimization and arrest rates for 1980 for various subgroups of the population). While the overall victimization rate for 1980 was 35.0 that figure varied from 0.9 for Hispanics under 15 and for white females under 15 (e.g., there was only 1 homicide victim for every 111,111 residents in these subgroups) to 343.6 for black males 25-44 (e.g., there was 1 homicide victim for every 291 black males 25-44 in the Dade population). Thus black males 25-44 were 381 times greater (or 38,000% greater) to be killed in 1980 in Dade than were Hispanics under 15 or white females under 15. Though this variation in victimization was great the variation in arrest rates was even greater. While several subgroups of those under 15 had no arrests and thus a rate of 0.0 (e.g., females, Anglos and Hispanics under 15), black males 15-24 had a rate of 295.9 (e.g., there was one arrest of a black male 15-24 for every 338 in the Dade population). Obviously 295.9 is infinitely greater than 0.0. If one takes the lowest non-zero rate (0.7 for males under 15) and compares it to the 295.9 rate we can see that the latter rate (for Black males, 15-24) was 423 times greater (or 42,200% greater) than the former rate (for males under 15). Thus the range in arrest rates is greater than the range for victimization rates across subgroups of the Dade population based on age, sex and race/ethnicity.

It also appears (Table 6.3) that the victimization rate distribution across the age groups is much "flatter" than the arrest rate distribution. For example, the victimization rate rises 1,568% (3.4 to 60.1) for those 15-24 from those under 15 while the arrest rate rises 13,400% (0.3 to 40.7). Likewise, the victimization rate drops more slowly for the 45-64 and 65 & up age groups than does the arrest rate (e.g., the victimization rate for the 25-44 age group decreases by 52% to the 45-64 group while the arrest rate decreases by 66%).

It is also interesting to note the relative extent to which various subgroups of the population are at risk for being homicide victims versus being arrested as a criminal homicide offender (see Table 6.3). Whereas a Dade County resident is overall 2.1 times as likely to be a victim as to be arrested as a killer, this ratio varies sharply by subgroups of the population. In general the very young (those under 15) and the elderly have a greater disparity in the victim/killer ratio. Those under 15 are 11.3 times as likely to be a victim as to be a killer and those 65 & up are 8.1 times as likely to be killed as to kill. On the other hand, those 15-24 are only 1.5 times as likely to be killed as to kill. In fact, black males from 15-24 were more likely to be arrested (a rate ratio of 0.8:1) than to be killed.

It is also interesting to note (from Table 6.3) that the male to female arrest rate ratio was 9.8:1 while the racial male to female rate ratios were 9.8:1 for Blacks (Black males to Black females) and 7.4:1 for Whites (White males to White females). Also a Black Dade resident was 11.3 times as likely (per capita) to be arrested as an Anglo and 3.8 times as likely (per capita) as an Hispanic. Likewise, Hispanics were 3.0 times as likely (per capita) to be arrested as an Anglo. Finally when one considers age as a predictor of arrest rates one finds that the ranges across subgroups of age are even greater than that for sex or ethnicity. For example, the arrest rate for those 15-24 was 54.4 compared to 0.3 for those under 15 and

1.6 for those 65 and over. Thus those 15-24 were 181 times as likely to be arrested as those under 15 and 34 times as likely as those 65 and over. Thus it would appear that age is the best predictor of arrest rates followed by sex and then ethnicity.

Chapter Four examined changes over time in victimization rates and thus it is appropriate at this point to indicate changes over time in arrest rates by subgroups of the population (see Table 6.4). However, since arrest figures are more difficult to obtain the comparison (in Table 6.4) will be from 1974 (from a previous study by the author) to 1980. Though the arrest rate in Dade in 1980 was up 19% for the population as a whole (from 13.8 per 100,000 in 1974 to 16.4 in 1980), it is down 16% for females, down 22% for Anglos and down 4% for Blacks. By contrast the Hispanic arrest rate was up 127% over this 6 year period. The subgroup with the greatest decrease over this period was 15-24 Anglos (down 55%) and 15-24 females (down 49%). On the other hand the subgroup with the greatest percentage increase in arrest rates was males 65 and over (up 264%) though this percentage increase is based on very small rates (1.1 to 4.0).

MOTIVES OF 269 ARRESTED OFFENDERS

The previous discussion of motive (in chapter Five and based on Table 5.4) was from the point of view of the 569 victims. Since multiple offenders are arrested in some cases and none in others, it is important to examine motive/circumstance from the point of view of the 269 offenders actually charged with criminal homicide (see Table 6.5). The most common circumstances underlying the homicides for which the 269 were charged was "other argument," 39.4%. An additional 16.4% were involved in domestic arguments and thus a total of 55.8% of the 269 arrested offenders killed during some type of argument. A total of 33.9% killed during some type of felonious act (13.8% during a robbery; 6.7% during a rape, burglary or other felony; and 13.4% during a drug rip-off). The remaining 10.4% of the arrested offenders killed during miscellaneous circumstances.

When motive of arrested offender is broken down by sex (see Table 6.5) of offender it appears that males were far more likely than females (36.5% to 10.7%) to kill during a felony (robbery, burglary, drug sale,

etc.) while females were far more likely than males
(64.3% to 10.8%) to kill during a domestic argument.
This tendency held up when sex of offender was broken
down by race in that white (66.7) and Black (62.5%)
females were more likely to kill during domestic
arguments than white males (12.0%) or Black males
(9.8%). A more complete analysis of all female
offenders is found in a separate study by this author
(Wilbanks, 1983b). That study examines the 47
offenders identified as female and follows those cases
through to final disposition.

With respect to ethnicity of offender it appears
that Black offenders were more likely (38.9%) than
Hispanic (27.4) or Anglo (27.7%) offenders to kill
during another felony. This tendency was especially
pronounced in robbery as 21.5% of all Blacks (as
opposed to 8.3% for Anglos and 2.4% for Hispanics)
arrested had been involved in a robbery. Robbery
homicides were not, however, characteristic of Black
females (only 1 of 16 arrests in this race/sex subgroup
was for a robbery/homicide).

VICTIM/OFFENDER RELATIONSHIP FOR 269 ARRESTED OFFENDERS

Most of the 269 arrested offenders killed someone
they knew (see Table 6.6). A total of 32.7% of the
arrestees killed an acquaintance; 12.6% killed a crime
partner; 9.7% killed a sex partner or rival; 7.8%
killed their husband or wife; and 4.5% killed some
other family member (40.6% killed a stranger).

When victim/offender relationship for the 269
arrestees was broken down by age, sex and ethnicity it
appears that those 15-24 (43.6%); males (30.3%) and
Black males (39.9%) were more likely to kill strangers
while both black (37.5%) and white females (33.3%) were
more likely to kill their spouse than were white males
(4.6%) and Black males (4.5%). However, it should be
noted that these percentage figures apply to the
percent of all homicides committed by this category of
offender and should not be interpreted as meaning that
more husbands are killed by wives than wives by
husbands. In fact, wives (11) or female sex partners
(18) were more likely to be killed by males than were
husbands (10) or sex partners (8) by females.

CHAPTER SEVEN:

THE POLICE ROLE

POLICE CLEARANCE RATE

There are four police departments in Dade County that investigate homicides. Metro handles all the homicides in the county not handled by the three major city departments (Miami, Miami Beach, and Hialeah). The clearance rate for homicide is much higher than that found for other crimes since this crime is usually the result of a conflict between people who know each other. The FBI reported that 72% of all criminal homicides were cleared by local police in the U.S. for 1980. However, this figure is down from the 86% reported for 1970 (UCR, 1970:10). In 1980 in Dade County the police cleared 338 (59.4%) of the 569 homicides that occurred in the county. Most (233) were cleared by arrest of one or more offenders while 85 were cleared by justifiable homicides and 20 by the death of the offender (see Table 7.1). However, when only criminal homicides are considered (i.e., excluding justifiable homicides), the clearance rate dropped to 51.1% (for 462 cases). The Dade figure of 51.1% is thus comparable to the national figure of 72% for 1980.

There was no significant (as measured by chi square) variation in the clearance rate across the four departments with Metro having a slightly higher rate (60.9%) in criminal homicides followed by Miami (58.6%), Miami Beach (57.9%) and Hialeah (43.8%). There was little variation in clearance (arrest, justifiable and offender dead categories) percentages by age, sex and ethnicity of offender (see Table 7.1). The variation in clearance rates is more a function of the type of homicides handled by each department than by any factor associated with the investigating department. When a regression equation was calculated for all criminal homicides with cleared (or not cleared) as the dependent variable and several victim, event and offender characteristics as the independent variables, the results indicate that the identification of the department is not significant in explaining clearances.

Furthermore, little variance in whether the case was cleared was explained by the case variables when used as independent variables in the regression equation. The best predictor of whether the criminal homicide was cleared was whether the victim/offender relationship was "crime partners", a category that largely involved drug rip-offs (i.e., crime partner cases were unlikely to be cleared) and yet this predictor accounted for only 5% of the variance in whether the case was cleared. Five other predictors (if the offender was male, if the offender was female, if the victim was not an Hispanic, if the murder was not a robbery and if the case was victim precipitated) were the next variables to enter the step-wise regression equation (and raised the R squared to .25) and to predict that a case would be cleared.

There appear to be several types of homicides that have relatively high clearance rates while other types have lower rates (see Table 7.2). For example, those homicides that were judged to be victim precipitated (victim was first to use force or was engaged in a criminal act when killed by the offender) had a clearance rate of 94.1%. Other types of homicides with high clearance rates were those with female offenders (87.0%); husbands and wives (86.8%); heterosexual partners (86.7%); domestic arguments (83.3%); sex rivals (75.0%); only one offender (74.0%); black victims (73.9%); victims under 15 (70.0%); and drunk victims (66.1%).

By contrast several types of homicides appear to be more difficult to solve. Low clearance rates were found for those involving Columbian victims (19.4%); homosexual partners (20.0%); Columbian offenders (22.2%); crime partners (29.3%); drug rip-offs (31.9%); robbery (38.5%); two or more offenders (41.0%); Hispanic victims (44.3%); and victims 65 & over (46.9%).

The 51.1% clearance rate for 1980 Dade County criminal homicides is probably largely due to the changing nature of homicides in the county. In 1974 (Wilbanks, 1979a) the criminal homicide clearance rate in Dade was 76.1% and thus in a period of six years the clearance rate has dropped from approximately 3 in 4 to 1 in 2 cases. But in 1974 the number of cases involving drug rip-offs, Columbian victims and offenders, robberies, and elderly victims (all categories shown in Table 7.2 to have low clearance rates) was not nearly as great as 1980. What has changed over the six year period has not been so much the efficiency of the police in investigating various types of homicides but the type of homicides that occurred. The decreasing clearance rate nationwide has also been largely due to the changing nature of homicides (more felony-related and fewer "domestics") in the U.S. The country and Dade County are now simply experiencing more of the difficult cases and fewer (relatively speaking) of the easy ones.

This is not to say that no factor related to the police departments has contributed to the decline in the clearance rate. The police are quick to point out that caseloads for each detective are much higher than in years past. The growing prevalence of difficult ("whodunits") cases led the Miami homicide bureau to create a special team of detectives to work only on these cases. Likewise, Metro created a special team of detectives to deal with the drug homicides (which have a low clearance rate). This unit shares information with other departments on the activities of various drug gangs.

HOMICIDES BY THE POLICE

No discussion of the police role in homicide would be complete without mention of homicide committed by the police since so much public attention involves this topic. In 1980 14 persons were killed (for a list of these 14 cases see case index in Appendix B) by the police and all were ruled justifable homicides. The 14 police homicides represent a rate of 0.9 per 100,000 citizens which is higher than that of most recent years (Table 5.3 indicates that in 1970 and 1971 the rate was higher---at 1.3 and 1.1). However, this rate of 0.9 is far below the rate of 16.3 for 1925-26. In fact, a Dade citizen in 1925-26 was 18 times more likely (16.3/0.9=18) to be killed by the police than a Dade citizen in 1980. Furthermore, in 1925-26 homicides by the police comprised 18% (38 of 216) of the homicides occurring in those years. By contrast only 2% (14 of 569) of the 1980 homicides were committed by the police.

It is surprising that the homicide rate by the police has not risen with the general homicide rate since much of the literature (see Geller, 1982; Matulia, 1982) on this topic indicates that for several jurisdictions at one point in time the police homicide rate is strongly and positively correlated with the general homicide rate. Thus this study provides evidence that the positive correlation between the general homicide rate and the police rate applies to the same jurisdiction over time as well as across jurisdictions at one point in time. The correlation coefficient (r) for the general and police rate for this 28 year period (1956-1983) was +.41.

There is some data on the police homicide rate in other urban areas and thus it is possible to place the Dade figure of 0.9 into a comparative perspective. A comprehensive analysis of police use of deadly force (Matulia, 1982) funded by the International Association of Chiefs of Police (IACP) found that for the period of 1975 to 1979 the rate for the city of Miami (figures are not provided for Dade and other counties) was 0.51 which ranked Miami 27 (below the median) of 52 cities surveyed. New Orleans (with a rate of 2.13) had the highest police homicide rate over this time period. Another study (Sherman and Langworthy, 1979) found police homicide rates to be as high as 33.0 for Chicago over a seven year period and 24.8 for New York County over a five year period. Thus the Chicago rate for this 7 year period was 36 times greater than the Dade County rate for 1980. Given the high violent crime and murder rate one would expect the city's police department to have one of the highest police homicide rates in the nation. It does not.

There is also considerable discussion on the racial aspects of police homicides in Dade County and throughout the nation. Nationwide approximately 50% of police homicide victims have been Black (Fyfe, 1982 and Milton et al, 1977). Dade County is no different in that 50% of the 14 victims of police shootings in 1980 were Black (135B, 166B, 168B, 180B, 182B, 214B and 499B) while 5 were Anglo (017A, 088A, 102A, 105A and 313A) and 2 were Hispanic (191L and 570L). It should be noted that 4 of the 7 Black victims were killed during the May riots.

In terms of rates the police homicide rate against Blacks was 2.50, against Anglos, 0.65 and against Hispanics, 0.34. Thus Blacks were 3.8 times as likely to be killed by the police as were Anglos and 7.4 times as likely to be killed by police as were Hispanics. If the ethnic groups are reduced to two racial groups the Black to White rate ratio is 4.5:1 (2.50/0.55=4.5). This ratio is below the 4.9:1 Black to White rate ratio of felony arrests in Dade County for 1980 (Wilbanks, 1982c). The 4.5:1 Black to White rate ratio is greater than the 3.1:1 (79.2/25.8) rate ratio of Black to White homicides in general. Overall there is little evidence here that Blacks are disproportionately victims of police homicides when their greater involvement in felony arrests and homicides in general are considered. This conclusion confirms that of others (see Fyfe, 1982 and Matulia, 1982) who have reached the same conclusion in studies of other jurisdictions.

HOMICIDES AGAINST THE POLICE

Far more academic literature and studies have been devoted to homicides by the police than against the police. In Dade County in 1980 two police officers (425A and 464A) were killed. One (425A) was working an off-duty job picking up money from a restaurant when he was robbed and killed by four Black males in two separate cars. The second (464A) was killed by a Black male in a chase and arrest situation after the officer stopped the perpetrator for suspicion of burglary. Both police officers were White males. Nationwide 29% of police officers killed were killed during a robbery or burglary while in Dade this was the case for both killings of police. Also nationwide 93% of the offenders were males and 43% were Black while in Dade both shooters were males and Black.

The 1980 Dade County ratio of police killed to those killed by the police was 1:7 (2 to 14). This ratio is below that for the nation as a whole as that rate has been declining over the years and reached 1:3 for 1970 to 1974 (Milton et. al., 1982:60). Or in other terms Dade County had 2.2% of all criminal homicides in the U.S. in 1980 (515 of 23,044) and 1.9% of all police officers killed 2 of 104). In short, Dade County appears to be similar to the rest of the nation in the extent to which police officers are killed.

CHAPTER EIGHT:

THE PROSECUTION ROLE

INTRODUCTION:

As indicated earlier the role of the prosecutor begins before the case actually comes to court. In Dade County assistant state attorneys (ASA's) are on call 24 hours a day with the medical examiner's office and are on the scene of all homicide cases in the county to aid in the investigative process. The assistant district attorneys are also actively involved in the investigation and work with police detectives to ensure that no mistakes are made that might result in the case being eventually thrown out of court. Arrest warrants are issued only with the approval of the state attorney's office and, as mentioned earlier, the standard of evidence appears to be more stringent than simple probable cause. The ASA determines the nature of the charge as well as whether an arrest warrant will be issued.

Almost all homicide cases are initially charged (see Table 8.1) as first (41.7%) or second degree (49.8%) murder as opposed to manslaughter (5.9%), third degree murder (0.7%) or "other" (1.9%). The "other" category involved five cases. Two offenders (430A and 460B) were charged with leaving the scene of an accident (in which a fatality occurred) and failure to stop and render aid. Two other offenders (536B and 264L) were charged with attempted murder. The fifth was a co-defendant who was charged only with the unlawful possession of a shotgun (091B).

The nature of the initial charge does vary by age, sex, and ethnicity of offender (see Table 8.1). Males were more likely than females (43.6% to 25.0%) to be charged with Murder I as were Anglos (63.9%) than Blacks (38.3%) or Hispanics (38.1%). Black Females were the least likely (18.8%) to be initially charged with Murder I. (For a discussion of possible race and sex bias in charging see Chapter Ten.)

CASES CHARACTERISTIC OF MURDER I CHARGE

Murder I by definition involves premeditation and intent or felony murder. Most Murder I cases (N=112) involve some type of felonious act other than the murder. Cases in which the initial charge against the offender(s) is Murder II (N=134) generally involve intent but not premeditation. Most involve "domestics" or homicides between acquaintances and are what are commonly thought of as "passion" crimes in that one or both parties becomes angry during an argument/confrontation and kills the other. Often one or both parties have been drinking.

The common law and Florida law require that convictions for Murder I involve premeditation and intent and that the premeditation be proven to be "uninfluenced or uncontrolled by a dominating passion sufficient to obscure" that premeditation (Tien Wang Vs. State of Florida, 1983). In other words, "Premeditation is a fully formed conscious purpose to kill, which exists in the mind of the perpetrator for a sufficient length of time to permit of reflection, and in pursuance of which an act of killing ensues....Premeditation does not have to be contemplated for any particular period of time before the act, and may occur a moment before the act...It must exist for such time before the homicide as will enable the accused to be conscious of the nature of the deed he is about to commit and the probable result to flow from it insofar as the life of the victim is concerned." (Tien Wang Vs. State of Florida, 1983.

Thus though it is possible to convict a person of Murder I in a passion killing, the state would have to prove that the defendant did reflect upon his intended act and consider the consequences. Since premeditation usually must be proven by circumstantial evidence it is almost impossible to find a passion killing where the circumstantial facts would not also be consistent with a lack of premeditation and thus Murder II. This evidentiary problem is illustrated in the conviction of Case no. 556A (see full narrative in Appendix B). In this case a Dade jury convicted a man of Murder I in what appeared to be a passion killing. The appellate court overturned the conviction and reduced it to Murder II since the circumstantial facts presented at trial were not inconsistent with a lack of premeditation.

Some scholars (Sudnow, 1965; Zimring, 1976; and Boris, 1979) have suggested that prosecutors have stereotypical views of the proper kind of case that should result in a Murder I charge and that that view

is based on notions of desert rather than legal
distinctions involving premeditation. However, there
is no evidence in the 1980 Dade data that such
considerations of desert are utilized by prosecutors in
Dade in formulating the initial charge.

DISPOSITIONS FOR 269 ARRESTS

Obviously not all persons charged for 1980 Dade
County cases were convicted. Convictions did result in
62.1% of the 240 cases (see Table 8.3) in which a final
disposition was reached by July of 1982 (27 cases were
still pending final disposition). Sixty of the 240
cases (25%) were dismissed while thirty-one (12.9%)
were found not guilty. This distribution of final
outcomes (guilty, not guilty, dismissed) did not differ
significantly by age, sex or race/ethnicity of offender
(see Table 8.3). For example, whereas the overall
percentage of convictions was 62.1% the comparable
figures for male and female offenders were 61.4% and
68.0%. Likewise, the conviction percentages for Anglo
offenders was 71.8%; for Black offenders, 60.6%; and
for Hispanics 60.6%.

PLEA BARGAINING

It is difficult to discern from the police and
court records whether a "bargain" has been struck
between the state and the defendant or whether the
defendant decided to plead guilty with no concessions.
However, it is generally assumed that the defendant
receives a "quid pro quo" for his/her plea. This
concession may involve the promise of a more lenient
sentence, the dropping of other charges or the
reduction of the criminal homicide charge. There is
strong evidence (see Table 8.2) that those defendants
pleading guilty do receive charge reductions. Of the
43 offenders charged with Murder I who pleaded guilty
only 3 pled "on the nose" (e.g., to the original charge
of Murder I. A total of 33 of the 43 initially charged
with Murder I were allowed to plead to Murder II while
6 pled to manslaughter. By contrast of those who went
to trial on a charge of Murder I (33 offenders), 14
were found guilty of Murder I. However, 14 were found
guilty only of Murder II while 10 were acquitted. Thus
it appears that those who go to trial stand a
surprisingly good chance (23% or 10 of 43) of acquittal
or charge reduction (44% or 19 of 43). On the other

hand, they also stand a good chance (33% or 14 of 43) of being convicted of Murder I with the concomitant mandatory penalty of life or death.

Those offenders charged with Murder II (38) who pled guilty appear to have received less of a concession in the way of charge reduction (18 of 38 pled to the initial charge of Murder II) though 20 of 38 did plead to manslaughter. Since the sentence for Murder II can range from probation to life in prison (without the mandatory 25 years before parole), it is likely that those who pled to the initial charge did receive some concession on the sentence. However, 39% (18 of 46) of those charged with Murder II who went to trial were acquitted and only 39% (18 of 46) were convicted of the original charge of Murder II. Also, 37 Murder II cases were dismissed before trial. Thus of the 83 Murder II offenders who refused to plead guilty, 55 (66%) were not convicted. Thus it appears that those who were charged with Murder II and who refused to plead guilty fared very well. Of course it may be that the cases against those who pled guilty were much stronger than those who refused to plead (and that this is in fact why they pled guilty) and thus that the high attrition rate (66%) for those charged with Murder II who refused to plead guilty is really a reflection of weak cases.

It is also interesting to note (from Table 8.2) that almost twice as many Dade murderers pled guilty as were convicted at trial (87 to 48). The predominance of convictions via pleas over trial (73 to 55) also resulted in a follow-up of all 1974 Dade murder cases (Wilbanks, 1979a). It does appear, however, that the conviction rate for 1980 Dade residents charged with criminal homicide (rate of 62% for adult offenders reaching final disposition ---149 of 240) is down from the 75% (128 of 170) for 1974 (Wilbanks, 1979a). This reduction in the conviction rate is largely due to the increase in dismissals after arrest but before trial. Only 8% (14 of 170) of 1974 adult offenders reaching a final disposition had the charges dropped while 25% (60 of 240) of such cases involving 1980 offenders resulted in dismissals (Wilbanks, 1979a). There has been little change in six years in the proportion of cases that go to trial which result in convictions. Sixty-one percent (55 of 90) of 1974 adult cases going to trial resulted in convictions compared to sixty-seven percent (62 of 93) of 1980 adult cases.

It should be noted, however, that the convictions at trial are often for a reduced charge and thus charge reductions occur with trial as well as with pleas. In 1980 cases 58% (19 of 33) of those going to trial on Murder I charges (and who were convicted) were convicted of Murder II (14), Murder III (3) or other (3) charges. In 1974 the comparable figure was only

38% (15 of 40) and thus trials in 1980 for Murder I were less likely to convict on the initial charge. However, the opposite result applies to trials in Murder II cases. In 1980 Murder II trials (which resulted in convictions) 36% (10 of 28) were convicted of lesser charges (2 of Murder III, 7 of manslaughter and 1 of other charges) compared to 73% (11 of 15) for 1974 Murder II trials (Wilbanks, 1979a).

ATRRITION OF CASES AT THE PROSECUTORIAL LEVEL

A surprisingly large number of the 269 arrests did not result in convictions. In fact only 149 convictions resulted from the 269 arrests. If the attrition of cases is depicted (see Figure 8.1) is appears that many cases are lost at the court level. This relatively large number of cases is even more surprising when one remembers that those who are initially charged are charged not on the basis of simple probable cause since prosecutors require a more stringent standard. Why are so many cases lost? The public image is that of people "getting away with murder" because of legal technicalities such as suppressed confessions or evidence thrown out because of improper searches.

An analysis of the reasons for attrition was conducted by Robert Blum, a student at Florida International University, under the direction of the author. A total of 91 cases (60 dismissals plus 31 found not guilty at trial) were "lost" after arrest in that the cases were nolle prossed, dismissed by the judge or resulted in acquittals in court. The office of the State Attorney of Dade County maintains in its files of all cases a "disposition form" that is completed by the prosecuting attorney at the conclusion of each case. These disposition forms include narrative data on the circumstances of the homicide event along with a statement by the ASA as to why he/she perceived the case was "lost." In some cases additional information as to the reasons for attrition of cases was gleaned from other documents in the files and from personal conversations with the prosecuting attorneys.

Unfortunately 44 of the 91 cases were not included in the analysis of attrition since the files were out or the disposition form was incomplete or missing. Thus the attrition analysis consisted of 47 cases. Of this total 33 (70%) were nolle prossed by the state or dismissed in court before trial while the remaining 14 (30%) were acquitted at trial.

The case attrition analysis found three general categories of "lost" cases. First, the majority (25 of 47 or 53%) of cases were lost due to problems with witnesses. Either witnesses could not be found, had fled, were uncooperative or unreliable, had changed their testimony, had lied under oath, had a criminal record, etc. Most (19) of the 25 "bad or no witness" cases were dismissed by the state or the judge before trial while the remaining 6 were acquitted at trial as the judge or jury simply did not believe the witnesses were credible to convict beyond a reasonable doubt.

A listing of abbreviated case narratives (for a full narrative see Appendix B) for the three categories of "lost" cases will now be given to provide insight into the nature of the reason(s) for attrition.

EXAMPLES OF BAD WITNESS CASES LOST BEFORE TRIAL

(Case 022A)---The state had two witnesses and both lived at the Rescue Mission where the crime took place. One was considered incompetent to testify. The second had a history of mental problems but agreed to give a deposition and cooperate with the state. At one point this unstable witness even threatened the life of the ASA. At the time of the trial this witness could not be found. After rescheduling the trial several times the state had to dismiss.

(Case 064L)---The state had no eyewitness who could identify the four men caught in the van as the "shooters." The wounded victim could not identify these men and no fingerprints on the guns (thrown from the fleeing van) could be matched to the occupants.

(Case 078B)---The only witness who admitted to seeing the shooting fled to New York and was never found. A second witness did not see the actual shooting but was told of it by the first and missing witness. Later the second witness became abusive when called to give a deposition and refused to cooperate. At a later hearing the earlier statements of this witness were excluded and thus the state was left with no case.

(Case 081B)---The only witness to the murder could not be found for the bond hearing or trial (the witness had said earlier that he had been threatened by the defendant and told to change his story). A continuance was denied and the charges were dropped.

(Case 083B)---The only witness willing to testify was a transient with a questionable background. This witness failed to appear at the trial date (near end of 180 day speedy trial rule) and the Judge dismissed.

(Case 211B)---The state had few witnesses. One witness was in the house but said he was in the toilet and only heard the shot. Two other witnesses said they saw the defendant with two others running from the house. However, they later refused to cooperate and disappeared. The defendant was on probation at the time of his arrest and remained in jail for a year awaiting trial. The state then dropped the charges.

(Case 263L)---The only witness was a 13 year old boy who gave police a description of the man who shot the victim. However, the defendant did not fit this description and later the witness changed his story and said that he suffered from epileptic seizures, had a metal plate in his head and had a bad memory. Charges were dismissed.

(Case 264L)---The only witness claimed the victim was shot by someone in a moving car but ballistics showed that the victim was shot from 3-4 feet away. One week later the witness was himself arrested for attempted armed robbery and decided not to testify. No deal was sought for his testimony since his story did not match the physical evidence.

(Case 269B)---There was no witness to dispute the claim by the defendant that the gun had gone off by accident.

(Case 308A)---The witness changed his mind and would not testify in connection with his deposition which linked the defendant with the crime. The witness claimed that his original statement had been coerced by the police. The witness did not actually see the crime but was approached by the defendant who gave an inculpatory statement. In the absence of other evidence the charges were dismissed.

(Case 323L)---Three other occupants of the car were unable to identify the defendant as the shooter. Three other witnesses who supposedly identified the defendant could not be found for numerous trial dates and so the charges were dropped (the defendant was in jail for almost a year awaiting trial).

(Case 337A)---The state had two witnesses. The first saw the shooting but then disappeared. The second witness was drunk at the time but overheard a conversation 20 minutes before the shooting about the intent to rob the victim. However, her testimony was inconsistent with prior statements and the physical evidence. This witness also had 35 prior arrests. Lacking credible witnesses, the state dismissed the charges.

(Case 349A)---The night clerk at the motel claimed he saw a man leaving the room in a hurry and took down his license plate number. Police then picked up the defendant but he admitted only to being in the area. The night clerk and another employee later refused to cooperate. Lacking physical evidence and cooperative witnesses, the state dismissed.

(Case 356A)---The only evidence against the second defendant was the testimony of the co-defendant (who was convicted and got life) and the latter refused to testify so the state dismissed.

(Case 357L)---The defendant was the only survivor of the three offenders who tried to extort money from a man. The later testified that the defendant was not armed, never threatened him or tried to extort money from him. Since there were no other live witnesses to prove that the defendant was engaged in a felony (thus felony murder) which resulted in a death, the charges were dismissed.

(Case 479L)---The only witness to the shooting was present at the bond hearing but upon advice from his attorney he pled the fifth amendment. This witness also resisted later attempts to have him testify and eventually disappeared (though a $10,000 material witness bond was issued the witness could not be found before the 180 day speedy trial period ended).

(Case 517B)---The state had no witnesses that actually saw the murder and thus the charges were dismissed.

(Case 550B)---The state's case was based on statement of one witness who changed her story after being threatened by the defendant (she claimed the police forced her to make a false statement) and on the statement of the defendant which was inconsistent with the testimony of the medical examiner. The Judge dismissed the charges before trial.

(Case 558L)---All physical evidence indicated that the victim was killed by the co-defendant (who was still at large). The available witnesses changed their stories. The gun the defendant had was not tied to any death and since there were other guns found in the house the defense could have claimed self-defense.

EXAMPLES OF BAD WITNESS CASES LOST AT TRIAL

(Case 241A)---Eyewitness testimony at trial was not believed by the jury (in opinion of ASA). However, since the defendant was on probation at the time (violation hearing was held in conjunction with trial), he was revoked and received one year in county jail.

(Case 248B)---Evidence at trial showed that eyewitnesses were 100 yards from crime scene and only saw victim and offender together a few minutes before (i.e., they did not claim to see the shooting). One witness said he was unsure of his identification and the second witness suffered from mental problems and lacked credibility. A third witness (14 years old) "froze" on the stand. The jury evidently found reasonable doubt.

(Case 259A)---The main witness would not cooperate or testify. The state arrested him for contempt but when he was brought to court he passed out in the hall and thus did not testify at the trial. The jury acquitted the defendant.

(Case 292B)---Two state witnesses disappeared and the only remaining witness was facing a pending rape charge. Furthermore, there was also testimony that the defendant earlier in the day had been robbed by the victim and thus the jury may have felt the victim precipitated his own death. skip 1

(Case 319A)---The state's witness who was called to testify to dispute the defendant's self-defense claim admittedly testified falsely while under oath and earlier had given a false statement to the police. Also, the defense presented extensive evidence that the defendant's common-law husband (the victim) was an alcoholic and constantly beat the defendant and her children. The jury acquitted.

(Case 367A)---The first three defendants all blew the whistle on each other and implicated this defendant (who was acquitted). Since the state only had the testimony of the co-defendants, the jury evidently found a reasonable doubt.

Second, 32% (15 of 47) of the cases examined in the attrition analysis were "lost" due to the view of the judge or jury that the defendant acted in self-defense or, failing that, that he/she at least acted with no culpable negligence. Of these 15 cases, 8 were dismissed by the state or judge before trial while the remaining 7 were found not guilty at trial (in these cases the ASA believed the judge/jury viewed the cases as self-defense---or at least that self-defense could had not been ruled out beyond a reasonable doubt).

EXAMPLES OF SELF-DEFENSE CASES DISMISSED BEFORE TRIAL

(Case 097B)---The victim was 6 foot tall and weighed 213 lbs. while the defendant was 5'5" and 136 lbs. The Judge dismissed the case as he felt the defendant feared for his life and had no prior record (while the victim had an extensive prior arrest record).

(Case 146L)---The charges against the three friends of the drug dealer victim were dismissed because (at least after conviction of the shooter) it was felt that the "real" killer had been punished; the three were only helping a friend; they were not culpable in that they only followed in another car and witnessed the shooting; and one of the three testified against the shooter.

70

(Case 183B)---Charges were dismissed since the
defendant was first stabbed and later shot in both legs
by the victim. When the defendant (now on crutches)
saw the victim again a friend gave him a gun and he
shot the victim. The judge felt this was self-defense
since the defendant was already incapacitated and was
terrified of the victim.

Case 192L)---The judge dismissed the charges
against the woman in the auto (after her gun which she
carried for self-defense discharged) since he felt that
the state had no evidence of culpable negligence.
(This was a dispute over a parking space.)

(Case 291B)---The victim had a reputation of
always carrying a gun when gambling. The defendant had
argued with the victim earlier and when he returned the
victim had a gun in his lap under a towel. The
defendant then drew a gun and shot the victim. All
witnesses claimed it was self-defense and the state saw
no way to successfully prosecute.

(Case 428B)---During the investigation it was
found that the state's witness had concealed a material
piece of evidence which showed that the defendant had
acted in self-defense after the victim attacked her
with a belt-buckle (the hidden evidence). State
decided the defendant acted in self-defense and
dismissed.

(Case 449B)---In a domestic argument the victim
went for a knife but the defendant got to it first.
The victim then lunged at the defendant and was impaled
with the knife. The state decided that self-defense
was either probable or could not be disproved.

(Case 533B)---In a probation violation hearing
preceding the trial the judge decided that the
defendant had killed the victim in self-defense and
thus the state had failed to show that the defendant
had violated his probation. The charges (for the new
crime) were also dropped at this time since the judge
ruled the defendant acted in self-defense.

EXAMPLES OF SELF-DEFENSE CASES DETERMINED AT TRIAL

(Case 024B)---The jury evidently believed that the
two defendants were not culpable since they said they
were trying to flee a robbery attempt (while they were

buying drugs) and the victim was dragged from their fleeing car and killed. Or perhaps the jury believed that the victim was more culpable than the defendants.

(Case 051L)---The jury (in this parking lot dispute) evidently believed that the defendant, who "only" put his hand on the gun of the shooter and yelled, "shoot him," was not culpably negliglent.

(Case 224B)---The jury evidently believed the defendant's story that he came to borrow a shotgun from his old girlfriend and that when the victim came at him the gun discharged (thus defendant was not culpable). Another witness had testified that the defendant had caught the girlfriend and the victim "in the act" and had shot the victim. Either the jury believed the accidental discharge story or had doubt about the state's story.

(Case 238L)---Defendant was charged with felony murder in a drug rip-off that resulted in the "accidental" death of the victim. The judge (bench trial) evidently believed either than the participation of the defendant in the underlying felony (robbery) had not been proved or that the victim was even more culpable as he had a record of armed robbery.

(Case 272B)---The verdict of acquittal was a shock to the ASA. He believed that some jurors believed the defendant acted in self-defense since the victim or one of the friends "could have" had a gun and thus the defendant felt threatened (jurors told ASA this). The state pushed for a parole revocation after the acquittal and the defendant was returned to prison for two years (based on same evidence presented to the jury).

(Case 447B)---The jury felt that the co-defendant was not culpable and was only in the wrong place at the wrong time. Also the defendant testified at the second trial of the co-defendant (who got life sentence).

(Case 484B)---The jury felt that the shooting was justifiable in that the defendant grabbed the gun from the victim and tried to persuade him to leave. But when the victim went for another gun, the defendant shot the victim. The picture of the victim showed him clutching a pistol.

The third and final category of "Lost" cases

involves those in which the defendant, in the terms of
the public, "got off on a technicality" or a legal
issue was raised by the defense that could not be
denied. Fifteen percent (7 of 47) of the lost cases
analyzed fell into this category. Three of the 7
involved cases of felony murder where the underlying
felony could not be proven while an additional three
involved confessions suppressed by the court.

EXAMPLES OF CASES LOST DUE TO "TECHNICALITIES"

(Case 091B)---Both defendants gave statements that
were suppressed by the court since they were given
under a police threat of first degree murder charges.
The robbery victim who gave a statement was later
killed by a girlfriend and thus the state had no case
left.

(Case 118B)---Judge ruled that since the defendant
was not in the house during the shooting the felony
murder rule did not apply. The judge also suppressed a
confession given by the defendant since he was not
advised of his rights prior to the interview. This
case went to trial and the defendant was acquitted.

(Case 459B)---The judge suppressed the confession
of the defendant as to his intent to commit the
underlying felony (a robbery, thus felony murder) and
thus the state had no other evidence of his intent and
so dropped the charges.

(Case 086B)---Charges dismissed due to speedy
trial rule.

(Case 398A)---The Medical Examiner ruled that the
cause of death was not the contusion inflicted by the
defendant but drowning. Since victim had alcohol level
of .25, judge dismissed since it appears victim drowned
due to being drunk not due to being unconscious when he
fell into the canal after being struck by the
defendant.

(Case 271L)---Second defendant agreed to testify
against the first defendant and thus charges were
dropped.

(Case 133L)---Defendant was charged with felony
murder since his alleged accomplice was killed in a
robbery attempt. Defendant testified that he was just

73

riding in a car with the accomplice/robber when the latter decided (without knowledge of this defendant) to rob a pedestrian. The court ruled that there was no evidence that the defendant intended to engage in robbery and thus no evidence of the underlying felony in the charge of felony murder.

ATTRITION DUE TO INCOMPETENCE AND INSANITY

The public appears to be convinced not only that most homicide cases are lost by "technicalities" but that one of the major reasons for people "getting away with murder" is the insanity defense. Though it is likely that the public is not clear as to the difference between insanity and incompetence there is probably also the impression that fewer killers escape punishment via incompetency proceedings. However, this is incorrect as far more murder cases involve incompetency proceedings (and "escape" via this avenue) than the insanity defense (see Laboratory..., 1972, for a critique of the use of incompetency).

A separate analysis of all 1980 Dade homicide offenders that were the subject of a psychiatric evaluation was conducted by Eileen Chafetz (a graduate student in Criminal Justice at Florida International University) under the direction of the author. Though there is no data from Dade County to indicate what proportion of insanity acquittals involve murder cases, a study in New York State (Steadman, 1980) found that about half of the Not Guilty by Reason of Insanity (NGRI) cases there (from 1976 to 1978) were murder cases. A total of 40 offenders were examined by a psychiatrist at the direction of the court. Thus only 14.9% of the 1980 offenders were considered by the court to be so mentally disordered that their condition might preclude them from aiding in or understanding their own defense or that it might have been a causative factor in the criminal homicide.

Only 8 of the 40 (20.0%) were "successful" in that they either delayed their trial indefinitely by being declared incompetent or were found not guilty by reason of insanity (NGRI). Of the 8 only 6 were found NGRI (the remaining two are still incompetent to stand trial and are in the custody of the Department of Mental Health Services---DMHS). It should be noted that the 6 NGRI cases for 1980 is much greater than the single NGRI case found in the follow-up of all 1974 offenders in Dade County (Wilbanks, 1979a).

Furthermore it appears (see Table 8.4 and Figure 8.2) that those who went the "nut route" had a higher conviction rate than those who did not. Of the 209 offenders who reached final disposition without being ordered to undergo a psychiatric exam, 120 or 57.4% were convicted. On the other hand, of the 37 who had a psychiatric exam (the "nut route") and reached a final disposition, the conviction rate was 78.4% (29 of 37). (The conviction rate for all 246 offenders reaching a final disposition was 60.6% (149 of 246). Of course, it may be that those who submitted to a psychiatric exam did so as a last resort since the case against them was so strong and this was their only "out".

Nevertheless, there is no evidence here that those who pled incompetent or insanity "got off easier." In fact, the opposite appears to be the case. The sentences of those convicted also appear (see Table 8.4 and Figure 8.2) more severe than those for offenders who did not go through a psychiatric exam. Thus there is no evidence here that going the "nut route" is less likely to result in a conviction or that this strategy will result in a lesser sentence. For example, 69% (20 of 29) of those who were subjected to a mental exam but who were convicted eventually got 10 years or more in prison (9 of the 20 got life).

The examination of the 40 cases involving psychiatric evaluations as compared to the other 229 arrestees in this study leads to several conclusions that are opposite to what is commonly perceived by the public. Each of the "myths" will be discussed in turn. Each of these myths was also identified by the National Commission on the Insanity Defense (1983). The Dade data confirm the conclusions of that national commission in that the myths they identified also are negated by the data on dispositions for 1980 Dade County homicides.

Myth No. 1----Many criminal defendants plead insanity and most are acquitted.

Many persons apparently believe that the insanity defense and/or incompetency is raised in most cases of violence. Yet the National Commission on the Insanity Defense (1983) cited several studies that indicated that the insanity defense was used in less than 1% of

the felony cases. However there was no study cited
that looked at the use of this defense solely in murder
cases. The present study provides evidence on the
frequency of use of insanity/incompetence in all
homicide cases in one jurisdiction (Dade County,
Florida, for 1980). Mental examinations were conducted
in only 40 of 269 cases in which an arrest was made.
Six were NGRI and 2 are still incompetent. However,
interpreting these figures as indicating successes is
questionable since the probability of conviction was
greater for the 40 than for the other 229 arrestees
(who did not attempt to use incompetence/insanity).

Myth no. 2-----The insanity defense causes major
problems for the Criminal Justice System.

Citizens seem to believe that the insanity defense
is but part of the overextension of rights to criminal
defendants and thus the public anger has been displaced
to the most obvious loophole. However, this concern
ignores the other problems that plague the system.
Most of the homicide cases that are lost are the result
of witness failure to cooperate or unreliable
witnesses.

Myth No. 3----The Insanity Defense allows
Defendants to Fool Juries and Escape Punishment.

It is significant that no Dade jury found any
homicide arrestee NGRI. The only six cases in which
this disposition resulted were by a bench trial (two
cases----See Table 8.4) and by the entering of a plea
in which both the prosecution and the defense
stipulated to the court that the defendant was insane
(three cases---see Table 8.4). The final case (478A)
was tried in front of a jury but the judge dismissed
the jury and issued a directed verdict of NGRI.

Furthermore those defendants who "escaped
punishment" may not view their plight in the same
manner as the public. The two defendants declared
incompetent are still in custody though one (case
005A---see Table 8.4) may be released soon since he
evidently did "fool" or "con" the prosecutor, defense,
judge and psychiatrists. A second (case 315L) was NGRI
and was released only to commit a second murder (see
narrative of 315L in discussion of Myth No. 6). The
four other cases are still in custody of DMHS (two are

76

in a state hospital, one is in a halfway house and one
is on out-patient status in Dade).

Myth No. 4----The Insanity Defense is a Rich Man's Defense

Of the eight "successful" insanity/incompetence
cases, 6 were represented by public defenders
(indicating that they were not rich). Of the 26 cases
who were originally referred for psychological
evaluations but did not pursue an insanity claim at
all, 21 had public defenders or special appointed
public defenders (5 had private counsel). Only 8 of
the 40 cases involving insanity/incompetence retained
an expert (psychiatrist or psychologist) on their
behalf. Only one of the 8 "successful" cases retained
an expert in private practice.

Myth No. 5----Insanity trials are a "circus" of conflicting expert testimony that confuses the jury.

First, juries were presented with insanity
defenses in only three cases as the court did not allow
(or defendants changed their mind) this defense in ten
other cases. In one case (478A) the jury never got to
decide the case as the judge issued a directed verdict
of NGRI since all five psychiatrists unanimously
testified that the defendant was insane at the time of
the offense. In another case (417L) the jury heard the
insanity defense but acquitted on other grounds. In
the third case (403L) the jury found the defendant
guilty. As indicated earlier, all five experts agreed
in one case (478A) while in the other two the defense
did present one expert who represented the defense as
opposed to the three psychiatrists appointed in both
cases by the court.

This lack of conflict may partly be due to the
practice in Dade courts of consulting both the state
and defense before the appointment of expert witnesses
(psychiatrists). Though the defense may object to an
appointment it appears that they do not often object to
the degree that they call other witnesses. The defense
appears to drop the NGRI plea (this occurred in 10
cases) after the examination (by the court appointed
psychiatrist) fails to provide evidence of insanity.
In short, there is little evidence of conflict in the
testimony of expert witnesses. Three of the six

successful insanity defenses were stipulated to by the
state and defense in a plea to the court. Two others
were bench trials in which the defense called no
special "defense" psychiatrists (as opposed to those
appointed by the court). The remaining case was the
directed verdict of NGRI after five psychiatrists
agreed the defendant was insane. Thus there was
obviously no circus of conflicting testimony from
psychiatrists called by the the state and the defense.

Myth No. 6----Most insanity acquittees or persons
declared incompetent go free immediately or within a
short period of time following their trial.

Only one NGRI had been released by DMHS by July
1983 (and been rearrested). However, this case was
quite notable and resulted in a good deal of publicity.
The offender (315L) was a Mariel refugee and was found
NGRI after a bench trial in April of 1981. After only
six weeks in the custody of DMHS he was found competent
and released to his sister. Six months later he was
arrested for killing (by hitting him 14 times in the
head with a steel pipe) an acquaintance whom he thought
was making fun of him. The offender admitted to police
that he had also stabbed two other men since his
release and that he was on his way to kill two other
people when he was arrested. Though this case is
"real" it is the exception and other research (Ribner
and Steadman, 1981) has demonstrated that ex-patients
have lower recidivism rates than ex-offenders (prison
inmates). A second is likely to be released soon
(005A), a third is in outpatient status and the fourth
is in a DMHS halfway house. These periods of
incarceration (or "treatment") are longer than that
served by many offenders who were convicted and
sentenced (several got probation with or without
several months in jail).

Myth No. 7----Those who plead insanity or
incompetence were less likely to be convicted.

As discussed earlier, the conviction rate for
those going through a psychiatric exam was 78.4%
compared to 57.4% for other defendants.

OFFENDERS PROSECUTED IN JUVENILE COURT

Six offenders were prosecuted for homicide in juvenile court (see Figure 8.1). Five of the six were adjudicated as delinquent while one (016B) was not adjudicated. However, this juvenile who appears to have accidently shot another juvenile with a gun they had taken in a burglary, was placed in an intensive community program as a condition of probation (for earlier burglaries he had committed). Four of the five adjudicated delinquents were sent to a juvenile training school. Three of the four were involved in a burglary (see case 375L) when the homeowner shot their companion burglar and each was charged with the felony murder of the companion. The fourth killed a carnival operator (case 096A) when the victim called him a name. One juvenile (case 460B) was placed on probation after running over a Black male with his car in an attempt to flee what he felt was a dangerous situation. No information was found on the length of sentence for the four juveniles sent to training school but such committments are generally for less than a year.

CHAPTER NINE:

SENTENCING CONVICTED OFFENDERS

INTRODUCTION

A total of 149 offenders were convicted and
sentenced from the 240 offenders convicted at the close
of the data collection process (July 15, 1982, for
search of court records). This chapter will examine
the variation in sentences for these 149 cases by type
of final charge; by age, sex, and race/ethnicity of
offender; and by other potential predictor variables.
It should be remembered that the 149 convicted
offenders represent the final step in the attrition of
offenders from the 454 persons identified by name by
the police to those who were actually convicted (see
Figure 8.1).

VARIATION IN SENTENCE BY FINAL CHARGE

Obviously the most important factor in determining
the sentence of an offender is the nature of the final
charge (see Table 9.1). Seventeen offenders were
convicted of Murder I, 83 of Murder II, 5 of Murder
III, 38 of manslaughter and 6 of other charges. The
range in sentences for Murder I was quite small since
the judge has only two options (death or life in prison
with a 25 year mandatory minimum before eligibility for
parole). Seventeen of the 149 persons were convicted
of Murder I. Five of the 17 received the death penalty
with the remaining 12 receiving the life sentence.
Since so much literature exists on the alleged
arbitrary nature of the death penalty, some attention
will be given to each of these cases and the extent to
which these offenders represent the "worst" offenders
of the 17 (or of the 149).

SENTENCES FOR FIRST DEGREE MURDER

The five cases in which the offender received the
death penalty will now be summarized (more detailed
narratives can be found in Appendix A) to be followed
by the 12 in which the offender got a life sentence.
Under Florida law the life sentence for Murder I
requires that the offender not be eligible for parole
for 25 calendar years.

(Case 005A)---An anglo male, 27, received the death penalty for a quadruple murder drug rip-off. Three offenders stabbed the four victims, placed them in a car on a freeway and set the car afire. The second offender got life after pleading guilty and the third was acquitted by reason of insanity.

(Case 052B)---An anglo male, 24, got out of prison and was given a place to stay with his prison roommate's mother (she was black). When she refused him the use of her car he waited by her bed with a shotgun until she awoke and then shot her. After a jury trial he was sentenced to death.

(Case 103L)---An Hispanic male, 44, killed another drug-dealer in a rip-off. The victim was killed in a brutal fashion. After a jury trial the offender received the death penalty.

(Case 252B)---A black male, 24, shot and killed three drug-dealers in the home of one of the victims. He received three consecutive death penalties.

(Case 524L)---Two Columbian drug-dealers where bound, gagged and shot in their residence by two Columbian hit men from a rival drug gang. One offender, 22, was caught, tried and sentenced to death.

The 12 offenders receiving life in prison (with 25 year minimum) were the following:

(Case 057A)---Four elderly anglos (two couples living near each other) were stabbed to death in their homes in the same evening by a 17 year old black male who burglarized their homes. He pled guilty and received life in prison.

(Case 072A)---A black male, 32, attempted to rob an anglo male, 61, on the street. He slammed the victim against the wall and threw him to the ground (causing fatal lacerations). After a jury trial he was sentenced to life in prison.

(Case 110L)---An Hispanic female, 32, was sentenced to life after a jury trial for a bar murder. The offender shot the boyfriend of a friend who was in the bar in retaliation for his treatment of her girlfriend.

(Case 138A)---An anglo victim, 74, was found

82

stabbed brutally in his home and robbed. After a jury trial a black male, 20, was sentenced to life.

(Case 194A)---A black male, 19, beat and killed a woman who found him burglarizing her home. He pled and got life.

(Case 226B)---The offender was a black male, 38, who had been harassing a grocer's family. One day he went to the store and shot one family member. After a jury trial he was sentenced to life.

(Case 255A)---A black male, 18, shot and killed a woman in her car when she resisted a robbery attempt at a red light. He pled and got life.

(Case 332A)---An anglo male, 23, beat and killed a family friend and neighbor after she discovered that he had been stealing from her. After a jury trial he got life.

(Case 356A)---An 80 year old Anglo male was robbed in his room by an Anglo female prostitute, 25. After a jury trial she got life.
(Case 367A)---An 84 year old anglo male was beaten by four black males at his shop in a robbery. One received a life sentence.

(Case 516B)---A 13 year old black female was stabbed and raped in her home during a burglary by a black male, 17. After a jury trial he received life.

(Case 556A)---A 62 year old Anglo (Oriental) male stabbed his father-in-law when he went to his house to get his wife (who had left him). After a jury trial he got life.

Given the information provided at this point (and in the more detailed case narratives in Appendix B), it is difficult to discern what factors differentiate between life and death cases. Prior record is one factor but there was no systematic inclusion of prior record in the case files examined. However, the nature of the event does not appear to be significantly different between the 5 receiving death and the 12 receiving life. When a step-wise regression equation was calculated for death or life as the dependent variable and various case variables as the independent or predictor variables, the best predictor was whether or not the victim was totally innocent (rather than precipitating or participating in the murder). Thus knowing whether the victim was innocent accounted for 36% of the variance (R squared =.36) in death versus life (i.e., those who killed an innocent victim were more likely to receive a life sentence).

The second variable to enter the equation (raising the R squared to .62 was whether the murder involved a White offender on a Black victim (i.e., if a White offender killed a Black victim the offender was more likely to receive death). This result is opposite of what one would expect if racial disparity (against Black victims) existed for 1980 Dade Murder I cases. However, it should be noted that this result is based on a small sample and that case 052B was reputed to be the "first time on record that a white in Florida was condemned to death for killing a black" (Reider, 1983). The third variable to enter the equation was whether the murder was a "domestic" rather than felony related (i.e., those who killed in domestics were less likely to receive death) and raised the R squared to .77. It is somewhat surprising that whether or not the offender pled guilty rather than demanded a trial was not one of the best predictors (however, whether a plea or trial was related to the sentence for Murder I with a zero-order correlation coefficient of r=.30----meaning that those who pled were less likely to receive death).

SENTENCES FOR SECOND DEGREE MURDER

The most striking feature of sentences for Murder II is the wide variation (from probation to life in prison). While (see Table 9.1) two of the offenders convicted of Murder II got simple probation (with no jail time as a condition) and an additional 14 got 5 years or less in jail/prison, 34 received a life sentence (with no minimum) for the same crime. The median sentence for Murder II was 30 years in prison. A comparison of the 14 most lenient sentences with the 34 most severe sentences fails to distinguish any major factors to account for this vast difference. Granted no data was found in the files as to prior record of the offender (the pre-sentence investigations were not available to the researcher), it is still surprising that such a wide range in sentences exists.

A step-wise regression equation was calculated with the dependent variable being the years received (probation being given a score of 0 years and life a score of 51 years) in the sentence. The predictor or independent variables were 25 case variables. The first variable to enter the equation was whether the victim was White (i.e., those who killed White victims got more severe sentences). However, before racial bias is inferred the reader is referred to Chapter Ten which is devoted to testing for racial bias at four decision points, including sentencing. The first variable achieved an R squared of .15 (i.e., it accounted for 15% of the variance in sentences for Murder II). The second variable to enter the equation was whether or not the offender pled guilty (i.e., those who pled got lesser sentences) and raised the R squared to .23. The third variable to enter the equation was whether the offender was male (i.e., male offenders got more severe sentences) and raised the R squared to .29. The only other variable to enter the equation and account for more than 1% of the variance was whether the offender was White and the victim Black (i.e., these cases got more severe sentences). Again, this result is opposite of what one would expect if racial discrimination (against Blacks) existed.

It should be noted at this point that this vast discretion in sentencing for Murder II changed markedly on October 1, 1983, when sentencing guidelines went into effect in Florida. These guidelines call for presumptive sentences based on offense and offender scores as recorded on a "scoresheet" presented in open court.

Those who are not interested in the statistical presentation above will be interested in comparing the six cases resulting in the most lenient sentences for Murder II (probation with or without the condition that the offender spend a number of months in county jail) with six cases (chosen randomly from the 34) receiving a life sentence.

NARRATIVES OF THE SIX MOST LENIENT MURDER II SENTENCES

(Case 139B)---A black male, 40, was shot by his wife while he was watching TV (she had a history of being battered---see narrative in Appendix B) apparently after the most recent argument had ended. She pled to Murder II and was given 10 years probation (with adjudication withheld) and allowed to move to Tenn. and be supervised under the Interstate Compact.

(Case 467B)---A black female, 44, shot her boyfriend in a domestic dispute. She was first declared incompetent but then allowed to plead to Murder II. She was given probation with the condition that she serve one year in the county jail and complete an alcohol program.

(Case 128B)---A black Hispanic male, 31, was charged with the felony murder of his burglar companion when the latter was shot by the homeowner. The surviving burglar pled to Murder II and burglary and was given probation with condition that he serve 5 months in county jail (which he had already done at time of sentencing).

(Case 130B)---A black female, 34, stabbed her husband in the neck during an argument following heavy drinking by both. After a jury trial she received probation with special condition that she serve a year in county jail and complete an alcohol program.

(Case 174B)---A 58 year old black male stabbed a 24 year old black male in a drunken dispute they had over whiskey stolen during the May riots. After a jury trial the offender got probation with special condition that he serve one year in the county jail. The sentence was soon modified to allow work release and later so that it could be served on weekends.

(Case 277B)---A black male, 24, stabbed another black male, 32, during a fist fight when a bystander handed the offender a knife. Offender pled to Murder II and received probation with condition that he serve a year in the county jail.

NARRATIVES OF SIX OF THE LIFE SENTENCES FOR MURDER II

(Case 005A)---An Anglo male received a life sentence for a quadruple murder drug rip-off. Three offenders (one got death the other NGRI) stabbed the four victims, placed them in a car on a freeway and set the car afire. The offender pled to Murder II and received life.

(Case 074L)---A Latin male killed another drug dealer for drugs and money. After a trial he was convicted of Murder II (charged with Murder I) and received life.

(Case 271L)---A Black male offender, 19, with a companion robbed and shot an old man sitting on a bus bench evidently because the victim only gave them $2 for their efforts. He pled to Murder II and received two concurrent life terms.

(Case 400L)---Five Mariel refugees started an argument with a barmaid when the victim attempted to intervene and was shot to death. After a jury trial the offender received a life sentence.

(Case 425A)---Two Black males, 17 and 18, received life sentences after pleading to Murder II and robbery in the killing of a police officer who was working off-duty picking up money for a restaurant.

(Case 496L)---A Latin male, 37, killed another Latin male in an argument at a night club over a bill. The offender was found guilty at trial and sentenced to life.

SENTENCES FOR MANSLAUGHTER

Thirty-eight offenders were convicted and sentenced for manslaughter. The sentences (see Table 9.1) ranged from probation for three offenders (049B, 233L, and 518B) to one (051L) who received 20 years in prison. The probation sentences all involved domestic disputes with two involving a male killing a girlfriend (049B and 518B) while the other involved a man killing another man who made comments to his girlfriend. By contrast the offender receiving the most severe sentence (20 years) killed a man and shot at other members of his family in a dispute over a parking space. Six offenders received 15 years for manslaughter. Two involved a husband killing his wife (148A and 094B); one killed a prostitute in a fight (350B); one involved a tenant/landlord dispute (418A); one involved threats between two males (067B); and one (167A) was a riot killing. A stepwise regression equation was calculated to determine the best predictors of the sentence in the 38 manslaughter cases. The best predictor was whether the offender pled guilty (i.e., those who did got lesser sentences) and this predictor alone achieved an R squared of .17. The second variable to enter the equation was whether the offender and victim were acquainted or strangers (i.e., offenders who were acquaintances got lesser sentences) and achieved an R squared of .24.

87

AGE, SEX AND RACE/ETHNICITY IN SENTENCES

There was some variation in sentences for the 149 convicted offenders by age, sex and race/ethnicity of offender when one examines all convictions regardless of offense of conviction (see Table 9.2). This difference in sentencing patterns was most pronounced for male and female offenders as 53.0% of the female offenders got 5 years or less while only 24.2% of male offenders received such a lenient sentence. Also 37.9% of male convictees got life or death compared to only 22.8% of female offenders. There were no obvious differences in sentences by race/ethnicity. Chapter Ten will examine the possible existence of race and sex bias in sentencing.

CHAPTER TEN:

RACE AND SEX BIAS

INTRODUCTION

The public's perception of the legitimacy of the criminal justice system is closely tied to its perception of the fairness of that system. Thus it is difficult to have faith in a system that one believes is unfair due to discrimination by race, sex or some other "non-legal" factor. Furthermore, the belief or disbelief in the basic fairness/justice of the criminal justice system is more than an academic matter as there is some evidence that a belief in the basic unfairness or injustice of the system may actually conribute to criminal activity. Offenders may "neutralize" (Sykes and Matza, 1957) their conscience when violating the law by a belief that the injustice of the system makes it unworthy of obedience. Two of the techniques of neutralization described by Sykes and Matza (1957) as being utilized by offenders are denial of the victim (e.g., the offender maintaining that he is not the offender but a victim of oppression and discrimination) and condemnation of the condemners (e.g., the offender maintaining that he is no more a "crook" than the corrupt politicians or brutal cops who condemn him).

Davis (1974) interviewed a sample of blacks (not necessarily offenders) in several social settings in an attempt to discover the explanations blacks give for the higher crime rate among blacks. He found seven types of explanations to be most prominent and described them as a "core of different and unique motives" that were "preconditons to (criminal) behavior but not necessarily precursors of behavior" (p. 74). The uniqueness of this set of explanations is questionable since Davis did not compare the responses of blacks to other racial groups. However, he maintains that these explanations may become motives for violation of the law since they represent a "justification for no obligation" to the law.

The idea that criminals may be motivated by rationalizations about the injustice of the law and the criminal justice system is not new as Sutherland's theory of differential association (1939) maintained that people learn both techniques of criminality and rationalizations (or in Davis' term, neutralizations) for it from personal interaction with others. These rationalizations were seen by Sutherland as motives of criminal behavior. Critics of this view (Nettler, 1978:271) point out that such an explanation confuses reasons with motives and that the justifications which criminals give for their behavior should not be confused with the actual motives which impel that behavior.

Given the commonly expressed belief that the criminal justice system discriminates against members of minority groups, the poor, women, etc. it is surprising that little research exists that has attempted to test the "discrimination hypothsis." It also appears that the term "discrimination" is not properly understood by the public (and some academics) in that it is equated with disparity. Clearly, there is a difference between "differentiation" (discriminating or treating individuals or groups differently for a valid and legal reason) and "disparity" (discrimination based on "non-legal" criteria). In short, disparity refers to unwarranted differences in dispositions among individuals or groups while differentiation refers to different (whether warranted or unwarranted) dispositions among individuals or groups (Parisi, 1982).

For example, blacks (or women or the poor) may receive more severe dispositions for a particular offense (e.g., burglary). This "fact" represents "differentiation" but not necessarily "disparity" since the differentiation may be based on legal differences between blacks and whites. Such potential legal differences might include the greater prevalence of a prior record among the black offenders, the amount of goods stolen, the age of the offenders, etc. On the other hand, if the differentiation found to exist cannot be accounted for by legal criteria (e.g., greater liklihood of prior record), there is some evidence that disparity exists in the treatment of blacks and whites. However, a simple assertion that disparity exists is seldom possible since most studies do not control for all (or even the most important) of the potential legal variables that might explain differentiation. Thus it is always possible that differentiation exists due to some (unmeasured) legal criteria that have not been controlled.

Several studies have addressed the issue of discrimination by race and sex by the criminal justice system. Kleck (1981) made an exhaustive review of all empirical studies of race and criminal sentencing published in the United States through 1979. He found 40 studies of non-capital sentencing and 17 of capital sentencing which examined the race factor. Likewise, (Parisi, 1982) reviewed a comparable number of sentencing studies which related sex of the offender to disposition. The general conclusions of these two reviews is that little evidence exists of racial or sexual disparity (rather than differentiation) in sentencing.

Kleck (1981) found that of the 40 studies examining race and non-capital sentence length only 8 supported the discrimination (disparity) hypothesis. "Mixed" results were found in 12 and 20 produced evidence contrary to the discrimination hypothesis. However, the evidence for the disparity hypothesis is weaker than this tabulation would indicate since most of the 8 which found disparity either failed completely to control for prior criminal record or did so using the crudest possible measure of prior record (a simple dichotomy). Of the 17 studies of capital sentencing only 7 produced evidence favoring the disparity hypothesis but none of these controlled for prior record.

Parisi (1982) found that studies of possible sexual discrimination in sentencing produced evidence of more lenient or equal sentences for females rather than more severe sentences. However, she also pointed out the failure of most such studies to control for relevant legal factors that might affect disposition. She also pointed out the possibility that a result of equal sentences might be considered disparity if the females differed significantly from the males on such factors as prior record and seriousness of the offense. For example, if women are less likely to have a prior record and commit less serious offenses then "equal" sentences for females and males would be indicative of disparity. Thus it may be that a study which reports no discrimination (equal sentences) but fails to determine if the two groups (males and females) are equal has not proven no discrimination. It may be that the females should have received less severe sentences due to lesser offenses and a lesser prior record. In short, disparity may be present without differentiation in dispositions if there is differentiation (based on legal criteria) in the two groups.

Only one study (Curran, 1979) has examined either race or sex discrimination with Dade County data. She found that there was a "chivalry" factor (less severe sentences) for two time periods (1971 and 1975-76) but no sex difference for another period (1965-66).

Radelet (1981) agrees that prior studies of the race factor in capital and non-capital sentencing have been contradictory to the hypothesis of racial discrimination (disparity) against black defendants. However, he suggests that the failure to find evidence of racial discrimination at sentencing may be due to three limitations of prior studies. First, he suggests that prior studies have focused on the characteristics (e.g., race and sex) of the offender but not the victim. Second, he says that such studies have failed to distinguish among differences in the crime itself (e.g., such as domestic versus felony homicides). Third, he suggests that studies of racial discrimination have focused on the sentencing decision while ignoring possible racial disparity at earlier decision points in the criminal justice system. Radelet claims to have found racial disparity at the charging stage (but not at sentencing) in capital cases in several Florida (including Dade) counties in that those who killed whites were more often charged with first degree murder even after the type of homicide (domestic versus felony) was controlled.

Nettler (1978:70) contends that the public is incorrect in believing the criminal justice system discriminates against minorities. He suggests that most studies of police decision-making do not support the disparity hypothsis and thus the perception of the public that the police "pick on" minorities and thus inflate the "official" crime rate for minorities. Likewise, Hindelang (1978, 1979) found that official crime statistics are not distorted by the police since victimization surveys also indicate similar (to official statistics) ratios of black to white and male to female offenders.

Also, in a comprehensive study by the Rand Corporation (Petersilia, 1983) of possible race bias in the criminal justice systems of California, Michigan, and Texas, the author found that the races were, in general, treated similarly when important legal factors were controlled. The sentencing stage represented one exception to this conclusion in that differences between sentence length and time served did not disappear when numerous controls were introduced. However, the author suggests several interpretations of this result aside from the view that racial disparity existed.

Given the background of the prior literature in this area, this chapter will examine discrimination (both differentiation and disparity) at four decision stages of the criminal justice system to determine if "discrimination" based on race and sex can be found. If differentiation exists at any or all of the four points an attempt will be made to see if that differentiation represents disparity (e.g., legal differences will be controlled). Also, an attempt will be made to overcome the three limitations described by Radelet (1981) by examining the race and sex of both offender and victim, controlling for type of homicide, and examining three decision stages prior to sentencing.

THE METHODOLOGY

The four decision stages at which possible race and sex "discrimination" was examined were the following:

(1) The decision as to whether or not to charge the 454 identified offenders (269 were charged/arrested while 185 were not)

(2) The decision as to type of charge for the 269 persons arrested (112 were charged with Murder I, 134 with Murder II and 23 with other charges)

(3) The decision as to whether or not the 240 persons charged and reaching a final disposition in adult court were found guilty (149 were found guilty and 91 were found not guilty or charges were dismissed)

(4) The sentencing decision for the 149 persons found guilty (6 got probation, 91 got a term of years in jail/prison, 47 got a life sentence and 5 received the death penalty). The disposition was "final"" only in terms of the trial process as appellate court decisions were not considered. For example, one of the five receiving the death penalty was released from death row after the Florida Supreme Court overturned his conviction and set him free---he was not remanded for a new trial (see case 524L in Appendix B).

Differentiation in disposition at the four decision stages was examined for seven offender/victim independent variables:

(1) Sex of offender
(2) Ethnicity of offender
(3) Race/sex of offender
(4) Ethnicity of victim
(5) Sex of victim
(6) Victim/offender relationship by sex
(7) Victim/offender relationship by ethnicity

Tables were generated via the CROSSTABS program of the Statistical Package for the Social Sciences (SPSS) for these seven independent variables and the four dependent variables (the four decision stages, each with its decision options). The cross-tabulations thus indicate the extent to which differentiation resulted at each decision point for the seven offender/victim variables.

Since the crosstabulations do not control for other variables any differentiation cannot be viewed as evidence of disparity. For example, it may be that differences in the percentage of male and female offenders arrested (as opposed to identified but not arrested) is due to the strength of the physical evidence, the willingness of witnesses to testify, the availability of witnesses, whether the homicide was "felony-related" or a "domestic," etc. It is also possible that such differentiation is due to the consideration of improper (non-legal) factors such as race and/or sex of the offender or victim. Though it was impossible to control for all of the possible variables that might impact upon the decision at each of the four stages, an attempt was made to determine the relative importance of selected factors, both legal and non-legal.

At each of the four decision stages a step-wise regression equation was generated via SPSS with a dichotomized dependent variable (e.g., charged versus not charged; Murder I versus other charges; convicted or not) for the first three stages and a continuous dependent variable for the sentencing stage (with probation given a sentence score for years in prison of 0; life with no minimum a score of 51; life with 25 year minimum a score of 99 and death a score of 150). The independent variables measured and thus "eligible" for selection as efficient predictors were the following:

LEGAL FACTORS

(1) Whether or not the victim and offender were acquainted
(2) Whether or not the victim and offender were strangers
(3) Whether or not the victim was "innocent" (versus victim-participated or victim-precipated
(4) Whether or not the victim precipitated the assault
(5) Whether or not the homicide was a "domestic"
(6) Whether or not the homicide was "felony-related"
(7) Whether or not the victim was legally drunk at the time of assault
(8) Whether or not a gun was used in the fatal assault
(9) Whether or not the offender was charged with Murder I (used only for sentencing decision)

NON-LEGAL FACTORS

(10) Whether or not the offender was black
(11) Whether or not the offender was latin
(12) Whether or not the offender was male
(13) Whether or not the offender was a white female
(14) Whether or not the offender was a black male

(15) Whether or not the victim was black
(16) Whether or not the victim was male
(17) Whether or not the homicide was white offender on black victim
(18) Whether or not the homicide was black offender on white victim
(19) Whether or not the homicide was male offender on female victim
(20) Whether or not the homicide was female offender on male victim

These 20 potential predictor varibles were utilized to determine which individual (and which of the two categories--legal versus non-legal) variables were the most efficient predictors. If disparity exists one would expect the non-legal variables to account for a significant degree of the variance in the dependent variable. Though the major non-legal factors were measured in the study it is obvious that the major legal factors (strength of evidence, availability of witnesses, prior record, etc.) were not measured at the first three decision stages. The most important legal factor, the nature of the charge (Murder I versus other charge), was measured and utilized as a predictor at the sentencing stage. Thus there was no expectation that a substantial portion of the variance at the first three decision stages would be accounted for (unless signifiant disparity existed) in the absence of a measurement of the most important legal factors.

RESULTS

The first decision stage was whether or not a charge was lodged against the 454 identified offenders. There was some differentiation in charging versus not charging for various subgroups of offenders based on race and sex characteristics of victim and offender. Overall 59.3% (269) of the 454 identified offenders were arrested. Some of the subgroups with arrest percentages above this figure were cases involving male offenders (61.2%), black offenders (68.3%), white female offenders (70.6%), and black male offenders (70.7%). Other subgroups with arrest percentages above the average were cases with female victims (77.2%), Black offenders on Hispanic victims (82.4%) and Black offenders on Anglo victims (80.4%). However, this differentiation is not necessarily disparity since legal factors may account for these differences.

A step-wise regression equation was generated via SPSS with the charge/not charged dichotomy as the dependent variable and the 20 independent variables listed earlier. The first predictor to enter the equation was whether or not the victim precipitated the assault (those who did were more likely to be arrested) with this variable accounting for 22% of the variance in the disposition. This result is meaningful in that one of the major reasons identified offenders were not charged was the view that the homicide was justifiable and a major determinant of that decision involved the frequent "first use" of deadly force by the victim or the victim engaging in a felony (such as an armed robbery) which resulted in his death.

The remaining predictors only increased the multiple R squared by 8% (to 30%). Thus 70% of the variance in charged/not charged could not be accounted for by the predictor variables utilized. Only three other predictors explained an additional 1% of the variance and those were all legal factors (whether the victim was drunk, whether the homicide was felony-related, and whether the offender was a stranger). Thus though differentiation exists when the decision to charge is considered, disparity (differentiation based on non-legal factors) does not appear to exist. Or phrased another way, one cannot predict the arrest decision from knowledge of the race and/or sex of the offender or victim after controlling for (some) legal factors.

The second decision point was whether the charge was Murder I or a lesser charge. Overall 41.6% (112) of the 269 arrested offenders were charged with Murder I. However, some differentiation was found in that several case subgroups had a higher percentage of arrests for Murder I. Among these subgroups were cases involving white male offenders (47.2%), Hispanic offenders (63.9%), black offenders on Anglo victims (70.3%), and Hispanic victims (67.6%).

The regression equation indicates that legal factors were more efficient predictors of the dependent variable (whether or not the charge was Murder I) than were non-legal factors. Only 12% of the variance in the dependent variable was accounted for by the independent variables selected for inclusion in the equation. Only two, both of these legal factors, accounted for more than 1% of the variance. Whether or not the victim was totally innocent (versus victim participated or precipitated) was the first predictor selected and accounted for 6% of the variance (i.e., those who killed innocent victims were moe likely to be charged with Murder I). The second predictor chosen, whether the victim and offender were acquainted, accounted for an additional 1% of the variance (i.e., those who killed acquaintances were less likely to be charged with Murder I). Again, though differentiation exists when the decision as to the exact charge is considered, disparity does not appear to exist. In short, one cannot explain the nature of the charge by the race and/or sex of the offender or victim when (some) legal factors are controlled.

The third decision point at which race and sex bias were tested was whether the offender was found guilty. Overall 62.1% (149) of the 240 arrestees reaching final disposition by July 15, 1982, were found guilty. However, differentiation existed at this decision point as some subgroups of cases had guilty percentages greater than 62.1%. Among these subgroups were those with female offenders (68.0%), Hispanic offenders (71.8%), black female offenders (69.2%), female victims (65.9%), Anglo offenders on Anglo victims (70.4%), and Anglo victims (70.1%).

However, the differentiation by subgroups indicated above does not appear to be disparity from the regression equation generated for this decision point. The dependent variable for this equation was whether or not the offender (in the 240 cases reaching final disposition in adult court by July 15, 1982) was found guilty. Since no measures of strength of evidence were utilized it is not surprising that only 8% of the variance in outcome was accounted for by the combination of all the predictor variables. Whether or not a gun was used accounted for 2% of the variance (those who used guns were more likely to be found guilty) and was the first predictor to enter the equation. The next three factors to enter the equation (whether the homicide was felony-related, whether the victim and offender were acquainted and whether the victim precipitated the assault) were also "legal" factors and each accounted for an additional 1% of the variance in outcome. Thus, we cannot explain the outcome (whether guilty or not) of the 240 cases by knowledge of the race and/or sex of the offender or victim when (some) legal factors are controlled.

The fourth and final decision point was the severity/length of the sentence received by the 149 convicted offenders. Overall 35.0% of the 149 convicted offenders received the three most severe sentences (life with no minimum, life with a 25 year minimum and death). However, some differentiation did occur in that some case subgroups had percentages beyond the 35.0%. For example, higher severe sentence percentages were found for Hispanic offenders (52.1%), White male offenders (48.2%) and Anglo offenders on Anglo victims (51.0%).

The differentiation that appears in these tables does not appear to be disparity when the step-wise regression equation is examined. The variable which should be the best predictor, whether the final charge was Murder I or a lesser charge, accounted for 58% of the variance in sentence for the 149 cases in which a conviction was obtained. Two non-legal factors were the second and third factors to enter the equation. Whether the victim was white or not entered second (i.e., those who killed Whites received greater sentences) and explained an additional 3% of the variance and whether the offender was male or not

entered third (i.e., male offenders got more severe
sentences) and accounted for an additional 2% of the
variance. The predictive power of whether the victim
was white remained strong (changing the R squared by
3%) when all legal variables were forced to enter the
equation first before the program selected any
non-legal factor. All of the non-legal predictors
increased the R squared by 6% after legal factors were
forced to enter the equation first. Whether the
offender was a white female (i.e., they got lesser
sentences) accounted for 2% of this total.

Separate regression equations were generated for
all offenders convicted of Murder I (N=17), Murder II
(N=83) and manslaughter (N=38). The best predictor of
life versus death for Murder I convictions was whether
or not the victim was totally innocent (i.e., those who
killed innocent victims were more likely to get life
rather than death) and accounted for 36% of the
variance in the sentences for Murder I. The second
variable to enter the equation was whether the case
involved a White offender on a Black victim (i.e.,
Whites who killed Blacks were more likely to get death)
and accounted for an additional 26% of the variance.
This result is opposite what one would expect if race
bias (against Blacks) existed.

The regression equation with the 83 Murder II
sentences as the dependent variable indicated that the
best predictor of the sentences (which ranged from
probation to life----see discussion in Chapter Nine)
was whether the victim was White (i.e., those who
killed White victims were more likely to get severe
sentences) and accounted for 15% of the variance in
sentences. The predictive ability of this variable
remained strong even after all legal variables were
forced into the equation first as whether the victim
was White still raised the R squared by 14% when it
entered the equation. Of course this result does not
prove disparity exists since other important legal
controls that were not included may have (if utilized)
reduced the predictive ability of this variable.

The regression equation on the 38 manslaughter
sentences indicated that the best predictor of the
sentences (which ranged from probation to 20 years) was
whether the offender pled guilty or went through a
trial (i.e., those who pled guilty received lesser
sentences) and accounted for 17% of the variance.
However, the second predictor to enter the equation was

99

whether the case involved a White offender on a Black victim (i.e., Whites who killed Blacks got less severe sentences----a result opposite to that found for Murder I sentences) and accounted for an additional 10% of the variance. The predictive ability of this variable remained undiminished even after all other legal variables were forced to enter the equation first.

Thus at the sentencing level knowledge of the race and/or sex of the offender or victim does slightly improve our ability to predict the sentence once (some) legal variables are controlled. However, though the latter represents some evidence of disparity it should be noted that disparity is not "proven" since most major legal factors were not measured in this study.

CUMULATIVE DISPARITY ACROSS THE SYSTEM

The discussion thus far has considered disparity at several individual points in the criminal justice system but has not examined possible cumulative bias across the system. It is quite possible that a particular group (e.g., Blacks and/or males) may face a series of decisions across the criminal justice system that result in cumulative discrimination. For example, it is often (and correctly) pointed out that Blacks are incarcerated at a much higher rate than are Whites in the U.S. The latest figures available (Christianson, 1982; Blumstein, 1982) indicate that Blacks are approximately seven times as likely to be incarcerated as Whites. Though there is agreement on this racial "gap" in incarceration, there is disagreement in explaining the reasons for the gap. Some (Christianson, 1980a & 1980b) suggest either implicitly or explicitly that the gap is a product of racially disproportionate decisions at various stages of the criminal justice system (e.g., at arrest, at conviction, at sentencing). Others (e.g., Blumstein, 1982) assert that the racial gap in incarceration rates is explained largely by racially disproportionate arrest rates with the later decision points (conviction and sentencing) simply maintaining the disproportionality found at the arrest stage. In short, one position sees the racial gap in incarceration as the cumulative result of discriminatory decisions across the criminal justice system while the other sees the gap as resulting from a gap in offense levels (as represented by arrest rates) rather than from discriminatory decisions in the criminal justice system.

One way to shed light on this controversy is to examine changes in the racial gap at various decision points across the criminal justice system to see if the gap in Black and White arrest rates found at the arrest stage is stable across the criminal justice system or whether the gap in arrest rates cumulates from decision point to decision point so that a greater gap (cumulates) results at the sentencing stage. Furthermore, since it can be argued that the arrest decision is discretionary on the part of the police and thus may represent racially biased decisions, it would be useful to examine the racial gap at the suspect level before anyone is arrested. Obviously, many persons are not arrested due to a lack of physical evidence, witness problems, flight or death of the perpetrator, the offense being viewed as justifiable, etc.

The dispositional data for identified offenders in all 569 homicide cases in 1980 in Dade County were examined at seven decision points:

(1) whether or not the suspect was identified by race and/or sex;
(2) whether or not the suspect was identified by name;
(3) whether or not the suspect was arrested;
(4) whether or not the arrestee was convicted;
(5) whether or not the person convicted was sentenced to jail/prison time or probation;
(6) Whether or not the person sentenced to jail/prison time received eleven or more years in prison;
(7) Whether or not the person sentenced received the death penalty.

Table 10.1 presents data on six of these decision points (the final two decision points are combined) with respect to the gap in terms of disposition percent at each stage. It is obvious from Table 10.1 that the Black offender subgroup does not have the highest percent of unfavorable disposition at each of the six decision points. Both Anglos (91%) and females (96%) were more likely to be identified by name than Blacks (79%). White females (71%) were more likely to be arrested than Blacks (68%). Anglos (64%) and females (61%) were more likely to be convicted than Blacks (56%). Anglos (96%) and Hispanics (98%) were more likely to get jail/prison time than were Blacks (95%). Finally, Anglos (72%) and Hispanics (67%) were more likely to receive 11 years of more in prison than were Blacks (56%).

Furthermore, Blacks were not treated as a homogenous category of offenders as the percent of dispositions at each stage were sharply different at three decision points (identification by name, arrest, and eleven or more years in prison) for Black males as contrasted to Black females. The difference in percent of disposition for male versus female offenders was greater at all but one decision point (arrest) than was the case for Black versus White offenders. Thus sex was a better predictor of disposition than was race.

Table 10.2 presents racial (and sex and age) gaps at seven points in the criminal justice system. At first glance it might appear that the race gap grows larger as the offenders move through the system. In other words, while the rate ratio/gap begins at 4.0:1 at the level of identification by race/sex, it increases to 5.6:1 at the point of the incarceration decision. However, the positive cumulation in the size of the Black/White gap appears to be limited to Black male offenders as the gap actually narrows for Black versus White female offenders (from 8.4:1 to 4.6:1 at the incarceration decision). Furthermore, the increase in the racial gap appears to be due to the tendency of Hispanic Whites (rather than Anglo Whites) to receive more favorable outcomes at the seven points. In fact, the ethnic (as opposed to the racial) gap for Black to Anglo offenders actually narrows (from 10.1:1 to 9.7:1 at the incarceration decision) as one moves across the system.

In other terms the ethnic gap between Black and Anglo offenders is narrowed by 4% as one moves across the first five decision points of the system (to incarceration); by 15% as one moves to the sixth point (length of sentence); and by 86% as one moves to the final point (death penalty). Likewise, the ethnic gap between Hispanic and Anglo offenders is also narrowed---by 42% across the first five decision points; by 42% to the sixth point; and by 70% to the final point. Certainly there is no evidence from the Dade data that the largely Anglo decision-makers in the criminal justice system are discriminating against Black and/or Hispanic offenders. In fact, a case can be made that (without controls for differences among offenders and types of homicides) that the system is discriminating against Anglos as the ethnic gaps narrowed rather than widened.

Table 10.3 presents the Dade data from a different perspective. This table indicates the attrition from identified suspects to sentencing. For example, of every 100 Dade homicide offenders by race and/or sex, 74 were identified by name, 44 were arrested, 25 were convicted, 24 were sentenced to jail/prison time, 14 were sentenced to 11 or more years (or life or death), and 1 received the death penalty. The variation in this attrition did not vary significantly by race, ethnicity or sex of the offenders.

SUMMARY AND CONCLUSIONS

This study examined the dispositions of all offenders in 1980 homicide cases in Dade County to determine if there was evidence of discrimination by race or sex. Differentiation was found in that some subgroups of the cases (by race and/or sex of offender or victim) did have differing percentages for certain outcome options at the four decision points. However, the direction of those differences was not consistently in the direction predicted by the discrimination hypothesis (that blacks and women receive more severe dispositions compared to other subgroups) since whites and men appear to often receive more severe outcomes. For example, male offenders received more severe dispositions than females at three of the four decision points (the exception being whether convicted or not). Black offenders received more severe dispositions only at the first decision point (whether arrested if identified). Cases involving female victims resulted in more severe dispositions in only the first three decision points (not at sentencing). Cases involving anglo victims resulted in more severe dispositions at three of the decision points (the exception being the first stage (whether arrested if identified).

Furthermore, the differentiation that does appear is not equivalent to disparity (unjustified differentiation) in that the best predictors of the outcome of the case at each of the four decision points are legal rather than non-legal factors. In short, with the exception of the sentencing stage, there is absolutely no evidence to suggest disparity by race and/or sex characteristics of offenders or victims when (some) legal factors are controlled.

Also, there does not appear to be any cumulative discrimination against Blacks or females as one moves across the criminal justice system in that the gap in Black versus White and female versus male offenders does not increase across the various decision points. It is clear from the 1980 Dade data that the higher incarceration rates for Blacks is due to their greater representation in the pool of suspects rather than to cumulative discriminatory decisions across the system.

The following qualifications to this summary should be considered before the inevitable misinterpretations arise:

(1) This conclusion does not necessarily "prove" that discrimination by race or sex did not exist in the handling of 1980 homicide offenders from arrest to sentencing. It is one thing to assert that there was no evidence of discrimination and another to say that no evidence was found. It is quite possible that discrimination (disparity) by race or sex did exist for individual cases but that such discrimination was not so prevalent that it could be demonstrated for groups (such as for all black or female offenders). Or it may be that in some individual cases a black (or woman) may have received a more severe disposition than a white in a comparable case while in another the black may have received a less severe disposition. This combination of some more severe and some less severe dispositions would thus cancel each other and produce an overall result of "equality" of sentences. It should be pointed out that leniency can also be the result of racial and sexual stereotypes (cf. Kleck, 1981; Parisi, 1982) in that a subgroup may be viewed as less responsible due to cultural or hereditary characteristics. However, no evidence was found in this study of a linear or consistent bias for or against blacks or female offenders.

(2) The disposition for blacks and females may be so inter-correlated with some legal factors that it is not possible to separate out the effects of race. Swigert and Farrell (1976) suggested that prior studies of sentencing and homicide did not find a race bias due to the correlation of race with social class, type of legal representation, extent of prior record, etc. In short, the race or sex bias may operate through a legal factor and thus not appear in the regression equation.

(3) Equality of sentencing does not necessarily mean

that justice is achieved. Justice is not attained if unequal cases receive equal treatment. This point is sometimes made in opposing "determinate" or "fixed" sentences in that such a scheme attempts to impose equal sentences on unequal cases. Thus evidence of little or no differentiation does not necessarily mean no disparity exists since disparity can exist without differentiation (if the cases are unequal).

Thus the results of this study are consistent with the survey of prior literature in the area of race (Kleck, 1981) and sex (Parisi, 1982) bias in that little or no evidence of disparity was found at the four decision stages from arrest to sentencing. It appears that the common belief on the part of blacks (and many women) that "their" subgroups are discriminated against in the criminal justice system are not supported for 1980 homicide offenders in Dade County at the four decision points from arrest to sentencing. This result receives additional importance when one considers the literature discussed earlier that indicates that black criminality is, in part, a product of a "justification for no obligation" based on a belief in discrimination. The results reported here and the similar results found by others should caution against sweeping generalizations about discrimination in the criminal justice system in Dade County in the absence of empirical support. The evidence that does exist would appear to contradict that hypothesis.

CHAPTER ELEVEN:

NEWSPAPER COVERAGE

INTRODUCTION

The public learns of homicides committed in the community from the mass media. Though television covers crime the news shows are limited in time and thus most homicides are not reported on the local news. Newspapers do devote considerable space to crime news, especially homicide. However, all homicides are not even reported by newspapers. Thus the public cannot hope to learn all pertinent facts about homicides since the ones reported are only a sample of all that occur.

There are several other problems faced by the reader who wants to learn about homicide from newspaper accounts. First, the details available for a particular homicide are not all available the day the story breaks in the newspaper. Sometimes the victim's name is not even known and usually the identity of the offender(s) is unknown. Though this information may become avilable within a few days (most homicides are solved quickly if at all) the details/facts available later are not "news" at that point and thus rarely does a follow-up story appear giving more details on a homicide reported days earlier. Second, dispositional data is seldom provided in the newspaper. By the time the case has gone to court and a final disposition reached (whether conviction or not), the case is no longer news. Sentences are generally only reported if the case is especially notable or if the sentence is extreme (i.e., probation or death). Thus the reader's impression of sentences for homicide convictions is likely to be quite skewed since the typical or average sentence is seldom reported. Third, newspaper coverage provides little aggregate data on homicide since reporting is on a case by case basis. Thus readers are not likely to learn the percentage of county homicides that involve drug rip-offs, domestic disputes, black on white cases, etc.

This chapter will report on an analysis of the coverage of 1980 Dade homicides by the Miami Herald. The author with Cheryl Little, a student at Florida International University, clipped all articles appearing in the Herald in 1980 to 1982 that referred to any of the 569 homicides occurring in Dade County in

107

1980. A second student, Ira Vilinsky, under the direction of the author, coded all articles clipped so that a computer analysis could be conducted. The purpose of the analysis was to determine what factors were good predictors of whether or not a homicide was covered by the Herald, the type of coverage and the extent of coverage.

PREDICTORS OF WHETHER CASE WAS REPORTED

Overall 59.6% (or 339 of 569) of the 1980 Dade County homicides were mentioned/covered by the Miami Herald. There were some types of cases which were always covered while other types were reported at a rate significantly below the average (59.6%). One may take a high reporting percentage as an indication that the Herald considered this type of case as "newsworthy" since these types of cases were selected from all cases available to the newspaper. Several types of cases had a 100% reporting rate. All of the cases (N=14) involving police officers shooting citizens were reported in the Herald as were all 17 of the homicides that resulted directly from the May riots. Likewise all 12 cases involving citizens killed by burglars were reported by the Herald as were both of the cases involving police officers killed by felons. Other types of cases with relatively (significantly higher than 59.6%) high reporting rates were those involving Latin female victims, 78.8%; those involving heterosexual lovers, 76.7%; those with victims under 15, 70.0%; and those involving white offenders on black victims, 69.7%.

On the other hand some homicide cases were (as indicated by a low reporting rate) seen as being less newsworthy. Only 1 of 7 (14.3%) cases involving a prostitute/"john" relationship was reported. Likewise only 3 of 10 (30%) of the cases involving homosexual lovers were reported. Other types with low reporting percentages were cases involving black female victims, 38.2%; those with victims 65 or over, 40.6%; and those where felons were killed by citizens, 50.0%. In each of these cases one might argue that the type of victims in these cases have less status than other victim types.

There was little difference in reporting rates by sex of victim (59.3% for males and 61.0% for females) or ethnicity of victim (Anglo, 60.3%; Blacks, 55.9% and

108

Latins, 62.9%). However, there was considerable variation by age of victim (under 15, 70.0%; 15-24, 63.7%; 25-44, 59.9%; 45-64, 58.4%, and 65 and up, 40.6%).

An attempt was made through the statistical technique of multiple regression analysis to identify those factors related to the victim, the offender or the event that were good predictors of whether or not the Herald covered a particular homicide. However, no potential predictor accounted for even 1% of the variance in the dependent variable (whether or not the case was reported) and thus it does not appear that any characteristics of the victim or offender "determined" whether or not a case was reported.

However, an analysis of day-by-day coverage of homicides did point to a possible explanation for the selection of homicides cases for mention in the Herald. It appears that the day of occurrence of a homicide does correlate with whether the case is reported. For example, homicides occurring on Sunday were reported 74.5% of the time while those occurring on Tuesday were reported only 48.5% of the time. Perhaps more manpower (reporters) was available on certain days or there was simply more important non-crime news to cover on certain days.

There was also monthly variation in the reporting rate. Interest by the Herald in homicide stories appeared to peak in the two months after the May riots since the reporting percentages for June and July were 75.0% and 77.4%, respectively. Attention to homicide by the Herald reached a low in September as only 34.3% of the homicides occurring in that month were reported in the Herald. Thus a homicide was more than twice as likely to be covered by the Herald if it occurred in June or July rather than in September.

Thus it appears that whether a homicide was covered by the Herald was better predicted by when the event occurred than by any characteristic of the victim or offender. This conclusion was confirmed by another regression analysis which found that the best predictor from a "pool" of day of occurrence variables plus victim/offender/event variables was whether or not the homicide occurred in September or March (the two low reporting months). The second variable to enter the step-wise regression equation was whether or not the homicide occurred on Sunday. The third predictor variable in the equation was whether the homicide occurred in June or July (the two high reporting months). These three predictors achieved together a Multiple R of .28 and a R squared of .08.

PREDICTING TYPE OF COVERAGE

Homicides are so numerous in Dade County that it is quite common to have two or more homicides occur in one day. Thus the Herald often covers homicides by one story about all the homicides that occurred the previous day. A total of 155 (45.7%) of the 339 homicides reported by the Herald were found in group stories as opposed to 184 in stories about only one homicide. Obviously, group stories were more likely to be utilized on days when several homicides occurred the previous day. However, individual stories were often devoted to a homicide even if several occurred the previous day if that homicide was considered to be sufficiently newsworthy. However, a regression analysis failed to discover any case factors that served as good predictors of whether a homicide appeared in an individual or group article. The first variable (whether the homicide was female offender on male victim) to enter the equation produced an R squared of only .01.

The analysis of the 339 homicides reported by the Herald also recorded the number of articles in which mention of each homicide occurred. Approximately one-third (33.6%) of 1980 homicides mentioned by the Herald were considered so newsworthy that several articles appeared with information on one homicide. However, 66.4% of the homicides mentioned by the Herald were mentioned in only one article. An additional 20.1% were mentioned in two articles with the remaining 13.5% being mentioned in 3 or more articles. The most frequent motive involved in cases mentioned in more than two articles was drug rip-off (34.8%) followed by riot (13.0%) and non-domestic argument (13.0%).

There were 14 cases in which 7 or more articles were devoted to (or mentioned) a single homicide. The 14 cases appearing to the Herald to merit this "follow-up attention" largely involved multiple killings. Seven of the 14 cases involved drug rip-offs and were comprised of one quadruple killing (cases 005A, 006L, 007L and 008L) and a triple murder (252B, 253B and 254B). In both of these multiple killings one

110

offender was tried and received the death penalty and thus many of the follow-up articles involving the trial process. In addition 5 of the 14 were killings involving a burglary with four of the five (057A-060A) being victims in a quadruple killing. In this case a single Black male killed two elderly couples during burglaries. He received a life sentence but was killed in prison when he tried to escape by taking a female hostage. The fifth burglary case to result in 7 or more articles was the "911" (the police emergency number) case in which a teenage girl called 911 to report a break-in and the operator, thinking the situation was not serious, did not code the call as an emergency. The resulting delay in police response led to her death by the intruder. A number of articles appeared on this case decrying the reaction of the authorities. The remaining two cases of the 14 receiving the most frequent coverage were one of the riot cases (217A) and one (464A) of the two cases involving police officers being killed.

A regression equation also found that the best predictor of the number of articles devoted to a particular homicide was the number of victims involved in a particular homicide event (i.e., whether the case involved multiple victims). The R squared with the first predictor was .38. The second predictor variable to enter the equation was whether the victim was Hispanic (i.e., fewer articles were devoted to homicides involving Hispanic victims). The third predictor to enter the equation was whether the victim was totally innocent rather than a precipitator or participator (i.e., innocent victims produced more articles). These three variables produced an R squared of .42 indicating that 42% of the variance in the number of articles devoted to the homicide could be explained by the combination of these three variables.

EXTENT OF COVERAGE

The research team also coded the number of column inches devoted to each of the 339 homicides covered by the Herald and found that number ranged from 1 (for 17 cases) to 553 (for one of the riot cases---case no. 217A). Over 100 column inches were devoted to 20 cases but these were largely Riot caes (11 of the 20) with 4 additional cases being victims of the same quadruple burglary murder (cases 057A-060A) mentioned earlier and three others part of the triple murder drug rip-off

111

(cases 252B-254B) mentioned earlier. When a regression equation was run the best predictor of the number of column inches was the number of victims in the homicide event (i.e., whether the homicide was part of a multiple killing) producing an R squared of .34. The second predictor to enter the equation was whether the victim was totally innocent rather than a precipitator or participator (i.e., innocent victims like the quadruple burglary murders merited more column inches). The second variable raised the R squared to .36.

COMPARISON OF HERALD COVERAGE IN 1925-26 WITH 1980

A total of 167 homicide cases were reported in the Herald for Dade County in 1925-26. This total represents 77% of the 216 homicides recorded on death certificates for this two-year period. There is some conflict between homicide information found on death certificates and that found in the Herald. Death certificates indicate that there were 57 white victims of homicide in 1925-26 while the Herald reported 72 white victims. On the other hand while death certificates indicate that there were 163 black victims the Herald reported only 95. Thus the Herald reported more white victims but fewer black victims than did death certificate data.

In 1925-26 race of victim was a prominent part of the stories found in the Herald as Black victims were indicated by the designation, "a negro", after the name of the victim was given. In 1980 the race of the victim was not routinely provided in the Herald homicide stories as 47% of the stories did not give the race of the victim.

It is interesting to note that homicide in Dade County was not big news in the Herald in 1925-26. The front page of the Herald was always filled with "foreign" (out of South Florida) crime stories along with a picture of some notable visitor (usually a prominent man in business or politics) who was (as the caption of the article indicated) enjoying his visit to the area. The suggestion to the reader was that the rest of the world had crime while South Florida was a vacation paradise. The Herald in one issue (July 10, 1926:1) pointed out that a "crime wave" existed in rural Tennessee when three murders occurred there in three years. There was no suggestion that a crime wave existed in the vacation paradise of South Florida though the homicide rate for the area for 1925-26 was 12 times the national rate. Homicides in Miami (86% of the homicides then occurred in the city) were generally confined to page 2 of each issue of the Herald in 1925-26 and described very briefly in a list of events under the heading, "Around the City."

The Herald's coverage in 1980 is quite different from that of 1925-26. In 1980 the newspaper openly acknowledged the homicide problem and indicated that Dade had one of the highest murder rates in the United States. It is almost as if the thesis of the Herald's coverage in 1925-26 was that homicide was not a problem in the community while in 1980 it was that homicide was our greatest problem. And since the Herald's stories indicated that 97% of the victims (whose address was given) had Dade County addresses the impression was left that the problem was not due to "them" (those from outside the county) but to "us" (Dade residents). Also the extent of coverage in 1980 was much more substantial than that found in 1925-26 as many lengthy articles appeared on individual homicides and "group" stories focused on the homicides of the day rather than on various crime and non-crime events of the day (as was the case in 1925-26).

Also in 1980 there is no indication that the Herald devoted more prominent or extensive coverage to homicides involving White victims while this was the case in 1925-26. For example, in 1925-26 40% of the stories of white homicide victims appeared on page one compared to 3% for black victims. Likewise, the Herald devoted two or more stories to only 12% of black victims compared to 26% of white victims. The number of stories devoted to white versus black victims did not vary significantly in 1980.

CHAPTER TWELVE

SUMMARY AND CONCLUSIONS

The reader may feel inundated with figures, rates and statistics after reading the first eleven chapters of this volume. And yet some figures and facts should be repeated in this chapter for two reasons. First, the more important figures may have become lost in a sea of figures and thus need to be repeated for emphasis at this point. Second, some facts are more pertinent to the development of theories and explanations and thus should be repeated before any discussion of theory. In short some of the figures represent facts that the theory must fit. The important facts presented in each of the first eleven chapters will be presented and followed by a discussion of theory.

CHAPTER ONE---DEFINITIONS AND DATA SOURCES

1. The two national data sources (FBI and NCHS) are inadequate for a detailed study of homicide victims and offenders in a single jurisdiction.

2. Homicide victimization can be studied in Dade County from 1917 to 1955 only by examining death certificate data from the State of Florida and the Miami Herald since files in the office of the medical examiner are only available from 1956.

3. Studies of homicide victims require gathering data from only one office (the medical examiner) while studies of victims and offenders require that data be gathered from the medical examiner, the police and the courts.

CHAPTER TWO----HISTORICAL PERSPECTIVE

1. 1980 was not the peak year for homicides and other types of violent death for Dade County. That "distinction" belongs to the period of 1925-26. The homicide rate for these two years was more than three times the rate of 1980.

2. The homicide rate in Dade County has fluctuated over the 65 year period from 1917 to 1982 with two

peak periods, 1925-26 and 1980. At the current time (August of 1983) the rate appears to be retreating from the second peak (1980) by a gradual decline.

3. Homicide rates generally rise and fall with two other forms of violent death, accidents and suicides, as there is a strong positive correlation among these three forms of death over the 65 year period from 1917 to 1982. Thus the factors that "cause" increases or decreases in one appear to similarly affect the other two.

4. Homicide, accident and suicide rates over the 65 year period for Whites and Blacks tend to rise and fall together suggesting that the factors that affect one race affect the other.

5. The 1925-26 period differed from 1980 primarily in the magnitude of rates (e.g., the former being three times greater than the latter) since the patterns of homicide differed little in the two time periods. In short, there were more homicides of all types in 1925-26.

CHAPTER THREE---COMPARATIVE PERSPECTIVE

1. The figures available in the FBI's Uniform Crime Reports do indicate that Miami had the highest murder rate of all U.S. cities in 1980 while Dade County had the highest murder rate of the 259 Standard Metropolitan Statistical Areas. However, this "fact" is questioned because of the large number of non-resident victims that contribute to the rate and because of the population base utilized in the calculations.

2. An examination of murder rates over time for selected metropolitan areas indicated that Dade County has not always led the nation or the state in murder.

3. The percentage increase in Dade County's murder rate from 1960 to 1980 was much less than that for many other metropolitan areas and the gap between Southern and non-Southern metropolitan areas has almost closed.

4. The sharp increase in Dade's murder rate in 1979 and 1980 was matched only by the sharp rise in

116

1925-26. However, unlike 1925-26 the 1979-80 increase was not matched by other South Florida counties.

CHAPTER FOUR---PATTERNS OF VICTIMIZATION

1. The homicide victimization rate for Dade County in 1980 was 35.0 per 100,000 (thus 1 person was a victim of homicide for every 2,857 persons in the resident population).

2. Victimization varied sharply by age as those 25-44 were 20 times as likely to be killed as those under 15.

3. Victimization varied by sex as males were five times as likely (rate of 61.1/11.7=5.2) to be killed as were females. It appears that this "gender gap" is widening in that the male to female victimization rate ratio for earlier periods was lower (1959-61=2.6; 1969-71=4.2; 1974-76=4.4).

4. Victimization varied by race as Blacks were 3 times as likely to be killed as were Whites (79.2/25.8=3.1). The race gap is narrowing in that the Black to White victimization rate ratio for earlier periods was higher (1959-61=9.4; 1969-71=7.6; 1974-76=5.3).

5. Blacks have a victimization rate twice that of Hispanics (79.2/36.1=2.2) while the Hispanic rate is twice that of Anglos (36.1/17.9=2.0). Thus Blacks are four times more likely to be killed than Anglos (79.2/17.9=4.4).

6. The victimization rate for Mariel Refugees (about 84) is approximately equal to that of Blacks and, when the disproportionate numbers of males and young among the Marielitos are considered, the rate is actually below that of Blacks.

7. From 1959-1961 to 1980 the victimization rate in Dade County increased by 215% (from 11.1 to 35.0 per 100,000). Most subgroups of the population experienced similar increases though the greatest increases were for those 65 & up (361%); White Males (612%); White males 65 & up (1,307%); White males 15-24 (457%); and White females 15-24 (534%). There was actually a decrease in rates over this 20 year

period for 4 of the 5 age groups among non-White females (e.g., down 49% for non-White females under 15). However, in general victimization is up for subgroups of the population.

8. The variation in the victimization rate for the overall population (35.0) is so wide that one subgroup (Black males 25-44) was 382 (343.6/0.9=382) times as likely to be killed as another subgroup (White females under 15). Thus the 35.0 figure is rather meaningless if viewed as an indication of the risk of being killed of a particular individual (of a particular age, sex and race). In short, homicide is not a random event but occurs with regularity against certain subgroups.

CHAPTER FIVE---CHARACTERISTICS OF THE EVENT

1. Sixteen percent of the 569 Dade homicides in 1980 were justifiable or excusable with the remaining 84% being criminal. Thus in 86 homicides no one was charged since the police and prosecutor viewed the shooting as either authorized by law (justifiable) or accidental (excusable).

2. 72% of all Dade homicides were committed with a gun (60% by handguns). Also 88% of the increase in Dade's homicide rate from 1956 to 1982 was due to the increase in gun homicides. Knife and blunt instrument rates remained stable over this 27 year period.

3. The most frequent motive for 1980 Dade homicides was a domestic or other argument (41%) with drug rip-offs being the second most frequent motive (20%). The third most frequent motive was self-defense (13%) followed by robbery (11%).

4. Though the motive pattern for Dade County homicides in 1980 was similar to that of the rest of the nation (with the exception of drug rip-offs), the magnitude of rates was different. Thus a Dade resident was 3 times as likely to be killed in an argument and 4 times as likely to be killed in a robbery/murder as the average U.S. resident. Thus it is clear that Dade's high overall rate is not due just to an inordinate number and rate of drug murders----Dade is high in all motive categories.

5. The distribution of victim/offender relationships is little different from the national pattern though the rates are much higher for each category. Approximately 28% of Dade victims in 1980 were killed by strangers and approximately 68% by acquaintances (10% by family members; 9% by sex partners or rivals; 20% by crime partners; and 29% by other acquaintances). However, the rates for each victim/offender category are much higher than for the nation. Thus Dade residents were both more likely to be killed by a stranger and by a family member of acquaintance than was the average U.S. resident. In short, Dade residents were not only in danger from the violent stranger but also from the violent family member and acquaintance.

6. Dade killings were intra-ethnic rather than inter-ethnic with respect to Black and Hispanic victims (i.e., Blacks were killed by Blacks and Hispanics by Hispanics) but inter-ethnic with respect to Anglo victims (Anglos were more often killed by Blacks or Hispanics).

7. In general males were killed by males and females were killed by males. Only 1 homicide in 569 involved a female killing a female. Thus Dade county was actually below the national average of female on female killings for 1980.

8. 15% of Dade victims in 1980 clearly precipitated their own demise by being the first to show or use deadly force. An additional 57% "participated" in their demise by engaging in such "risky" actions as drinking or arguing with the offender or by engaging in a crime. The victim was totally "innocent" in only 24% of the cases (did nothing to contribute to the events leading to his/her death).

9. 20% of all 1980 victims (and 25% of those tested) were legally drunk at the time of their death. In addition 26% of the victims tested for other (than alcohol) drugs had some trace of such drugs in their bodies.

10. The most frequent location of the assault/homicide was a home (37% of the 569 victims in 1980).

11. The victimization rate varied sharply by city (68.3 in Miami; 19.8 in Miami Beach; 11.0 in Hialeah; and 28.6 in Dade areas not in one of these three cities) and across the 237 census tracts of the county. If census tracts are viewed as little neighborhoods then 24% of the 237 tracts/neighborhoods had no residents who were killed in 1980. The victimization rates for the census tracts ranged from 0.0 (for the 57 with no victims) to 925 for one tract in downtown Miami. With respect to the actual location of the assault (rather than to the residence of the victim regardless of where killed), 65 of the 237 tracts had no homicides occurring in their boundaries. Yet one tract (in center of Overtown) had 21 homicides within its boundaries in 1980.

12. Dade County reached a plateau of 52.5 homicides per month for a 24 month period from May of 1980 to April of 1982. This plateau was preceded by a plateau of 27.0 per month for the 24 preceding months and was followed by a plateau of 37.8 for the 20 months after April of 1982 to the end of 1983 (when data collection ceased). Thus homicides in Dade in recent years have not increased or decreased gradually but rather have jumped up to or down to different plateaus rather suddenly.

CHAPTER SIX----OFFENDER CHARACTERISTICS

1. 269 offenders were arrested in the 569 homicides occurring in 1980 for an arrest rate of 16.4 per 100,000.

2. The variation in the arrest rate for subgroups of the population was great. Some subgroups (e.g., females 65 & over) had no arrests and thus a rate of 0.0 while Black males 15-24 had an arrest rate of 295.9. Thus the overall arrest rate of 16.4 is rather meaningless if utilized as a measure of the probability of a resident of a particular age, sex and race being arrested.

3. Overall a Dade resident was 2.1 times as likely to be a victim as to be arrested as a murderer. This overall figure varied sharply by subgroup as those 65 & over were 8 times as likely to be killed as to be arrested while Black males from 15-24 were actually more likely to be arrested than to be killed.

4. Males were 10 times more likely to be arrested for murder in 1980 than were females (31.3/3.2=9.8). Thus the gender gap for murder is widening as in 1974 males were only 7 times as likely to be arrested (25.9/3.8=6.8). In fact the arrest rate for females was actually down 16% from 1974 to 1980 while the male arrest rate was up 25%.

5. From 1974 to 1980 the arrest rate was up 19%. However, this increase varied sharply by ethnic group as the arrest rate was actually down 22% for Anglos and 4% for Blacks but up 127% for Hispanics. Thus the increase in the Dade County arrest rate from 1974 to 1980 was due to the increase in the Hispanic arrest rate and to the growing numbers of Hispanics in the population.

CHAPTER SEVEN---THE POLICE ROLE

1. Nationwide in 1980 the police cleared 72% of criminal homicides while in Dade only 51% were cleared or solved (by arrest or the decision not to charge). This clearance rate in Dade was down sharply from the 76% clearance rate for the county in 1974. It appears that the lower clearance rate in Dade for 1980 (compared to the U.S. for the same year and for 1974 in Dade) was largely due to the changing nature of homicides in the county. Dade homicides in 1980 were comprised of a greater proportion of the difficult to solve cases than was the case for the nation as a whole in 1980 or for Dade in 1974.

2. Homicides by the police in Dade are not keeping pace with the rapid increase in the general homicide rate. The rate of homicides by the police has remained relatively stable over a 27 year period while there has been a great increase in the general rate. However, in the peak year of 1925-26 an estimated 18% of all homicides were by the police (compared to 2% in 1980). Dade's police homicide rate is far below that found in many other metropolitan areas even though Dade has one of the highest overall homicide rates and there is generally a positive correlation between the police rate and the general rate (i.e., most cities with high murder rates have high police rates and most with low murder rates have low police rates).

CHAPTER EIGHT---THE PROSECUTION ROLE

1. 62% (149) of the 240 offenders prosecuted as adults and reaching a final disposition were convicted. But 25% (60) of the 240 cases were dismissed before trial and 13% (31) were found not guilty. The conviction rate of 62% for 1980 is down from the 75% for 1974. However, when cases that actually reach trial are considered, there is no decrease in conviction rate from 1974 to 1980. The lower conviction rate for 1980 (62% down from 75% in 1974) is largely due to the increase in dismissals as in 1974 only 8% of arrestees had their cases dismissed before trial while that figure was 25% in 1980.

2. Most cases which were "lost" before or at trial were not lost due to such legal "technicalities" as suppressed confessions or evidence but rather to witness problems (either non-credible witnesses or a complete lack of witnesses).

3. The majority (87 of 149) of convicted offenders pled guilty and did so in return for a reduction in charges or a more lenient sentence.

4. A total of 40 of the 269 persons arrested in 1980 murder cases were examined by a psychiatrist at the direction of the court. Only 8 of the 40 were "successful" in that they either delayed their trial indefinitely by being declared incompetent or were found not guilty by reason of insanity (6 were found NGRI). Also those who were examined by a psychiatrist were more likely than those who were not to be convicted and given a severe sentence. The analysis of the 40 exposed seven myths commonly believed about the use of the insanity defense.

CHAPTER NINE---SENTENCING

1. Seventeen persons were convicted of Murder I for a 1980 Dade murder with 5 receiving the death penalty and 12 a life sentence. Sentences for the 83 persons convicted of Murder II ranged from probation to life. Sentences for the 38 persons convicted of manslaughter ranged from probation to 20 years in prison.

2. Males received more severe sentences than did

females though this difference was largely due to the domestic nature of their killings.

CHAPTER TEN---RACE AND SEX BIAS

1. No bias or disparity was found by sex or race of victim or offender for 1980 Dade homicides at four decision points: arrest, charge, conviction and sentence. Though "differentiation" (differences in outcome by sex and/or race of victim or offender) did occur, those differences were better explained by "legal" factors (i.e., such as whether the homicide was felony-related or domestic) than by the sex and race of victim or offender.

2. There was also no evidence of a cumulative bias against Blacks or females in that the arrest rate ratio gap between Black and White and male and female offenders did not increase across the different stages of the criminal justice system from identification of suspect by sex and race to sentence.

CHAPTER ELEVEN---NEWSPAPER COVERAGE

1. 60% of the 1980 homicides were mentioned by the Miami Herald with the reporting rate varying from 100% for police and riot homicides to 14% for those involving prostitutes and "johns." However, the best predictor of coverage was the month of occurrence as the Herald appears to have been more concerned with homicides in certain months of the year. The most extensive coverage (as measured by number of articles and number of total column inches) was given to police homicides, riot homicides and homicides involving multiple victims.

2. The Herald's coverage of homicide was quite different in 1925-26 as in the earlier period the newspaper downplayed the problem and even suggested that homicide elsewhere was a greater problem (in fact Dade's rate was 12 times the national rate). Also in 1925-26 more prominent coverage was given to White victims while this was not the case in 1980.

CRITIQUE OF EXPLANATIONS FOR HIGH MURDER RATES

The academic literature is replete with explanations for high rates of homicide (for the U.S. as a whole in comparison to other nations and for particular jurisdictions in the U.S. compared to others). And yet these theories or explanations all have the same problem---they often do not fit or explain the facts. Several such explanations will now be reviewed and an indication given of the extent to which each "fits the facts" summarized above for Dade County.

First, the most commonly heard explanation from laypersons for homicide is that those who kill are "crazy" as "no one in his right mind kills another human being." The evidence of this mental illness is, of course, the fact that the killer took another life (obviously a crazy act). Such reasoning is tautological (circular) in that the observer has no independent evidence of a crazy mind other than the act of murder and the latter is what one should be explaining. It is like saying that people kill because they are "hostile" and yet the only evidence of hostility is the fact that an individual killed someone. This type of explanation is actually a label ("I think all killers are 'nuts'") rather than an explanation. And yet in numerous criminology classes taught by this author the most commonly chosen theory (from a list of 11 that are found in the literature) for murder is that people kill because they are "crazy."

This explanation appears to most laypersons to be just good "common-sense." Unfortunately it is more common than sensical. This explanation would also imply that Americans are crazier than the Japanese, Swiss, and Germans (since these countries have lower murder rates than the U.S.) but less crazy than Mexicans and Columbians (since these countries have higher rates than the U.S.). Also such an explanation would imply that males in Dade County in 1980 were 10 times as likely to be crazy as females (since the arrest rate for males was 10 times that of females) and Blacks were 4 times as likely to be crazy as Anglos (since the Black arrest rate was 4 times the Anglo rate). Also it would follow that people/killers generally develop their craziness as young adults (since the very young and the elderly rarely kill) and become saner as they reach middle-age. Since few would suggest that these implications of the explanation are accurate it should follow that the explanation itself does not explain the facts of homicide.

Second, another common explanation for high homicide rates is the easy availability of guns, primarily handguns. Though there may be some truth to this "common-sense" view it should be pointed out that a two year federal effort to review the literature on the relationship between guns and crime (Wright, Rossi, and Daly, 1983) failed to confirm a direct causal relationship. Guns may deter as well as "cause" murder. Though this study did find that the knife and blunt instrument homicide rate was fairly stable over a 27 year period while the gun murder rate increased sharply (accounting for 88% of the increase in the overall homicide rate), it does not follow that the "more guns equal more murders" thesis has been proven. First, it may be that more persons in the 1980 population wanted to kill and chose a gun (the most deadly weapon) to accomplish that purpose. Second, there is no evidence that newly acquired guns (which have contributed to the "arming of Miami") are those that have been used to kill. Third, though increasing numbers of women have bought guns in the period from 1974 to 1980 there has been a decrease in the arrest rate for women. Guns are sometimes called the great "equalizer" and yet it appears that the gender gap for killers is widening rather than narrowing. Fourth, the jumping up to and dropping from the homicide "plateaus" over time as discussed in Chapter Five is not easily explained by the gun explanation. Certainly it is not obvious that guns were simply more available beginning in May of 1980 but less available beginning in May of 1982. In short, such an explanation does not fit well with the facts evident in a study of homicide trends over time.

On the other hand the groups who would appear to be less likely to be armed (women, the very young, and the elderly) are less likely to kill. Also one cannot read the 569 narratives without being impressed by the triviality of many of the arguments/disputes that led to murder and the apparent lack of a resolve (rather than "passion") to kill. In so many ases it appears that the offender was angry and armed and killed. What is unknown is whether the offender would have killed without the gun. In many cases this would not have occurred since the victim could run from a knife or blunt instrument and in others because the offender

125

would not have dared to approach the victim in "hand-to-hand combat."

   Third, another commonly heard (around Dade County) explanation for Dade's high murder rate and the sharp increase in 1980 is that Dade is "infected" with large numbers of illegal aliens and/or drug dealers whose presence artificially inflated the homicide rate from what it would have been without the influence of "outsiders." Though it is clear that Dade's murder rate is partly the result of large numbers of drug murders and murders involving aliens, it is also clear that Dade has high murder rates for non-drug motives and family and acquaintance murders. In short, Dade has high rates for all types of murders not just drug murders and murders involving aliens. Furthermore, the "alien and drug" theory does not explain the jumping up to and falling from the homicide plateaus in recent years. Though Mariel refugees did arrive in large numbers and contribute to the sudden and sharp increase in homicides in May of 1980 they only account for 25% of the increase experienced in that year. And surely the drug traffic did not change dramatically and abruptly in May of 1980 and then again in May of 1982 (when the sharp decline began).

   The problem with the first three explanations (too many crazy people, too many guns, too many aliens and drug dealers) is not that there might not be some validity to these views but that each seeks to find a scapegoat for the homicide problem in the county and to maintain the fiction that Dade would be OK were it not for certain "alien" factors (alien forces affecting the minds of some, alien weapons and alien persons and crooks). These explanations ignore the possibility that there may be something wrong with the core values and "real" residents of Dade County. The fact remains that over a long period of time (not just since the arrival of the Marielitos or other Hispanics) Dade County has killed its own at a rate far exceeding most other metropolitan areas. This killing has been "across the board" in that victims and offenders of all ages, both sexes and all ethnic groups have been involved as victims and offenders at rates exceeding that of most other jurisdictions. The homicide problem does not involve just "them" but "us" (unless one defines "them" as all killers----an explanation which is, of course, tautological).

126

TWO EXPLANATIONS THAT FIT MOST OF THE FACTS

If the answer (to why Dade has such a high homicide rate and why the rate peaked in 1980) does not lie in too many crazy people, too many guns or too many aliens and drug dealers, what answer does fit the "facts"? First, as suggested in Chapter Two, Dade County may have experienced such stress in 1925-26 with the "boom, bust and blow" that the county went through the equivalent of a domestic "war" in which a temporary culture existed that broadened the rationalizations that approved of violence. That temporary culture may have dissipated in a few months as the period of stress ended and the county settled down to normal.

In a similar vein one could argue that 1980 was another period of stress so different in magnitude from the years between 1926 and 1980 that 1980 might also be considered as a "war year." There was the riot, the arrival of 125,000 refugees, the continuation of the drug wars, the arming of the county, the fear and even paranoia on the part of many residents. In such a period of stress it is likely that more acts of violence will occur in the absence of restraints. And it may be that the very restraint that normally inhibits the individual from taking another life (i.e., the belief that it is wrong) was weakened in the atmosphere of fear. In short it may be that more individuals simply came to believe that some people "needed killing."

This hypothesis, as stated in Chapter Two, is derived from a scholarly study of homicide rates in countries after wars (Archer and Gartner, 1976) which found that the rationalizations for killing broadened after the war in the countries that won the war. The attitude seemed to be that its OK to kill our enemies in war since they threaten our national security and it must also be OK to kill our personal enemies who endanger our personal security (or ego, or love relationship, etc.). Perhaps the large number (86) of justifiable killings is an indication that residents increasingly saw more people as deserving of death. Chapter Eight also found a number of cases that were "lost" in court due to the perception of the judge or jury that the offender was not culpable since the victim was somehow deserving or at least as culpable as the offender.

Lundsgaarde (1977) claimed that there is a strong

correlation between justifiable homicides and the
general homicide rate not because more people tend to
kill in self-defense against criminals but because
potential offenders see cues in homicides ruled as
justifiable. They sense that homicides in certain
circumstances are OK and thus broaden those
circumstances to include their own situation (which may
simply involve an argument or domestic dispute). Thus
Lundsgaarde would argue that the more a society
justifies homicides in its midst (for "legitimate"
self-defense reasons) the more it stands in danger of
stimulating criminal homicides by sending the wrong
message (i.e., that homicide is OK under certain
circumstances) to potential offenders. It is likely
that most killers believe murder is wrong but that in
their case the homicide was deserving. If this is the
case then the question becomes where did they get the
idea that the circumstances under which they killed
legitimated their action?

If there is any validity to the view that the
justifications for killing are broadening due to a
crisis atmosphere in the county how does one explain
that some groups did not increase their "killing rate"?
The "facts" enumerated in this chapter indicate that
Anglos, Blacks, women and the police have not markedly
increased their proclivity to kill. However, male
killing rates are up and there has been a significant
increase in the arrest rate of Hispanics (and in their
victimization rate).

The stability of police homicides in the face of
growing violence in the community is testimony to the
policy restriction placed upon the police in their use
of deadly force. It is clear from the study of 1925-26
homicides that police were far more likely to kill
citizens than in 1980. But in 1925-26 there was little
policy to restrict the police. Today policy has
restricted the rationalizations to kill while in the
general population those rationalizations appear to
have broadened. Thus policy has reversed a
rationalization trend found in the general population.

It is more difficult to explain the decline in the
female arrest rate and the infrequent occurrence of
female on female homicide. If one assumes (as this
chapter has) that a temporary "war culture" existed in
Dade in 1980 it is difficult to see why females were
not proportionately affected. It may be that this
temporary war culture mentality was subcultural in

nature and was transmitted only among males.
Furthermore, since the arrest rate is up for Hispanics
and down for Anglos and Blacks it may be that these
subcultural attitudes (broadening of the
rationalizations to kill) are more predominant among
Hispanics. However, there is no independent evidence
of that subculture.

A second partial explanation for the upsurge in
Dade homicides in 1980 involves examining the
demographics of the changes in the victimization and
arrest rates from 1974 to 1980. As pointed out
earlier, Hispanic victimization is up sharply (up 300%)
while Anglo and Black victimization is only up
slightly. Likewise, the Hispanic arrest rate is up
127% while the Anglo and Black arrest rates are down.
Thus Dade's homicide upsurge is due to the increase in
the Hispanic arrest and victimization rates and to the
growing proportion of the Dade population that is
Hispanic.

However, this explanation does not explain why the
Hispanic victimization and arrest rates are up.
Perhaps the broadening of rationalizations to kill due
to the crisis atmosphere in the county has occurred
largely in the Hispanic community. And yet Hispanic
females do not appear to be a part of that subculture
as they are rarely involved in criminal homicides.
This view of a growing subculture of violence in the
Hispanic (male) community infers a functionalist
perspective in that the subculture is seen as deriving
from the conditions present in South Florida. However,
it may be that an "importation thesis" much akin to
that hypothesized by Irwin and Cressey (1962) with
respect to prisons is more valid. In short, it may be
that the large numbers of Hispanics arriving in Dade in
recent years have brought with them rather "liberal"
attitudes as to who "deserves to be killed." In this
view the South Florida conditions would be irrelevant
to the subculture since the area's only role would be
in attracting those from Latin American who already
hold those subcultural views. And yet it should be
pointed out that if subcultural beliefs are inferred
from high homicide rates then "native" Blacks have a
stronger adherence to violent subcultural beliefs than
do Hispanics (i.e., the victimization and arrest rates
for Blacks are much greater than those for Hispanics).

The reader may at this point be left with the
impression that the two above mentioned partial

129

explanations are inadequate. The intent is not to come up with "the" explanation for Dade's high homicide rate and its recent upsurge (and decrease) but to suggest that whatever explanation is set forth it should make some attempt to "fit the facts."

REFERENCES

ARCHER,D. and R. GARTNER (1976) "Violent Acts and Violent Times: A Comparative Approach to Postwar Homicide Rates." American Sociological Review, 41:937-963.

ARCHER,D., R. GARTNER, R. AKERT, and T. LOCKWOOD (1978) "Cities and Homicide: A New Look at an Old Paradox." Comparative Studies in Sociology 1, 73-95.

ATHENS, L.H. (1980) Violent Criminal Acts and Actors: A Symbolic Interactionist Study. Boston: Routledge & Kegan Paul.

BENSING, R. and O. SCHROEDER (1960) Homicide in An Urban Community. Springfield, Ill.: Charles C. Thomas.

BLOCK, R. (1977) Violent Crime: Environment, Interaction, and Death. Lexington, MA: D.C. Heath.

BLUM, A. and G. FISHER (1978) "Women Who Kill," pp. 187-197 in I.L. Kutash, S.B. Kutash, L.B. Schlesinger and Associates (eds.) Violence: Perspectives on Murder and Aggression. San Francisco: Jossey-Bass.

BLUMSTEIN, A. (1982) "On The Racial Disproportionality of United States' Prison Populations." The Journal of Criminal Law & Criminology, 73(3):1258-1281.

BORIS, S.B. (1979) "Stereotypes and Dispositions for Criminal Homicide." Criminology, 17(2):139-158.

BOUDOURIS,J. "A Classification of Homicide." Criminology, 11:525-540.

BROWN, R.M. (1979) "Southern Violence--Regional Problem or National Nemesis--Legal Attitudes Toward Southern Homicide in Historical Perspective." Vanderbilt Law Review, 32(1), 225-250.

CANTOR, D. and L.E. COHEN (1980) "Comparing Measures of Homicide Trends: Methodological and Substantive Differences in the Vital Statistics and Uniform Crime Report Time Series (1933-1975)." Social Science Reseaarch, 9, 121-145.

CHRISTIANSON, S. (1980a) "Corrections Law Developments: Legal Implications of Racially Disproportionate Incarceration Rates." Criminal Law Bulletin, 16(1):59-63.

CHRISTIANSON, S. (1980b) "Corrections Law Developments: Racial Discrimination and Prison Confinement--A Follow-up." Criminal Law Bulletin, 16(6):616-621.

Christianson, S. (1982) Disproportionate Imprisonment of Blacks in the United States: Policy, Practice, Impact and Change. Albany, N.Y.: School of Criminal Justice.

CONSTANTINO, J.P., L.H. KULLER, J.A. PERPER and R.H. CYPESS (1977) "An Epidemiological Study of Homicides in Allegheny County, Pennsylvania." American Journal of Epidemiology, 106, 314-326.

COUNT-VAN MANEN, G. (1977) Crime and Suicide in the Nation's Capital: Toward Macro-Historical Perspectives. New York: Praeger.

CURRAN, D.A. (1979) "Judicial Discretion and the Sex of the Defendant." Paper presented at the Southern Political Association.

CURTIS, L.A. (1974) Criminal Violence: National Patterns and Behavior. Lexington, MA: D.C. Heath.

CURTIS, L.A. (1975) Violence, Race and Culture. Lexington, MA: D.C. Heath.

DAVIS, J.A. (1974) "Justification For No Obligation: Views of Black Males Toward Crime and the Criminal Law." Issues in Criminology, 9:69-87.

Del Olmo, R. (1975) "Limitations for the Prevention of Violence: The Latin American Reality and Its Criminological Theory." Crime and Social Justice, Spring-Summer:21-29.

DODGE, R.W. and H.R. LENTZNER (1980) Crime and Seasonality. Washington, D.C.: U.S. Dept. of Justice.

DOERNER,W.G. (1975) "A Regional Analysis of Homicide Rates in the U.S." Criminology, 13(1), 90-101.

DOERNER,W.G. (1978) "Index of Southerness Revisited: The Influence of Wherefrom Upon Whodunit." Criminology, 16(May):47-66.

DUNCAN, J.W. and G.M. DUNCAN (1978) "Murder in the Family," pp. 171-186 in I.L. Kutash, S.B. Kutash, L.B. Schlesinger and Associates (eds.) Violence: Perspectives on Murder and Aggression. San Francisco: Jossey-Bass.

ERLANGER, H.S. (1978) "The Empirical Status of the Subculture of Violence Thesis." pp. 163-171 in Crime and Society. L. Savitz and N. Johnston (eds.). New York: John Wiley.

FORBES, T.R. (1977) "Inquests Into London and Middlesex Homicides."

GELLER,W.A. (1982) "Deadly Force: What We Know." Journal of Police Science Administration, 10:151-177.

GEORGE, P.S. (1975) Criminal Justice in Miami: 1896-1930. A Ph.D. Dissertation. Ann Arbor: Xerox University Microfilms.

GIVEN, J.B. (1977) Society and Homicide in Thirteenth-Century England. Stanford, CA: Stanford University Press. Yale Journal of Biology and Medicine, 50(2):207-220.

FYFE, J.J. (1981) "Race and Extreme Police-Citizen Violence," pp. 89-108 in R.L. McNeely and C.E. Pope (eds.) Race, Crime and Criminal Justice. Beverly Hills, CA:Sage.

GLASER, D. (1978) Crime in Our Changing Society. New York: Holt, Rinehart and Winston.

GOLDCAMP, J.S. (1976) "Minorities as victims of police shooting: Interpretations of racial disproportionality and police use of deadly force." Justice System Journal, 2:169-183.

GREENBERG, S.W. (1981) "Alcohol and Crime: A Methodological Critique of the literature." pp. 70-109 in J.J. Collins, Jr. (ed.) Drinking and Crime. New York: Guilford Press.

GURR, T.R. (1981) "Historical trends in violent crime: A Critical review of the evidence." pp. 295-353 in M. Tonry and N. Morris (eds.) Crime and Justice: An Annual Review of Research. Chicago: University of Chicago Press.

HENRY, A.F. and J.F. SHORT (1954) Suicide and Homicide. New York: Free Press, 1954.

HAGAN, J. (1974) "Extra-legal attributes and criminal sentencing: An assessment of a sociological viewpoint." Law and Society Review, 8:357-383.

HEFFERNAN, R., MARTIN, J.M. and A.T. Romano (1982) "Homicides Related to Drug Trafficking." Federal Probation, 46(3):3-7.

HEPBURN, J.R. (1973) "Violent behavior in interpersonal relationship." Sociological Quarterly, 14:419-429.

HINDELANG, M.J. (1969) "Equality under the law." Journal of Criminal Law, Criminology and Police Science, 60:306-313.

HINDELANG, M.J. (1974) "The uniform crime reports revisited." Journal of Criminal Justice, 2:1-17.

133

HINDELANG, M.J. (1979) "Sex Differences in Criminal Activity." Social Problems, 27(2):143-156.

HINDELANG, M.J. (1978) "Race and Involvement in Common Law Personal Crimes." American Sociological Review, 43:93-109.

HIRSCH, C.S., N.B. RUSHFORTH, A.B. FORD AND L. ADELSON (1973) "Homicide and Suicide in a Metropolitan County." Journal of the American Medical Association, 223:900-905.

Homicide Analysis, 1980. (1981) New York: Crime Analysis Unit, Office of Management Analysis, New York City Police Department.

IRWIN, J. and D. CRESSEY (1962) "Thieves, convicts and the inmate culture." Social Problems, 10:142-155.

JACOBSON, A.L. (1975) "Crime trends in southern and nonsouthern cities: A Twenty-Year Perspective." Social Forces, 54:226-241.

JONES, A. (1980) Women Who Kill. New York: Holt, Rinehart & Winston.

KOFOED, J. (1960) The Florida Story. New York: Doubleday & Co.

KLECK, G. (1981) "Racial discrimination in criminal sentencing: A critical evaluation of the evidence with additional evidence on the death penalty." American Sociological Review, 46:783-805.

KLEBBA, A.J. (1975) "Homicide trends in the U.S., 1900-1974" Public Health Reports, 90:195-204.

LABRATORY OF COMMUNITY PSYCHIATRY, HARVARD MEDICAL SCHOOL (1973) Competency to Stand Trial and Mental Illness. Rockville, MD: National Institute of Mental Health, Center for Studies of Crime and Delinquency.

LANE, R. (1979) Violent Death in the City: Suicide, Accident, and Homicide in Nineteenth-Century Philadelphia. Cambridge, MA: Harvard University Press.

LESTER, D. And G. LESTER (1975) Crime of Passion. Chicago: Nelson Hall.

LETCHER, M. (1979) "Black women and homicide." pp. 83-90 in H.M. Rose (ed.) Lethal Aspects of Urban Violence. Lexington, MA: D.C. Heath.

LIEBER, A.L. (1978) The Lunar Effect: Biological Tides and Human Emotions. Garden City, N.Y.: Doubleday.

LUCKENBILL, D.F. (1977) "Criminal homicide as a situated transaction." Social Problems, 25:176-186.

LUNDSGAARDE, H.P. (1977) Murder in Space City: A Cultural Analysis of Houston Homicide Patterns. New York: Oxford University Press.

MATULIA, K. (1983) A Balance of Forces: A Study of Justifiable Homicides By the Police. Gaithersburg, MD: International Association of Chiefs of Police.

MCWHINEY, G. and P.D. JAMIESON (1982) Attack and Die: Civil War Military Tactics and the Southern Heritage. University, AL: U. of Alabama Press.

"Miami's Police Force." (1927) Miamian, 7(May):18.

MILTON, C., HALLECK, J., LARDNER, J. and G. Albrecht (1977) Police Use of Deadly Force. Washington, D.C.: Police Foundation.

MUNFORD, R.S., R.S. KAZER, R.A. FELDMAN and R.R. STIVERS (1975) Criminology, 14:213-232.

NATIONAL CENTER FOR HEALTH STATISTICS (1982) Vital Statistics of the United States.

NATIONAL COMMISSION ON THE INSANITY DEFENSE (1983) Myths and Realities: A Report of the National Commission on the Insanity Defense. Arlington, VA: National Mental Health Association.

NETTLER, G (1978) Explaining Crime. Second Edition. New York: McGraw-Hill.

PARISI, N. (1982) "Are Females Treated Differently? A Review of The Theories and Evidence on Sentencing and Parole Decisions." pp. 205-220 in Judge Lawyer Victim Thief: Women, Gender Roles and Criminal Justice. N.H. Rafter and E.A. Stanko (eds.). Boston: Northeastern University Press.

PARKER, R.N. and M.D. SMITH (1979) "Deterrence, poverty, and type of homicide." American Journal of Sociology, 85(3): 614-624.

PETERSILIA, J. (1983) Racial Disparities in the Criminal Justice System. Santa Monica: CA: Rand Corporation.

POKORNY, A.D. (1965) "A comparison of homicide in two cities." Journal of Criminal Law, Criminology, and Police Science, 56:480-487.

POPE, C.E. and R.L. MCNEELY (1981) "Race, Crime and Criminal Justice: An overview," pp. 9-28 in R.L. McNeely and C.E. Pope (eds.) Race, Crime and Criminal Justice. Beverly Hills, CA: Sage.

POUSSAINT, A.F. (1982) "Black-On-Black Homicide: A Psychological Political Perspective." Paper presented at Second International Institute on Victimology, Bellagio, Italy.

RADELET, M.L. (1981) "Racial characteristics and the imposition of the death penalty." American Sociological Review, 46: 918-927.

REIDER, E. (1983) "Death Penalty Critics Claim a Different Bias." Miami Herald, July 25, 1983, p. 4A.

REIMAN, J.H. (1979) The Rich Get Richer and the Poor Get Prison. New York: John Wiley and Sons.

RIBNER, S.A. and H.J. STEADMAN (1981) "Recidivism Among Offenders and Ex-Mental Patients." Criminology, 19(3):411-420.

ROBERSON, C.E. (1976) Patterns of Victim Involvement in Criminal Homicide: A Case Study of San Francisco, California. A Ph.D. Dissertation. Ann Arbor: Xerox University Microfilms.

ROIZEN, J. (1981) "Alcohol and criminal behavior among blacks." pp. 207-251 in J.J. Collins, Jr. (ed.) Drinking and Crime. New York: Guilford Press.

ROMAN, P.M. (1981) "Situational factors in the relationship between alcohol and crime." pp. 143-151 in J.J. Collins, Jr. (ed.) Drinking and Crime. New York: Guilford Press.

ROSE, H.M. (1978) "The geography of despair," Annals of the Association of American Geographers, 68(4):453-464.

RUSHFORTH, N.B., A.B. FORD, C.S. HIRSCH, N.M. RUSHFORTH and L. ADELSON (1977) "Violent death in a metropolitan county," New England Journal of Medicine, 297:531-538.

SHERMAN, L.W. and R.H. LANGWORTHY (1979) "Measuring homicide by police officers," Journal of Criminal Law and Criminology, 70:546-560.

SHIN, Y. ET AL. (1977) "Homicide among blacks," Phylon, 38:398-407.

SILBERMAN, C. (1978) Criminal Violence, Criminal Justice. New York: Random House.

SILVERMAN, R.A. (1974) "Victim precipitation: An examination of the concept," pp. 99-110 in I. Drapkin and E. Viano (eds.) Victimology: A New Focus, Volume I: Theoretical Issues in Victimology. Lexington, MA: D.C. Heath.

SMITH, M.D. and R.N. PARKER (1980) "Type of homicide and variation in regional rates," Social Forces, 49(1):136-147.

STEADMAN, H.J. (1980) "Insanity Acquittals in New York State, 1965-1978."" American Journal of Psychiatry, 137(3):321-326.

SUDNOW, D. (1965) "Normal Crimes: Sociological Features of the Penal Code in the Public Defender's Office." Social Problems, 12:255ff.

SUTHERLAND, E.H. (1939) Principles of Criminology. Third Edition. Philadelphia: J.B. Lippincott.

STAPLES, R. (1974) "Violence and Black America," Black World, May, 17-24.

SWARTZ, J. (1975) "Silent killers at work." Crime and Social Justice, 15-20.

SWIGERT, V.L. and R.A. FARRELL (1976) Murder, Inequality and the Law. Lexington, MA: D.C. Heath.

SYKES, G. and D. MATZA. (1957) "Techniques of Neutralization: A Theory of Delinquency." American Sociological Review, 22:664-670.

TEBEAU, C. (1971) A History of Florida. Coral Gables, FL: University of Miami Press.

Tien Wang v. the State of Florida (1983). 426 Southern Reporter, 2nd Series, 1004-1008.

TINDALL, G. (1965) "The Bubble in the Sun." American Heritage, 16:110ff. "Trouble in Paradise." (1981) Time Magazine, Nov. 23, 1981:22-32,

Uniform Crime Reports. Washington, D.C. U.S. Dept. of Justice.

VERKKO, V. (1967) "Static and Dynamic Laws of Sex and Homicide," pp. 36-44 in Studies in Homicide. M. Wolfgang (ed.). New York: Harper & Row.

VOSS, H.L. and J.R. HEPBURN (1965) "Patterns in criminal homicide in Chicago," Journal of Criminal Law, Criminology and Police Science, 59:449-508.

WEST, D. (1966) Murder Followed By Suicide. Cambridge: Harvard University Press.

WILBANKS, W. (1979a) "Homicide and the criminal justice system in Dade County, Florida," Journal of Crime and Justice, 2:58-74.

WILBANKS, W. (1979b) "Homicide victimization rates," Victimology, 4(2):305-309.

WILBANKS, W. (1981a) "Does alcohol cause homicide?" Journal of Crime and Justice, 4, 149-170.

WILBANKS, W. (1981b) "A test of Verkko's static and dynamic 'laws' of sex and homicide," International Journal of Women's Studies, 4(2):173-180.

WILBANKS, W. (1981-82) "Trends in violent death among the elderly." International Journal of Aging and Human Development, 14(3):167-175.

WILBANKS, W. (1982a) "Fatal accidents, suicide and homicide: Are they related?" Victimology, 6(1-2).

WILBANKS, W. (1982b) "Murdered women and women murderers: A critique of the literature," pp. 151-180 in N.H. Rafter and E.A. Stanko (eds.) Judge Lawyer Victim Thief: Women, Gender Roles and Criminal Justice. Boston: Northeastern University Press.

WILBANKS, W. (1983a) "Female Homicide Offenders in the U.S." International Journal of Women's Studies, 6(4).

WILBANKS, W. (1983b) "The Female Homicide Offender in Dade County, FL." Criminal Justice Review, 8(2).

WILBANKS, W. and D. MURPHY (1983) "The elderly homicide offender in the U.S., 1980," in D.J. Newman, E. Newman, and M. Gerwitz (eds.) Boston: Oelgeschlager, Gunn and Hain.

WOLFGANG, M. (1958) Patterns in Criminal Homicide. Philadelphia: University of Penn. Press.

WOLFGANG, M.E. (1959) "Suicide by means of victim-precipitated homicide." Journal of Clinical and Experimental Psychopathology, 6:335-349.

WRIGHT, J.D., ROSSI, P. and K. DALY (1983) Under the Gun: Weapons, Crime and Violence in America. New York: Aldine.

WRIGHT, R.K. and J.H. DAVIS (1977) "Studies in the epidemiology of murder: A proposed classification." Journal of Forensic Sciences, 22(2):464-470.

ZIMRING, F. (1976) "Punishing Homicide in Philadelphia: Perspectives on the Death Penalty." The University of Chicago Law Review, 43(2), 227-252.

APPENDIX A

TABLES AND FIGURES

to skip a page to make tables start on odd no.

Table 2.1 Dade County Homicide, Suicide and Accident
Rates by Race of Victim, 1917 to 1983

Year	Total Homicide Rate	White Homicide Rate	Non-White Homicide Rate	Total Suicide Rate	White Suicide Rate	Non-White Suicide Rate	Total Accident Rate	White Accident Rate	Non-White Accident Rate
1917	19.8	12.1	37.0	8.5	12.2	0.0	65.2	65.3	64.8
1918	13.1	3.7	34.5	10.4	7.5	17.2	125.3	134.8	103.4
1919	9.7	10.4	8.1	2.4	3.5	0.0	89.6	100.3	64.5
1920	18.9	8.8	44.1	8.4	8.8	7.4	105.0	111.8	88.2
1921	20.9	11.9	45.8	17.4	23.8	0.0	66.2	64.1	71.9
1922	34.2	15.9	88.2	20.8	27.9	0.0	92.3	89.6	100.0
1923	26.0	10.3	74.9	5.2	6.9	0.0	72.7	75.5	64.2
1924	34.6	9.0	117.6	16.1	19.6	4.9	114.1	90.4	191.2
1925	102.6	38.9	318.2	29.0	36.2	4.5	226.9	209.4	286.4
1926	110.1	29.1	392.4	23.5	26.6	12.7	324.6	313.6	362.9
1927	55.1	16.5	192.9	37.0	45.2	7.9	126.6	114.7	169.3
1928	37.4	18.2	107.0	13.5	15.2	7.4	88.2	93.2	70.1
1929	31.0	12.2	100.7	17.7	20.6	6.9	104.0	96.4	131.9
1930	35.2	12.2	121.7	23.5	28.8	3.2	100.8	97.8	111.8
1931	33.4	12.4	113.6	23.0	27.3	6.3	91.8	95.2	78.9
1932	34.4	13.4	115.5	29.4	36.2	3.0	78.1	73.1	97.3
1933	29.8	12.7	96.8	26.2	29.2	14.7	84.1	78.6	105.6
1934	28.5	10.0	101.7	29.6	35.7	5.6	109.5	105.1	127.1
1935	30.4	12.2	103.8	25.5	28.4	13.7	109.5	102.8	136.7
1936	26.7	9.8	96.4	22.3	24.0	15.2	99.5	98.4	104.1
1937	26.0	5.6	111.6	22.8	25.9	9.5	107.5	107.1	109.3
1938	21.9	5.7	91.1	26.6	30.7	8.9	77.4	70.8	75.6
1939	23.6	7.2	94.3	16.9	20.3	2.1	66.4	62.3	83.9
1940	21.8	5.5	94.0	18.1	22.3	0.0	79.2	76.8	90.0
1941	22.9	5.7	100.2	17.2	20.1	3.9	76.2	73.5	89.1
1942	17.6	5.9	71.7	15.2	17.7	3.9	68.5	64.0	89.1
1943	15.4	4.9	64.8	12.1	14.6	0.0	98.8	104.5	72.4
1944	12.0	3.1	54.4	17.5	20.0	5.6	81.5	83.3	73.2
1945	14.8	3.0	73.5	13.6	15.6	3.7	84.1	89.9	55.1
1946	14.7	3.3	75.7	17.2	19.4	5.3	74.7	73.5	81.0
1947	14.1	5.0	65.8	11.6	13.0	3.4	73.3	69.0	97.8
1948	11.3	3.0	61.7	15.7	17.7	3.2	70.5	69.8	74.7
1949	13.8	4.7	72.1	16.8	19.2	1.6	46.3	43.5	64.3
1950	12.4	3.4	72.1	11.6	12.9	3.0	52.7	49.5	73.6

141

Year	Total Homicide Rate	White Homicide Rate	Non-White Homicide Rate	Total Suicide Rate	White Suicide Rate	Non-White Suicide Rate	Total Accident Rate	White Accident Rate	Non-White Accident Rate
1951	10.8	3.6	58.4	12.6	14.1	2.8	56.0	53.5	72.3
1952	13.7	5.8	65.1	15.2	16.6	6.5	52.3	50.5	63.8
1953	9.4	3.9	46.7	13.0	14.6	2.5	53.0	48.9	80.7
1954	10.4	4.0	53.8	12.9	13.9	6.0	50.0	44.1	89.7
1955	11.3	5.3	50.3	15.1	16.4	6.4	50.5	45.9	80.2
1956	10.3	3.3	56.1	13.0	14.6	2.0	52.8	47.0	91.5
1957	9.6	2.7	55.4	13.3	14.8	2.7	47.0	44.3	65.3
1958	10.6	4.0	53.5	16.0	18.2	1.6	47.8	44.7	67.4
1959	11.7	4.8	53.6	15.9	18.0	3.1	47.8	44.3	68.9
1960	15.6	5.3	41.2	15.5	17.6	3.5	46.9	44.8	58.9
1961	9.8	3.9	42.9	17.3	19.8	2.7	41.7	38.6	59.2
1962	10.3	5.2	39.2	17.7	20.3	3.3	45.2	42.1	62.8
1963	9.2	5.2	31.4	17.3	19.6	4.4	45.9	44.0	56.6
1964	9.3	3.8	40.6	16.5	18.4	5.5	47.4	46.4	52.7
1965	10.8	5.6	40.0	17.8	19.8	6.5	47.7	45.1	62.4
1966	11.9	4.6	52.4	15.8	17.8	4.6	51.5	47.1	75.9
1967	13.0	7.0	46.4	13.6	15.0	5.5	49.5	45.0	74.5
1968	13.4	7.0	48.8	14.9	16.8	4.2	52.0	46.6	81.7
1969	15.0	7.5	56.4	16.8	18.6	6.7	55.0	51.8	72.4
1970	19.2	10.1	68.8	18.2	20.3	6.6	51.2	49.8	58.7
1971	20.0	9.8	75.2	17.9	19.7	7.9	52.3	47.5	78.2
1972	16.9	7.7	66.7	18.7	21.2	5.2	52.7	49.9	68.2
1973	20.5	11.2	70.4	21.1	23.9	6.0	52.2	49.3	67.6
1974	19.2	10.3	67.3	22.2	24.7	8.5	45.4	42.6	60.1
1975	20.0	12.1	62.5	19.9	22.5	5.8	41.1	36.9	63.8
1976	15.0	9.1	47.1	20.0	22.0	9.2	37.5	35.9	45.7
1977	16.1	10.6	45.0	22.7	35.3	9.1	38.1	36.1	48.9
1978	16.6	9.3	56.0	20.2	22.5	8.5	37.5	38.5	52.5
1979	22.7	15.9	58.8	19.0	20.0	10.6	43.9	42.1	60.4
1980	35.0	24.2	98.0	18.5	21.8	4.3	50.9	51.6	79.6
1981	34.6	27.1	96.9	17.1	19.5	10.4	48.0	50.3	67.8
1982	30.2	25.1	76.1	20.2	25.0	8.5	43.7	43.9	71.2
1983	24.2			17.0			39.7		

Table 2.2

Homicide Rate for Dade County Compared to the U.S.,
Florida and Selected Florida Counties, 1920 to 1980

Jurisdiction	1920	1924	1925	1926	1927	1930	1940	1950	1960	1970	1980
U.S.	6.8	8.1	8.3	8.4	8.4	8.8	6.3	5.3	4.7	8.3	11.3
Florida	19.1	28.0	35.1	49.3	35.7	24.7	21.2	13.0	9.1	14.5	15.6
Dade County	18.9	34.6	102.6	110.1	55.1	35.2	21.8	12.4	15.6	19.2	35.0
Broward	0.0	7.7	63.1	123.2	58.7	24.9	22.6	14.5	12.3	19.7	17.7
Palm Beach	21.4	43.9	53.9	109.8	58.1	40.5	25.0	13.9	11.0	13.8	10.6
Monroe	5.1	0.0	7.0	35.4	7.1	0.0	7.1	3.3	14.6	7.4	12.7
Duvall	35.2	65.0	63.2	93.2	60.9	32.8	23.8	14.8	11.4	17.6	14.0
Hillsborough	13.6	29.4	36.0	60.4	38.9	20.8	15.5	10.0	9.8	13.2	13.1
Leon	16.6	10.3	20.0	33.8	32.7	21.3	19.0	17.4	6.7	9.4	8.7
Alachua	41.0	6.2	30.7	57.7	42.0	37.8	38.9	14.0	12.2	18.0	9.3

Table 2.3

All Accident Rate for Dade County Compared to the U.S., Florida and Selected Florida Counties, 1920 to 1980.

Year

Jurisdiction	1920	1924	1925	1926	1927	1930	1940	1950	1960	1970	1980
U.S.	70.0	73.8	76.5	77.2	77.1	79.8	73.2	60.6	52.3	56.4	47.9
Florida	75.6	81.7	119.9	172.2	115.6	104.9	89.6	68.6	58.1	66.5	52.6
Dade	105.0	114.1	226.9	324.6	126.6	100.8	79.2	52.7	46.9	51.2	50.9
Broward	272.6	100.0	210.4	661.3	129.2	94.6	95.5	50.0	53.0	62.1	49.7
Palm Beach	123.3	122.8	282.7	282.0	127.9	139.0	103.8	73.2	68.0	69.5	59.5
Monroe	51.2	41.7	105.2	141.5	92.9	88.1	56.8	60.1	60.5	32.4	83.9
Duval	96.9	111.3	128.0	139.4	129.9	120.2	84.2	72.0	60.6	70.1	49.2
Hillsborough	75.9	59.5	111.0	140.5	102.9	82.7	87.2	58.8	51.3	62.0	50.9
Leon	66.5	82.5	69.8	101.3	121.4	161.9	101.1	34.9	62.0	50.1	36.3
Alachua	63.1	86.9	89.0	94.1	105.1	119.3	114.0	54.0	59.5	68.0	36.3

Table 3.1

Twenty Cities (Over 300,000) With Highest Murder and
Non-negligent Manslaughter Rates for the U.S., 1980
According to Figures in Uniform Crime Reports, 1980

1. Miami, Fl 65.5 (220)

2. St. Louis, Mo.............. 49.9 (225)

3. Newark, N.J................ 49.4 (163)

4. Atlanta, Ga................ 47.6 (201)

5. Cleveland, Ohio............ 46.3 (265)

6. Detroit, Mich.............. 45.7 (547)

7. New Orleans, La............ 39.1 (218)

8. Houston, Texas............. 39.1 (633)

9. Dallas, Texas 35.4 (319)

10. Los Angèles, Calif......... 34.2 (1,010)

11. Washington, D.C............ 31.5 (200)

12. Kansas City, Mo............ 29.8 (133)

13. Chicago, Ill............... 28.9 (863)

14. Baltimore, Md.............. 27.5 (216)

15. Philadelphia, Pa........... 25.9 (436)

16. New York, N.Y.............. 25.8 (1,812)

17. Las Vegas, Nev............. 23.9 (92)

18. Memphis, Tenn.............. 23.6 (152)

19. Long Beach, Calif.......... 23.0 (82)

20. San Antonio, Texas......... 20.8 (164)

Cities (over 300,000) with lowest rates
were Minneapolis (9.7), San Jose, Calif
(9.9), Tulsa (10.1), and Milwaukee (11.7).

Table 3.2

Ten S.M.S.A.'s (over 300,000 population) With Highest
Murder and Non-negligent Manslaughter Rates for the U.S.,
1980 According to Figures in Uniform Crime Reports, 1980

1. Miami, FL (includes all of Dade County)... 32.7
   (515)

2. Houston, TX (includes Brazoria, Ft. Bend,
   Harris, Liberty, Montgomery, and
   Waller counties......................... 27.6
   (799)

3. Las Vegas, Nev (includes Clark County).... 23.4
   (103)

4. Los Angeles—Long Beach, Calif (includes
   Los Angeles County)..................... 23.3
   (1,731)

5. New Orleans, La (includes Jefferson,
   Orleans, St. Bernard and St. Tammany
   parishes)............................... 22.3
   (264)

6. New York, N.Y.—N.J. (includes Bronx,
   Kings, New York, Putnam, Queens,
   Richmond, Rockland, and Westchester
   counties, N.Y. and Bergen county, N.J.). 21.0
   (1,903)

7. Bakersfield, Calif (includes Kern county). 20.9
   (84)

8. Mobile, Ala (includes Baldwin and Mobile
   counties)............................... 20.5
   (90)

9. Fresno, Calif (includes Fresno county).... 20.1
   (102)

10. Shreveport, La (includes Bossier, Caddo
    and Webster parishes)................... 19.6
    (74)

S.M.S.A.'s (over 300,000) with lowest rates were
Madison, Wis (1.6), Lancaster, Pa (2.2) and
Davenport, Iowa (2.3).

Table 3.3

Murder and Non-negligent Manslaughter Rates for
1960 to 1980 for the U.S., Population Groups,
And Selected SMSA's

	1960	1965	1970	1975	1976	1977	1978	1979	1980	% Change 1960 to 1980	% Change 1979 to 1980
United States	5.1	5.1	7.8	9.6	8.0	8.8	9.0	9.7	10.2	+100%	+ 5%
Rural U.S.	6.4	5.1	6.4	8.1	7.8	7.8	7.5	7.4	7.5	+ 17%	+ 14%
Other Cities	3.8	3.5	4.4	5.5	5.3	5.0	5.2	5.7	5.8	+ 53%	+ 18%
U.S. SMSA's	4.9	5.4	8.7	10.6	9.5	9.7	9.9	10.9	11.5	+135%	+ 5%
Atlanta	10.7	11.5	20.4	15.7	14.0	11.3	13.9	20.2	14.4	+ 35%	- 29%
Birmingham	17.5	13.3	13.7	19.2	16.6	16.7	15.2	16.6	16.5	- 6%	- 1%
Chicago	6.7	6.9	12.9	13.9	13.4	13.7	13.0	14.3	14.5	+116%	+ 1%
Cleveland	5.3	5.7	14.5	17.0	15.1	14.2	13.2	16.7	15.9	+200%	- 5%
Dallas	10.1	10.3	13.4	15.3	14.5	15.2	15.3	18.3	18.1	+ 79%	- 1%
Detroit	5.1	6.2	14.7	17.9	18.1	14.1	15.2	13.8	16.1	+216%	+ 17%
Houston	10.9	10.7	16.9	19.1	16.5	18.0	23.5	30.0	27.6	+153%	- 8%
Los Angeles	4.4	6.1	9.4	14.3	13.8	16.0	17.4	20.0	23.3	+430%	+ 16%
Miami	9.6	8.9	15.6	18.3	13.6	15.6	17.0	21.3	32.7	+241%	+ 54%
Mobile	13.0	9.5	12.2	15.0	17.6	22.2	18.6	20.1	20.5	+ 58%	+ 2%
Nashville	11.5	10.9	12.6	15.7	12.4	12.1	12.9	13.5	13.5	+ 17%	----
New York City	4.0	6.1	10.5	18.0	17.5	17.1	16.8	19.8	21.0	+425%	+ 1%
San Antonio	6.7	7.8	9.5	14.7	14.3	16.8	14.9	17.9	17.5	+161%	- 2%
Seattle	2.9	2.7	4.4	5.7	4.4	4.3	5.8	5.1	6.7	+131%	+ 31%
Washington, DC	6.9	8.2	11.4	12.0	10.1	10.3	9.7	9.3	10.7	+ 55%	+ 15%
Ft. Lauderdale	16.2	8.2	14.0	14.3	10.9	9.1	10.8	14.1	17.4	+ 7%	+ 23%
Tampa-St. Pete	6.1	6.0	9.5	11.1	7.7	7.0	8.4	7.4	8.1	+ 33%	+ 9%
Jacksonville,	11.2	11.1	18.2	15.5	15.3	13.2	13.7	12.0	12.4	+ 11%	+ 3%

147

Table 4.1

Trends in Homicide Victimization Rates
For Dade County by Age, Sex, Race and
Sex-Race; For 1959-61, 1969-71, 1974-76
and 1980

	Total Rate	0 - 14	15 - 24	25 - 44	45 - 64	65 - up	Males	Females	Whites	Non-White	White Males	White Females	Non-White Males	Non-White Females
1959-61	11.1	1.6	15.7	21.4	11.1	2.8	16.1	6.3	5.0	46.8	6.6	3.3	70.3	24.0
1969-71	19.0	2.7	24.4	37.9	19.9	7.6	31.6	7.6	9.6	72.9	14.9	4.7	127.3	23.8
1974-76	18.2	2.9	23.9	34.6	16.8	9.1	30.9	7.1	10.9	57.6	18.3	4.4	98.9	21.1
1980	35.0	3.4	60.1	68.6	32.7	12.9	61.1	11.7	25.3	79.2	47.0	9.7	167.9	26.7
% Change from 1959-61 to 1980	+215%	+113%	+283%	+221%	+195%	+361%	+280%	+86%	+416%	+69%	+612%	+194%	+139%	+11%

148

Table 4.2

Trends in Homicide Victimization Rates
For Dade County by Age-Sex-Race Subgroups
For 1959-61, 1969-71, 1974-76, and 1980

	White Males					White Females				
	0 - 14	15 - 24	25 - 44	45 - 64	65 - up	0 - 14	15 - 24	25 - 44	45 - 64	65 - up
1959-61	0.6*	11.0	11.2	8.4	1.5*	1.0*	2.9	5.4	3.6	2.2
1969-71	1.4	15.2	27.8	18.4	8.9	2.0	5.0	6.2	6.3	2.5
1974-76	2.6	19.5	31.1	19.9	14.7	0.9*	6.1	6.7	3.5	4.4
1980	2.7*	63.5	87.1	43.4	21.1	0.9*	18.4	13.9	10.1	4.3
% Change 1959-61 to 1980	+350%	+457%	+678%	+417%	+1,307%	-10%	+534%	+157%	+181%	+95%

	Non-White Males					Non-White Females				
1959-61	3.0*	91.4	130.6	91.3	34.9	5.1*	18.7	49.5	26.3	15.7*
1969-71	8.5	157.8	267.7	220.4	92.5	3.7*	27.0	52.8	18.0	21.2*
1974-76	7.1	100.7	224.4	131.3	41.4	5.4	33.7	35.2	18.9	0.0*
1980	12.8*	225.0	343.6	191.5	85.0*	2.6*	51.9	43.7	19.8*	11.7*
% Change 1959-61 to 1980	+327%	+146%	+163%	+110%	+144%	-49%	+178%	-12%	-24%	-25%

149

Table 4.3

Number of 1980 Homicide Victims and Victimization Rates Per 100,000 Residents for Subgroups of Dade County by Race, Sex, and Age.

	All Ages	0 – 14	15 – 24	25–44	45 – 64	65 – up
Whites (Anglos & Latins)	347	4	79	160	78	26
	1,345,600	215,553*	193,829*	328,350*	308,847*	233,472*
	(25.8)	(1.9)	(40.8)	(48.7)	(25.3)	(11.1)
Non-Latin Whites	137	3	30	45	37	22
	764,570	144,358**	127,036**	203,908**	168,852**	120,040**
	(17.9)	(2.1)	(23.6)	(22.1)	(21.9)	(18.3)
Latin Whites	210	1	49	115	41	4
	581,030	109,920**	96,488**	154,959**	128,318**	91,224**
	(36.1)	(0.9)	(50.8)	(74.2)	(32.0)	(4.4)
Blacks	222	6	67	107	35	6
	280,379	78,272*	49,029*	61,125*	36,372*	14,398*
	(79.2)	(7.7)	(136.7)	(175.1)	(96.2)	(41.7)
All Males	469	8	115	228	92	25
	767,882	148,930*	120,052*	182,930*	156,765*	100,813*
	(61.1)	(5.4)	(95.8)	(124.6)	(58.7)	(24.8)
All Females	100	2	31	39	21	7
	857,899	144,895*	122,796*	206,545*	188,454*	147,057*
	(11.7)	(1.4)	(25.2)	(18.9)	(11.1)	(4.8)
White Males	281	3	61	136	61	20
	597,499*	109,767*	96,064*	156,158*	140,573*	94,932*
	(47.0)	(2.7)	(63.5)	(87.1)	(43.4)	(21.1)
White Females	66	1	18	24	17	6
	682,552*	105,786*	97,765*	172,192*	168,269*	138,540*
	(9.7)	(0.9)	(18.4)	(13.9)	(10.1)	(4.3)
Black Males	188	5	54	92	31	5
	112,001*	39,163*	23,998*	26,772*	16,187*	5,881*
	(167.9)	(12.8)	(225.0)	(343.6)	(191.5)	(85.0)
Black Females	34	1	13	15	4	1
	127,195*	39,109*	25,031*	34,353*	20,185*	8,517*
	(26.7)	(2.6)	(51.9)	(43.7)	(19.8)	(11.7)
Total	569	10	146	267	113	32
	1,625,979	307,746	270,016	433,643	359,090	255,286
	(35.0)	(3.4)	(60.1)	(68.6)	(32.7)	(12.9)

Note: The population figures are from the 1980 census when there is no *. When the population figure appears with one * the figure is from a 1979 estimate of the subgroup from figures provided by the University of Florida (comparable figures from the 1980 census were not available for race by sex by age). When the population figure appears with two *'s the figure is extrapolated from the 1980 census figure (for all ages) with the count for each age subgroup estimated by assuming that this subgroup would have the same percentage of persons in each age subgroup as the general population.

There was one Black Male victim whose age was not determined thus the total number of victims for all Blacks (N=222), Black Males (N=188), and Males (N=469) includes one more victim than a summation of victims in the age categories would indicate.

Table 4.4

A Comparison of Victimization Rates for Homicides
Occurring in Dade County in 1925-26 versus 1980

	1925-1926	1980	Ratio of Rate for '25-'26 to 1980 Rate & % Difference
Number of Homicides (from death certificates)	216	**569**	
Rate per 100,000	106.5 (1:939)	35.0 (1:2,857)	Ratio=3:1 or 204% greater
White Victimization Rate (from death certificates)	33.7 (1:2,967)	25.8 (1:3,875)	Ratio=1.3:1 or 31% greater
Black Victimization Rate (from death certificates)	356.6 (1:280)	79.2 (1:1,263)	Ratio=4.5:1 or 350% greater
White Victimization Rate (estimated from Herald sample—No./.77)	60.0 (1:1,667)	25.8 (1:3,875)	Ratio=2.3:1 or 130% greater
Black Victimization Rate (estimated from Herald)	269.1 (1:371)	79.2 (1:1,263)	Ratio=3.4:1 or 240% greater
Male Victimization Rate (estimated from Herald)	148 (1:676)	61.1 (1:1,637)	Ratio=2.4:1 or 142% greater
Black Male Victimization Rate (from Herald)	273 (1:366)	167.9 (1:596)	Ratio=1.6:1 or 63% greater
White Male Victimization Rate (from Herald)	67 (1:1,492)	47.0 (1:2,128)	Ratio=1.4:1 or 43% greater
Female Victimization Rate (from Herald)	44 (1:2,272)	11.7 (1:8,547)	Ratio=3.8:1 or 276% greater
Black Female Victimization Rate (from Herald)	104 (1:961)	26.7 (1:3,745)	Ratio=3.9:1 or 290% greater
White Female Victimization Rate (from Herald)	14 (1:7,142)	9.7 (1:10,309)	Ratio=1.4:1 or 44% greater

Table 4.4

A Comparison of Victimization Rates for Homicides
Occurring in Dade County in 1925-26 versus 1980

	1925-1926	1980	Ratio of Rate for '25-'26 to 1980 Rate & % Difference
	(continued)		
Gun Homicide Rate (from Death certificates)	82.3	25.4	Ratio=3.2:1 or 224% greater
Knife Homicide Rate (from Death certificates)	17.3	4.7	Ratio=3.7:1 or 268% greater
Other Weapon Rate	6.4	5.2	Ratio=1.2:1 or 23% greater
Estimated Robbery/Murder Rate (conservative estimate from Herald sample)	8.4	4.0	Ratio=2.1:1 or 110% greater
Estimated Argument/Murder Rate (conservative estimate from Herald sample)	40.4	14.2	Ratio=2.8:1 or 184% greater
Estimated Police Homicide Rate (from Herald sample)	16.3 (N=33)	0.9 (N=14)	Ratio=18.1 or 1,710% greater
Estimated Police Homicide Rate With White Male Victims (from Herald sample)	14.9 (N=19)	1.2 (N=7)	Ratio=12.4:1 or 1,142% greater
Estimated Police Homicide Rate With Black Male Victims (from Herald Sample)	69.3 (N=14)	6.2 (N=7)	Ratio of 11.2:1 or 1,018% greater

The estimated rates from the Miami Herald sample were
calculated by increasing the actual number found on the
pages of the Herald by 29% (since the total number of
homicides found in the Herald was 29% less than the
"real" number of homicides as reported by death certificates).

Table 4.5

A Comparison of Characteristics of 1925–26
Versus 1980 Homicides for Dade County

		1925–26		1980	
		No.	%	No.	%
Race of O and V When Both Known	Black on Black Homicides	63	43%	169	34%
	White on White Homicides	56	38%	228	47%
	White on Black Homicides	18	12%	33	7%
	Black on White Homicides	9	6%	59	12%
		146	100%	489	100%
Sex of O and V When Both Known	Male on Male Homicides	111	78%	369	75%
	Male on Female Homicides	17	12%	81	16%
	Female on Male Homicides	9	6%	45	9%
	Female on Female Homicides	5	4%	1	0.2%
		143	100%	496	100%
Victim/Offender Relationship	Acquaintances	63	38%	330	58%
	Married or Relative	15	9%	54	10%
	Strangers	45	27%	161	28%
	Unknown	44	26%	24	4%
		167	100%	569	100%
Place of Occurrence When Known	On the Street	43	32%	83	15%
	In a Home	65	48%	212	37%
	Other	27	20%	274	48%
		135	100%	569	100%
Time of Day When Known	Killed during Day	37	29%	267	47%
	Killed during Night	90	71%	302	53%
		127	100%	569	100%
Day of Week When Known	Killed Friday – Sunday	85	51%	340	60%
	Killed Monday – Thursday	82	49%	229	40%
		167	100%	569	100%

Table 5.1 Age, Sex and Race of Victim by Legal Type of Homicide for All Homicides Occurring in Dade County in 1980

	Criminal Homicide	Justifiable Homicide	Excusable Homicide	Criminal— Felony Murder	Total
0 - 14	9 90.0%	1 10.0%	0 0.0%	0 0.0%	10
15 - 24	114 78.1%	27 18.5%	0 0.0%	5 3.5%	146
25 - 44	208 77.9%	47 17.6%	3 1.1%	9 3.3%	267
45 - 64	99 87.6%	10 8.8%	2 1.8%	2 1.8%	113
65 & up	31 96.9%	1 3.1%	0 0.0%	0 0.0%	32
Males	367 78.3%	84 17.9%	4 0.9%	14 3.0%	469
Females	95 95.0%	2 2.0%	1 1.0%	2 2.0%	100
Non-Latin Whites	115 83.9%	14 10.2%	4 2.9%	4 2.9%	137
Blacks	161 72.5%	56 25.2%	1 0.5%	4 1.9%	222
Latins	186 88.6%	16 7.6%	0 0.0%	8 3.8%	210
Total	462 81.2%	86 15.1%	5 0.9%	16 2.9%	569

Table 5.2 Age, Sex and Race of Victim by Type of Weapon Used to Kill the Victim for All Homicides Occurring in Dade County in 1980

	Handgun	Rifle or Shotgun	Unknown Gun	Knife	Blunt Object	Hands, feet	Other	Total
0 - 14	2 20.0%	1 10.0%	0 0.0%	1 10.0%	2 20.0%	4 40.0%	0 0.0%	10
15 - 24	97 66.4%	13 8.9%	4 2.7%	17 11.6%	6 4.1%	5 3.4%	4 2.8%	146
25 - 44	176 65.9%	23 8.6%	13 4.9%	36 13.5%	6 2.2%	10 3.7%	3 1.1%	267
45 - 64	60 53.1%	6 5.3%	6 5.3%	21 18.6%	10 8.8%	6 5.3%	4 3.5%	113
65 & Over	6 18.8%	0 0.0%	2 6.3%	7 21.9%	7 21.9%	8 25.0%	2 6.3%	32
Male	290 61.8%	35 7.5%	22 4.7%	69 14.7%	26 5.5%	20 4.3%	7 1.5%	469
Female	52 52.0%	8 8.0%	3 3.0%	13 13.0%	5 5.0%	13 13.0%	5 5.0% .	100
Non-Latin White	60 43.8%	5 3.6%	6 4.4%	22 16.1%	16 11.7%	20 14.6%	8 5.8%	137
Black	130 58.6%	29 13.1%	3 1.4%	40 18.0%	11 5.0%	7 3.2%	2 0.9%	222
Latin	152 72.4%	9 4.3%	16 7.6%	20 9.5%	4 1.9%	6 2.9%	3 1.4%	210
Total	342 60.1%	43 7.6%	25 4.4%	82 14.4%	31 5.4%	33 5.8%	13 2.3%	569 100%

Table 5.3

Violent Death Rates for Dade County, FL, 1956–1983

Year	Population	Med. Examiner Homicide Rate	U.C.R. Homicide Rate	Firearm Hom. Rate	Knife Homicide Rate	Other Method Hom. Rate	% of Tested Victims with Alcohol	Med. Examiner Suicide Rate	Motor Vehicle Accident Rate	All Other Accident Rate	Rate of Hom. By Police	Rate of Hom. By Police Or Citizen
1956	757,700	9.4	----	5.4	2.6	1.3	44%	12.0	16.2	19.3	0.4	0.4
1957	834,550	10.2	----	5.7	3.0	1.4	67%	14.6	19.7	21.9	0.2	0.4
1958	879,000	11.7	----	7.3	2.8	1.7	44%	18.0	18.0	23.0	0.6	0.9
1959	909,930	11.9	11.2	7.5	2.4	2.0	64%	16.9	16.9	23.5	0.9	1.3
1960	935,047	11.3	9.6	6.2	2.6	2.4	63%	16.3	17.9	22.9	0.4	0.9
1961	990,950	9.9	9.1	6.4	2.2	1.4	64%	10.1	15.3	20.6	0.1	0.3
1962	1,056,620	10.7	8.2	5.9	1.8	3.0	69%	17.1	21.2	19.6	0.5	0.7
1963	1,081,390	9.2	8.0	6.1	1.5	1.6	58%	17.5	15.7	19.3	0.3	0.3
1964	1,093,600	10.1	6.2	7.1	1.5	1.5	56%	17.5	18.5	24.3	0.3	0.3
1965	1,120,200	11.5	8.9	8.5	1.7	1.3	58%	19.1	16.7	23.1	0.1	0.4
1966	1,154,000	12.5	10.7	8.2	2.2	2.1	69%	16.5	23.7	25.0	0.8	1.1
1967	1,200,000	14.3	11.3	10.3	2.2	1.8	56%	14.8	19.5	23.1	0.6	0.8
1968	1,240,000	14.2	12.5	9.4	2.3	2.4	62%	14.8	26.6	24.9	0.7	1.2
1969	1,280,000	15.1	12.8	10.9	1.3	3.0	48%	17.0	24.1	25.6	0.9	1.0
1970	1,267,792	20.5	15.6	14.9	2.4	3.2	48%	20.7	23.4	26.0	1.3	2.1
1971	1,307,669	20.6	17.1	15.1	2.5	3.0	48%	19.2	24.4	25.1	1.1	1.5
1972	1,342,475	17.5	14.3	13.1	1.3	3.1	52%	19.4	22.9	31.6	0.4	0.9
1973	1,373,609	20.1	15.7	15.3	1.6	3.2	51%	21.7	24.7	24.6	0.7	0.9
1974	1,413,102	19.0	17.4	11.7	1.6	1.5	56%	22.3	19.2	24.8	0.4	0.8
1975	1,437,993	20.5	18.3	14.8	2.2	3.4	53%	19.9	18.6	23.8	0.5	1.2
1976	1,449,300	15.4	13.6	9.1	1.7	2.4	50%	20.6	17.3	20.4	0.3	0.6
1977	1,468,270	17.0	15.6	10.1	2.5	4.3	54%	23.0	18.9	19.5	0.3	0.4
1978	1,528,000	17.9	17.0	12.4	1.5	3.9	49%	20.9	18.6	20.2	0.3	0.6
1979	1,519.247	24.2	21.3	16.3	3.0	4.8	50%	19.0	22.1	21.7	0.8	1.3
1980	1,625,781	35.0	32.7	25.4	4.7	5.2	43%	18.6	27.4	23.0	0.9	3.0
1981	1,732,000	35.6	31.9	27.2	4.0	4.8	----	16.3	24.1	19.0	0.6	----
1982	1,739,000	30.7	29.8	24.1	2.8	3.9	----	20.5	23.2	19.4	0.6	----
1983	1,734,000	24.2	----	17.4	2.7	4.2	----	17.0	20.4	19.3	0.5	----

Note: The "Accident Rate" includes all non-motor vehicle accidents and largely involves drownings, home accidents, drug overdoses, burns, and even airplane crashes (the 1972 rate includes 96 deaths from an Eastern Airline crash in the Everglades). The "% of Tested Victims with Alcohol" refers to those victims who tested positive. Data begins with 1956 since records were not available earlier.

Table 5.4 Age, Sex and Race of Victim by Motive/Circumstance for all Homicides Occurring in Dade County in 1980

	Domestic Argument	Other Argument	Robbery	Rape, Burglary Or Other Felony	Drug Rip-Off	Self-Defense	Other	Unknown	Total
0 - 14	0 0.0%	1 10.0%	0 0.0%	1 10.0%	0 0.0%	1 10.0%	7 70.0%	0 0.0%	10
15 - 24	15 10.3%	36 24.7%	11 7.5%	4 2.7%	33 22.6%	26 17.8%	10 6.8%	11 7.5%	146
25 - 44	28 10.5%	91 34.1%	21 7.9%	4 1.5%	66 24.7%	36 13.5%	14 5.2%	7 2.6%	267
45 - 64	21 18.6%	29 25.7%	22 19.5%	6 5.3%	17 15.0%	9 8.0%	6 5.3%	3 2.7%	113
65 & up	2 6.3%	8 25.0%	11 34.4%	5 15.6%	0 0.0%	1 3.1%	3 9.4%	2 6.3%	32
Male	32 6.8%	153 32.6%	59 12.6%	10 2.1%	98 20.9%	71 15.1%	28 6.0%	18 3.8%	469
Female	34 34.0%	12 12.0%	6 6.0%	10 10.0%	18 18.0%	2 2.0%	12 12.0%	6 6.0%	100
Non-Latin Whites	14 10.2%	24 17.5%	32 23.4%	13 9.5%	19 13.9%	11 8.0%	19 13.9%	5 3.6%	137
Blacks	29 13.1%	70 31.5%	20 9.0%	4 1.8%	32 14.4%	47 21.2%	12 5.4%	8 3.6%	222
Latins	23 11.0%	71 33.8%	13 6.2%	3 1.4%	65 31.0%	15 7.1%	9 4.3%	11 5.2%	210
Total	66 11.6%	165 29.0%	65 11.4%	20 3.5%	116 20.4%	73 12.8%	40 7.0%	24 4.2%	569

Table 5.5 Age, Sex and Race of Victim by the Victim/Offender Relationship for all Homicides Occurring in Dade County in 1980

	Husband/Wife	Other Family	Sex Partners Or Rivals	Acquaintances	Crime Partners	Strangers	Felon Killed By Citizen	Felon Killed By Police	Citizen Killed by Felon	Police Killed by Felon	Unknown	Total
0 - 14	0 0.0%	5 50.0%	0 0.0%	2 20.0%	0 0.0%	0 0.0%	1 10.0%	0 0.0%	1 10.0%	0 0.0%	1 10.0%	10
15 - 24	7 4.8%	3 2.1%	9 6.2%	39 26.7%	32 21.9%	22 15.1%	12 8.2%	5 3.4%	7 4.8%	0 0.0%	10 6.8%	146
25 - 44	21 7.9%	3 1.1%	24 9.0%	87 32.6%	65 24.3%	22 8.2%	16 6.0%	11 4.1%	9 3.4%	2 0.7%	7 2.6%	267
45 - 64	8 7.1%	5 4.4%	17 15.0%	26 23.0%	18 15.9%	12 10.6%	1 0.9%	1 0.9%	20 17.7%	0 0.0%	5 4.4%	113
65 & up	2 6.3%	0 0.0%	2 6.3%	8 25.0%	1 3.1%	7 21.9%	0 0.0%	0 0.0%	11 34.4%	0 0.0%	1 3.1%	32
Males	18 3.8%	13 2.8%	32 6.8%	148 31.6%	100 21.3%	55 11.7%	29 6.2%	17 3.6%	39 8.3%	2 0.4%	16 2.8%	469
Females	20 20.0%	3 3.0%	20 20.0%	14 14.0%	16 16.0%	9 9.0%	1 1.0%	0 0.0%	9 9.0%	0 0.0%	8 8.0%	100
Non-Latin Whites	4 2.9%	7 5.1%	12 8.8%	26 19.0%	16 11.7%	23 16.8%	5 3.6%	5 3.6%	31 22.6%	2 1.5%	6 4.4%	137
Blacks	21 9.5%	5 2.3%	22 9.9%	73 32.9%	31 14.0%	28 12.6%	15 6.8%	9 4.1%	7 3.2%	0 0.0%	11 5.0%	222
Latins	13 6.2%	4 1.9%	18 8.6%	63 30.0%	69 32.9%	13 6.2%	10 4.8%	3 1.4%	10 4.8%	0 0.0%	7 3.3%	210
Total	38 6.7%	16 2.8%	52 9.1%	162 28.5%	116 20.4%	64 11.2%	30 5.3%	17 3.0%	48 8.4%	2 0.4%	24 4.2%	569

158

Table 5.6   Ethnicity of Victim by Ethnicity of First Offender; Sex of Victim by Sex of First Offender; and Ethnicity/Sex of Victim by Ethnicity/Sex of First Offender; for All Homicides Occurring in Dade County in 1980

	Race of First Offender						Sex of First Offender			
	Non-Latin Whites	Blacks	Latins	Unknown	Total		Males	Females	Unknown	Total
Non-Latin White	45 32.8%	43 31.4%	20 14.6%	29 21.2%	137	Male	369 78.7%	45 9.6%	55 11.7%	469
Blacks	19 8.6%	169 76.1%	14 6.3%	20 9.0%	222	Females	81 81.0%	1 1.0%	18 18.0%	100
Latins	8 3.8%	16 7.6%	155 73.8%	31 14.8%	210					

Race/Sex of First Offender	Non-Latin White Males	Non-Latin White Females	Black Males	Black Females	Latin Males	Latin Females	Unknown	Total
Non-Latin White Males	25 24.0%	4 3.8%	34 32.7%	1 1.0%	16 15.4%	1 1.0%	23 22.1%	104
Non-Latin White Females	15 45.5%	1 3.0%	7 21.2%	0 0.0%	3 9.1%	0 0.0%	7 21.2%	33
Black Males	18 9.6%	0 0.0%	113 60.1%	28 14.9%	12 6.4%	1 0.5%	16 8.5%	188
Black Females	1 2.9%	0 0.0%	27 79.4%	0 0.0%	1 2.9%	0 0.0%	5 14.7%	34
Latin Males	8 4.5%	0 0.0%	14 7.9%	1 0.6%	123 69.5%	8 4.5%	23 13.0%	177
Latin Females	0 0.0%	0 0.0%	1 3.0%	0 0.0%	24 72.7%	0 0.0%	8 24.2%	33
Total	67 11.8%	5 0.9%	196 34.4%	30 5.3%	179 31.5%	10 1.8%	82 14.4%	569

(Race/Sex of Victim)

159

Table 5.7 Age, Sex and Race of Victim by the Degree of Involvement of the Victim for all Homicides Occurring in Dade County in 1980

	No Participation	Victim Participated	Victim Precipitated	Unknown	Total
0 - 14	8 80.0%	1 10.0%	1 10.0%	0 0.0%	10
15 - 24	25 17.1%	86 58.9%	27 18.5%	8 5.5%	146
25 - 44	42 15.7%	172 64.4%	43 16.1%	10 3.7%	267
45 - 64	37 32.7%	58 51.3%	13 11.5%	5 4.4%	113
65 & up	22 68.8%	7 21.9%	1 3.1%	2 6.3%	32
Males	100 21.3%	268 57.1%	81 17.3%	20 4.3%	469
Females	34 34.0%	56 56.0%	4 4.0%	6 6.0%	100
Non-Latin Whites	63 46.0%	55 40.1%	13 9.5%	6 4.4%	137
Blacks	35 15.8%	127 57.2%	49 22.1%	11 5.0%	222
Latins	36 17.1%	142 67.6%	23 11.0%	9 4.3%	210
Total	134 23.6%	324 56.9%	85 14.9%	26 4.6%	569

Table 5.8 Age, Sex and Race of Victim by the Amount of Alcohol Found in Body of Victim for all Homicides Occurring in Dade County in 1980

	No Alcohol	.01 to .09	.10 to .19	.20 to .45	Not Tested Or Unknown	Total
0 - 14	5 50.0%	0 0.0%	0 0.0%	0 0.0%	5 50.0%	10
15 - 24	79 54.1%	29 19.9%	23 15.8%	4 2.7%	11 7.5%	146
25 - 44	132 49.4%	47 17.6%	47 17.6%	20 7.5%	21 7.8%	267
45 - 64	56 49.6%	16 14.2%	12 10.6%	10 8.8%	19 16.8%	113
65 & up	14 43.8%	4 12.5%	3 9.4%	2 6.3%	9 28.1%	32
Male	230 49.0%	82 17.5%	72 15.4%	34 7.2%	51 10.9%	469
Female	57 57.0%	14 14.0%	13 13.0%	2 2.0%	14 14.0%	100
Non-Latin White	71 51.8%	20 14.6%	13 9.5%	4 2.9%	29 21.2%	137
Black	108 48.6%	35 15.8%	37 16.7%	20 9.0%	22 9.9%	222
Latin	108 51.4%	41 19.5%	35 16.7%	12 5.7%	14 6.7%	210
Total	287 50.4%	96 16.9%	85 14.9%	36 6.3%	65 11.5%	569

161

Table 5.9 Age, Sex and Race of Victim by Type of Place of Occurrence for All Homicides Occurring in Dade County in 1980

	Home of Victim	Other Home	Parking Lot	Public Bldg	Near or in Bar	Street, Sidewalk	Field, Canal	Motor Vehicle	Unknown	
0 - 14	6	2	1	0	0	1	0	0	0	10
	60.0%	20.0%	10.0%	0.0%	0.0%	10.0%	0.0%	0.0%	0.0%	
15 - 24	20	21	7	25	11	26	19	16	1	146
	13.7%	14.4%	4.8%	17.1%	7.5%	17.8%	13.0%	11.0%	0.7%	
25 - 44	59	33	15	43	30	27	30	30	0	267
	22.1%	12.4%	5.6%	16.1%	11.2%	10.1%	11.2%	11.2%	0.0%	
45 - 64	47	6	4	15	6	22	5	7	1	113
	41.6%	5.3%	3.5%	13.3%	5.3%	19.5%	4.4%	6.2%	0.9%	
65 & Up	17	1	1	3	0	6	1	3	0	32
	53.1%	3.1%	3.1%	9.4%	0.0%	18.8%	3.1%	9.4%	0.0%	
Male	101	54	25	80	46	79	42	42	0	469
	21.5%	11.5%	5.3%	17.1%	9.8%	16.8%	9.0%	9.0%	0.0%	
Female	48	9	3	6	1	4	13	14	2	100
	48.0%	9.0%	3.0%	6.0%	1.0%	4.0%	13.0%	14.0%	2.0%	
Non-Latin White	48	9	6	23	5	17	13	15	1	137
	35.0%	6.6%	4.4%	16.8%	3.6%	12.4%	9.5%	10.9%	0.7%	
Black	53	29	14	39	15	38	19	15	0	222
	23.9%	13.1%	6.3%	17.6%	6.8%	17.1%	8.6%	6.8%	0.0%	
Latin	48	25	8	24	27	28	23	26	1	210
	22.9%	11.9%	3.8%	11.4%	12.9%	13.3%	11.0%	12.4%	0.5%	
Total	149	63	28	86	47	83	55	56	2	569
	26.2%	11.1%	4.9%	15.1%	8.3%	14.6%	9.7%	9.8%	0.4%	100%

Table 5.10

Sex and Race of Victim by Census Tract of Residence
of Victim for Tracts With Greatest Numbers of
Homicides---All 569 Homicides in Dade County, 1980

Total		Males		Females		Anglos		Blacks		Latins	
No.	Tract	No.	Tract	No.	Tract	No.	Tract	No.	Tract	No.	Tract
13	19.02	12	19.02	3	4.07	5	37.01	13	19.02	7	36.02
12	4.07	11	31.00	2	3.01	5	39.04	12	31.00	7	43.00
12	10.04	10	10.04	2	6.01	4	78.02	11	10.04	7	49.00
12	14.00	10	34.00	2	10.01	3	2.07	9	4.07	5	24.00
12	31.00	9	4.07	2	10.04	3	4.07	9	14.00	4	9.01
11	34.00	9	14.00	2	14.00	3	11.03	9	15.02	4	37.02
9	15.02	9	37.02	2	15.02	3	37.02	9	34.00	4	44.00
9	18.03	9	43.00	2	17.01	3	42.00	8	18.03	4	52.00
9	37.02	8	18.03	2	39.04	3	68.00	7	4.03	3	6.01
9	43.00	8	36.02	2	42.00	2	1.03	7	18.02	3	17.03
8	36.02	7	15.02	2	49.00	2	2.03	6	10.01	3	26.00
7	10.01	7	18.02	2	57.02	2	2.04	6	18.01	3	27.01
7	18.02	6	4.03	2	84.01	2	2.05	5	17.02	3	29.00
7	49.00	6	113.00	2	93.03	2	3.01	5	19.01	3	30.02
6	9.01	5	9.01	2	100.01	2	9.03	5	23.00	3	53.01
6	18.01	5	10.01	2	101.12	2	40.00	5	72.00	3	57.01
6	19.01	5	10.03	2	105.00	2	43.00	4	10.03	3	57.02
6	24.00	5	17.02			2	45.00	4	17.01	3	60.01
6	52.00	5	18.01			2	52.00	4	20.02	3	64.00
		5	19.01			2	77.03	4	83.03	3	84.01
		5	24.00			2	100.01	4	105.00	3	90.01
		5	27.00			2	101.03	4	113.00		
		5	37.00			2	101.08				
		5	49.00								
		5	52.00								
		5	72.00								
		5	100.08								

28=Out of Dade Co.	22=Out of Dade Co.	6=Out of Dade Co.	15=Out of Dade Co.	3=Out of Dade Co.	10=Out of Dade Co.
18=Unknown	17=Unknown	1=Unknown	2=Unknown	5=Unknown	11=Unknown
180 of 237 tracts had 1 or more homicides of residents	161 of 237 tracts had 1 or more homicides	74 of 237 tracts had 1 or more homicides	82 of 237 tracts had 1 or more homicides	64 of 237 tracts had 1 or more homicides	100 of 237 tracts had 1 or more homicides
		of residents	of residents of residents	of residents	of residents

Tract 37.02 had rate of 925.0 Tract 34.00 had rate of 446.4

Tract 37.02 had rate of 638.3 Tract 34.00 had rate of 240.0

Tract 101.12 had rate of 94.3 Tract 17.01 had rate of 88.0

Tract 37.01 had rate of 762.2 Tract 37.02 had rate of 560.7

Tract 31.00 had rate of 213.8 Tract 34.00 had rate of 200.2

Tract 37.02 had rate of 919.5 Tract 43.00 had rate of 260.3

163

Table 5.11

Sex and Race of Victim by Census Tract Where Homicide
Occurred for Tracts with Greatest Numbers of Homicides,
For all 569 Homicides in Dade County, 1980

Total		Males·		Females		Anglos		Blacks		Latins	
No.	Tract	No.	Tract	No.	Tract	No.	Tract	No.	Tract	No.	Tract
21	34.00	20	34.00	3	48.00	5	15.01	15	34.00	9	49.00
14	14.00	11	15.02	3	115.00	5	39.04	12	14.00	7	24.00
13	15.02	11	37.02	2	2.04	4	37.02	12	15.02	7	36.02
11	31.00	10	15.01	2	3.01	3	1.03	9	31.00	6	52.00
11	37.C2	10	31.00	2	10.01	3	2.03	8	4.03	6	101.12
10	15.01	9	14.00	2	14.00	3	3.01	7	10.04	6	115.00
9	10.04	9	113.00	2	15.02	3	37.01	7	18.01	5	13.00
9	49.00	8	4.03	2	21.00	3	42.00	7	19.02	5	34.00
9	113.00	8	10.04	2	22.01	3	48.00	6	18.03	5	53.02
9	115.00	8	36.02	2	39.04	3	68.00	5	4.06	5	54.02
8	4.03	7	13.00	2	42.00	3	78.03	5	4.07	5	113.00
8	13.00	7	24.00	2	49.00	3	90.01	5	10.01	4	48.00
8	24.00	7	28.00	2	52.00	3	101.08	5	15.01	4	101.03
8	36.02	7	37.01	2	53.02	3	114.00	5	17.02	3	2.03
8	37.01	7	49.00	2	76.04	3	115.00	5	23.00	3	5.02
7	4.06	6	4.06	2	88.01			5	28.00	3	7.01
7	4.07	6	4.07	2	100.01			5	37.02	3	9.01
7	17.02	6	17.02	2	101.12			5	83.03	3	27.01
7	18.01	6	18.01					4	4.05	3	37.01
7	18.03	6	18.03					4	4.08	3	64.00
7	19.02	6	19.02					4	72.00	3	76.04
7	28.00	6	90.01					4	113.00	3	90.02
7	48.00	6	101.08							3	91.00
7	90.01	6	114.00							3	101.02
7	101.12	6	115.00							3	101.08
7	114.00									3	101.09

172 of 237 tracts had 1 or more homicides committed there	153 of 237 tracts had 1 or more homicides committed there	77 of 237 tracts had 1 or more homicides committed there	86 of 237 tracts had 1 or more homicides committed there	73 of 237 tracts had 1 or more homicides committed there	100 of 237 tracts had 1 or more homicides committed there

*Figures in this table include 32 victims who appear to have
been "dumped" in a tract rather than killed there.

**No rates were calculated by tract since the fact that a homicide
occurred in a tract may have little relationship to the number
of residents of the tract (the victim may have been from another
tract. Rates were calculated by tract for residence of victim.

Table 5.12 Age, Sex and Race of Victim by Time of Day of Occurrence
For All Homicides Occurring in Dade County in 1980

	8 PM to 2 AM	2 AM to 8 AM	8 AM to 2 PM	2 PM to 8 PM	Unknown	Total
0 - 14	0 0.0%	1 10.0%	3 30.0%	3 30.0%	3 30.0%	10
15 - 24	50 34.2%	25 17.1%	25 17.1%	27 18.5%	19 13.0%	146
25 - 44	79 29.6%	50 18.7%	45 16.9%	67 25.1%	26 9.7%	267
45 - 64	40 35.4%	15 13.3%	24 21.2%	27 23.9%	7 6.2%	113
65 & up	8 25.0%	2 6.3%	6 18.8%	11 34.4%	5 15.6%	32
Male	155 33.0%	80 17.1%	80 17.1%	115 24.5%	39 8.3%	469
Female	23 23.0%	13 13.0%	23 23.0%	20 20.0%	21 21.0%	100
Non-Latin White	42 30.7%	23 16.8%	23 16.8%	27 19.7%	22 16.1%	137
Black	64 28.8%	39 17.6%	42 18.9%	62 27.9%	15 6.8%	222
Latin	72 34.3%	31 14.8%	38 18.1%	46 21.9%	23 11.0%	210
Total -	178 31.3%	93 16.3%	103 18.1%	135 23.7%	60 10.5	569 100%

165

Table 5.13 Age, Sex and Race of Victim by Day of Week of Assault for All Homicides Occurring in Dade County in 1980

	Monday	Tuesday	Wednesday	Thursday	Friday	Saturday	Sunday	Unknown	Total
0 - 14	0	2	0	3	2	1	2	0	10
	0.0%	20.0%	0.0%	30.0%	20.0%	10.0%	20.0%	0.0%	
15 - 24	22	16	13	17	14	30	26	8	146
	15.1%	11.0%	8.9%	11.6%	9.6%	20.5%	17.8%	5.5%	
25 - 44	39	33	28	28	37	48	44	10	267
	14.6%	12.4%	10.5%	10.5%	13.9%	18.0%	16.5%	3.7%	
45 - 64	17	12	11	14	9	25	23	2	113
	15.0%	10.6%	9.7%	12.4%	8.0%	22.1%	20.4%	1.8%	
65 & up	5	3	6	4	3	3	7	1	32
	15.6%	9.4%	18.8%	12.5%	9.4%	9.4%	21.9%	3.1%	
Males	72	53	47	58	56	88	85	10	469
	15.4%	11.3%	10.0%	12.4%	11.9%	18.8%	18.1%	2.1%	
Females	12	13	11	8	9	19	17	11	100
	12.0%	13.0%	11.0%	8.0%	9.0%	19.0%	17.0%	11.0%	
Non-Latin Whites	24	13	18	21	9	22	23	7	137
	17.5%	9.5%	13.1%	15.3%	6.6%	16.1%	16.8%	5.1%	
Blacks	29	22	22	20	33	42	50	4	222
	13.1%	9.9%	9.9%	9.0%	14.9%	18.9%	22.5%	1.8%	
Latins	31	31	18	25	23	43	29	10	210
	14.8%	14.8%	8.6%	11.9%	11.0%	20.5%	13.8%	4.8%	
Total	84	66	58	66	65	107	102	21	569
	14.8%	11.6%	10.2%	11.6%	11.4%	18.8%	17.9%	3.7%	

Table 5.14

Age, Sex and Race of Victim by Month of the Assault for All Homicides Occurring in Dade County in 1980 and Number of Homicides Each Month from 1975 to 1983

	Jan.	Feb.	March	April	May	June	July	Aug.	Sept.	Oct.	Nov.	Dec.	Year
0 – 14	1	0	1	1	1	0	0	0	3	1	2	0	10
	10.0%	0.0%	10.0%	10.0%	10.0%	0.0%	0.0%	0.0%	30.0%	10.0%	20.0%	0.0%	
15 – 24	9	8	10	8	24	12	12	14	16	6	14	13	146
	6.2%	5.5%	6.8%	5.5%	16.4%	8.2%	8.2%	9.6%	11.0%	4.1%	9.6%	8.9%	
25 – 44	15	12	21	17	23	22	29	22	28	21	35	22	267
	5.6%	4.5%	7.9%	6.4%	8.6%	8.2%	10.9%	8.2%	10.5%	7.9%	13.1%	8.2%	
45 – 64	6	11	8	1	8	11	8	11	14	13	11	11	113
	5.3%	9.7%	7.1%	0.9%	7.1%	9.7%	7.1%	9.7%	12.4%	11.5%	9.7%	9.7%	
65 & up	1	3	0	0	7	3	4	2	6	1	3	2	32
	3.1%	9.4%	0.0%	0.0%	21.9%	9.4%	12.5%	6.3%	18.6%	3.1%	9.4%	6.3%	
Males	30	26	30	20	53	39	42	38	66	34	55	36	469
	6.4%	5.5%	6.4%	4.3%	11.3%	8.3%	9.0%	8.1%	14.1%	7.2%	11.7%	7.7%	
Females	2	8	10	7	10	9	11	11	1	9	10	12	100
	2.0%	8.0%	10.0%	7.0%	10.0%	9.0%	11.0%	11.0%	1.0%	9.0%	10.0%	12.0%	
Non-Latin Whites	10	9	13	4	14	16	11	15	16	11	11	7	137
	7.3%	6.6%	9.5%	2.9%	10.2%	11.7%	8.0%	10.9%	11.7%	8.0%	8.0%	5.1%	
Blacks	8	11	19	10	32	19	24	16	22	17	28	16	222
	3.6%	5.0%	8.6%	4.5%	14.4%	8.6%	10.8%	7.2%	9.9%	7.7%	12.6%	7.2%	
Latins	14	14	8	13	17	13	18	18	29	15	26	25	210
	6.7%	6.7%	3.8%	6.2%	8.1%	6.2%	8.6%	8.6%	13.8%	7.1%	12.4%	11.9%	
Total	32	34	40	27	63	48	53	49	67	43	65	48	569
	5.6%	6.0%	7.0%	7.0%	11.1%	8.4%	9.3%	8.6%	11.8%	7.6%	11.4%	8.4%	
1975	31	21	32	22	26	22	30	16	39	22	12	26	299
1976	17	17	12	27	20	22	22	25	22	15	12	19	230
1977	18	16	21	18	37	18	29	18	15	17	22	20	249
1978	13	22	33	8	22	16	23	22	25	25	26	39	274
1979	27	25	25	26	26	28	28	39	45	36	27	33	365
1980	32	34	40	27	63	48	53	49	67	43	65	48	569
1981	46	63	54	64	49	46	50	53	50	45	51	52	623
1982	53	53	48	48	39	48	40	57	44	34	30	43	537
1983	34	35	36	42	33	41	30	42	31	21	41	34	420

27.0 Monthly Average for May 1978 to April 1980
52.5 Monthly Average for May 1980 to April 1982 (up 94% from May '78 – Ap '80)
37.8 Monthly Average for May 1982 to Dec. 1983 (up 40% from May '78 – Ap '80)
(down 28% from May '80 – Ap '82)

167

Table 6.1

Age, Sex, Ethnicity and Race/Sex of 454 Identified Offenders in 569 Homicide Cases Occurring in Dade County in 1980 by Whether or Not the Identified Offender Was Charged/Arrested

	Total of Identified & Unidentified	Identity Unknown	Offender Not Charged	Offender Dead	Insufficient Evidence to Charge	At Large	Arrested	Total of Identified offenders
Unknown	247	197	29	2	16	3	0	50
1 to 14	1	0	0	0	0	0	1 100%	1
15 to 24	147	5	10 7.0%	2 1.4%	15 10.6%	5 3.5%	110 77.5%	142
25 to 44	220	18	42 20.8%	10 5.0%	19 9.4%	11 5.4%	120 59.4%	202
45 to 64	55	3	10 19.2%	3 5.8%	3 5.8%	2 3.8%	34 65.4%	52
65 & up	7	0	1 14.3%	1 14.3%	1 14.3%	0 0.0%	4 57.1%	7
Males	554	160	67 17.0%	18 4.6%	50 12.7%	18 4.6%	241 61.2%	394
Females	50	2	3 27.1%	0 0.0%	4 8.3%	3 6.3%	28 58.3%	48
Unknown Sex	73	61	12 100.0%	0	0	0	0	12
Non-Latin Whites	75	7	20 29.4%	6 8.8%	6 8.8%	0 0.0%	36 52.9%	68
Blacks	277	59	38 17.4%	4 1.8%	20 9.2%	7 3.2%	149 68.3%	218
Latins	244	93	19 12.6%	8 5.3%	26 17.2%	14 9.3%	84 55.6%	151
Unknown	81	64	15 88.2%	0	2 11.8%	0	0	17
White Males	300	98	38 18.8%	14 6.9%	30 14.9%	12 5.9%	108 53.5%	202
White Females	19	2	1 5.9%	0 0.0%	2 11.8%	2 11.8%	12 70.6%	17
Black Males	245	57	27 14.4%	4 2.1%	18 9.6%	6 3.2%	133 70.7%	188
Black Females	30	0	11 36.7%	0 0.0%	2 6.7%	1 3.3%	16 53.3%	30
Unknown	83	66	15 88.2%	0	2 11.8%	0	0	17
Total	677	223	92 20.3%	18 4.0%	54 11.9%	21 4.6%	269 59.3%	454

168

Table 6.2 Number and Rate of Dispositions for 677 Offenders in 569 Homicide Cases Occurring in Dade County in 1980 by Age, Sex, Ethnicity and Sex/Race of Offender

	Total	Identity Unknown	Offender Not Charged	Offender Dead	Insufficient Evidence to Charge	At large	Arrested
Unknown	247	197	29	2	16	3	0
1 to 14	1	0	0	0	0	0	1
	0.3	0.0	0.0	0.0	0.0	0.0	0.3
15 to 24	147	5	10	2	15	5	110
	54.4	1.9	3.7	0.7	5.6	1.9	40.7
25 to 44	220	18	42	10	19	11	120
	50.7	4.2	9.7	2.3	4.4	2.5	27.7
45 to 64	55	3	10	3	3	2	34
	15.3	0.8	2.8	0.8	0.8	0.6	9.5
65 & up	7	0	1	1	1	0	4
	1.6	0.0	0.4	0.4	0.4	0.0	1.6
	677	223	92	18	54	21	269
Males	554	160	67	18	50	18	241
	72.1	20.8	8.7	2.3	6.5	2.3	31.4
Females	50	2	13	0	4	3	28
	5.8	0.2	1.5	0.0	0.5	0.3	3.3
Unknown Sex	73	61	12	0	0	0	0
	677	223	92	18	54	21	269
Non-Latin Whites	75	7	20	6	6	0	36
	9.8	0.9	2.6	0.8	0.8	0.0	4.7
Blacks	277	59	38	4	20	7	149
	98.8	21.0	13.6	1.4	7.1	2.5	53.1
Latins	244	93	19	8	26	14	84
	42.0	16.0	3.3	1.4	4.5	2.4	14.5
Unknown	81	64	15	0	2	0	0
	677	223	92	18	54	21	269
White Males	300	98	38	14	30	12	108
	50.2	16.4	6.4	2.3	5.0	2.0	18.1
White Females	19	2	1	0	2	2	12
	2.8	0.3	0.2	0.0	0.3	0.3	1.8
Black Males	245	57	27	4	18	6	133
	218.7	50.9	24.1	3.6	16.1	5.4	118.7
Black Females	30	0	11	0	2	1	16
	23.6	0.0	8.6	0.0	1.6	0.8	12.6
Unknown	83	66	15	0	2	0	0
Total	677	223	92	18	54	21	269
	41.6	13.7	5.7	1.1	3.3	1.3	16.4

Table 6.3 A Comparison of Homicide Victimization and Arrest/Offender Rates
For Subgroups of the Dade County Population by Sex, Race and Ethnicity

All — 1,625,979

Age Group	V Rate	O Rate	Rate Ratio
0-14	3.4	0.3	11.3:1
15-24	60.1	40.7	1.5:1
25-44	68.6	27.4	2.5:1
45-64	32.7	9.2	3.6:1
65-up	12.9	1.6	8.1:1
All	35.0	16.4	2.1:1

Black — 280,379

Age Group	V Rate	O Rate	Rate Ratio
0-14	7.7	1.3	5.9:1
15-24	136.7	155.0	0.9:1
25-44	175.1	93.3	1.9:1
45-64	96.2	38.5	2.5:1
65-up	41.7	6.9	6.0:1
All	79.2	53.1	1.5:1

Male — 767,882

Age Group	V Rate	O Rate	Rate Ratio
0-14	5.4	0.7	7.7:1
15-24	95.8	86.6	1.1:1
25-44	124.6	55.8	2.2:1
45-64	58.7	18.5	3.2:1
65-up	24.8	4.0	6.2:1
All	61.1	31.3	2.0:1

White Male — 597,499

Age Group	V Rate	O Rate	Rate Ratio
0-14	2.7	0.0	-----
15-24	63.5	20.0	3.2:0
25-44	87.1	23.3	3.7:1
45-64	43.4	9.9	4.4:1
65-up	21.1	0.0	-----
All	47.0	11.8	4.0:1

Female — 857,899

Age Group	V Rate	O Rate	Rate Ratio
0-14	1.4	0.0	-----
15-24	25.2	4.9	5.1:1
25-44	19.9	8.2	2.3:1
45-64	11.1	2.1	5.3:1
65-up	4.8	0.0	-----
All	11.7	3.2	3.7:1

White Female — 682,552

Age Group	V Rate	O Rate	Rate Ratio
0-14	0.9	0.0	-----
15-25	18.4	1.0	18.4:1
25-44	13.9	4.6	3.0:1
45-64	10.1	1.2	8.4:1
65-up	4.3	0.0	-----
All	9.7	1.6	6.1:1

Anglo — 764,570

Age Group	V Rate	O Rate	Rate Ratio
0-14	2.1	0.0	-----
15-24	23.6	8.7	2.7:1
25-44	22.1	10.3	2.1:1
45-64	21.9	1.2	18.3:1
65-up	18.3	1.7	10.8:1
All	17.9	4.7	3.8:1

Black Male — 112,001

Age Group	V Rate	O Rate	Rate Ratio
0-14	12.8	2.6	4.9:1
15-24	225.0	295.9	0.8:1
25-44	343.6	183.0	1.9:1
45-64	191.5	74.1	2.6:1
65-up	85.0	17.0	5.0:1
All	167.9	119.6	1.4:1

Hispanic — 581,030

Age Group	V Rate	O Rate	Rate Ratio
0-14	0.9	0.0	-----
15-24	50.8	23.8	2.1:1
25-44	74.2	26.5	2.8:1
45-64	32.0	13.2	2.4:1
65-up	4.4	1.1	4.0:1
All	36.1	14.1	2.6:1

Black Female — 127,195

Age Group	V Rate	O Rate	Rate Ratio
0-14	2.6	0.0	-----
15-24	51.9	20.0	2.6:1
25-44	43.7	23.3	1.9:1
45-64	19.8	9.9	2.0:1
65-up	11.7	0.0	-----
All	26.7	11.8	2.3:1

	V Rate	O Rate
Male to Female Rate Ratio............	5.2:1	9.8:1
White to White Female Rate Ratio....	4.8:1	7.4:1
Black Male to Black Female Rate Ratio...	6.3:1	10.1:1
Black to Anglo Rate Ratio...........	4.4:1	11.3:1
Black to Hispanic Rate Ratio........	1.7:1	3.8:1
Hispanic to Anglo Rate Ratio........	2.0:1	3.0:1

170

Table 6.4 A Comparison of Arrest Rates by Age, Sex, and Ethnicity of Offender for Dade County Homicides, 1974 and 1980

	All Ages	0-14	15-24	25-44	45-64	65 & up
All	13.8 to 16.4 +19%	0.0 to 0.3 +—%	39.9 to 40.7 +2%	24.2 to 27.4 +13%	5.6 to 9.2 +64%	0.5 to 1.6 +220%
Males	25.9 to 31.3 +25%	0.0 to 0.7 +—%	70.9 to 86.6 +22%	43.6 to 55.8 +28%	9.6 to 18.5 +93%	1.1 to 4.0 +264%
Females	3.8 to 3.2 -16%	0.0 to 0.0 -----	9.7 to 4.9 -49%	7.2 to 8.2 +14%	2.3 to 2.1 -9%	0.0 to 0.0 -----
Anglos	6.0 to 4.7 -22%	0.0 to 0.0 -----	19.4 to 8.7 -55%	12.2 to 10.3 -16%	1.6 to 1.2 -25%	0.0 to 1.7 +—%
Hispanics	6.2 to 14.1 +127%	0.0 to 0.0 -----	11.9 to 23.8 +100%	11.6 to 26.5 +128%	5.0 to 13.2 +164%	0.0 to 1.1 +—%
Blacks	55.1 to 53.1 -4%	0.0 to 1.3 +—%	131.1 to 155.0 +18%	87.1 to 93.3 +7%	31.4 to 38.5 -23%	8.6 to 6.9 -20%

*There were 195 arrests in 1974 Dade homicides and 269 arrests in 1980 Dade homicides.

171

Table 6.5

Age, Sex, Ethnicity and Sex/Race of all 269 Arrested Offenders for 1980 Dade County Homicide Cases by Motive of Offender

	Domestic Argument	Other Argument	Robbery	Rape, burglary, other felony	Drug Rip-off	Other	Total
1 to 14	0 0.0%	1 100.0%	0 0.0%	0 0.0%	0 0.0%	0 0.0%	0
15 to 24	7 6.4%	28 25.5%	28 25.5%	14 12.7%	18 16.4%	15 13.6%	110
25 to 44	26 21.7%	55 45.8%	9 7.5%	2 1.7%	16 13.3%	12 10.0%	120
45 to 64	11 32.4%	18 52.9%	0 0.0%	2 5.9%	2 5.9%	1 2.9%	34
65 & up	0 0.0%	4 100.0%	0 0.0%	0 0.0%	0 0.0%	0 0.0%	4
Male	26 10.8%	101 41.9%	35 14.5%	18 7.5%	35 14.5%	26 10.8%	241
Female	**18 64.2%**	**5 17.9%**	**2 7.1%**	**0 0.0%**	**1 3.6%**	**2 7.1%**	**28**
Non-Latin White	6 16.7%	11 30.6%	3 8.3%	2 5.6%	5 13.9%	9 25.0%	36
Black	23 15.4%	53 35.6%	32 21.5%	8 5.4%	18 12.1%	15 10.1%	149
Latin	15 17.9%	42 50.0%	2 2.4%	8 9.5%	13 15.5%	4 4.8%	84
White Male	13 12.0%	51 47.2%	4 3.7%	10 9.3%	18 16.7%	12 11.1%	108
White Female	8 66.7%	2 16.7%	1 8.3%	0 0.0%	0 0.0%	1 8.3%	12
Black Male	13 9.8%	50 37.6%	31 23.3%	8 6.0%	17 12.8%	14 10.5%	133
Black Female	**10 62.5%**	**3 18.8%**	**1 6.3%**	**0 0.0%**	**1 6.3%**	**1 6.3%**	**16**
Total	44 16.4%	106 39.4%	37 13.8%	18 6.7%	36 13.4%	28 10.4%	269

Table 6.6

Age, Sex, Ethnicity and Sex/Race of All 269 Arrested Offenders
for 1980 Dade County Homicide Cases Victim/Offender Relationship

	Husband/Wife	Other Family	Sex Partners or Rivals	Acquaintances	Crime Partners	Strangers	Felons Killed by Citizen or Police but Felony Murder	Total
1 to 14	0	0	0	1	0	0	0	1
	0.0%	0.0%	0.0%	100.0%	0.0%	0.0%	0.0%	
15 to 24	2	1	6	29	15	48	9	110
	1.8%	0.9%	5.5%	26.4%	13.6%	43.6%	8.2%	
25 to 44	12	8	14	46	17	19	4	120
	10.0%	6.7%	11.7%	38.3%	14.2%	15.8%	3.3%	
45 to 64	7	3	5	10	2	7	0	34
	20.6%	8.8%	14.7%	29.4%	5.9%	20.6%	0.0%	
65 & up	0	0	1	2	0	1	0	4
	0.0%	0.0%	25.0%	50.0%	0.0%	25.0%	0.0%	
Male	11	9	18	83	34	73	13	241
	4.6%	3.7%	7.5%	34.4%	14.1%	30.3%	5.4%	
Female	10	3	8	5	0	2	0	28
	35.7%	10.7%	28.6%	17.9%	0.0%	7.1%	0.0%	
Non-Latin White	1	5	5	11	5	8	1	36
	2.8%	13.9%	13.9%	30.6%	13.9%	22.2%	2.8%	
Black	12	5	14	44	16	32	26	149
	8.1%	3.4%	9.4%	29.5%	10.7%	21.5%	17.5%	
Latin	8	2	7	33	13	14	7	84
	9.5%	2.4%	8.3%	39.3%	15.5%	16.7%	8.3%	
White Male	5	5	9	43	18	20	8	108
	4.6%	4.6%	8.3%	39.8%	16.7%	18.5%	7.4%	
White Female	4	2	3	1	0	2	0	12
	33.3%	16.7%	25.0%	8.3%	0.0%	16.7%	0.0%	
Black Male	6	4	9	40	16	53	5	133
	4.5%	3.0%	6.8%	30.1%	12.0%	39.9%	3.8%	
Black Female	6	1	5	4	0	0	0	
	37.5%	6.3%	31.3%	25.0%	0.0%	0.0%	0.0%	
Total	21	12	26	88	34	75	13	269
	7.8%	4.5%	9.7%	32.7%	12.6%	40.6%	4.9%	

173

Table 7.1 Age, Sex and Race of Victim by Disposition Status of First Offender for All Homicides Occurring in Dade County in 1980

	Arrest	At Large	Identity Known But Insufficient Evidence to Charge	Offender Dead	Justifiable Offender Not Charged	Unknown	Total
0 - 14	6	0	3	0	1	0	10
	60.0%	0.0%	30.0%	0.0%	10.0%	0.0%	
15 - 24	56	5	10	4	25	46	146
	38.4%	3.4%	6.8%	2.7%	17.1%	31.5%	
25 - 44	108	12	18	11	48	70	267
	40.4%	4.5%	6.7%	4.1%	18.0%	26.2%	
45 - 64	50	0	9	4	10	40	113
	44.2%	0.0%	8.0%	3.5%	8.8%	35.4%	
65 & up	13	1	3	1	1	13	32
	40.6%	3.1%	9.4%	3.1%	3.1%	40.6%	
Males	189	14	34	6	82	144	469
	40.3%	3.0%	7.2%	1.3%	17.5%	30.7%	
Females	44	4	9	14	3	26	100
	44.0%	4.0%	9.0%	14.0%	3.0%	26.0%	
Non-Latin Whites	57	0	15	7	17	41	137
	41.6%	0.0%	10.9%	5.1%	12.4%	29.9%	
Blacks	108	6	8	4	52	44	222
	48.6%	2.7%	3.6%	1.8%	23.4%	19.8%	
Latins	68	12	20	9	16	85	210
	32.4%	5.7%	9.5%	4.3%	7.6%	40.5%	
Total	233	18	43	20	85	170	569
	40.9%	3.2%	7.6%	3.5%	14.9%	29.9%	100%

174

Table 7.2 A Comparison of Types of Cases with Low Versus High Clearance Rates for 1980 Dade County Homicides

<u>High Clearance Types</u>

Victim Precipitated........ 94.1% (85)		Columbian Victim.............. 19.4% (31)	
Female Offenders............87.0% (46)		Sex Partner/homosexual........ 20.0% (10)	
Husband/Wife V/O Rel....... 86.8% (38)		Columbian Offender............ 22.2% (18)	
Sex Partner/heterosexual... 86.7% (30)		Crime Partners................ 29.3% (116)	
Domestic Argument.......... 83.3% (66)		Drug Rip-Off.................. 31.9% (116)	
Sex Rivals................. 75.0% (12)		Robbery/Homicide.............. 38.5% (65)	
One Vs. Multiple Offenders. 74.0% (384)		Two or More Offenders......... 41.0% (115)	
Black Victims.............. 73.9% (222)		Latin Victim.................. 44.3% (210)	
Victim Under 15............ 70.0% (10)		Victim 65-up.................. 46.9% (32)	
Victim Drunk............... 66.1% (121)			
Male Offender.............. 64.9% (450)			
Friend/Acq. as V/O Rel..... 64.2% (123)			
Weapon not Gun............. 62.9% (159)			
Mariel Offender............ 61.5% (39)			
Female Victim.............. 61.0% (100)			

Overall (for 569 homicides) the Clearance Rate was 59.4% (338 of 569). The Clearance Rate for Criminal Homicides was 51.1% (236 of 462) while the Rate for Justifiable Homicides was 97.7 (84 of 86). Clearances include arrests, Offender died, and no charge (self-defense).

175

Table 8.1

Age, Sex, Ethnicity and Sex/Race of All 269 Arrested Offenders for 1980 Dade County Cases by Initial Charge

	Murder I	Murder II	Murder III	Manslaughter	Other	Total
1 to 14	0 0.0%	1 100.0%	0 0.0%	0 0.0%	0 0.0%	0
15 to 24	53 48.2%	43 39.1%	1 0.9%	10 9.1%	3 2.7%	110
25 to 44	51 42.5%	63 52.5%	1 0.8%	4 3.3%	1 0.8%	120
45 to 64	6 17.6%	26 76.5%	0 0.0%	1 2.9%	1 2.9%	34
65 & up	2 50.0%	1 25.0%	0 0.0%	1 25.0%	0 0.0%	4
Males	105 43.6%	114 47.3%	2 0.8%	15 6.2%	5 2.1%	241
Females	7 25.0%	20 71.4%	0 0.0%	1 3.6%	0 0.0%	28
Non-Latin Whites	23 63.9%	7 19.4%	1 2.8%	3 8.3%	2 5.6%	36
Blacks	57 38.3%	78 52.3%	0 0.0%	12 8.1%	2 1.3%	149
Latins	32 38.1%	49 58.3%	1 1.2%	1 1.2%	1 1.2%	84
White Males	51 47.2%	49 45.4%	2 1.9%	3 2.8%	3 2.8%	108
White Females	4 33.3%	7 58.3%	0 0.0%	1 8.3%	0 0.0%	12
Black Males	54 40.6%	65 48.9%	0 0.0%	12 9.0%	2 1.5%	133
Black Females	3 18.8%	13 81.3%	0 0.0%	0 0.0%	0 0.0%	16
Total	112 41.7%	134 49.8%	2 0.7%	16 5.9%	5 1.9%	269 100%

Table 8.2   Initial Charge by Final Charge by Plea Versus Trial
For All 1980 Dade Homicides Reaching Final Disposition
In Adult Court   (N=240)

Plea

Initial Charge	Murder I	Murder II	Murder III	Manslaughter	Other	Total
Murder I	3	33	0	6	1	43
Murder II	0	18	0	20	0	38
Murder III	0	0	0	0	0	0
Manslaughter	0	0	0	4	1	5
Other	0	0	0	0	1	1
Total	3	51	0	30	3	87

Trial

Initial Charge	Murder I	Murder II	Murder III	Manslaughter	Other	Not Guilty	Total
Murder I	14	14	3	0	2	10	43
Murder II	0	18	2	7	1	18	46.
Murder III	0	0	0	0	0	1	1
Manslaughter	0	0	0	1	0	1	2
Other	0	0	0	0	0	1	1
Total	0	32	5	8	3	31	93

Dismissed Before Trial

Initial Charge	Dismissed Before Trial
Murder I	13
Murder II	37
Murder III	1
Manslaughter	7
Other	1
	60

177

Table 8.3

Age, Sex, Ethnicity and Race/Sex of 240 Offenders Charged in 569 Homicides Occurring in Dade County in 1980 by Whether the Offender Was Convicted

	Guilty	Not Guilty	Dismissed	Total
1 to 14	0 0.0%	0 0.0%	0 0.0%	0
15 to 24	62 66.0%	10 10.6%	22 23.4%	94
25 to 44	66 58.4%	15 13.3%	32 28.3%	113
45 to 64	20 66.7%	6 20.0%	4 13.3%	30
65 & up	1 33.3%	0 0.0%	2 66.7%	3
Males	132 61.4%	28 13.0%	55 25.6%	215
Females	17 68.0%	3 12.0%	5 20.0%	25
Non-Latin White	23 71.8%	4 12.5%	5 15.6%	32
Blacks	83 60.6%	19 13.9%	35 25.5%	137
Latins	43 60.6%	8 11.3%	20 28.2%	71
White Male	58 63.7%	11 12.1%	22 24.2%	91
White Female	8 66.7%	1 8.3%	3 25.0%	12
Black Male	74 59.7%	17 13.7%	33 26.6%	124
Black Female	9 69.2%	2 15.4%	2 15.4%	13
Total	149 62.1%	31 12.9%	60 25.0%	240

Table 8.4 Dispositional Status of 40 Defendants Ordered by
Court to Undergo Psychiatric Exam----From the 269
Persons Arrested in all 1980 Dade County Homicides

Case No.	Ethnicity Sex & Age Defendant	Found Incompetent At One Point?	Plea or Trial	Verdict	Sentence or Current Status
002	L,M,55	yes	Pending	Pending	still incompetent, custody DHRS
005	A,M,36	yes	plea/stip.	N.G.R.I.	Release Pending
028	BL,M,23	no	jury trial	guilty	Prison, 50 years
063	L,M,47	no	jury trial	guilty	Prison, Life
077	B,M,20	no	plea	guilty	Prison, 10 years
109	L,M,48	no	plea	guilty	Prison, Life
129	B,M,47	no	jury trial	guilty	Prison, Life
147	B,M,53	no	jury trial	guilty	Probation with 1 year jail
212	L,M,47	no	plea	guilty	Prison, 10 years
221	B,M,20	no	plea	guilty	Prison, Life
242	O,F,29	no	plea	guilty	Prison, 15 years
259	B,M,20	no	jury trial	guilty	Prison, 20 years
261	B,M,30	no	jury trial	guilty	Prison, 3 years
263	L,M,24	no	dismissed	dismissed	---------
266	L,M,21	no	plea	guilty	Prison, Life
286	B,F,46	no	plea	guilty	Prison, 5 years
315	L,M,28	yes	bench trial	N.G.R.I.	Released, rearrest in 2nd murder
339-40	L,M,34	no	plea	guilty	Prison, Life
366	A,M,19	no	plea	guilty	Prison, 15 years
403	L,F,19	no	jury trial	guilty	Prison, 1-3 years
410	B,F,42	no	plea	guilty	Probation with 11 months jail
417	L,M,41	yes	jury trial	not guilty	---------
418	B,M,39	no	plea	guilty	Prison, 15 years
419	B,F,22	yes	plea/stip.	N.G.R.I.	in custody, DHRS
423	BL,M,25	no	jury trial	guilty	Prison, Life
430	A,M,47	no	plea/stip.	N.G.R.I.	Outpatient, DHRS
443	L,M,37	no	Pending	Pending	Pending
465	B,M,48	no	plea	guilty	Prison, 10 years
467	B,F,44	yes	plea	guilty	Probation
471	BL,M,24	yes	bench trial	N.G.R.I.	in custody, DHRS
474	A,F,34	no	plea	guilty	Prison, 7 years
478	A,M,35	yes	jury trial	dir. verdict of acquittal	-------
483	L,M,38	yes	Pending	Pending	still incompetent, custody DHRS
486/502	L,M,28	no	plea	guilty	Prison, 10 years
509	L,M,18	no	plea	guilty	Prison, Life
514	A,F,26	no	plea	guilty	Probation with 6 months jail
518	B,M,47	yes	plea	guilty	Probation
538	L,M,27	no	jury trial	guilty	Prison, Life
552	L,M,33	no	plea	guilty	Prison, 15 years
563	L,M,51	no	bench trial	guilty	Prison, 15 years

*L=Latin/Hispanic; B=Black; BL=Black Latin; A=Anglo; M=Male; F=Female;
N.G.R.I.=Not Guilty By Reason of Insanity

179

Table 9.1

Final Charge by Sentence for all Homicides Occurring in Dade County in 1980 for which a conviction was obtained in Criminal Court

	Murder I	Murder II	Murder III	Manslaughter	Other	Total
Probation	0	2	0	3	1	6
0 to 5 Years in jail/prison	0	14	0	18	3	35
6 to 10 Years in prison	0	10	1	8	1	20
11 to 20 Years in prison	0	13	0	9	1	23
21 to 134 Years in prison	0	10	3	0	0	13
Life, no min.	0	34	1	0	0	35
Life, 25 year minimum	12	0	0	0	0	12
Death Sentence	5	0	0	0	0	5
Total	17	83	5	38	6	149

Table 9.2

Age, Sex, Ethnicity and Race/Sex of 149 Convicted Offenders in 569 Homicides Occurring in Dade County in 1980 by Sentence

	Probation	0 to 5 Years in jail/prison	6 to 10 Years in prison	11 to 20 Years in prison	21 to 134 Years in prison	Life, no min.	Life with 25 year minimum	Death Sentence	Total
1 to 14	0	0	0	0	0	0	0	0	0
15 to 24	1 1.6%	13 21.0%	5 8.1%	11 17.7%	5 8.1%	17 27.4%	7 11.3%	3 4.8%	62
25 to 44	3 4.5%	12 18.2%	14 21.2%	9 13.6%	6 9.1%	15 22.7%	5 7.6%	2 3.0%	66
45 to 64	1 5.0%	10 50.0%	1 5.0%	3 15.0%	2 10.0%	3 15.0%	0 0.0%	0 0.0%	20
65 & up	1 100.0%	0 0.0%	0 0.0%	0 0.0%	0 0.0%	0 0.0%	0 0.0%	0 0.0%	1
Males	4 3.0%	28 21.2%	17 12.9%	20 15.2%	13 9.8%	35 26.5%	10 7.6%	5 3.8%	132
Females	2 11.8%	7 41.2%	3 17.6%	3 17.6%	0 0.0%	0 0.0%	2 11.8%	0 0.0%	17
on-Latin hites	1 4.3%	5 21.7%	1 4.3%	4 17.4%	0 0.0%	7 30.4%	3 13.0%	2 8.7%	23
Blacks	4 4.8%	22 26.5%	13 15.7%	15 18.1%	7 8.4%	13 15.7%	8 9.6%	1 1.2%	83
Latins	1 2.3%	8 18.6%	6 14.0%	4 9.3%	6 14.0%	15 34.9%	1 2.3%	2 4.7%	43
White Males	2 3.4%	9 15.5%	6 10.3%	7 12.1%	6 10.3%	22 37.9%	2 3.4%	4 6.9%	58
White Females	0 0.0%	4 50.0%	1 12.5%	1 12.5%	0 0.0%	0 0.0%	2 25.0%	0 0.0%	8
Black Males	2 2.7%	19 25.7%	11 14.9%	13 17.6%	7 9.5%	13 17.6%	8 10.8%	1 1.4%	74
Black Females	2 22.2%	3 33.3%	2 22.2%	2 22.2%	0 0.0%	0 0.0%	0 0.0%	0 0.0%	9
Total	6 4.0%	35 23.5%	20 13.4%	23 15.4%	13 8.7%	35 23.5%	12 8.1%	5 3.4%	149

Table 10.1 Race, Ethnic and Sex Dispositional Differentials for Six Decision Stages of the Criminal Justice System---For All Offenders Associated with All 569 Homicides Occurring in Dade County, Fl, in 1980

	Total Number Offenders Identified by Race	Number and Percent Of Offenders Identified By Name	Number and Percent Of Offenders Identified By Name Who Were Arrested	Number and Percent Of Arrested Offenders Who Were Convicted	Number and Percent Of Convicted Offenders Who Received time in Jail/Prison	Number and Percent Of Incarcerated Offenders Who Received 11 or More Years in Prison, Life, or Death
All	596	437 (73%)	269 (62%)	149 (55%)	143 (96%)	88 (62%)
Blacks	277	218 (79%)	149 (68%)	83 (56%)	79 (95%)	44 (56%)
Whites	319	219 (69%)	120 (55%)	66 (55%)	64 (97%)	44 (69%)
Anglos	75	68 (91%)	36 (53%)	23 (64%)	22 (96%)	16 (72%)
Hispanics	244	151 (62%)	84 (56%)	43 (51%)	42 (98%)	28 (67%)
Males	554	394 (71%)	241 (61%)	132 (55%)	128 (97%)	83 (63%)
Females	50	48 (96%)	28 (58%)	17 (61%)	15 (88%)	5 (29%)
White Males	300	202 (67%)	108 (53%)	58 (54%)	56 (97%)	41 (73%)
White Females	19	17 (89%)	12 (71%)	8 (67%)	8 (100%)	3 (38%)
Black Males	245	188 (77%)	133 (71%)	74 (56%)	72 (97%)	42 (58%)
Black Females	30	30 (100%)	16 (53%)	9 (56%)	7 (78%)	2 (29%)

182

Table 10.2 Race, Ethnic, Sex and Age "Gaps" (Rate Ratio) in Disposition Rates For Seven
Decision Stages of the Criminal Justice System---For All Offenders Associated
With All 569 Homicides Occurring in Dade County, FL, in 1980

	Total Offender Rate Ratio	Offenders By Name Rate Ratio	Arrested Offender Rate Ratio	Convicted Offender Rate Ratio	Offenders With Jail/Prison Time Rate Ratio	Offenders With 11 Or More Years, Life, or Death Rate Ratio	Death Penalty Rate Ratio
Black to White	4.0:1 98.8/24.9	4.5:1 77.8/17.1	5.6:1 53.1/9.4	5.7:1 29.6/5.2	5.6:1 28.2/5.0	5.0:1 15.4/3.1	1.2:1 0.36/0.31
Black to Anglo	10.1:1 98.8/9.8	8.7:1 77.8/8.9	11.3:1 53.1/4.7	9.9:1 29.6/3.0	9.7:1 28.2/2.9	8.6:1 15.4/1.8	1.4:1 0.36/0.26
Hispanic to Anglo	4.3:1 42.0/9.8	2.9:1 26.0/8.9	3.1:1 14.5/4.7	2.5:1 7.4/3.0	2.5:1 7.2/2.9	2.5:1 4.5/1.8	1.3:1 0.34/0.26
Black to Hispanic	2.4:1 98.8/42.0	3.0:1 77.8/26.0	3.7:1 53.1/14.5	4.0:1 29.6/7.4	3.9:1 28.2/7.2	3.4:1 15.4/4.5	1.1:1 0.36/0.34
Black Male White Male	4.3:1 218.7/50.2	5.0:1 167.9/33.8	6.6:1 118.7/18.1	6.8:1 66.1/9.7	6.8:1 64.2/9.4	5.9:1 36.6/6.2	1.3:1 0.9/0.7
Black Fem. White Fem.	8.4:1 23.6/2.8	9.4:1 23.6/2.5	7.0:1 12.6/1.8	5.9:1 7.1/1.2	4.6:1 5.5/1.2	4.0:1 1.6/0.4	------
Male to Female	12.4:1 72.1/5.8	9.2:1 51.3/5.6	9.5:1 31.4/3.3	8.6:1 17.2/2.0	9.8:1 16.7/1.7	17.1:1 10.2/0.6	----- 0.65/---
15-44 to 45 & up	5.2:1 52.2/10.1	5.1:1 48.9/9.6	5.3:1 32.7/6.2	5.4:1 18.2/3.4	5.9:1 18.2/3.1	8.2:1 10.7/1.3	----- 0.71/---
Total Rate	41.6	27.9	16.4	9.2	8.8	5.1	0.31

Table 10.3 Attrition Of Offenders Processed by The Criminal Justice System From Identification by Race/Sex to Death Penalty---For All Offenders Associated With All 569 Homicides Occurring in Dade County, FL, 1980

	Total Offenders Identified by Race/Sex	Percent Total Offenders Identified By Name	Percent Total Offenders Arrested	Percent Total Offenders Convicted	Percent Total Offenders Sent to Jail/Prison	Percent Total Offenders Incarcerated for 11 or More Years, Life, Death	Percent Total Offenders Receiving Death Penalty
All	100	74	44	25	24	14	1 (0.8)
Black	100	79	54	30	29	16	1 (0.4)
White	100	69	38	21	20	12	1 (1.2)
Anglo	100	91	48	31	30	18	3 (3.5)
Hispanic	100	62	35	18	17	11	1 (0.8)
Male	100	71	44	24	23	14	1 (0.9)
Female	100	97	56	34	29	10	0 (0.0)

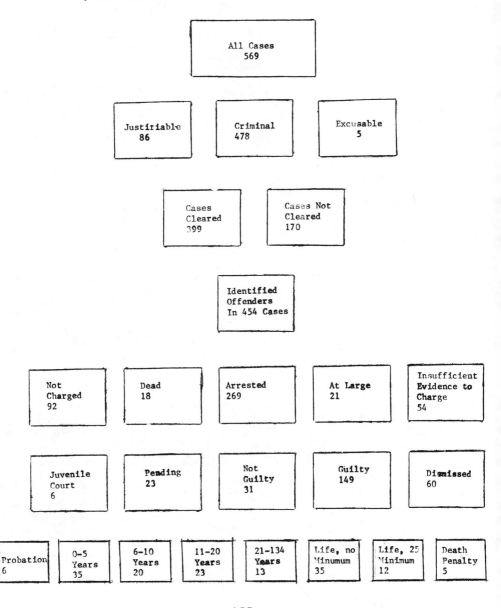

Figure 8.1   Attrition of 569 Cases and 454 Offenders
From 1980 Dade County Homicides As Processed
By The Criminal Justice System

185

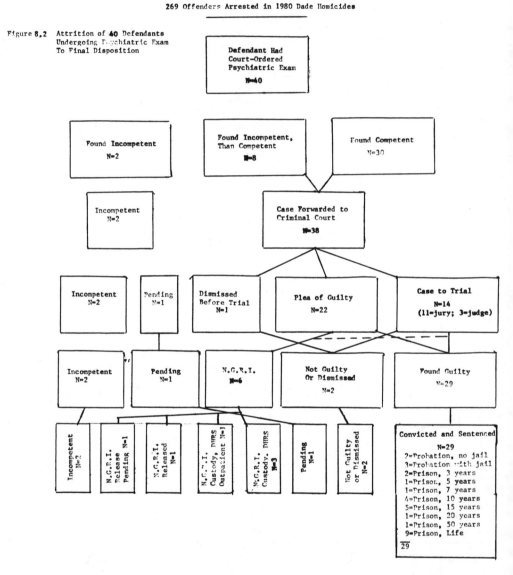

Figure 8.2   Attrition of 40 Defendants
Undergoing Psychiatric Exam
To Final Disposition

186

APPENDIX B

INDEXES AND NARRATIVES FOR 1980 HOMICIDE CASES

LIST OF CASE NUMBERS FOR VARIOUS TYPES OF 1980
HOMICIDES

Death Sentences---005, 052, 103, 252, 524

Probation Sentences---049, 096, 139, 196, 233,
460, 467, 518

Life Sentences With 25 Year Minimum---057, 072,
110, 138, 194, 226, 255, 332, 356, 367, 516, 556

Life Sentences With No Minimum---005, 023, 023,
040, 063, 074, 109, 160, 163, 171, 220, 266,
271, 298, 339, 351, 359, 391, 400, 404, 416,
420, 422, 423, 425, 425, 447, 451, 464, 492,
496, 509, 515, 538

Victim Precipitated---004, 009, 015, 017, 029,
030, 035, 041, 044, 065, 075, 085, 088, 091,
095, 102, 105, 126, 128, 133, 135, 143, 152,
155, 159, 162, 166, 168, 169, 170, 180, 182,
188, 189, 191, 208, 214, 216, 218, 245, 250,
258, 270, 280, 287, 288, 295, 296, 306, 315,
319, 320, 327, 335, 341, 357, 358, 384, 385,
393, 402, 404, 406, 415, 419, 422, 427, 428,
439, 445, 446, 449, 466, 472, 499, 511, 513,
518, 523, 532, 554, 555, 560, 566, 570

Riot Victims---163, 164, 165, 167, 171, 176, 177,
178, 180, 182, 185, 217, 244

Elderly Victims in 60's---013, 039, 052, 063, 072,
145, 171, 188, 205, 235, 241, 244, 308, 333,
334, 347, 365, 374, 395, 418, 436, 481, 493,
500, 512, 527, 556
Elderly Victims in 70's----010, 060, 138, 187,
194, 213, 246, 259, 266, 289, 332, 454, 488, 546

Elderly Victims in 80's---059, 190, 356, 363, 367

Mariel Victims---191, 247, 258, 263, 264, 284,
285, 301, 305, 316, 343, 354, 357, 358, 371,
375, 376, 380, 399, 404, 412, 420, 423, 427,
439, 441, 469, 471, 472, 473, 483, 486, 505,
510, 515, 523, 547, 548, 549, 551, 555, 562,
567, 572

Mariel Offenders---149, 253, 263, 266, 281, 289,
315, 343, 348, 354, 357, 358, 371, 375, 399,

400, 404, 411, 420, 423, 469, 471, 472, 483,
485, 509, 510, 512, 515, 547, 548, 548, 551,
552, 557, 558, 562, 567

Haitian Victims---517, 539

Killers At Large----010, 018, 021, 026, 151, 181,
261, 274, 301, 314, 316, 354, 396, 397, 412,
443, 501, 504, 553

Killers Died Before Trial---045, 092, 119, 121,
145, 157, 172, 173, 215, 234, 239, 251, 268,
363, 441, 530, 562

Killers to Juvenile Court---016, 096, 375, 460

Elderly Killers---022, 030, 219, 233, 363, 398,
402, 426, 512, 513

Female Killers---010, 043, 046, 062, 065, 079,
093, 095, 105, 110, 123, 130, 139, 143, 184,
186, 192, 228, 230, 242, 250, 265, 286, 295,
296, 304, 319, 320, 321, 329, 356, 403, 406,
410, 428, 429, 432, 445, 449, 453, 467, 474,
490, 504, 514, 560, 564, 573

Homicides By Police----017, 088, 102, 105, 135,
166, 168, 180, 182, 191, 214, 303, 499, 570

Justifiable Homicides---009, 015, 017, 030, 035,
044, 065, 075, 076, 085, 088, 095, 097, 102,
105, 124, 126, 135, 142, 143, 152, 155, 158,
159, 162, 166, 168, 169, 170, 180, 182, 188,
189, 191, 201, 206, 208, 210, 214, 216, 228,
230, 245, 250, 258, 270, 280, 287, 288, 295,
296, 303, 306, 320, 324, 329, 335, 341, 368,
384, 385, 389, 392, 393, 402, 406, 414, 415,
419, 427, 428, 439, 445, 446, 472, 499, 511,
513, 523, 532, 533, 537, 554, 555, 560, 566, 570

190

001A 002L 004A 005A 006L 007L 008L 009B 010B 011L   012B
013L   014A 015L 016B 017A 018B 019L 020L 021L 022A 023A
024B 026L 027L 028B 029L 030L 031L 032B 033L 034A   035B
036L   037B 038B 039A 040A 041B 042L 043A 044L 045L 046L
047L 048A 049B 050A 051L 052B 053A 054B 055L 056L   057A
058A   059A 060A 061B 062B 063L 064L 065B 066L 067B 068L
069A 070B 071B 072A 073L 074L 075B 076A 077B 078B   079L
080A   081B 082L 083B 084L 085B 086B 087B 088A 089L 090A
091B 092A 093A 094B 095B 096A 097B 098B 099B 100B   101B
102A   103L 104A 105A 106L 107L 108L 109L 110L 111B 112L
113L 114A 115L 116A 117L 118B 119L 120B 121A 123B   124B
125L   126B 127L 128L 129B 130B 131B 132A 133L 134L 135B
136B 137B 138A 139B 140L 141B 142L 143L 144L 145A   146L
147B 148A 149L 150B 151B 152B 153B 155B 156L 157L   158B
159L 160B 161B 162B 163A 164A 165A 166B 167A 168B   169B
170B   171L 172B 173B 174B 175A 176B 177B 178B 179B 180B
181B 182B 183B 184B 185A 186B 187L 188B 189B 190A   191L
192L   193B 194A 195L 196A 197L 198B 199B 200B 201B 202L
203L 204B 205A 206A 207A 208A 209A 210B 211B 212L   213A
214B   215A 216B 217A 219L 220B 221B 222B 223A 224B 225L
226B 228B 229B 230B 231A 232A 233L 234A 235A 236L   237A
238L   239L 240B 241A 242A 243B 244A 245B 246A 247L 248B
249L 250B 251L 252B 253B 254B 255A 256B 257B 258L   259A
260A   261B 262B 263L 264L 265B 266A 267B 268A 269B 270A
271L 272B 273L 274B 275B 276B 277B 278L 279A 280B   281L
282L   283L 284L 285L 286B 287B 288B 289L 290L 291B 292B
293L 294B 295B 296B 297L 298A 299L 300A 301L 302L   303A
304B   305L 306B 307B 308A 309B 310A 311A 312L 313B 314L
315L 316L 317B 318L 319A 320B 321B 322A 323L 324B   325B
326L   327B 328L 329B 330B 331L 332A 333A 334B 335A 336L
337A 338B 339A 340A 341A 342L 343L 344L 345B 346A   347A
348A   349A 350B 351L 352L 353L 354L 355B 356A 357L 358L
359A 360B 361B 362L 363A 364L 365B 366A 367A 368A   369A
370A   371L 372B 373L 374A 375L 376L 377L 378A 379L 380L
381B 382B 383L 384B 385B 386B 387B 388B 389B 390B   391B
392B   393B 394L 395A 396L 397L 398A 399L 400L 401A 402B
403L 404L 405L 406B 407B 408L 409L 410B 411L 412L   413L
414A   415A 416L 417L 418A 419L 420L 421L 422A 423L 424L
425A 426A 427L 428B 429B 430A 431L 432B 433L 434B   435B
436A   437A 438A 439L 440B 441L 442B 443L 444A 445B 446B
447B 448B 449B 450L 451L 452B 453A 454B 455A 456B   457B
458B   459B 460B 461B 462A 463A 464A 465B 466A 467B 468A
469L 470L 471L 472L 473L 474L 475L 476L 477B 478A   479L
480L   481B 482B 483L 484B 485A 486L 487A 488B 489A 490B
491L 492B 493L 494L 495B 496L 497L 498L 499B 500L   501L
502B   503A 504B 505B 506B 507L 508L 509L 510L 511B 512A
513B 514A 515L 516B 517B 518B 519B 520B 521A 522L   523L

524L   525B 526B 527B 528L 529L 530B 531A 532B 533B 534B
535A 536B 537B 538B 539B 540L 541L 542L 543L 544A   545B
546B   547L 548L 549L 550B 551L 552L 553B 554B 555L 556A
557L 558L 559A 560B 561B 562L 563L 564L 565L 566L   567L
568A 569B 570L 571B 572L 574L

001 Victim=Anglo Male, 23; Jan. 1, 1980; Tract=114.00; 9999; PSD;   The victim and a friend came to Miami from California to complete a deal for drugs. The V was last seen negotiating a deal with some Latin Males in Miami. V was found shot in the back of the head on a rocky road in far south Dade. V was a college student in Calif. Police believe V was killed by Latin Male drug dealers.

offender=Unknown Latin Males

004 Victim=Anglo Male, 29; Jan. 5, 1980; Tract=90.01; 2030; PSD;   The Victim and another Anglo Male along with a Black Male went to the home of a known drug dealer to rip-off the dealer. All three were armed and upon their arrival one of the robbers shot at the dealer but missed him and accidently hit this victim/robber. At some point the dealer shot and wounded one of the offenders (the Anglo Male who survived). The three robbers fled and the B/M drove the two wounded to the hospital and then fled. After the V died the two surviving robbers were charged with felony murder in the death of their companion.

Offender=Black Male, 27 (Glaspar, Horace); (80-535A); charged with attempted robbery and Murder II; pled to attempted robbery and Murder II; Judge 12; Sentenced to 7 years in prison.
Offender=Anglo Male, 30 (Patterson, Gerald); charged with attempted robbery and Murder II; pled to Murder II and attempted robbery; Judge 12; Sentenced to 7 years on these charges to begin at expiration of another 3 year sentence for possession of cocaine in another unrelated case.

005 Victim=Anglo Male, 25; Jan. 8, 1980; Tract=9999;
0200; PSD;   A passerby enroute to work saw car
on I-95 parked and on fire. Witness stopped and
extinguished fire. Closer investigation revealed
four dead bodies in the car (3 Latin Males, 1
Anglo Male) and all were wrapped in blankets. Two
were in the trunk, one in rear seat and one in
front seat. Police believe that the quadruple
murder involved a drug rip-off. The four were
stabbed and beaten at a residence and taken to
this location. Three Anglo males were arrested
and charged with Murder I, kidnapping and robbery.
(See 006, 007, & 008 in Latin List for other 3
victims.)

Offender=Anglo Male, 27; (Bolander, Bernard);
(80-640); charged with four counts of Murder I,
robbery & kidnapping; jury trial; Judge 03; death
penalty.
Offender=Anglo Male, 42; (Macker, Joseph); charged
with four counts of Murder I & kidnapping; pled to
Murder II, kidnapping and robbery (4 counts);
Judge 03; sentenced to life in prison.
Offender=Anglo Male, 34; (Thompson, Paul); charged
with four counts of Murder I; bench trial; Judge
03; not guilty by reason of insanity; Committed to
DHRS.

014 Victim=Anglo Male, 42; Jan. 15, 1980; Tract=70.02;
0230; MPD;   Victim was found in his apt., nude,
feet bound, wash cloth in mouth & hands tied.
Police believe the V was killed by a homosexual
partner who then ransacked the house taking a
number of items. Blood was all over the apt.

Offender=Unknown Male

194

017 Victim=Anglo Male, 29; Jan. 19, 1980; Tract=48.00;
     1610; PSD;   Victim entered a gift shop at Miami
     International Airport and pulled out a handgun
     (which was later found to be a toy gun). The V
     pointed the "gun" at several people and stated he
     would kill them. Three police officers arrived on
     the scene & V pointed the gun at them. Verbal
     attempts to make V surrender were ineffective.
     All 3 officers fired at V and V died at the scene.

     Offender=Three Police Officers; no charges filed.
     Justifiable Homicide.

022 Victim=Anglo Male, 47; Jan. 22, 1980; Tract=37.02;
     1900; MPD;   The Victim was involved in a
     confrontation with the offender in front of a
     downtown rescue mission. During an argument the V
     took away a cane from the O (who had been using it
     as a weapon) and then walked away. The O followed
     him and stabbed the V with a pocket knife. The V
     had alcohol level of .16. The O had a long record
     of arrests for assault and murder.

     Offender=Black Male, 69; (Neal, Waymond);
     (80-1226); Charged with Murder I; Judge 13;
     Charges were dismissed. There were 2 witnesses.
     Both W's lived in rescue mission where murder took
     place. One W was considered incompetent to
     testify, 2nd had history of mental problems but
     agreed to give deposition. However, this W later
     threatened life of prosecutor and did not show up
     for trial. After several continuances state
     dropped charges since had no witness.

023 Victim=Anglo Male, 57; Jan. 22, 1980;
Tract=100.08; 1145; PSD;   The Victim owned a
nursery and lived by his place of business. V and
his wife were sleeping when they heard the dogs
barking.   V got his handgun and went (on a
golfcart) to investigate. He got off the cart and
was approached by three Black Males who attempted
to rob him. The V was shot by the robbers since
they were former employees of the V and knew that
he could identify them. The robbers believed the
owner kept a lot of money on the premises.

Offender=Black Male, 23; (Tillman, Phillip);
(80-23916); charged with Murder I, attempted
robbery and use of firearm; Judge 29; Pled to
Murder II, robbery and use of firearm; Sentenced
to 30 years in prison.
Offender=Black Male, 23; (Whitfield, Vance);
charged with Murder I, attempted robbery and use
of firearm; Judge 29; Pled to Murder II, robbery
and use of firearm; Sentenced to life (suspended
entry on firearm count) in prison.
Offender=Black Male, 21; (Washington, Drew);
charged with Murder I, attempted robbery and use
of firearm; Judge 29; Pled to Murder II, robbery &
use of firearm; Sentenced to life in prison
(suspended entry on firearm count).

027 Victim=Anglo Male, 33; Jan. 25, 1980;
Tract=100.05; 070; PSD;   The Victim was on duty
at a convenience store when unknown person(s)
entered and robbed the store. V was killed during
the robbery.

Offender=unknown

034 Victim=Anglo Female, 22; Feb. 17, 1980 (found);
Tract=110.00; 9999; PSD;   Victim had a history
of drug arrests and police believe she was killed
in some type of drug dispute or drug rip-off. She
died by drowning and methaqualue intoxication.
Police suspect two Anglo Males were involved in
this murder.

Offender=Unknown but probably two Anglo Males

039　Victim=Anglo Male, 66; Feb. 4, 1980;　Tract=4.07;
0235; PSD;　　Victim was driving a van when he
was shot in the head (by unknown person).　After
being shot the V's van hit a fence and tree (but
gunshot was primary cause of death).　Police have
no idea who shot the V.

　　　Offender=Unknown

040　Victim=Anglo Male, 54; Feb. 4, 1980;　Tract=78.02;
1315; PSD;　　Victim came home and found his home
in disarray.　While walking thru his residence he
was confronted by two burglars (White Males).　One
burglar shot the V and then both fled.

　　　Offender=White Male, 22; (Jackson, Kelly W.);
(80-1920); charged with Murder I, armed burglary &
assault; pled to Murder II, armed burglary &
assault; Judge 05; Sentenced to two concurrent 15
year prison terms (this O was not the shooter).
Offender=White Male, 17; (Keith, Robert);　charged
with Murder I, armed burglary & assault; Judge 05;
Sentenced to life in prison (this offender was the
shooter).

043　Victim=Anglo Male, 55; Feb. 7, 1980;　Tract=2.01;
1330; PSD;　　Victim lived with his girlfriend &
according to neighbors they frequently argued and
were in argument on this date.　The O took the V's
handgun and fired two shots at him (but missed).
V ran from the residence and O fired another shot
through the window (V was already outside the
house) and hit the V.

　　　Offender=Anglo Female, 29; (Harrison, Patricia);
(80-2081); charged with Murder II and use of
firearm; pled to manslaughter (state abandoned
firearm charge); Judge 10; Sentenced to five years
in prison (The O had extensive prior arrest
record.)

048   Victim=Anglo Male, 54; Jan. 26, 1980; Tract=44.00;
      2300; MBPD;   The Victim was a local drunk who
      hung around a particular bar along with the
      Offender and an Anglo Female, 37.   All 3   were
      drinking when at one point V hit the female
      knocking her to the floor.   The 0 then struck
      (with fist) the V and said, "This is for her." The
      V was taken to the hospital and eventually died
      from the injuries received in this bar fight.
      Prosecutor's office ruled that the death was an
      excusable homicide since it was a mutual bar fight
      and the 0 did not intend to inflict a fatal
      injury.

      Offender=Anglo Male; no charges filed,   ruled
      excusable homicide.

050   Victim=Anglo Male, 59; Sept. 14, 1980; Tract=41.01
      MBPD;   The Victim and Offender were homosexual
      lovers and lived together in a hotel. Both V and
      0 were heavy drinkers. 0 was violent and   abusive
      and had beaten the V in the past as he feared V
      would leave him.   It was a typical "battered-wife"
      syndrome but with homosexuals. On this date V and
      0 argued and in subsequent fight V slipped and hit
      his head on stairs. V was also stabbed.

      Offender=Anglo Male, 21; Identity known but not
      enough evidence to charge

053   Victim=Anglo Female, 20; Feb. 16, 1980 (found);
      Tract=101.12;   9999;   PSD;   Victim   was   a
      prostitute whose nude body was found floating in a
      canal in advanced stage of decomposition.   Police
      believe she was probably killed by a "trick" who
      had picked her up while she was working as a
      prostitute.

      Offender=Unknown Male

057 Victim=Anglo Male, 59;
058 Victim=Anglo Female, 52;
059 Victim=Anglo Male, 83;
060 Victim=Anglo Female, 77; Feb. 21, 1980; Tract=39.04; 0100; PSD; (a quadruple murder) The four victims were two married couples who lived near each other. On the same night they were all killed by the same lone Black Male offender who broke into the two houses and stabbed to death the residents (who were asleep). The houses were also burglarized. The O was caught a short distance from the two homes by police in a car owned by one of the couples and with merchandise taken from the two homes. Both female victims had also been raped.

Offender=Black Male, 17; (Mitchell, Ray Anthony); (80-2885); charged with four counts of Murder I, 2 counts of robbery and sexual battery, 2 counts of burglary, 2 counts of grand theft; pled to same 10 counts; Judge 07; sentenced to life in prison. In 1981 the O and another inmate took a female hostage in a state prison. The V was killed by police who rushed the two kidnappers to rescue the hostage.

069 Victim=Anglo Male, 37; March 1, 1980; Tract=1.03; 0300; PSD; The victim was an escapee from a Conecticut prison who had been living in Miami for 4 months under an alias. Witnesses in his apt. building heard a shot and V was found shot to death in the parking lot. Police have no suspect and no motive in this killing.

Offender=Unknown

072   Victim=Anglo Male, 61; Feb. 28, 1980; Tract=43.00;
      0337; MBPD;   The Victim was walking on the
      street when he was approached by a Black Male
      robber who (according to a witness) slammed the V
      bodily into the side of a building and then pushed
      the V to the ground (causing head lacerations
      which were the cause of death). The O then went
      thru the V's pockets and took some money and fled.
      The witness called the police.

      Offender=Black Male, 32; (Baker, John); (80-3293);
      charged with Murder I and robbery; jury trial;
      Judge 11; guilty on Murder I and robbery;
      Sentenced to life in prison.

076   Victim=Anglo Male, 26; Jan. 7, 1980; Tract=3.03;
      2200; PSD;   Victim and a friend (the Offender)
      had been involved in a fist fight in V's apt. V
      complained of gas pains shortly afterward and was
      admitted to the hospital. V did not survive
      surgery.

      Offender=Anglo Male, 27; no charges filed;
      prosecutor ruled that case was either justifible
      or "non-prosecutable."

080   Victim=Anglo Female, 21; Mar 11, 1980 (found);
      Tract=3.01; 9999; PSD;   Victim was found in
      advanced stage of decomposition in a densely
      wooded area. She was clad only in a shirt.
      Police believe she was raped and then shot in the
      head.

      Offender=Unknown Male

088   Victim=Anglo Male, 36; Mar 17, 1980; Tract=78.03;
      2100; PSD;   The Victim abducted another White
      Male, 41, at gunpoint and forced the abducted man
      to drive him away in his van. Police were advised
      of the abduction and were in pursuit of the van
      when the V and the driver (the abductee) began a
      struggle over the gun. Both fell out of the van
      and police subsequently shot the V several times.

      Offender=Three metro police officers; no charges
      filed, justifiable homicide

090 Victim=Anglo Female, 30; Mar 17, 1980; Tract=84.01; 0100; PSD; Victim was visiting the home of a social worker friend who had taken the O (Anglo Male, 16) into his home to help him. The O shot the visiting V when he was alone with her. Police believe the O is a "mental case."

Offender=Anglo Male, 16; (Savier, Jay); (80-6022); charged with Murder II and possession of controlled substance; pled to manslaughter; Judge 01; Sentenced as a Youthful Offender to state prison for up to 4 years (with remainder of 6 year term to be served on parole).

092 Victim=Anglo Male, 56; Feb. 16, 1980; Tract=3.01; 2030; PSD; Victim was a customer in a grocery store and was walking to his car in the parking lot when a Black Male attempted to rob him. V was shot in the robbery attempt.

Offender=Black Male, 46; (Pew, John); charged with Murder I and robbery; O committed suicide (hung himself) while in jail awaiting trial.

093 Victim=Anglo Male, 23; Mar 22, 1980; Tract=8.02; 2120; HPD; A Latin female knocked at V's door asking for the V. As he came to the door the L/F stepped back and at least two Latin Males opened fire on the V. The V ran to his bedroom and got his handgun. More gunshots were exchanged and V was fatally wounded. The V was involved in drug trade and police believe killing was dispute over drugs.

Offender=Two Latin Males and Latin Female

096　Victim=Anglo Male, 18; Mar 24, 1980; Tract=89.03; 1145; PSD;　　The Victim was carnival employee at Youth Fair.　Offender was at the fair on a high school field trip.　O got off the ride but exited the wrong way and V said, "Hey nigger, get off on the other side." A fight ensued and V knocked O to ground.　O left and returned with a knife and stabbed the V.

Offender=Black Male, 15; charged with manslaughter; waiver to adult court denied; tried in juvenile court; Judge 31; Adjudicated delinquent for agg. battery and committed to Div. of Youth Services where O placed in a training school for 3 months and then furloughed.

102　Victim=Anglo Male, 27; Mar 27, 1980; Tract=82.01; 1255; PSD;　　The Victim, the son of a policeman, was killed while attempting to rob the manager of a fast-food restaurant.　V was observed circling the parking lot (the police had the restaurant staked out because of a rash of such robberies) and eventually robbing the manager as the latter exited his business.　The police confronted the robber, a shiny object was observed in the O's hands (he used a knife in the robbery) & the O was perceived to have made a threatening move.　The officers fired and V was killed.

Offender=Two Metro Police Officers; no charges filed, justifiable homicide.

104　Victim=Anglo Female, 20; Mar 29, 1980 (found); Tract=115.00; 9999; PSD;　　The Victim was an alcoholic who hung around the bars in S. Dade area and apparently traded sexual favors with anyone who would buy her a drink.　She was last seen 3 weeks before her body was found, in an advanced stage of decomposition, in a field near a street.

Offender=Unknown

105 Victim=Anglo Male, 23; Mar 30, 1980; Tract=78.03; 0220; PSD; Victim had been creating a disturbance at a motel and police were called. Upon arrival the police were attacked by V and V attempted to take officer's revolver. A back-up unit arrived and one officer struck V in the head but V then fled and was pursued by police. V was caught in parking lot and again fought over the officer's gun. The V gained possession of the officer's gun but a female officer, who had arrived on the scene, shot and killed the V.

Offender=Metro Police Officer (female); no charges filed; justifiable homicide.

114 Victim=Anglo Female, 39; Ap 9, 1980; Tract=100.05; 1210; PSD; The Victim and her old boyfriend became involved in an argument inside V's room and new boyfriend attempted to go to her aid. The new boyfriend saw that the old boyfriend had a rifle and so he shot at the old boyfriend. The shot grazed the old boyfriend's hand and struck the victim, killing her. The V had alcohol level=.18.

Offender=Anglo Male, 31; no charges filed, prosecutor ruled that this was case of excusable homicide since O was justified in shooting at the boyfriend and killing of V was not intended.

116 Victim=Anglo Male, 31; Ap. 8, 1980 (found); Tract= 101.08; 9999; PSD; The Victim was incarcerated at a work release facility and a few days before did not return to the facility after work after he had been involved in a minor traffic accident and had fled the scene. V was then found, slightly decomposed, in a field in some bushes. He had been dealing drugs and had told friends he was going to do a big deal soon. Police believe he was killed in a dispute over drugs. V had alcohol level=.16.

Offender=Unknown

121 Victim=Anglo Female, 31; Ap 19, 1980; Tract=76.02;
     1700, PSD;   Victim was recently divorced from
     her husband (the Offender) but O wanted to
     reconcile, V did not. O had been harassing V
     (burglarizing her house, etc.) and on this date
     confronted V as she returned to her home with her
     3   year   old   daughter (O's stepdaughter).   O
     approached her on the front lawn, engaged her in
     brief conversation, then pulled a gun and shot her
     twice.   O fled to Nevada but there committed
     suicide (2 days after the murder). Police did not
     learn of the suicide until later and looked for
     the O for over a year.

     Offender=Anglo Male, 41; (Warden, David);   no
     charges filed, offender committed suicide.

132 Victim=Anglo Male, 23; Ap 27, 1980;   Tract=22.02;
     1235; PSD;   The Offender and the Victim were
     involved in an altercation. O then went to his
     car and returned with a handgun and shot the
     victim (O claimed he was trying to break up a
     fight between V and another, hit V over the head,
     and gun discharged, killing the V.

     Offender=Anglo   Male,   21;   (Fultz,   Anthony);
     (80-7574); charged with Murder II; Judge 13;
     charge dismissed

138 Victim=Anglo Male, 74; May 4, 1980; Tract=37.02;
     1805; MPD;   Police believe that the Victim was
     killed (throat was cut and almost cut in two with
     stab wound to abdomen) during a robbery/burglary.
     Police found shaving cream sprayed on inside door
     knob, V-8 juice and sugar and salt were poured
     over upper portion of V's body. Dresser drawers
     had been ransacked. Police report that this M.O.
     has been found in 2 or 3 other cases.   Police
     found O's fingerprints at scene.

     Offender=Black Male, 20; (Peavy, Robert L.);
     (82-3193); Charged with Murder I, robbery and
     burglary; Judge 06; Jury trial; guilty of Murder
     I, robbery and burglary; Sentenced to death
     penalty plus (consecutive) two life terms.

145 Victim=Anglo Female, 62; May 7, 1980; Tract=89.01;
     9999; PSD;   Victim was involved in a domestic
     altercation with her son. The son shot his mother
     and then shot himself (both were found dead in
     bed).

     Offender=Anglo Male, 37; (Bojarczuk, Robert); no
     charges filed, Offender committed suicide

148 Victim=Anglo Female, 40; May 11, 1980; Tract=1.01;
     0530; PSD;   The Victim and the Offender (her
     husband) had been legally separated after
     longstanding marital difficulties (V had filed
     numerous complaints with police in community in
     upstate N.Y. for assault by the O). On a Friday
     night in N.Y. they met in a bar, got drunk
     together and decided to fly to Miami for a weekend
     trip (they withadrew $1,000 from the bank). Upon
     arrival in Miami they rented a motel room and
     began to argue. Members of the Chicago Police
     Dept. were staying in the hotel and heard the V
     and O arguing (and V pleading for O not to hit her
     anymore). The V was found dead (strangled) in the
     room the next morning by the maid.

     Offender=Anglo Male, 37; (Pettit, Wm.);
     (80-17699); charged with Murder I; pled to
     manslaughter; Judge 22; Sentenced to 15 years in
     prison.

163 Victim=Anglo Male, 15;
164 Victim=Anglo Male, 15;
167 Victim=Anglo Male, 21; May 17, 1980; Tract=15.01;
     2130; MPD;   The Three victims were stopped by a
     mob of Blacks during the May riots. They were
     dragged from the car and beaten to death. Five of
     the members of the mob were identified by a Black
     witness and prosecuted.

     Offender=Black Male, 21; (Capers, Leonard);
     (80-9587); charged with 3 counts of Murder I; jury
     trial; Judge 04; guilty on 3 counts of
     manslaughter; Sentenced to 3 consecutive 15 year
     sentences (thus total of 45 years).
     Offender=Black Male, 19; (Lane, Nathaniel);
     charged with 3 counts of Murder I; jury trial;
     Judge 04; jury acquitted him on 2 of the counts
     and mistrial on the third. A second and a third
     trial also resulted in a mistrial and then
     prosecutor dropped the charges. State felt that
     three trials were enough and felt they would not
     get a conviction.
     Offender=Black Male, 24; (Capers, Lawrence);
     charged with 3 counts of Murder I; jury trial;
     Judge 04; guilty on 3 counts of manslaughter;
     sentenced to 3 consecutive 15 year terms (thus
     total of 45 years).
     Offender=Black Male, 16; (Lightsey, Samuel);
     charged with 3 counts of Murder I; jury trial;
     Judge 04; guilty of 3 counts of Murder II;
     Sentenced to 3 consecutive life terms.
     Offender=Black Male, 20; (Moore, Patrick); charged
     with 3 counts of Murder I; jury trial; Judge 04;
     not guilty on all 3 counts.

165 Victim=Anglo Male, 22; May 17, 1980; Tract=17.02;
     2250; PSD;   Victim was stopped by mob of Blacks
     during May riots and drug from his car. He was
     stabbed then his body was placed in the street to
     stop other cars and thus he was run over by
     several vehicles.

     Offender=Unknown Black Males

206

175   Victim=Anglo Male, 42; May 18, 1980; Tract=90.01; 9999; PSD;   (This case occurred during the May riots but was not riot-related). The Victim had a long history of criminal activity (drug sales, use, sale of weapons, etc.) and was somewhat paranoid. On this night the V and some friends were in an office when the V stated people were coming in thru the concrete ceiling and several people started firing their weapons (shooting at the phantom invaders). V was accidently shot in the leg and bled to death. Prosecutor considered the case as non-prosecutable as it was either an accident or excusable homicide.

Offender=Anglo Male; no charges filed, considered accident or excusable homicide.

185   Victim=Anglo Female, 54; May 17, 1980; Tract=15.02; 2130; PSD;   Victim was enroute home during the May riots. A mob of Blacks stopped her car, stoned it, poured gasoline on the car and set it afire. V managed to escape the vehicle but had 25% burns on her body. However, the crowd continued to stone her (she died of the burns).

Offender=Unknown Blacks

186   Victim=Anglo Male, 15; May 18, 1980; Tract=10.01;
     0300; PSD;   (This case occurred during May
     riots but was not riot related.) Victim came home
     "stoned" (alcohol level=.16) and his mother
     evidently killed him with a claw hammer and knife.
     Her other children had left home and the V was the
     youngest and was about to move from home (she was
     upset about this and argued over this with V).
     After killing him she wiped the weapons clean and
     wrapped his body in a waterbed liner and kept him
     in the house for 6 days (kept spraying his body
     with disinfectant).

     Offender=Anglo Female, 49 (Janca, Joan);
     (80-9506); charged with Murder II; jury trial;
     Judge 12; Acquitted by jury. Defense contended
     that the mother did not kill her son and that she
     did not contact police for 6 days because she was
     shocked at discovering her son dead. Perhaps the
     jury believed that story or had a doubt about the
     state's version.

190   Victim=Anglo Male, 82; May 18, 1980; Tract=37.01;
     1030; MPD;   (This murder was during the riots
     but apparently not riot related.) The Victim was
     walking near his hotel when he was assaulted and
     robbed and killed (strangled with his necktie).

     Offender=Unknown

194   Victim=Anglo Female, 75; Ap 23, 1980; Tract=2.04;
     1000; PSD;   The Victim was out in her yard when
     she entered her home and was confronted by a Black
     Male who was burglarizing her home. He beat her
     up and she died a month later of her injuries.

     Offender=Black Male, 19; (Rozier, Michael);
     (80-7112); charged with Murder I, burglary &
     robbery; pled to Murder I and burglary; Judge 10;
     Sentenced to 2 concurrent life terms.

196 Victim=Anglo Female, 57; Oct 27, 1980; Tract=2.04;
     1210; PSD;   The younger offender was forced   at
     gunpoint to drive a car by the older offender (who
     was a drug dealer). The two offenders had met at
     a bar when the older O decided to get revenge   on
     some other drug dealers. He forced second O to
     drive and they followed a second vehicle (occupied
     by other drug dealers).   When   first   O shot at
     second vehicle the fire was returned and driver
     (the younger O) ducked (while the   car   was   still
     moving).   When   driver   looked   up again he saw a
     woman in path of car but couldn't stop. The woman
     (the V) was killed and thus the offenders were
     charged with felony murder in her death. Second O
     agreed to testify against first O.

     Offender=Anglo Male, 28; (Weir, David); (81-1357 &
     81-2958); charged with Murder III; (this O was
     shooter);   charges   dismissed   since 3 critical
     witnesses   changed   their   story   when   gave
     depositions.
     Offender=Anglo Male, 22; (Derringer, Neal T.);
     charged with manslaughter and leaving scene of
     accident; pled to leaving scene of accident; Judge
     14; Sentenced to 4 years of probation   (and
     adjudication withheld).

205 Victim=Anglo Male, 65; June 5, 1980;   Tract=31.00;
     0715; MPD;   The Victim was a vagrant who often
     slept by railroad tracks. It appears that he   was
     beaten (with a wooden 2 by 4 found near the body)
     and robbed. The V's head was split open so widely
     that it was thought at first a train had run   over
     him.

     Offender=Unknown

209

206   Victim=Anglo Male, 23; June 4, 1980; Tract=88.02;
      0330; PSD;   Two Latin Males were outside of a
      bar and made a pass at one of the nude dancers who
      worked in the bar. One of the other dancers told
      the bouncer there was trouble outside (and V
      overheard the report). Bouncer and the V went
      outside and V grabbed one of the L/M's around the
      neck. Bouncer fired a warning shot and the two
      L/M's fled.   V became angry that bouncer had
      stopped the fight and swung at the bouncer (who
      still had gun in his hand) and knocked him to the
      ground. Bouncer (from the ground) fired twice at
      the V and he was killed. No charges were filed
      and a week later the same bouncer shot two other
      patrons at the same lounge in an altercation (they
      were not killed).

      Offender=Anglo Male, 29;   no   charges   filed;
      justifiable homicide

207   Victim=Anglo Male, 59; Mar 7, 1980; Tract=34.00;
      9999; MPD;   The Victim was assaulted by two
      Black Males in a strong-armed robbery. The V died
      of injuries 3 months later.

      Offender=Two Unknown Black Males

208   Victim=Anglo Male, 16; June 6, 1980; Tract=101.08;
      0125; PSD;   The Victim was attempting   to
      burglarize a home when he was discovered by the
      owner of the house. Owner picked up his rifle, V
      ran out of front door. They met in the yard, V
      grabbed the rifle and it went off killing the V.

      Offender=Anglo Male, 51;   no   charges   filed;
      Justifiable homicide

209   Victim=Anglo Female, 22;   June 6, 1980 (found);
Tract=107.01; 9999; PSD;   Victim was sgt. in Air
Force and was living on the base. V was in
process of divorcing her husband (A Black Male)
and already had another boyfriend. Police suspect
that the husband found out about the boyfriend and
killed her. However, there is not enough evidence
to arrest the O.

Offender=Black Male, 25; identity known but not
enough evidence to charge

213   Victim=Anglo Male, 74; June 8, 1980;   Tract=14.00;
1030; MPD;   Victim left his house to buy a
newspaper and was attempting to make a phone call
from a pay phone when a Black Male juvenile
attempted to rob him. O had a knife and a gun. V
knocked knife out of O's hand and O then shot the
V.

Offender=Unknown Black Male juvenile

215   Victim=Anglo Female, 29;   June 12, 1980;
Tract=102.00;   0630;   PSD;   The Victim was
divorced (with 12 year old son) and had been
dating the O for some time (O was alcoholic). V
and O became involved in an altercation during
which the O shot the V several times. O then shot
himself (and died several days later in the
hospital).

Offender=Anglo Male, 31; (Richards, David); no
charges filed; O committed suicide.

217   Victim=Anglo Male, 22; May 17, 1980; Tract=15.01;
      1800; MPD;   The Victim, his brother and his
      girlfriend were traveling in their vehicle (during
      the May riots) when a mob of Blacks threw rocks
      and bottles at their car and it went out of
      control. The car hit a young Black girl (she
      eventually lost one leg) and the crowd then pulled
      the two males out of the car and beat them.   The V
      died of his injuries.   Four Black Males were
      identified from the crowd and prosecuted.

      Offender=Black   Male,   20;   (James,   Frankie);
      (80-9386);   charged with Murder II, attempted
      Murder II, and agg. battery; jury trial; Judge 04;
      not guilty on all counts.
      Offender=Black Male, 18; (McCullough, James);
      charged with Murder II, attempted Murder II and
      agg. battery; jury trial; Judge 04; guilty of
      manslaughter; Sentenced to 15 years in prison.
      Offender=Black Male, 32;   (Williams,   Samuel);
      charged with Murder II, attempted Murder II, and
      agg. battery; Judge 04; Charges dismissed
      Offender=Black   Male,   22;   (Bradley,   Lonnie);
      charged with Murder II, attempted Murder II and
      agg. battery; Judge 04; charges dismissed.

223   Victim=Anglo Male, 35; June 17, 1980; Tract=67.02;
      2040; MPD;   The Victim was a prominent attorney
      who represented mostly drug dealers. He was found
      dead lying on the floor in hallway of his office.
      Police believe that he was killed after he made
      promises to a client that he could not keep.
      Police believe he was "hit" by three Latin Males.

      Offender=Unknown Latin Males

231   Victim=Anglo Male, 53; June 22, 1980; Tract=10.04;
      0317; PSD;   Victim was a firefighter who died
      fighting a fire that police believe was set by an
      arsonist (thus a felony murder).   The V got
      separated   from   the   other   firemen,   became
      disoriented, his portable air supply ran out, and
      he died due to loss of oxygen. Police believe the
      owner of the building may have hired someone to
      set the fire but do not have enough evidence to
      charge.

      Offender=Anglo Male; not enough evidence to charge

                              212

232   Victim=Anglo Female, 17; June 22, 1980; Tract=101.03; 1815; PSD;   The Victim was found dead floating in a canal with her throat slashed. V was a chronic hitch-hiker, popped a lot of pills (& other drugs), hung-out with a rough crowd. She was last seen hitch-hiking from an amusement center.

Offender=Unknown

234   Victim=Anglo Female, 30; June 23, 1980; Tract=78.02; 1000; PSD;   Victim and her boyfriend were involved in drug, primarily cocaine, trade (V was "mule" for her boyfriend) as was the offender (who roomed with V's boyfriend). Two weeks before the murder the O broke into V's home and stole jewelry & drugs. V threatened to expose him to DEA and was supposed to go to DEA in a day or so (O knew this). She was probably killed to keep her quiet. V had traces of four different drugs in her body when she was killed. Prosecutor did not believe police had enough evidence for a warrant, O then fled to Virginia where he was killed in an auto accident.

Offender=Anglo Male, 52; (Perdue, Roy); no charges filed, Offender later died in auto accident.

235   Victim=Anglo Male, 60; June 6, 1980; Tract=37.02; 1600; PSD;   The Victim was beaten over the head with a hammer during a burglary of his home.

Offender=Unknown

237   Victim=Anglo Male, 29; June 24, 1980; Tract=90.01; 1115; PSD;   Victim and his brother were driving home from a bar when they became involved in a traffic altercation with four Latin Males in a second vehicle. They then drove off but the second vehicle followed. The V pulled over and upon exiting his vehicle he and his brother became involved in another altercation. One of the Latin Males stabbed the V.

Offender=Unknown

241　Victim=Anglo Male, 61; June 25, 1980; Tract=67.02;
　　　2305; MPD;　　Victim was employed as bartender at
　　　a bar when two Black Males robbed the bar and　one
　　　shot the V

　　　Offender=Black Male, 26; (Brown, Anthony C.);
　　　(80-14011); charged with Murder I, robbery, use of
　　　firearm;　jury　trial; Judge 04; not guilty on all
　　　counts. Eyewitness testimony was　not　believed.
　　　However,　since　O was on probation at this time a
　　　violation hearing was held in conjunction with the
　　　trial and O was found in　violation　of　probation
　　　and　got　one　year　in　county　jail. This O was
　　　accomplice as the shooter was not caught.

242　Victim=Anglo Male, 40; June 25, 1980; Tract=84.04;
　　　9999; PSD;　　The　Offender　was　a　part-time
　　　girlfriend　of　the V (who lived with another girl
　　　at two different　apartments).　On　this　date　V
　　　asked　her　out to eat but instead took her to one
　　　of his apts. and suggested they have　sex.　They
　　　smoked marijuana and took "ludes" and then went to
　　　bed.　O began to feel cheap and "used" and while V
　　　was　lying　on　his　back　she took weight-lifting
　　　dumbells and beat him over the head, killing him.

　　　Offender=Orienal Female, 29; (Rivera, Monica);
　　　(80-11702);　charged　with　Murder　I and robbery;
　　　pled to Murder II and　grand　theft;　Judge　13;
　　　Sentenced to 15 years in prison.

244　Victim=Anglo　Female,　65;　May　18,　1980;
　　　Tract=18.03;　1230;　PSD;　This　Victim　was
　　　assaulted in her car by a mob of Blacks during the
　　　May riots. She died 5　weeks　later　of　injuries
　　　suffered in that attack.

　　　Offender=Unknown Blacks

246 Victim=Anglo Male, 78; June 8, 1980; Tract=37.01; 1945; MPD;   The Victim was an alcohol abuser and upon being admitted to hospital on the day of the assault said that he was beaten by unknown Black Male (he was punched in the face during an argument).   The V died 3 weeks later of injuries suffered in the assault.

Offender=Unknown Black Male

255 Victim=Anglo   Female,   27;   July   3,   1980; Tract=100.01;   2030;   PSD;   The Victim and her husband and child stopped at a red light and two Black Males approached their vehicle and attempted to rob them.   One robber opened the car door to get the V's purse. V was holding the baby in her arms.   The O shot her in the face for no apparent reason. The baby was splattered with blood.   One of the offenders (the shooter) was caught and prosecuted.

Offender=Black Male, 18; (Holmes, Tommy Lee); (80-13530);   charged with Murder I, attempted robbery, use of firearm; pled to Murder I and attempted robbery; Judge 12; Sentenced to life plus two 99 year terms (for rapes in another case).   Court retained jurisdiction for first 1/3 of the sentence.

259 Victim=Anglo Male, 71; July 4, 1980; Tract=10.03; 0030; PSD;   The Victim was killed during a burglary of his home when burglar found V asleep on his couch (killed with sharp instrument).   The O ransacked the house, took several things and the V's car. O was arrested after police found the car (O had given it to friends) and traced it back to O.

Offender=Black Male, 19; (Fleming, Ernest); (80-12486); charged with Murder I, burglary and grand theft; jury trial; Judge 22; guilty on burglary and grand theft (acquitted of Murder I); Sentenced to 20 years in prison (15 years for burglary plus 5 more for grand theft). Primary witness did not cooperate and failed to testify against O.   Also the W passed out in hall before he was to testify & at one point was arrested to get him to court to testify.

262   Victim=Anglo Female, 51; July 5, 1980; Tract=7.03;
       1800; HPD;   The Victim did not approve of a
       love affair between her daughter and a Black
       (Haitian) male. V told daughter she could not
       date the O anymore and O went to talk to her about
       this but during the argument he stabbed and
       strangled her.

       Offender=Black Male, 35; (Barratteu, Jacques);
       (80-12391); charged with Murder II; jury trial;
       Judge 14; guilty on Murder II; Sentenced to 134
       years in prison.

266   Victim=Anglo Female, 78; July 9, 1980;
       Tract=42.00; 2350; MBPD;   The Victim was beaten
       and strangled during a burglary of her home. O,
       after police found his fingerprints at the scene,
       confessed that he saw an open door and walked into
       the apt. The V was sleeping but woke up as he was
       going thru the refrigerator. V screamed. The O,
       a Mariel refugee, spoke to her in Spanish but she
       didn't understand him.   V then picked up a fork
       (this is O's story) and came at O and he hit her,
       knocking her down---then beat and strangled her.

       Offender=Latin Male, 21; (Morejon, Alberto);
       (80-14639); charged with Murder I and burglary;
       pled to Murder II and burglary; Judge 05;
       Sentenced to two consecutive life terms.

268 Victim=Anglo Female, 38; July 9, 1980; Tract=68.00; 9999; MPD; The Victim was found dead in her apt. hanging by the neck from the bedroom door (she had been stabbed several times). Police found her diary listing approximely 50 boyfriends (the diary served as the basis for a two-part article in Herald's Sunday Magazine) and believed that one of them killed her. An ex-boyfriend was later found in Broward County to have committed suicide and objects from this V's apt. were found in his possession. Police believe he killed her after a quarrel. Victim was also into the drug scene and her diary was filled with references to smoking marijuana and taking cocaine. Traces of cocaine were found in V's body.

Offender=Anglo Male, 35; (Knowles, Dennis); no charges filed, Offender committed suicide.

270 Victim=Anglo Male, 39; July 12, 1980; Tract=31.00; 0915; MPD; Owner of a store promised to get Victim some illegal drugs but instead sent V to a "set-up" where V was ripped-off (was cut and beaten and robbed). Upon release from the hospital V returned to store & argument ensued with owner. V pulled a knife and threatened owner. They struggled, falling to the floor. The owner called out to a bystander, "Get my gun and shoot him in the ass." The bystander did exactly that---shot V twice in the ass. The V finally let go of the knife and subsequently bled to death.

Offender=Anglo Male, 21; no charges filed, justifiable homicide.

279 Victim=Oriental Female, 26; July 20, 1980; Tract=21.00; 0420; MPD; Victim and her boyfriend were living together but V was also dating another Oriental man. The V and O argued over her affair. O (the live-in boyfriend) prayed then asked V if they couldn't work this out--she said they could not. At that point the O stabbed her.

Offender=Oriental Male, 26; (Chua, Boon Eng); (80-13216); charged with Murder I; pled to Murder II; Judge 13; Sentenced to 3 years in prison.

298 Victim=Anglo Male, 25; July 31, 1980;
Tract=109.00; 0440; PSD; The Offender came to
residence of the V to resolve a drug dispute. V
let him in and then they argued and O shot V and
another Anglo Male who was in the house. O was
former roommate of the two victims and they were
all involved in drug traffic. Only one person
(this V) died.

Offender=Anglo Male, 20; (Steele, Ricky);
(80-14012); charged with Murder I, attempted
Murder I and use of firearm; jury trial; Judge 09;
acquitted on attempted Murder but convicted of
Murder II and use of firearm; Sentenced to life in
prison.

300 Victim=Anglo Male, 24; July 31, 1980; Tract=1.01;
9999; PSD; Victim was found shot to death in
men's restroom (of public beach). Police believe
that he was killed in a dispute over drugs and
that the O is an Anglo Male who has killed 3
others in drug disputes (2 in W. Palm Beach &
another in 1981 in Dade).

Offender=Anglo Male, 21; identity known but not
enough evidence to charge

303 Victim=Anglo Male, 33; July 31, 1980;
Tract=106.01; 2100; PSD; Victim was involved
in a drug deal with DEA agents. As the deal was
completed police moved in to make arrests. V
tried to drive away (escape) & police chased him.
V was shot a total of 32 tims by nine federal
agents. Two of those involved in the drug deal
were charged with felony murder in the death of
the victim but charges later dropped (determined
that they were the wrong men).

Offender=Nine federal agents; no charges filed;
justifiable homicide

308   Victim=Anglo Male, 65; Sept. 24, 1980;
Tract=50.00; 2130; MPD; Victim and Offender
were involved in dispute over their illegal
(organized) crime activity which included
gambling. V was found shot to death next to his
vehicle on the front lawn of his home. V had
alcohol level of .25. He had been in bar with
friends earlier in the evening.

Offender=Anglo Male, 41; (Laderman, Gerald);
(80-19752); charged with Murder I; Judge 01;
Charges dismissed (witness refused to testify).
The witness changed his mind and would not testify
at trial to support original statement linking O
to crime. W also accused police of coercion in
original statement but state found this untrue.

310   Victim=Anglo Male, 32;
311   Victim=Anglo Male, 39; Aug. 4, 1980; Tract=68.00;
1930; MPD; The younger victim was a drug
dealer who was shot and killed by his body guard
in a dispute over drugs and money. The older V
was just an innocent bystander who happened to be
at first victim's house when younger victim was
shot.

Offender=Anglo Male, 33; (Smith, Ernest);
(80-14804); charged with two counts of Murder I
and use of firearm; jury trial; judge 05; not
guilty on all three counts. O told 2 female
roommates how he killed the 2 V's; acquaintance of
V was witness to beating 2 days before when O
threatened to kill V at later date; and another
female heard O threaten V on phone the next day
(she later denied this story). Both female
witnesses changed their story. The Male witness
who saw the beating and heard the threat was not
located until the trial began and Judge ruled to
exclude this W since he was found so late. Since
no credible evidence remained the judge directed a
verdict of acquittal at the end of state's case
and thus jury never had to decide the case.

319 Victim=Anglo Male, 55; Aug. 10, 1980; Tract=4.07;
     2015; PSD;   Victim and Offender lived together
     for a month. O decided to move out and as doing
     so took a gun that was in the house. V argued
     over her taking the gun. V, who had alcohol level
     of .24, also got into a shoving match with one of
     her kids over some property they were taking from
     the house. V said he would call police but then O
     said, "No, you won't," and shot him in back.   V
     then turned around and O shot him two more times.

     Offender=Black Female, 33; (Hooks, Beatrice);
     (80-14762); charged with Murder II and use of
     firearm; jury trial; Judge 06; not guilty
     (witnesses gave contradictory testimony and was
     testimony about history of alcoholism and constant
     physical abuse by O of V and her children.   State
     witness used to disprove self-defense admitted
     testifying falsely while under oath and gave false
     statement to police earlier.

322 Victim=Anglo Male, 54; Aug. 12, 1980; Tract=1.03;
     0601; PSD;   Victim was attendant at a gas
     station. Police found him on floor of his office,
     below the open and empty cash register (evidently
     a robbery/murder).

     Offender=Unknown

332 Victim=Anglo Female, 73; Aug. 19, 1980;
     Tract=93.05; 1200; PSD;   The Victim and
     Offender had known each other for several years
     and she considered the O and his brother and
     sisters like her own grandchildren.   Then the
     family moved away. O would return on occasion and
     visit the V. On this occasion he spent the night
     at her house and V found out O had stolen from her
     and buglarized homes in the neighborhood. O asked
     V for money and V refused. O then beat her to
     death with a porcelain lamp.

     Offender=Anglo Male, 23; (Love, Raymond);
     (80-15528); charged with Murder I; jury trial;
     Judge 20; guilty of Murder I; Sentenced to life in
     prison with 25 year mandatory minimum before
     parole.

333 Victim=Anglo Male, 69; Sept. 26, 1980; Tract=24.00; 1445; MPD; Victim drove into parking lot of a supermarket and was walking over to a large garbage container when he was confronted by two unknown Black Males in an apparent robbery. A struggle ensued and V was knocked to ground & shot. Victim was a retired policeman (had been one of first officers hired when Metro police dept. began).

Offender=Two Unknown Black Males

335 Victim=Anglo Male, 29; Aug. 24, 1980; Tract=76.04; 0245; PSD; The Victim was burglarizing a home when he was shot by the owner. V had been arrested 5 weeks earlier for burglary.

Offender=Anglo Male; No charges filed; justifiable homicide

337 Victim=Anglo Male, 25; Aug. 24, 1980; Tract=15.01; 2200; MPD; The Victim frequented a bar where drugs and prostitution were common. On this occasion he was outside of this bar (in his car) and was talking with a prostitute trying to negotiate a price when a Black Male approached and attempted to rob him. V tried to drive off but his car stalled. The O shot V with revolver. O was from Bahamas.

Offender=Black Male, 20; (Thomas, Michael); (80-15967); charged with Murder II and use of firearm; Judge 10; charges dismissed; Two witnesses were available. First W (who actually saw the shooting) could not be found. Second W was drunk at time and overheard a conversation 20 minutes before shooting about O intending to rob the V. However, her statements were contradictory and inconsistent with the physial evidence (this W also had 35 prior arrests).

339   Victim=Anglo Male, 23;
340   Victim=Anglo Male, 24; Aug. 25, 1980; Tract=29.00;
      2130; MPD;   The two Victims were attending a
      minor league baseball game at the local stadium.
      Both victims had been drinking (alcohol level of
      .13 and .16) and got involved in an altercation
      with a Latin Male who shot them.

      Offender=Latin Male, 33; (Perez, Jose Thomas);
      (80-15802); charged with 2 counts of Murder I,
      attempted murder; use of firearm; pled to Murder
      II (2 counts), attempted Murder I, and use of
      firearm; Judge 05; Sentenced to two consecutive
      life terms.

341   Victim=Anglo Male, 21; Aug. 25, 1980; Tract=1.03;
      0320;   PSD;   The Victim was in process of
      robbing a convenience store when he was shot and
      killed by the store clerk.

      Offender=Anglo Male, 39; no charges filed,
      justifiable homicide.

346   Victim=Anglo Male, 22; Aug. 28, 1980;
      Tract=100.08; 9999; PSD;   The Victim was found
      shot to death in a parking lot by police. Police
      have no idea what happened in this case. The body
      was dumped here but police don't know where he was
      shot.   The V was known to frequently get "stoned"
      and walk around gazing at the moon.

      Offender=Unknown

347   Victim=Anglo Male, 61; Aug. 28, 1980;
      Tract=101.08; 0945; PSD;   Victim was retired
      police officer and had just arrived from N.Y. He
      took a job as a security guard at a bank and was
      unlocking the bank when he was approached by 3
      Latin Males. A confrontation ensued and V was
      shot by one of the Latin Males.

      Offender=Three Unknown Latin Males

348 Victim=Anglo Male, 52; Aug. 27, 1980; Tract=44.00; 2115; MBPD; Victim retired one month earlier in N.Y. and moved to Dade. V was sitting on a bus bench with 2 friends when 3 Latin Males (all Mariel Refugees) approached and said (as one pointed a gun), "money, money." V gets up, says "Wait" and starts to walk away when one O shot him in back of head. The 3 O's then fled. Police later learn that the 3 had committed a number of robberies that same evening. One of those arrested in another robbery (there was not enough evidence to arrest in this case) who is thought to have been involved in this killing was in prison in Cuba for 3 different murders (bar killings).

Offender=Three Black Latin Males, shooter is 24; no charges filed, insufficient evidence to charge.

349 Victim=Anglo Female, 26; Aug. 29, 1980; Tract=66.00; 2330; MPD; Victim was a prostitue who took her "date" to a motel. Clerk later saw an Anglo Male who had rented the room run to his car and then found the V dead (strangled). O was arrested and while being interviewed in homicide office tried to cut his throat with a knife---he was not successful.

Offender=Latin Male, 35; (Perez, Luis); (80-16228); charged with Murder I; Judge 02; Charges dismissed. The night clerk claimed he saw Anglo Male leaving room in hurry & took license no of his car. Police picked up O but he denied crime. However, then night clerk and 2nd employee refused to cooperate and there was no physical evidence to tie the O to the murder scene.

356   Victim=Anglo   Male,   80;   Tract=37.01;   9999;
MPD;   Victim   lived   in an old hotel.   The O, an
Anglo Female prostitute, and a Black Male went   to
the V's room to rob him.   Female O got him to open
door   by   offering   sex   and then V was beaten and
choked   to   death.   They   got $37   from   the
robbery/murder.

Offender=Anglo   (Mulatto)   Female,   25;   (Miller,
Theresa);   (80-16665);   charged   with Murder I and
robbery;   jury trial;   Judge 02;   guilty   on   both
counts;   Sentenced   to   life   in prison.   The O had
extensive prior record including violent offenses.
O was 8 months pregnant when sentenced.
Offender=Black   Male,   24;   (Williams,   Terry);
charged   with   Murder   I   and   robbery;   Judge 06;
Charges dismissed due   to   insufficient   evidence.
The   only evidence against the O was from female O
and she refused to testify against him.   However,
this   O   (a   transvestite)   was later arrested for
Murder I   in   a   case   involving   the   killing   of
another "john".

359   Victim=Anglo Male, 2; Sept. 4,   1980;   Tract=9.03;
9999;   PSD;   Victim   was   a   battered   child.
Evidently child had been battered   for   months   (O
confessed   to   2 months of beatings) as there were
numerous   bruises,   abrasions   and   even   burn   marks
(from cigarettes).   On this date it appears that V
was   punched   in the stomach by the O (his father)
and V died of this injury along with   impact   from
other injuries.

Offender=Anglo Male, 30;   (80-16553);   charged   with
Murder II and agg. child abuse;   jury trial;   guilty
on   both   counts;   Judge 20;   Sentenced to life in
prison (suspended   entry on agg. child abuse).

363 Victim=Anglo Female, 80; Sept. 6, 1980;
     Tract=112.00; 1430; PSD;   This elderly female
     was "killed" by her husband in a suicide pact.
     The O and V had been married for 60 years and he
     was dying of cancer and she was dying of a stroke
     (she was in a nursing home). While visiting her
     they went to patio area and O shot his wife and
     then shot himself.

     Offender=Anglo Male, 82; (Ivins, Charles); no
     charges filed; Offender committed suicide.

366 Victim=Anglo Male, 25; Sept 7, 1980; Tract=7.01;
     2350;   HPD;   The   Victim   and   Offender   were
     patrons in a bar and an argument ensued.   They
     went outside of the bar where O hit V in face with
     a large rock.

     Offender=Anglo Male, 19; (Highland, Wm. Lee);
     (80-16812); charged with Murder I; pled to Murder
     II; Judge 01; Sentenced to 15 years in prison.

367   Victim=Anglo Male, 84; Sept 8, 1980; Tract=25.00;
       1900; MPD;   Victim lived at his repair shop and
       was found dead on the floor of his shop. Four
       Black Males attempted to rob him (one had worked
       for the V and told his 3 friends that the old man
       kept a lot of money in the shop). The four kicked
       and choked V to death.   One O was arrested in
       another case and confessed to this killing and
       implicated his companions.

       Offender=Black   Male,   20;   (Fair,   Kelvin);
       (80-16926);   charged with Murder I and robbery;
       jury trial; Judge 09; guilty on both counts;
       Sentenced to life in prison.
       Offender=Black Male, 20; (Cone, Jackie); charged
       with Murder I and robbery; Judge 38; Pending as of
       July 13, 1982.
       Offender=Black   Male,   16;   (Redding,   Dennis);
       charged with Murder I and robbery; pled to Murder
       II; Judge 38; guilty of Murder II; Sentenced to 15
       years in prison.
       Offender=Black   Male,   32;   (McIntosh,   Leroy);
       charged with Murder I & robbery; Judge 09; charges
       dismissed.   The first three O's all blew whistle
       on each other and implicated the fourth O but he
       would not talk. Since state only had testimony of
       the co-defendants the jury didn't buy the case
       against this O and he was acquitted.

368   Victim=Anglo Male, 20; June 26, 1980; Tract=12.03;
       9999; PSD;   Victim was involved in a fight with
       another Anglo Male after which blood came from his
       mouth and he was incoherent. V was known drug
       addict and had been released from county jail one
       week earlier (V had traces of five different
       drugs, including alcohol in his body). Prosecutor
       would not file charges since O was only witness
       and he said V started fight and he (the O) was
       only defending himself (since there was no witness
       to contradict this assertion the case was
       considered non-prosecutable).

       Offender=Anglo Male, 28; no charges filed;
       justifiable homicide or a non-prosecutable case.

369 Victim=Anglo Male, 28; Sept. 10, 1980; Tract=36.01; 0730; MPD; Victim was a taxi driver and was at this location to buy drugs. He was shot outside the taxi and then dragged inside where his body was found.

Offender=Unknown

370 Victim=Anglo Male, 18; Sept 10, 1980; Tract=71.00; 2150; MPD; The Victim and his sister were walking from the convenience store near their home when they were approached by two Black Males who attempted to take the female's purse and the shoulder bag from the the V. A struggle ensued and one O shot the V.

Offender=Two Unknown Black Males

374 Victim=Anglo Male, 68; July 16, 1980; Tract=14.00; 1600; MPD; Victim was walking down sidewalk when he was approached by two Black Male juveniles who asked him for $1. V said he didn't have a $1 and one O then shot V in knee. V later died of complications from that wound.

Offender=Two Unknown Black Male juveniles.

378 Victim=Anglo Male, 52; Sept 15, 1980; Tract=2.08; 0033; PSD; Victim owned a jewelry store and coin exchange but was also dealing in cocaine. V was also a fence and melted down stolen gold items. At time he was shot he was cutting cocaine. Police believe V was killed in a drug dispute or rip-off.

Offender=Unknown

395 Victim=Anglo Male, 69; Aug 17, 1980; Tract=45.00;
9999; MBPD;   Victim was "peaceful old drunk"
who left a bar on this date and was beaten and
robbed by a Black Male, 41, who is known to have
preyed on drunks in this area. V, though injured,
went home and found later lying on his apt. floor
(naked) with water flooding the apt. V said he
was OK but owner came back the next day and V was
lying on the floor dead (died of injuries in the
robbery). The O had robbed this V before and was
arrested and convicted and sentenced (to time
served). O had also served time in the past for
murder.

Offender=Black Male, 41; identity known but not
enough evidence to charge

398 Victim=Anglo Male,   53;   Sept.   15,   1980;
Tract=42.00;   1930;   MPD;   Victim and another
Anglo Male were in argument on canal bank. The O
struck the V on top of had with whiskey bottle and
began choking him. Both men fell into the canal,
still fighting. O was pulled out of the water by
another companion but V drowned. The two others
then finished the bottle. V had alcohol level of
.20.

Offender=Anglo   Male,   65;   (Quinland,   Jim);
(80-17479); charged with manslaughter; Judge 09;
charges dismissed (lack of evidence). The O, V
and Witness were all alcoholics. Also Medical
Examiner said cause of death was drowning and
contusions thus insufficient to cause death or
unconsciousness. Judge 09 dismissed on defense
motion.

414 Victim=Anglo   Male,   37;   Sept   30,   1980;
Tract=114.00;   1240;   PSD;   The   Victim and
Offender and others were all drinking and an
argument ensued. V pulled a gun on O during the
argument but then put it away. Then the V went to
his boat (O still in car). When V came back
toward the car O thought he was in danger and shot
and killed the victim.

Offender=Anglo   Male,   52;   no   charges   filed;
justifiable homicide.

415   Victim=Anglo Male, 57; Sept 16, 1980; Tract=37.02;
       1030;   MPD;   The   Victim,   a   homosexual,
       approached a Black Male (in his 30's) in park
       across from downtown Miami and propositioned him.
       O told V to go away and leave him alone. V went
       to his car and got a night stick and went back to
       the O and threatened him. O then threw a rock at
       V hitting him in head. V fell and cracked his
       head in the fall (and died of this injury).
       Though identity of O is unknown it appears from
       witnesses   that   his act would be justifiable
       homicide.

       Offender=Unknown Black Male in 30's, probably
       would be justifiable homicide.

418   Victim=Anglo Male, 68; Sept. 8, 1980; Tract=27.02;
       1500; MPD   Victim was manager of apt. building
       and attempted to quell a disturbance on 3rd floor
       of his apt. building. After having argument with
       person causing disturbance O went to his room and
       returned with a knife and stabbed the V in
       abdomen.

       Offender=Black   Male,   39;   (Borders,   Paul);
       80-16836); charged with Murder II; Judge 08; pled
       to manslaughter; Sentenced to 15 years in prison.

422   Victim=Anglo Male, 47; Oct 5, 1980; Tract=40.00;
       9999; MBPD;   Victim was homosexual and had in
       the past taken pictures of homosexual acts with
       the offender.   O was angry because V was showing
       people these pictures. O confronted V about this,
       an altercation ensued, and V was beaten &
       strangled.   O then took V's money and fled to
       Tampa where he was arrested. It appears that the
       O tied up the V so that he would strangle himself
       no matter which way he moved.

       Offender=Anglo Male, 30; (Frederick, Christopher
       D.); (80-21554); charged with Murder I, robbery
       and kidnapping; pled to Murder II, robbery and
       kidnapping; Judge 02; Sentenced to life in prison.

                             229

425 Victim=Anglo Male, 38; Oct 11, 1980; Tract=78.03;
2340; PSD;   Victim was a police officer who was
working off-duty job and was picking up money from
a restaurant in shopping center when a vehicle
pulled up and occupants tried to rob the V.   A
second car was also involved in the robbery. The
two cars were occupied by four Black Males. The
two O's who got life terms were in the first car
and were direct participants in the robbery/murder
while the second two participated indirectly (were
in the second or "back-up" vehicle).

Offender=Black   Male,   18;   (Hicks,   Jerome);
(80-19545); charged with Murder I and robbery and
use of firearm; pled to Murder II, robbery and use
of firearm; Judge 07; Sentenced to life in prison
(court retained jurisdiction for 15 years).
Offender=Black Male, 17; (Brown, Freddie); charged
with Murder I, robbery & use of firearm; pled to
Murder II, robbery & use of firearm; Judge 07;
Sentenced to life in prison (court retained
jurisdiction for 20 years).
Offender=Black Male, 18; (Faniel, Frankie);
charged with Murder I, robbery & use of firearm;
Judge 08; jury trial; guilty of Murder II and
robbery; Sentenced to 4 years in prison as
Youthful offender to be followed by 2 years on
probation.
Offender=Black Male, 16; (Pittman, Terrace);
charged with Murder I, robbery & use of firearm;
Judge 08; jury trial; guilty of Murder II and
robbery; Sentenced to 4 years in prison as
Youthful Offender to be followed by 2 years on
probation.

426 Victim=Anglo Male, 42; Oct 5, 1980; Tract=94.00;
1930; PSD;   Victim lived at the health club run
by the offender. They had been arguing for some
time over rent and utility bills. On this
occasion both were leaving the premises at the
same time so V locked the gate so O couldn't get
out. This angered O so he shot victim. Then O
put the body in his van and took it to Palm Beach
and dumped it. O later confessed and led police
to the body. The O was 77 years old and died of
natural causes before he could be tried. V had
alcohol level=.22

Offender=Anglo Male, 77; (Wise, Gordon); Charged
with Murder I and use of firearm; Charges dropped
when O died.

430 Victim=Anglo   Female,   22;   Oct   13,   1980;
Tract=11.04;   1945;   PSD;   Victim was struck by
an automobile driven by a man who was an alcoholic
and had mental problems. O stated that he saw the
V and aimed his car toward her since she was a
devil. Medical Examiner ruled that the death was
a homicide but prosecutor did not and O was only
charged with leaving the scene of an accident and
failure to stop and render aid.

Offender=Anglo   Male,   47;   (Toepel,   Albert);
(80-019624); charged with leaving the scene of
accident and failure to stop and render aid; bench
trial; Judge 18; not guilty by reason of insanity.
O was required to continue out-patient treatment
for mental illness and to surrender his driver's
license.

436 Victim=Anglo Female, 61; Oct 20, 1980; Tract=5.03;
0100; PSD;   Victim was at home with her
daughter when an unknown Black Male entered the
apt. The V and the burglar struggled and the
burglar then shot the V and her daughter. The V
did not survive surgery.

Offender=Black Male, 23; identity known but not
enough evidence to charge.

437 Victim=Anglo Male, 55;
438 Victim=Anglo Female, 55; Oct 20, 1980; Tract=2.03;
     1550; PSD;   This married couple were found dead
     by police who were called to scene after shots
     were heard. Wife was shot and stabbed while
     husband was stabbed. Police believe the couple
     were robbed of their old jewelry.

     Offender=Unknown

444 Victim=Anglo Male, 50; Oct 23, 1980; Tract=77.02;
     2350; PSD;   The Victim was found shot to death
     in his home. The V's son was involved in the drug
     trade and many persons knew there was a lot of
     money in the house. Police believe V was robbed
     or that some type of drug rip-off was involved.

     Offender=Unknown but Police suspect a Latin Male
     and Female, both 26

453 Victim=Anglo Male, 1; Sept 19, 1980; Tract=71.00;
     9999; MPD;   The Victim was 10 month old infant
     and had obviously been battered for a period of
     weeks (there were many bruises in different stages
     of healing). V lived with his mother in a
     "commune" (7-8 persons in an old house). Mother
     was a rich kid in rich kids commune and appeared
     that baby was in the way of her lifestyle. Mother
     became pregnant in Calif. (doesn't know identity
     of father). Mother blamed battering on a
     boyfriend (and passed polygraph on this) but
     police still think she may have done it (police
     couldn't find the boyfriend she described).

     Offender=Unknown, but possibly mother of baby.

455 Victim=Anglo Male, 29; Oct 30, 1980; Tract=77.02;
     0645; PSD;   Victim was found shot to death on
     side of road. Police believe V was supposed to
     make a drug deal (for qualudes) shortly before.
     The O is believed to be the Latin Male who was to
     be the buyer in this deal.

     Offender=Latin Male, 24; identity known but not
     enough evidence to charge.

462 Victim=Anglo Male, 53; Nov 4, 1980; Tract=46.02;
     0030; PSD;   Victim was a homosexual and was
     last seen alive at a homosexual bar around
     midnight (shortly before the murder). V was found
     dead in his apt. on the bedroom floor with trauma
     to face and stab wounds in face and neck and back.
     A bedspread was knotted around his neck and pair
     of scissors embedded in back of his neck (V was
     nude). V had alcohol level of .16. Police
     believe the V was killed by another homosexual
     whom he had picked up in the bar.

     Offender=Unknown Male

463 Victim=Anglo Male, 53; Nov 5, 1980; Tract=54.01;
     0055; MPD;   Victim managed a hotel and upon
     answering door of his apt. was robbed by unknown
     person. Offender forced his way into the apt.
     with a gun and when a strugle ensued the V was
     shot. O took between $60-$70. Police suspect
     three Latin Males of this robbery/killing.

     Offender=Unknown, perhaps 3 Latin Males

464 Victim=Anglo Male, 41; Nov 5, 1980; Tract=103.00;
     0240; PSD;   Victim was a police officer and
     came to scene to back-up another officer who had
     stopped a suspicious car (driving with lights out)
     in a warehouse district. While the first officer
     was talking to the O he suddenly bolted and ran
     (he knew his car was stolen and that the officer
     would find this out). The V (as back-up) then
     gave chase into wooded area (V did not know O was
     armed). Shots were heard and V was found shot to
     death in the woods. O was found hiding a few feet
     away under some brush with gunshot wounds and v's
     handcuffs on one wrist.

     Offender=Black Male, 32; (Walker, Lonnie);
     (80-21484); charged with Murder I, use of firearm,
     grand theft, & unauthorized use of motor vehicle;
     jury trial; Judge 18; guilty of Murder II, grand
     theft & unauthorized use of vehicle; Sentenced to
     life in prison plus (consecutive) 3 years.

466   Victim=Anglo Male, 22; Nov 8, 1980; Tract=90.02;
      1215; PSD;   Victim and a companion were
      cruising a neighborhood looking for houses to
      burglarize. Upon breaking into one home they were
      confronted by the owner, an elderly man, who shot
      V in hallway as V fled. Son-in-law of homeowner
      arrived on scene & was told what happened. He and
      police captured the O thinking he was person who
      owner had shot at. But they then found the other
      burglar dead nearby. The fingerprints of this O
      were found on window and thus he charged with
      felony murder. He confessed but he was so stoned
      that Judge O7 threw out confession.   Judge also
      suppressed fingerprints but state appealed and
      won. The homeowner was not charged.

      Offender=Latin Male, 20;   (Coron,   Sebastian);
      charged with Murder II and burglary; Judge O7;
      pled to manslaughter and burglary; Sentenced to 10
      years in prison.

468   Victim=Anglo Male, 90; Nov 5, 1980; Tract=43.00;
      1845; MBPD;   Victim was found dead in his apt.
      Two days earlier V was approached by robbers
      outside of his hotel in the alley. V was grabbed
      by the throat during the robbery.   Since the
      robbery V had not been breathing well and Medical
      Examiner determined that V died of delayed effect
      of injuries sustained in that robbery.

      Offender=Unknown

478   Victim=Anglo Male, 54; Nov 15; 1980; Tract=39.04;
      0057; PSD;   Wife of Victim awoke after hearing
      shots and found her son standing over V's body
      with a gun in his hands. The son (offender) had
      been undergoing treatment for a mental disorder
      for over a year.

      Offender=Anglo   Male,   35;   (Baxter,   Richard
      Stephen); (80-22105); charged with Murder I; Judge
      19; Prosecution pending since O declared to be
      incompetent and is in S. Fla. mental hospital.

485 Victim=Anglo Male, 58; Nov 16, 1980; Tract=42.00;
     1830; MBPD;   Victim was sitting outside of apt.
     he owned when he became involved in an argument
     with a Mariel refugee (argument may have been over
     renting an apt. or over a deposit that was
     kept---the only witness spoke only Russian). O
     pulled out a knife and stabbed V. After V
     collapsed O pulled knife out of the body (it is
     believed V may have lived if knife had not been
     pulled out) and fled.

     Offender=Unknown Latin Male

487 Victim=Anglo Male, 36; Nov 17, 1980; Tract=105.00;
     1900; PSD;   Victim was having sex with a Black
     Female prostitute in his vehicle in a "hooker's
     park." Two or more Black Male juveniles approached
     the locked vehicle with guns and attempted to open
     the door. V tried to start the car to flee but
     was shot by one of the robbers. The prostitute
     was not working with the juveniles. It appears
     that the gang of robbers watched the prostitutes
     and followed cars which picked them up.

     Offender=Three Unknown Black Male juveniles

489 Victim=Anglo Male, 29; Nov, 1980 (found);
Tract=115.00; 9999; PSD Victim was found dead
floating in a canal. Since this area is in
Everglades National Park the case was referred to
the FBI. The FBI believes the case is
drug-related and has four suspects. The V and the
four O's were all involved in drug trade and lived
in midwest. They had been in prison together (in
another state) and were involved in selling drugs,
weapons and burglaries. The V (who was son of a
sheriff in midwestern state) and the four O's
regularly made trips to Florida to load marijuana
into a van to drive back to midwest. The four O's
became aware of attempt by V to "squirrel away" a
supply of marijuana so that he could secretly
return to Fl and sell the marijuana and keep the
proceeds for himself. They evidently killed the V
for trying to cheat them. V was shot in back of
head with 357 revolver. 3 of the 4 O's are still
free while one is back in prison for cocaine
charge. This gang is also suspect in some
homicides in midwest. At this point there is not
enough evidence to charge the four O's.

Offender=Three Anglo Males and One Latin Male, all
approximately 30 years old

493 Victim=Anglo (Phillipino) Male, 67; Nov. 17, 1980;
Tract=39.01; 0100; MBPD; V was a world famous
physician from the Phillipines who was here for a
convention after being brought to Houston to do
surgery. He was staying at a hotel on the beach
and was found dead (strangled) in his room wrapped
in a blanket with his hands tied behind him. The
motive is unknown. It did not appear to be a
robbery.

Offender=Unknown

503 Victim=Anglo Male, 35; ("John Doe"); Nov 3, 1980;
Tract=17.02; 1130; PSD; Victim was found dead
lying in the road by a passing motorist. Police
have no idea as to motive or suspect.

Offender=Unknown

236

512 Victim=Anglo Male, 64; Nov 27, 1980; Tract=36.02;
     1000; MPD;   Victim   entered   his   place   of
     business apparently during a burglary and   the   V
     was shot by unknown offender(s) who robbed him of
     his money and fled.   Police   later   arrested   two
     Mariel Refugees for this robbery/killing.

     Offender=Latin Male, 60; (Rodriguez,   Lazaro);
     (80-23503); charged with Murder I, armed robbery
     and burglary; bench trial; Judge 17; convicted   of
     Murder III and burglary; Sentenced to life plus 15
     years (consecutive).

514 Victim=Anglo Female, 1; Mar 4, 1980; Tract=3.01;
     9999; PSD;   Victim was infant who was battered
     by her mother.

     Offender=Anglo Female, 26; (Mashamesh, Francine);
     (80-21388); charged with manslaughter;   pled to
     manslaughter; Judge 17; Sentenced to 8   years   of
     probation with condition that offender spend 6
     months in county jail and   recommendation   that   O
     enter and complete a drug program.

521 Victim=Anglo Male, 30; Oct 31, 1980; Tract=2.09;
     2155; PSD;   Victim and Offender knew each other
     thru their girlfriends (who were both prostitutes)
     and both were involved in drug traffic.   Two days
     before V gave some money to O to buy cocaine but O
     couldn't complete deal. V was angry about this
     and when O came to his house they got into
     argument. Both were armed. V began hiting O with
     gun when gun discharged and killed the V.   O did
     not use his gun.

     Offender=There   actually   was   no   O   as   V   shot
     himself.   This   was   ruled   as excusable homicide
     since another man (Latin Male) was involved in the
     struggle.

531   Victim=Anglo Female, 23;
535   Victim=Anglo Male, 27; Dec 5, 1980; Tract=87.00;
       0200; PSD;   The Female Victim and her brother
       lived in a house where drugs were often sold.   The
       male victim was from Ohio and often made trips to
       Dade to buy drugs and always stayed with his lover
       (the   female   V).   It appears that someone came in
       to rip-off the occupants of the house knowing that
       a lot of cash was likely to be on hand (police
       think   robbers   got   away with $25,000).   Female V
       found hanging (strangled) from a doorknob and male
       V was found hanging (strangled) from the bathroom
       shower.   Both victims had "ludes" in their bodies.

       Offender=Unknown

544   Victim=Anglo Male, 19; Dec. 14, 1980; Tract=36.01;
       1739; MPD;   The Victim and a friend were parked
       in a car during a drug buy when   the   two Black
       Males (Jamaicans)   with whom they were dealing
       decided to rob them both and shot them both (only
       the V died).

       Offender=Two Unknown Black Males

556 Victim=Anglo Male, 62; Dec 20, 1980; Tract=12.03; 0110; PSD; The Victim was the step-father of the O's wife. The wife was disenchanted with the marriage to the O and initiated a separation. She also convinced him to return to his native Taiwan with the promise (never fulfilled) that she would send him a return ticket. The O found his way back to Florida and forced his wife to accompany him to Miami. The V (step-father) attempted (at the request of his step-daughter) to take her from the home of the O when the O pulled a knife, chased the V into a parking lot and stabbed him several times.

Offender=Oriental Male, 40; (Tien I. Wang); (80-24878); charged with Murder I, kidnapping and sexual battery; jury trial; Judge 14; guilty of Murder I and false imprisonment. Sentenced to life in prison plus (consecutive) 5 years in prison (acquitted of sexual battery). On appeal to the District Court of Appeal of Florida, Third District, the conviction was reduced to Murder II since evidence of the O's action was also consistent with the hypothesis that he acted in the heat of passion.

559 Victim=Anglo Male, 26; Dec 22, 1980; Tract=114.00; 2228; PSD; Victim was looking for a Black Male who had ripped him off on qualude deal the day before. O and two other Black Males approached the V's car (V was asking if they knew the B/M he was looking for) and evidently decided to rob the V. V was shot as he sat in the car. V had "ludes" in body.

Offender=Black Male, 22; (Bailey, William); (80-25470); charged with Murder I, use of firearm; Judge 22; pled to manslaughter; Sentenced to 3 years in prison.

568 Victim=Anglo Male, 48;
569 Victim=Anglo Female, 40; Dec 30, 1980;
     Tract=48.00; 1900; PSD;   This married couple
     owned a diamond exchange and were found dead by
     his secretary in his office 14 hours after they
     were last seen alive. Police believe they were
     killed as part of a swindle in which their
     business associate set them up for a meeting to
     liquidate some bonds but instead killed them.   The
     wife appears to have been an innocent bystander
     who just got in the way.

     Offender=Latin Male; identity known but not enough
     evidence to charge

009 Victim=Black Male, 27; Jan 9, 1980; Tract=31.00; 2240; MPD;   Victim was at a pool room when he became involved in an argument with a Black Female. V hit her with 2 pool balls. The owner of the place chased him out by firing shots at him and then took the B/F to the hospital. Owner left another B/M in charge of the place and left him his revolver. About an hour later the V returned to the pool hall with a gun. The B/M then shot the V twice in the chest (V had alcohol level of .15).

Offender=Black Male, 19; No charges filed; Justifiable homicide

010 Victim=Black Male, 70; Jan 10, 1980; Tract=37.02; 2000; MPD;   The Victim had been drinking all day (had alcohol level=.24) and was often in company of prostitutes. On this occasion it appears that he invited a prostitute up to his room and that she then robbed him and stabbed him with a butcher knife. The prostitute has been charged with murder before but beat the charge. She is now at large.

Offender=Black Female, 28; identity known but at large

012 Victim=Black Male, 37; Jan 14, 1980; Tract=34.00; 0105; PSD;   The Victim got into an argument with a Black Female. Another B/M intervened and was struck by the V who then got into his car and left. The B/F and B/M then got into a car and chased the V. Their car pulled alongside the V's car and the B/M fired 3 shots at the V and V was killed.

Offender=Unknown Black Male

241

016   Victim=Black Male, 13; Jan 19, 1980; Tract=100.08;
      1300; PSD;   The Victim was in the company of 3
      other Black Male juveniles when one of the B/M's
      (the O) took out a small handgun from his pocket
      and pointed it at the V and his friends. The gun
      went off striking V in abdomen. The V and the O
      were involved in burglaries and had stolen the gun
      in a burglary. Prosecution failed in effort to
      waive to adult court.

      Offender=Black Male, 14; charged with Murder II
      and use of firearm; tried in juvenile court; judge
      31;   not guilty but since O already on probation
      for several burglaries court ordered O to enter
      (as condition of probation) an intensive program
      in the community (court retained jurisdiction to
      see that order carried out at order carried out).

018   Victim=Black Male, 18; Jan 19, 1980;   Tract=34.00;
      1905; MPD;   The Victim was one of several Black
      (Jamaican) Males who were involved in a power
      struggle with American Blacks over the drug trade.
      On this occasion it appears that one of the
      American Blacks shot and killed a Jamaican Black.
      The V had been charged with a murder in 1979.

      Offender=Black Male; identity known but offender
      is at large (Frank Vargas)

024 Victim=Black Male, 23; Jan 21, 1980; Tract=76.03; 1050; MPD;   The Victim was leaning into a vehicle occupied by two Latin Males to sell them some marijuana. The two L/M's grabbed the V by the arms and held him inside of the car while they took off at a high rate of speed. Then they opened the door and threw him from the car. V was taken to the hospital, treated and released but was later found unconscious and died from these injuries.

Offender=Latin Male, 16; (Gonzalez, Luis); (80-1518); charged with Manslaughter; Judge 23; jury trial; not guilty.
Offender=Latin Male, 18; (Delgado, Procopio); charged with manslaughter; Judge 23; jury trial; not guilty. O's claimed they went to buy marijuana and when V stuck his head in their car he said he wanted money or his friend would shoot them (there was a fresh bullet hole in the car). So O's claimed they sped off with V hanging from the car. Neither O had criminal record. The jury evidently believed the O's or had a doubt about state's case.

028 Victim=Black Male, 22; Jan 25, 1980; Tract=13.00; 2000; MPD;   The Victim had shot the O's brother in the leg 4 hours earlier (in a dispute over drugs). O then found V at a pay phone inside of a convenience store and hit him over the head with a night stick and shot him (with a gun that had been stolen--not necessarily by this O--from a state trooper) in revenge for the V shooting his brother.

Offender=Black Male, 23; (Mercado, Ruben, Jr.); (80-1417); charged with Murder II and use of firearm; jury trial; Judge 01; guilty of both counts; Sentenced to 50 years on the murder charge and suspended entry on use of firearm.

032   Victim=Black Male, 22; Jan 31, 1980;   Tract=91.00;
      2025;   PSD;   Victim had gone to a warehouse
      where he had previously worked to pick up a
      paycheck. The security guard told V he couldn't
      go into the loading area with his vehicle but V
      did anyway. When V was leaving he was stopped by
      the guard and they argued. The guard says the V
      struck him once and that he (the O) then pulled
      his handgun and shot the V once in the head.

      Offender=Latin Male, 59; (DeLaPaz, Faustino A.);
      (80-1722);   charged   with Murder II, carrying
      concealed firearm; use of firearm, & agg. assault;
      jury trial; Judge 02; guilty of manslaughter, use
      of   firearm;   Sentenced   to   5 years on the
      manslaughter, suspended entry on use of firearm.

035   Victim=Black Male, 25; Feb 2, 1980;   Tract=15.01;
      1745;   MPD;   The   Victim   and Offender were
      involved in a dice game with several other Black
      Males when V pulled a knife in an argument. O
      then went and got a gun and returned. They argued
      again and V pulled a gun. O pulled his gun and
      shot and killed the V.

      Offender=Black Male, 31;   no   charges   field;
      Justifiable homicide.

038   Victim=Black Male, 42; Feb 4, 1980;   Tract=113.00;
      1230; PSD;   The Victim and 5 other persons were
      playing cards (gambling) when two unknown Black
      Males wearing stocking masks & armed entered the
      apt. in an apparent robbery. A struggle ensued
      and V was shot.

      Offender=Two Unknown Black Males

037   Victim=Black Male, 22; Feb 3, 1980; Tract=15.02;
     1941; PSD;   Victim and two Black Males were all
     dealing   in   drugs.   V attempted to rob the
     offenders (all had guns) but O's fired first and
     killed the V.

     Offender=Black   Male,   16;   (Hill,   Andrew);
     (80-1866); charged with Murder II; bench trial;
     Judge 28; not guilty
     Offender=Black Male, 22; (Eskridge,   Ulysses);
     charged with Murder II; bench trial; Judge 28; not
     guilty

041   Victim=Black Male, 24; Feb 5, 1980; Tract=20.01;
     0145; MPD;   Victim and Offender were drinking
     (V had alcohol level of .23) at a bar when they
     became   involved   in an argument over a dice game.
     V and O went outside of bar and continued arguing.
     V pushed O twice and on second push the O stepped
     back,   pulled a gun out and shot V once in chest.
     O then walked up to V lying on ground and fired
     another shot into head of V and fled.

     Offender=Black Male, 21; (Snell, Spencer); Charged
     with Murder II and use of firearm; pled to Murder
     II   and   use of firearm; Judge 13; Sentenced to 3
     years in prison. Suspended sentence on use of
     firearm.

049   Victim=Black Female, 21; Feb 12, 1980; Tract=4.07;
     2027; PSD;   Victim was involved in a verbal
     argument with her boyfriend. At one point the
     boyfriend (O) took out a gun (he says) to frighten
     her and the gun (he says) accidently discharged.
     V was shot in the head.

     Offender=Black   Male,   32;   (Crumity,   Willis);
     (80-2387); charged with manslaughter; pled to
     manslaughter; Judge 14; Sentenced to 3 years of
     non-reporting probation and adjudication withheld.

052 Victim=Black Female, 61; Feb 16, 1980; Tract=90.01; 9999; PSD; The Offender, an Anglo Male, was doing time in state prison with the V's son, a Black Male. O had nowhere to go upon release from prison so his friend arranged for O to stay with his mother. He had been out only a few weeks when he argued with his host over the use of her car (she wouldn't let him use it). The V went to bed and O waited by her bed with a shotgun on his lap for 2 hours for her to wake up. When she woke up he shot and killed her.

Offender=Anglo Male, 24; (Middleton, Wm.); (80-3289); charged with Murder I, grand theft and use of firearm; jury trial; Judge 10; guilty on all counts; Sentenced to death.

054 Victim=Black Male, 35; Feb 17, 1980; Tract=37.02; 1805; MPD; Victim was found dead in his car under a downtown expressway. The area is known as a place where prostitutes take their clients and other evidence suggests that this V was killed by a prostitute (or someone else who attacked him while they were in the car "doing business." V's shirt was unbuttoned and his jeans were pulled down. V was stabbed to death. V had alcohol level of .28. Fingerprints of a B/F were found in the car & she admitted to being in car but said when she left her boyfriend approached the car. A short time later he (the O/boyfriend) told her he had just stabbed a man.

Offender=Black Male, 23; (Williams, Howard R.); (82-3903); charged with Murder II; Judge 20; Pending

061 Victim=Black Male, 36; Feb 23, 1980; Tract=5.02; 1125; PSD; The Victim was a supervisor/clerk at a convenience store when 3 Black Males entered the store to rob it and shot the V (who was behind the counter. O's took the money and fled.

Offender=Three Black Males; identities known but not enough evidence to charge.

062 Victim=Black Male, 58; Feb 23, 1980; Tract=83.03;
1330; PSD;   Victim was involved in an argument
over money with his girlfriend.   During the
argument the girlfriend left the living room, got
kitchen knife, returned and stabbed the V once.
Both the V and O had been drinking (V had alcohol
level of .15).

Offender=Black Female, 25; (Brown, Edna Mae);
(80-3025); charged with Murder II; jury trial;
Judge 03; guilty of Murder III; Sentenced to 10
years of prison to be followed by 5 years of
probation.

065 Victim=Black Male, 38; Feb 25, 1980; Tract=5.03;
9999; PSD;   Victim and his girlfriend became
involved   in   a   domestic   quarrel   and   she
subsequently barricaded herself in the bedroom. V
then forced his way into the room and as he
approached the girlfriend, she fired 3 rounds with
a revolver and hit the V once in the head.

Offender=Black Female, 34; no charges filed;
justifiable homicide.

067 Victim=Black Male, 43; Feb 27,1980; Tract=104.00;
2100; PSD;   V threatened O with a shotgun. O
then fled in his vehicle and later V in his car
drove up alongside of O's car. At this point O
took a revolver from front seat and fired 3 shots
at V. V was unarmed at this time.

Offender=Black Male, 27; (Smith, Eddie James);
(80-3355); charged with Murder II, use of firearm;
jury trial; Judge 04; guilty of manslaughter & use
of firearm; Sentenced to 15 years in prison on
manslaughter (suspended entry on use of firearm).

070 Victim=Black Male, 27; Mar 2, 1980; Tract=15.02;
1662; PSD;   The Victim was standing near a
grocery store talking to an unknown Black Male
when they began to argue over a truck. The V
began to run and was chased by the O who chased
him for some distance before shooting him with a
handgun. V had alcohol level of .15.

Offender=Unknown Black Male

071   Victim=Black Male, 25; Mar 2, 1980; Tract=18.02;
      1810; PSD;   Victim and several friends were
      engaged in a card game in a parking lot when four
      Black Males approached and began watching. The V
      and one B/M became involved in a conversation
      which did not appear to be an argument. With no
      apparent provocation a second B/M punched the V in
      the stomach & V crouched over. When V rose up the
      first B/M shot the V.

      Offender=Black   Male,   18;   (Norris,   Audrey);
      (80-3953); charged with Murder II, use of firearm;
      bench trial; Judge 21; guilty on manslaughter and
      use of firearm; Sentenced to 15 years in prison to
      be followed by 5 years on probation.

075   Victim=Black Male, 33; Mar 8, 1980; Tract=28.00;
      0530; MPD;   Victim and another Black Male were
      drinking and gambling in a parking lot when they
      became involved in an argument which escalated
      into a fight. At one point the V pulled a gun and
      shot the O. After being shot, the O took the gun
      away from the V and shot the V, killing him.

      Offender=Black Male; no charges filed; justifiable
      homicide

077   Victim=Black Male, 53; Mar 9, 1980; Tract=31.00;
      0245; MPD;   Victim and his family and friends
      were having a birthday party (for the V).   V's
      daughter got into an argument with the offender
      over not wanting to have her picture taken with
      him.   The O pulled a gun and shot the V who had
      attempted to intervene in the dispute.

      Offender=Black   Male,   19;   (Yearby,   Kevin);
      (80-3989); charged with Murder II, use of firearm,
      and carrying a concealed weapon; pled to Murder
      II, use of firearm & carrying concealed weapon;
      Judge 23; Sentenced to 10 years in prison.

078 Victim=Black Male, 32; Mar 9, 1980; Tract=19.01;
     0345; MPD;   The   Victim and Offender were
     Jamaicans who were involved in drug traffic. They
     had argued earlier in the day over some marijuana
     and later O ambushed the V as he left a dance. V
     had alcohol level of .10.

     Offender=Black   Male,   26;   (Shaw,   Winston);
     (80-3961); charged with Murder II and use of
     firearm; Charges dismissed. The only eyewitness
     fled to NY; a 2nd witness claimed he was told of
     the events by eyewitness but then later claimed he
     did see the shooting. During second deposition
     2nd witness became abusive and decided not to give
     deposition. At a later hearing this witness's
     statements were excluded thus the state had no
     case.

081 Victim=Black Male, 27; Mar 12, 1980; Tract=15.01;
     0920; MPD;   Victim went to his brother-in-law's
     apt. and an argument ensued in the parking lot.
     The brother-in-law then went into his apt., got a
     gun, returned to the parking lot and shot the V.

     Offender=Black Male, 25; (Delaney, Michael);
     (80-4991); charged with Murder II and tampering
     with witness; Judge 14; Charges dismissed.   The
     only witness could not be found for the bond
     hearing or trial. Cont. denied thus case nolle
     prossed. The witness had said earlier that he was
     threatened by O to change his story.

083 Victim=Black Male, 57; Mar 14, 1980; Tract=37.02;
     2120; MPD;   Victim was involved in an argument
     while playing dice in a pool room. V was accused
     by O of using crooked dice. O demanded V's money
     & dice. When V put the money on the table, the O
     fired one shot that killed the V.

     Offender=Black Male, 28; (Hill, Clyde); (80-4747);
     charged with Murder II & use of firearm; Judge 07;
     Charges dismissed (witness didn't appear   and
     dismissed due to speedy trial rule). The only
     witness willing to testify was transient with bad
     background.   At trial date (near end of 180 days
     speedy trial limit) the witness failed to appear.
     Judge then dismissed charges.

085   Victim=Black Male, 44; Mar 15, 1980; Tract=34.00; 2020; MPD; Victim went into a bar for a robbery and pointed gun at barmaid. O then jumped over bar, took money from register (over $200) but as he was leaving there was a shoot-out between V and barmaid's boyfriend. V was killed.

Offender=Black Male; no charges filed; justifiable homicide

086   Victim=Black Female, 36; Mar 15, 1980; Tract=12.02; 0200; PSD; Victim was killed by her husband. After their marriage O wanted her to drop all of her old friends and even had the phone disconnected so she could not talk to them. However, V was still seeing an old boyfriend on the sly. V decided to leave her husband and V and O had apparently agreed to separate (with her going to boyfriend). On this date V was found shot to death in her home. Physical evidence indicated husband's cover story was not true and he had shot her.

Offender=Black Male, 38; (Osby, Raymond); (80-6036); charged with Murder II, use of firearm; Judge 21; Charges dismissed due to speedy trial rule.

087   Victim=Black Male, 19; Mar 16, 1980; Tract=9.02; 1835; PSD; Victim was at a movie theatre at a shopping center with two other companions. They became involved in an altercation with three other Black Males who were also at theatre. One of the 3 pulled a knife and stabbed the V (another V was also stabbed but did not die). The juvenile O was bound over for trial in adult court.

Offender=Black Male, 16; (Spaulding, Troy); (80-6080); charged with Murder II, agg. battery; pled to manslaughter and agg. battery; Judge 01; Sentenced to one year in jail to be followed by 8 years of probation (on both counts, concurrent). Also recommended work furlough privileges be granted during incarceration.

091　Victim=Black　Female,　31;　Mar　18,　1980;
Tract=21.00;　0730;　MPD;　Victim and two Black
Males went to home of another Black Male (who　was
drug　dealer) to rob him.　During the robbery the
drug dealer got into a struggle with the B/M
robber who told her to hit the dealer with the
sawed-off shotgun which she was holding.　She　did
this and the shotgun discharged and killed her
(the V).　The B/M then fled (with a second B/M who
was in the get-away car) with $750 taken in the
robbery.　The V had a long arrest record as did
the dealer (who was later killed in the May
riots--case no. 181).　The B/M robber and get-away
driver were both charged with felony murder in the
death of their companion.

Offender=Black　Male,　28;　(Simmons,　Lavern);
(80-4784); charged with manslaughter, robbery, use
of firearm, unlawful possession of shortbarrel
shotgun; Judge 13; This O was the robber.　Charges
were dismissed.
Offender=Black　Male,　23;　(McCall,　Gary　Lee);
charged with robbery & unlawful possession of
shortbarrel shotgun; Judge 13; (this O was
get-away driver).　Charges were dismissed.　Both
O's gave statements that were suppressed due to
police threats of 1st degree murder charge if they
did not.　The robbery victim was also later killed
by his girlfriend thus leaving the state with no
case.

094　Victim=Black　Female,　24;　Mar　23,　1980;
Tract=95.02; 2200; PSD;　Victim was involved in
verbal altercation at home with her common-law
husband.　The O got a rifle from a bedroom closet
and shot the V.　V had alcohol level of .10.

Offender=Black　Male,　39;　(Dudley,　Larry　C.);
(80-4980); charged with Murder II; pled to
manslaughter; Judge 14; Sentenced to 15 years in
prison.

095 Victim=Black Male, 21; Mar 24, 1980; Tract=10.01;
     0215; PSD;   Victim and his common-law wife
     became involved in a domestic argument. She got a
     shotgun and shot the Victim. He had often beaten
     her in the past and on this occasion was going
     toward her and she felt threatened.

     Offender=Black Female, 23; no charges filed;
     justifiable homicide

097 Victim=Black Male, 29; Mar 24, 1980; Tract=34.00;
     2330; MPD;   Victim and the Offender became
     involved in a verbal altercation during which the
     O cut the V on the arm and then walked away from
     him. The V followed and argument began again. O
     then stabbed the V in the chest. V had alcohol
     level of .32.

     Offender=Black Male, 20; (Gardner, Willie);
     (80-5073); charged with Murder II; Judge 21;
     Charges dismissed (granted motion to dismiss based
     on claim of self-defense). V was 6' tall and 213
     lbs and O was 5'5" and 136 lbs. Judge thus said
     it was self-defense given the fear of the smaller
     O. Also O had no prior record while V had
     extensive prior record.

098 Victim=Black Male, 40;
099 Victim=Black Male, 47;
100 Victim=Black Male, 35;
101 Victim=Black Male 31; Mar 26, 1980; Tract=4.05;
     1345; PSD;   The Four Victims were all found
     shot to death at a residence. Two Black Males
     were observed leaving the scene in one of the
     victim's car. Police believe the killings
     involved a drug rip-off.

     Offender=Two Unknown Black Males.

111   Victim=Black Male, 36; Ap 6, 1980; Tract=27.01;
       1200; MPD;   Victim was found stabbed to death
       in his apt. Police believe the victim was killed
       by another homosexual (V was known homosexual)
       whom V had picked up and taken to his apt.
       Fingerprints of O found in apt. and he confessed
       and said he went willingly to apt. but V coerced
       him into sex act he didn't want and so he got a
       knife from under the bed (they were in bed naked)
       and stabbed the V (O says he was only defending
       himself). He then tried to flee but found door
       locked so he ransacked the apt. to find the key
       and for money he felt he was owed for sexual
       favors. He finally had to break out. V had
       alcohol level of .21.

       Offender=Anglo   Male,   20;   (Herran,   Mario);
       (82-5203); charged with Murder I and burglary;
       Judge 37; Pending as of July 13, 1982.

118   Victim=Black Male, 29; Ap 13, 1980; Tract=4.03;
       9999; PSD;   Victim was found by a jogger shot
       (by shotgun) to death by side of road. V and two
       other B/M's went to a drug house to rip-off
       dealers (a B/M and B/F). Only the V went inside
       (this O hid by outside door and the other was in
       the car). The V pulled a gun and tried to rob the
       B/M dealer but a struggle over the gun ensued and
       the B/F, approximately 30, went and got a shotgun
       and pointed it at the B/M robber to scare him but
       the gun went off and killed him. Since both
       dealers were on probation they later dumped the
       body.   The dealers were given immunity to testify
       against this O for felony murder. V had alcohol
       level of .14.

       Offender=Black   Male,   27;   (Wright,   Eugene);
       (80-8607); charged with Murder II; Judge 02; jury
       trial; not guilty. This O was not the shooter
       (the B/F was shooter but this was considered
       justifiable) but was charged with felony murder
       since he was part of a robbery. However the judge
       dismissed the charge during the jury trial since
       the O was not in the apt. when the shooting
       occurred and thus the felony murder rule was not
       applicable. The judge had earlier suppressed the
       confession of O since he was not advised of his
       rights prior to the interview.

120   Victim=Black Male, 27; Ap 14, 1980; Tract=100.02;
       1845; PSD;   Victim and the O were acquaintances
       and became involved in argument at O's house. O
       got a shotgun and shot the V. V had alcohol level
       of .21.

       Offender=Black Male, 51;   (Barshaw,   Saladin);
       (80-6516); charged with Murder II and use of
       firearm; pled to Murder II and use of firearm;
       Judge 07; Sentenced to five years in prison to be
       followed by 5 years of probation.

123   Victim=Black Male, 46; Ap 20, 1980; Tract=57.02;
       1425; MPD;   Shoppers at a shopping center heard
       several shots and then observed a Latin Male and a
       Latin Female running from where the shots were
       fired. Police found the V shot behind   the
       steering wheel of a vehicle. Police have no
       motive and no suspect in this case.

       Offender=Unknown Latin Male and Latin Female

124   Victim=Black Male, 27; Ap 20, 1980; Tract=28.00;
       1750; MPD;   Offender walked out of a bar and
       bumped into the V who was standing by a baby
       carriage. V and O got into argument. V then went
       across the street and came back with a gun and
       shot at O (wounding him). O then pulled a gun and
       shot and killed the V.

       Offender=Black Male, 28;   no   charges   filed;
       justifiable homicide

126   Victim=Black Male, 14; Ap 22, 1980; Tract=100.06;
       0342; PSD;   Victim was burglarizing a residence
       when the owner woke up. The owner yelled at V and
       V attempted to flee out the door. Owner fired 2
       shots and killed V. V was drug addict (had needle
       tracks on both arms).

       Offender=Anglo Male, 35;   no   charges   filed;
       justifiable homicide

129 Victim=Black Female, 43; Ap 23, 1980; Tract=10.01;
     1745; PSD;   Victim and her husband (the
     offender) and their daughter were all involved in
     a domestic argument when V stepped between her
     daughter and her husband and was shot by the
     husband.

     Offender=Black   Male,   47;   (Turner,   Hoover);
     (80-7114); Charged with Murder I, use of firearm;
     pled to Murder II, attempted Murder I and use of
     firearm; Judge 19; Sentenced to two concurrent 15
     year terms in prison with mandatory minimum of 3
     years before parole in each.

130 Victim=Black Male, 37; Ap 26, 1980;   Tract=19.01;
     1600; MPD;   Victim and his wife were involved
     in a domestic disturbance after drinking together
     during most of the day (V had alcohol level of
     .42). Wife got a kitchen knife and stabbed V once
     in the neck. She had also stabbed him on three
     prior occasions.

     Offender=Black Female, 34; (Borders, Geraldine);
     (80-7288); Charged with Murder II; jury trial;
     Judge 12; guilty on Murder II; Sentenced to 10
     years on probation with special condition that
     serve one year in county jail and complete alcohol
     rehab. program.

131 Victim=Black Female, 20; Ap 27, 1980;   Tract=23.00
     MPD;   Victim and her common-law husband had
     been living together for two years and on this
     date were involved in argument. Husband (O) got a
     rifle from bedroom and (he claims) thinking it was
     unloaded placed it against his wife's chest. The
     gun went off accidently (he claims) and killed the
     V, who was pregnant. V had told a friend a few
     days before that O had drawn a gun on her and
     threatened her.

     Offender=Black Male,   22;   (Balkman,   Ernest);
     (80-7397); Charged with Murder II and use of
     firearm; pled to manslaughter and use of firearm;
     Judge 12; Sentenced to 12 years in prison
     (suspended entry of sentence for use of firearm).

135 Victim=Black Male, 39; May 3, 1980; Tract=4.09;
1720; PSD;   Police were dispatched to a
domestic disturbance and upon their arrival they
confronted the V who had just assaulted his wife
and then shot through the locked front door
injuring a child inside. When V turned toward the
officers with his gun the officers shot and killed
the V. V had alcohol level of .24.

Offender=Two Metro Police Officers; No charges
filed, justifiable homicide.

136 Victim=Black Female, 32; Ap 27, 1980; Tract=54.01;
2055; MPD;   Victim was pedestrian standing in
front of a bus bench when a car being chased by
police went out of control and hit her on the
sidewalk. V was dragged under the car for 1/2
mile from impact. V died of burns and blunt
trauma. The burglar who was being chased by the
police was charged with felony murder in the death
of this V.

Offender=Black Male, 27; (Rolle, Tyrone--no
relation to victim); (80-7353); Charged with
Murder I, burglary and Agg. Battery; pled to
manslaughter by culpable negligence in operating
motor vehicle; Judge 07; Sentenced to 12 years in
prison.

137 Victim=Black Female, 22; May, 1980 (found);
Tract=115.00; 9999; PSD;   Victim was found
strangled to death and floating in water at a
rockpit. V had been raped and had alcohol level
of .29. A similar incident of sexual battery had
occurred in this same area a few days before.

Offender=Unknown

256

139   Victim=Black Male, 40; May 5, 1980; Tract=4.07;
      2300; PSD;   Victim and his wife had been having
      domestic arguments in recent past. On this date V
      accused wife of having an affair with another man.
      The argument ended and V and O and their 14 month
      old child laid down to watch TV. Some time later
      O told V she was going to get diaper for the baby
      but instead went to night stand, got a gun and
      shot V several times (until she ran out of
      ammunition). She then called police and told them
      she shot him because of prior domestic incidents.
      Though she had often been assaulted in past the
      shooting at this particular moment seemed
      unprovoked.   O had been treated at hospitals in
      Miami and in Tenn. for injuries received from
      battering by the V. At one time she shot V in leg
      and shoulder but he did not press charges.

      Offender=Black Female, 41; (Evans, Delores);
      Charged with Murder I, use of firearm; pled to
      Murder II; Judge 04; Sentenced to 10 years
      probation (with adjudication withheld) and O
      allowed to move to Tenn. and be supervised there
      under interstate compact. The Judge took into
      account in his sentence the fact that the O was
      undergoing treatment for terminal cancer and had
      older children in Tenn.

141   Victim=Black Male, 17; May 7, 1980; 'Tract=31.00;
      2110; MPD;   Victim and O were acquaintances who
      became involved in argument over a stolen bicycle.
      O shot V with revolver. V had alcohol level of
      .11. Police believe the V was involved in several
      robbery/rapes of old women in the neighborhood
      (when their checks came in every month he would
      rob them).

      Offender=Black Male, 18; identity known but not
      enough evidence to charge.

147 Victim=Black Male, 33; May 10, 1980; Tract=19.02;
     2015; MPD;   Victim and a neighbor were arguing
     over a girl and a fight ensued. O then went and
     got a rifle from his 3rd floor apt. and came back
     and shot V. O was known as being a litle crazy
     and liked to shoot his rifle. V had alcohol level
     of .25.

     Offender=Black Male, 52; (Brown, John Henry);
     (80-8215); Charged with Murder II, use of firearm;
     jury trial; Judge 16; guilty of manslaughter and
     use of firearm; Sentenced to 4 years on probation
     with one year in county jail as special condition.

151 Victim=Black Male, 27; May 12, 1980; Tract=4.04;
     0300; PSD   V was a bouncer at a bar and became
     involved in a verbal altercation with a Black
     (Jamaican) Male. The V knocked the Jamaican (the
     O) to the ground but O then pulled a handgun and
     shot the V three times.

     Offender=Black Male, 25; identity known   (by
     nickname) but at large

152 Victim=Black Male, 19; Sept 16, 1980; Tract=15.02;
     2215; PSD;   Victim and two companions walked
     into a market and were refused service by the
     clerk. V pulled handgun and cocked it to threaten
     the clerk. The clerk pulled his own handgun and
     shot the V once. Clerk then ran to rear of store
     and V fired once. Clerk fired twice more killing
     the V.

     Offender=Black Male; No charges filed; Justifiable
     homicide

153 Victim=Black Male, 31; May 12, 1980; Tract=10.02;
     1700; PSD;   Victim and his two brothers were in
     a vehicle and became involved in an altercation
     with occupants (3 B/M's) of a second vehicle.   A
     short time later O saw the 3 B/M's again in a car.
     O stopped his car, went into the trunk and got a
     handgun. As vehicle passed by O fired two shots
     at car. Passenger in rear seat (the V) was hit in
     head.

     Offender=Black   Male,   33;   (Lowery,   Ellis);
     (80-8547); Charged with Murder II and use of
     firearm; Judge 14; Charges dismissed;

155 Victim=Black   Female,   21;   May   12,   1980;
     Tract=106.02; 1915; PSD;   Victim was shot by
     her brother during a domestic dispute.   The
     brother (O) had told V's parents about her
     shoplifting and she was angry about this.   She
     first   threatened   O with a knife which the O took
     away from her. V then threatened O with a kitchen
     fork. O then got a rifle (he claims) to scare
     her.   V grabbed at the gun and during the ensuing
     struggle the gun discharged (his story).
     Prosecutor ruled that the death was a justifiable
     and/or accidental.

     Offender=Black Male, 18;   No   charges   filed;
     Justifiable homicide

158 Victim=Black Male, 27; May 13, 1980; Tract=34.00;
     2150; MPD;   The Victim, a Jamaican, was killed
     in a shoot-out with a group of Jamaicans and a
     group of American Blacks (in a war over sale of
     drugs). The Jamaicans came and attacked the
     Americans and they shot back and killed the V. A
     bag of cocaine was found in V's pocket.

     Offender=Black Male; No charges filed; Justifiable
     homicide

160 Victim=Black Male, 19; May 16, 1980; Tract=10.04; 0200; PSD; Victim picked up a prostitute and was in front seat with her (parked). O was in a nearby bar, saw the two in the truck, and decided to rob them. O opened door and shot the V (prostitute got dressed and fled). Truck then rolled back and ran over (but did not kill) a wino who was sleeping nearby. Police found the killer thru fingerprints found at the scene. O was on probation and confessed.

Offender=Black Male, 24; (Hicks, Tyrone Melvin); (80-14324); Charged with Murder I and use of firearm; pled to Murder II and use of firearm; Judge 05; Sentenced to life in prison.

161 Victim=Black Male, 25; May 16, 1980; Tract=34.00; 2350; MPD; Victim was involved in a gambling argument with a group of brothers who squeezed O into a corner. O fled to his car, drove around the block, then came back and fired into the group. The V was hit and killed.

Offender=Unknown Black Male

162 Victim=Black Male, 25; May 16, 1980; Tract=10.04; 2315; PSD; Victim was coming out of a housing project with a gun in his hand when a group of Black Males who were gambling behind the projects got into a dispute with V about how he was handling the gun. V put gun to head of one B/M and pulled trigger (but gun didn't fire). Another B/M fled, got a shotgun and returned. When V pointed his gun at this B/M (the O) the O shot and killed him.

Offender=Black Male, 23; Offender never found but police believe the homicide would probably be ruled justifiable.

166   Victim=Black Male, 47; May 18, 1980; Tract=18.03; 0259; PSD;   Victim (during the May riots) was engaged in looting of a tire store when the police officer approached and ordered V to halt. V fired one shot at the police officer. Another officer, with a shotgun, then shot and killed the V.

Offender=Metro Police Officer; No charges filed; Justifiable homicide

168   Victim=Black Male, 21; May 18, 1980; Tract=15.02; 0310; MPD;   Three police officers were driving in an unmarked car (during the May riots) when they heard 3-4 shots. When they stopped their vehicle they saw a Black Male running behind the car with a gun. One of the officers got out of the car and fired 3-4 shots at the V.

Offender=Miami Police Officer; No Charges filed; Justifiable homicide

169   Victim=Black Male, 22;
170   Victim=Black Male, 17; May 18; 1980; Tract=18.01; 0330; PSD;   The two victims were killed by the same rifle during the May riots. A security guard panicked as a crowd broke into a drug store and fired several shots with his rifle, striking the two victims. The younger V had alcohol level of .14 (other had .04).

Offender=Anglo Male, 26; No Charges filed; Justifiable homicide

172   Victim=Black Male, 30;
173   Victim=Black Male, 23; May 18, 1980; Tract=31.00; 1410; MPD;   Two Black Males got into an argument over a girl (during the May riots but not riot related). Both pulled guns and shot at each other. Both died of these injuries. In other words, the two victims shot and killed each other.

Offender=Two Black Males were both the offenders and victims as they shot and killed each other.

174 Victim=Black Male, 24; May 18, 1980; Tract=72.00;
     1525; MPD;   The Victim and the O lived in the
     same apt. and were involved in a dispute over
     whiskey they had stolen during the May riots. At
     one point the O stabbed the V. Both had evidently
     been drinking (V had alcohol level of .17).

     Offender=Black Male, 58;   (Gainer, Lee W.);
     (80-8981); Charged with Murder II; jury trial;
     Judge 19; guilty of Murder II; Sentenced to five
     years of probation with special condition that O
     serve one year in county jail. Three weeks after
     the sentencing O received work release privileges
     and 9 months later sentence was modified to serve
     remainder of term (3 months) on weekends.

176 Victim=Black Male, 32; May 18, 1980; Tract=4.07;
     1648; PSD;   During the May riots a White Male,
     approximately 50, was in the riot area and it
     appears that several Black Male juveniles threw
     rocks at his pick-up truck. (A crowd of adults
     nearby tried to talk the juveniles out of this
     behavior.) The occupant of the pick-up got angry
     and fired shots into the (innocent) crowd striking
     the V. The V (who had alcohol level=.14) and the
     crowd were only conversing and drinking and were
     not involved in riotous behavior.

     Offender=Unknown Anglo Male, approximately 50

178 Victim=Black Male, 14;

177 Victim=Black Male, 38; May 18, 1980; Tract=10.01;
1830; PSD;   The two victims were shot during
the May riots by occupants of a blue pick-up truck
(occupied by four White Males) who were observed
shooting at other persons in the area. The 2
Victims were shot at two different locations (2
blocks apart) within a twenty minute period by an
occupant(s) of the same pick-up truck. The O was
arrested after he had bragged to others that he
had "just shot a nigger." O also had a shotgun
with him (both were killed with shotgun). O was
also on parole.

Offender=Anglo Male, 35; (Hembree, Paul);
(81-17355); Charged with Murder I and use of
firearm; Judge 22; Charges dismissed since
statements by witnesses were contradictory and no
one saw O shoot anyone.

179 Victim=Black Male, 51; May 18, 1980; Tract=31.00;
1930; MPD;   Victim was involved in an argument
with the O (during the May riots). They
challenged each other (both had guns). O shot the
V once. Both had been drinking.

Offender=Black Male, 42; (Young, Melvin);
(80-8978); Charged with Murder II and use of
firearm; pled to Murder II & use of firearm; Judge
10; Sentenced to 15 years in prison with 3 year
mandatory minimum.

180 Victim=Black Male, 40; May 18, 1980; Tract=22.02
MPD;   Victim (a Haitian) was shot and killed by
a Miami Police Officer as the V attempted to run
over the officer with a truck upon fleeing from a
burglary (during the May riots).

Offender=Miami Police Officer; No charges filed;
Justifiable homicide

181 Victim=Black Male, 18; May 19, 1980; Tract=25.00;
1013; MPD;   Victim went to residence of his 14
year old girlfriend and got into dispute with her
father. (The father, the O, had been charged with
the rape of this daughter and she had at one time
run away from home.) O followed V to his car and
either shot him or (as O claims) gun discharged as
O hit V over head with the gun. O fled and is
still at large. The V was the drug dealer in case
no. 091. This killing was during the May riots
but was not riot related.

Offender=Black Male, 49; (Graham, Kenneth);
identity known but still at large

182 Victim=Black Male, 33; May 19, 1980; Tract=19.02;
1635; MPD;   Victim was observed (during the May
riots) riding a bicycle around the pumps at a gas
station while he cursed police. One police
officer walked over to V who pulled out a knife.
V was put under arrest but then tried to flee on
his bike. He slashed at an officer with the knife
as he rode away and was shot by two officers.

Offender=Two Miami Police Officers; No charges
filed; Justifiable homicide

183 Victim=Black Male, 45; May 21, 1980; Tract=18.01;
1525; PSD;   Victim's car was vandalized by the
O during the May riots. The V shot and stabbed
the O in the leg after a dispute over the act of
vandalism. When O got out of hospital he went
looking for V, saw him on streetcorner and shot
him.

Offender=Black Male, 21; (Ealy, Anthony);
(80-9303); Charged with manslaughter; Judge 01;
Charges dismissed. Judge believed the O was
terrified and felt justifiably threatened by the V
since the V had earlier shot and stabbed the O and
O was on crutches when he spotted the V. The O
did not have a gun on him but was given a handgun
by a friend when they spotted the V. Judge
dismissed the charges since the O acted in
self-defense.

264

184   Victim=Black Male, 50; May 10, 1980;   Tract=15.02;
      1730; PSD;   Victim and his common-law wife were
      involved in an argument and V started chasing her.
      O grabbed a gun from a cabinet and shot the V.   V
      died a month later.

      Offender=Black Female, 46; (Williams, Cora Lee);
      (80-9467); Charged with Murder II and use of
      firearm; Judge 01; Charges dismissed (judge felt
      that homicide was justifiable)

188   Victim=Black Male, 68; May 23, 1980;   Tract=10.04;
      1845; PSD;   Victim and Offender shared an apt.
      and both had been drinking (V had alcohol level of
      .11) and arguing all day.   V produced a razor and
      began to cut O when O took a baseball bat and
      struck and killed the V.

      Offender=Black Male, 49;   No   charges   filed;
      Justifiable homicide

189   Victim=Black   Female,   23;   May   24,   1980;
      Tract=19.02;   1645;   MPD;   Victim   and   her
      boyfriend became involved in a domestic   argument.
      One of the parties obtained a handgun. According
      to boyfriend, V got the gun and threatened him, a
      struggle   ensued,   O   turned   gun toward V, gun
      discharged and V was killed. Prosecutor   felt   he
      could not prove otherwise.

      Offender=Black   Male,   33;   No   charges   filed;
      Justifiable homicide

193   Victim=Black Male, 30; May 28, 1980; Tract=101.14;
      2040; PSD;   Victim was shot by unknown   persons
      while standing by a convenience store. V was shot
      from a vehicle with a shotgun.   Police have a
      suspect and believe that the killing was
      drug-related (a dispute over selling of drugs).

      Offender=Anglo Male, 25; not enough evidence to
      charge

198 Victim=Black Male, 23; May 31, 1980; Tract=18.01; 9999; PSD; The Victim was a homosexual hustler and frequented a bar near the area (yard of an elementary school) where his body was found (V had been stabbed to death). Police believe V made a pick-up at the bar, went to the school area, an argument developed, O stabbed V numerous times (a pattern typical of homosexual killings). V had alcohol level of .10.

Offender=Unknown Male

199 Victim=Black Male, 23;
200 Victim=Black Male, 50; June 2, 1980; Tract=34.00; 1030; MPD; The two victims were evidently involved in a homosexual act in an abandoned house when unknown robbers found them, shot them to death, and robbed them. Both Victims were nude and had been tied up with cord & their own clothing. Both victims had been drinking (alcohol levels of .19 and .14). Police believe the robbers were two Black Males.

Offender=Two Unknown Black Males

201 Victim=Black Female, 34; Nov. 23; 1980; Tract=0240; 0200; PSD; Victim says (she lived for several hours in the hospital) she was picked up hitch-hiking by three Black Males who sexually assaulted her and threw her from the moving vehicle.

Offender=Three Unknown Black Males

204 Victim=Black Male, 33; June 5, 1980; Tract=106.01; 9999; PSD; Victim was found stabbed to death on a dirt roadway where there was a lot of blood and signs of a struggle. V was a Jamaican and was involved in selling drugs (marijuana) on a small scale. He was known to be desperate for money and was last seen getting into a car with two Latin Males. Police Suspect the Latin Males killed the V.

Offender=Unknown, probably two Latin Males

210   Victim=Black Male, 23; June 7, 1980; Tract=28.00;
      1650; MPD;   Victim had known the Offender for
      several years and on this date went to O's
      residence and entered the unlocked screen door. O
      asked the V to leave but V refused to leave and
      asked for money or a a "reefer" (drug).   O
      continued to ask V to leave but when he didn't O
      got kitchen knife. V and O became involved in a
      struggle and O stabbed V.

      Offender=Black Male, 28;   No   charges   filed;
      Justifiable homicide

211   Victim=Black   Male,   34;   March   25,   1980;
      Tract=36.01; 0845; MPD;   Victim was shot to
      death at his own home in a dispute over money owed
      for drugs. O was shot several times.

      Offender=Black   Male,   30;   (Floyd,   Freddie);
      (80-6240); Charged with Murder II and attempted
      Murder I; Judge 10; Charges dismissed. The state
      lacked witnesses. One W was in toilet at time of
      shooting. This W only heard the shot. The other
      witnesses said they saw O with 2 others running
      from the house. However, these witnesses did not
      cooperate and disappeared.   Since O was on
      probation at time of arrest and stayed in jail for
      1 year awaiting trial he did   receive   some
      punishment.

214   Victim=Black Male, 28; June 11, 1980; Tract=17.02;
      0153; PSD;   Victim, in early morning, for
      unknown reasons (he had alcohol level of .38)
      began firing shots at people in the street from a
      rifle.   Police were summoned & ordered the V to
      drop his gun. When V refused to drop the rifle,
      police officers fired at V, killing him.

      Offender=Two Miami Police Officers; No charges
      filed; Justifiable homicide.

216   Victim=Black Male, 25; June 12, 1980; Tract=14.00; 2130; MPD;   Victim and two other Black Males were attempting to rob a gas station when one of the employees shot the V.

Offender=Latin Male, 44; No charges filed; Justifiable homicide.

220   Victim=Black Male, 20;
221   Victim=Black Male, 22; June 15, 1980; Tract=15.02; 2100; PSD;   O and younger V grew up together. V was present when the O had robbed a drug dealer and told the O he wanted part of the take ($700). O met V at housing project and argument ensued. O shot this V and then as he was walking out of project with gun in his hand he passed by the second V who was sitting on a car talking to his girlfriend. The second V asked if the O had just shot "that guy" and O said he had and asked the second V what he planned to do about it. The girlfriend told the 2nd V to shut up and he said nothing else. This silence seemed to anger the O so he shot the 2nd V. First V had alcohol level of .14.

Offender=Black Male, 20; (Bendross, Nathaniel); (80-11042); Charged with Murder I (2 counts) and use of firearm (2 counts); pled to Murder II (2 counts); Judge 18; Sentenced to two consecutive life terms.

222   Victim=Black Male, 22; June 16, 1980; Tract=113.00; 2330; PSD;   Victim was walking on the street when he was approached by another Black Male who tried to rob him (grabbed at medallion from V's neck) at gunpoint. O had extensive past record for robbery. O also shot at V's brother who attempted to come to V's aid but missed him.

Offender=Black Male, 25; (Asia, Charles); (80-11174); Charged with Murder II, attempted Murder I, use of firearm, unlawful possession of firearm by convicted felon; Judge 13; Charges dismissed

224 Victim=Black Female, 55; June 17, 1980;
Tract=17.01; 2230; PSD;   Victim became involved
in a dispute with her boyfriend after she had been
in the company of another man for 2 hours.
Boyfriend came to this location with a shotgun
which was taken away from him. The argument was
apparently settled and the shotgun was given back
to O. O left but returned with the shotgun and V
got into struggle with the boyfriend over the gun.
At this point the O (boyfriend) shot the V. V had
alcohol level of .14. O fled the scene on foot.

Offender=Black Male, 49; (Eady, Artisce);
(80-11241); Charged with manslaughter; jury trial;
Judge 06; not guilty. Two different stories were
presented at the trial. O said he went to the
house to borrow shotgun from old girlfriend and
boyfriend came at him and shotgun discharged
accidently. State witness said O walked in and
saw his girlfriend and her boyfriend having sex
and shot the girlfriend. Jury either believed the
O's story or had a doubt about state's version.

226 Victim=Black Male, 37; June 20, 1980; Tract=34.00;
1830; MPD;   Victim was behind the counter at
his brother's grocery store when the O came into
the store with a rifle, walked up to the counter &
fired 2-3 shots at the V. O was a "nut" who said
someone in the V's family was harassing his
family. O said he meant to kill the V.

Offender=Black Male, 38; (Way, Clayton);
(80-11345); Charged with Murder I, attempted
Murder I (2 counts) use of firearm; jury trial;
Judge 09; guilty of Murder I and use of firearm;
Sentenced to life (suspended entry of sentence on
use of firearm).

228 Victim=Black Male, 18; June 21, 1980; Tract=4.07;
1225; PSD;   Victim entered O's bedroom and told
O not to be afraid as he just wanted to have sex.
O then got out her shotgun (by her bed) and
advised V to leave. When V put his right leg on
the bed he was shot by the O. O keeps a loaded
shotgun by her bed as she has been burglarized
several times. V had a knife in his possession
when he advanced on the O. O stated that she had
never seen the V before.

Offender=Black Female, 37; No Charges filed;
Justifiable homicide.

229 Victim=Black Male, 29; June 21, 1980; Tract=15.02;
1900;   PSD;   Victim lived near one O's
girlfriend and supposedly grabbed (fondled) her.
The V, the girl and the two O's (who were
brothers) got into an argument. At some point the
three males pulled guns and a shoot-out began.
The V was killed and the two offenders were
wounded. V had alcohol level of .24.

Offender=Black Male, 23; (Barnwell, Stanley);
(80-11405); Charged with Murder II, attempted
Murder II (2 counts), unlawful possession of short
barreled shotgun; Pending
Offender=Black Male, 32; (Barnwell, Paul); Charged
with Murder II, attempted Murder II (2 counts),
unlawful possession of short barreled shotgun;
Pending

230 Victim=Black Male, 31; June 13, 1980; Tract=71.00;
1930; MPD;   Victim had been involved in
domestic dispute with his wife (the O) and was
subsequently stabbed. O was first charged with
agg. battery (at time of incident) but when
husband died 9 days later further investigation
indicated that the wife acted in self-defense.

Offender=Black Female, 30; No charges filed;
Justifiable homicide

240   Victim=Black Male, 53; May 29, 1980; Tract=31.00; 1840; MPD;   Victim had been a small-time drug dealer for several years and was walking down the street when he was approached by a Black Male. An argument ensued and V was stabbed once (V died 2 weeks later). V was also a chronic drug abuser for 15 years.

Offender=Unknown Black Male, 25

243   Victim=Black Male, 40; June 26, 1980; Tract=4.03; 2130; PSD;   The V and O and several other Black Male juveniles were at V's apt. drinking and taking drugs when O at one point went up to V and asked him for a match (O didn't even smoke). O then began punching the V, V tried to defend himself, O then shot V for no apparent reason. O now says he hs no idea why he shot the V.

Offender=Black Male, 18; (Carter, Eugene); (80-11768); Charged with Murder II & use of firearm; pled to Murder II and use of firearm; Judge 10; Sentenced (as youthful offender) to 4 years in prison to be followed by 2 years on probation (with condition he perform community service).

245   Victim=Black Male, 26; June 27, 1980; Tract=28.00; 1400; MPD;   Victim was driving his car (with others as passengers) when he got involved in a traffic dispute with two unknown Latin Males. The argument ended but then the 2 L/M's followed the V and argument broke out again. V told his companions that he had been insulted and got out of the car with a gun. However, the L/M's also had guns and they shot first, killing V.

Offender=Two Unknown Latin Males

248   Victim=Black Male, 26; June 28, 1980; Tract=23.00; 2340; MPD;   Victim and the O were sitting on bleachers at a public park when they got into an argument (over money from sale of drugs) and a fight ensued. V attempted to flee but O beat him with a pipe and then stabbed him several times. V had alcohol level of .12.

Offender=Black Male, 25; (Hall, Ronald); (80-11998); Charged with Murder II; jury trial; Judge 17; not guilty. Evidence at trial showed eyewitnesses were 100 yards from crime scene. First W was unsure of his identification of O and 2nd W suffered mental problems and lacked credibility. Third W (14 year old) "froze" on the stand. The jury evidently had doubts.

250   Victim=Black Male, 47; June 29, 1980; Tract=83.01; 1935; PSD;   Victim became involved in a physical altercation with his girlfriend at her residence. Witnesses claim V was beating the O and had stabbed her with a paring knife. V apparently went outside of residence and when he attempted to re-enter he was shot by the O. V had alcohol level of .26.

Offender=Black Female, 30; No charges filed; Justifiable homicide

252   Victim=Black Male, 21;
253   Victim=Black Male, 34;
254   Victim=Black Male, 15; July 2, 1980; Tract=4.08; 0200; PSD;   The three victims were at the home of one victim when neighbors heard shots. Police found the three victims shot to death in the home. Police believe the triple killing to be drug-related as evidence of drug activity was found in the residence.

Offender=Black Male, 24; (Jones, Ronnie Lee); (80-12103); Charged with Murder I (3 counts), burglary, robbery, unlawful poss. of firearm by convicted felon, carrying concealed weapon, use of firearm; jury trial; Judge 22; guilty on all counts. The O served as his own attorney and also was cited for contempt for his conduct of the trial. He was sentenced to 3 consecutive death penalties plus one life term.

256 Victim=Black Male, 44; July 4, 1980; Tract=10.04;
    2100; PSD; Victim and O and others were
    involved in a card game and had been drinking all
    day (4th of July). At one point O confronted V
    over a $10 debt and argument ensued (others tried
    to break it up). Argument continued outside where
    a fight developed. O pulled out a pocket knife
    and stabbed V (V then bled to death). V had
    alcohol level of .14.

    Offender=Black Male, 53; (Harrison, Charlie);
    (80-12221); Charged with Murder II; pled to
    manslaughter; Judge 07; Sentenced to 4 years in
    prison to be followed by 3 years probation.

257 Victim=Black Male, 26; July 4, 1980; Tract=100.06;
    2345; PSD; Victim became involved in an
    altercation with another Black Male (O) over the
    O's involvement with V's wife. A struggle ensued
    and V was shot.

    Offender=Black Male, 26; (Fate, Clarke);
    (80-12243); Charged with manslaughter & use of
    firearm; pled to manslaughter and use of firearm;
    Judge 20; Sentenced to two concurrent 10 year
    prison terms.

260 Victim=Black Male, 19; July 6, 1980; Tract=93.02;
    0600; PSD; Victim was called out of his apt.
    at 6:00 AM by an unknown B/M (whom he evidently
    knew). They were standing next to V's van in the
    parking lot engaged in an argument. At one point
    O shot V (neighbor looked out window and saw a B/M
    fleeing the area). Motive is unknown.

    Offender=Unknown Black Male, approximately 20.

261 Victim=Black Female, 26; July 6, 1980;
Tract=22.01; 1951; MPD; Victim and others were
at a party. O arrived as the party broke up and
said that he wanted his girl back. O saw his
ex-girlfriend and told her he wanted to talk to
her but as she approachad him he shot her. O then
shot another woman and a male (only the girlfriend
died).

Offender=Black Male, 60; (Miller, Oswald); at
large

265 Victim=Black Male, 21; July 8, 1980; Tract=21.00;
1000; MPD; Victim was found in a motel room,
nude and beaten to death (with a lamp). Appears
that he was attacked while he was in bed. Police
believe that V was killed by a woman whom V was
trying to recruit as a prostitute for his
"stable." V was a pimp. O was not a prostitute at
this time. O may have been seeking revenge for
the attempted recruitment of another female.

Offender=Black Female, 20; (Torrey, Dorothy);
(80-13064); Charged with Murder I; pled guilty to
Murder II; Judge 22; Sentenced to 10 years in
prison.

267 Victim=Black Female, 15; July 9, 1980;
Tract=34.00; 0615; MPD; Victim was at her home
with her boyfriend. They then walked to a park
and an argument ensued (over drugs, marijuana).
The boyfriend (O) was high on drugs and shot the V
during the dispute.

Offender=Black Male, 18; (Williams, Tony);
(80-12526); Charged with manslaughter & use of
firearm; pled to manslaughter & use of firearm;
Judge 01; Sentenced as Youthful Offender to 4
years in prison to be followed by 2 years on
probation.

269   Victim=Black   Female,   16;   July   11,   1980;
Tract=14.00;   1900;   MPD;   The   Victim   and her
boyfriend (the O) were in a stolen   car   (which   V
had stolen) when O began argument over how she (V)
was   driving   the car.   At one point he shot the V
(with a   stolen   gun)   and   then   took   her   to   a
hospital (where he made up a story about her being
shot by someone else).

Offender=Black   Male,   21;   (King,   George);
(80-12639);   Charged   with   Murder   II,   use   of
firearm,   grand   theft   auto,   &   grand   theft   of
firearm;   Charges   dismissed.   O   claimed   he had
stolen the gun but it went off accidently and that
he didn't know car was stolen.   State felt Fl case
law would not   allow   successful   prosecution   for
manslaughter in this type of case without evidence
of culpable negligence.

272   Victim=Black   Female,   31;   July   13,   1980;
Tract=14.00;   0548;   MPD;   Victim was leaving a
private club with 3   other   people   (one   was   V's
date).   O   approached   and   touched   her   on   the
buttocks. V protested and a fight ensued. O then
went to his car and got a gun and fired   into   the
four.   One   male   tried to shield the V and he was
shot and paralyzed. V was shot and killed. V had
alcohol level of .16.

Offender=Black   Male,   22;   (Foster,   Willie R.);
Charged with   Murder   II, attempted Murder II, use
of firearm; jury trial; Judge 10;   not   guilty   on
all   counts   (even   though   one   surviving victim,
paralyzed and in a wheelchair, identified O as the
shooter). Verdict was a shock to the prosecution.
State had 3 eyewitnesses (including   paralyzed   V)
and   friend   who   was with O. The jurors may have
felt that the V or his friend "may" have had a gun
and thus O   felt   threatened.   Prosecution   then
charged   this   O   with parole violation and he was
revoked and went back to prison for 2 years.

274   Victim=Black Male, 27; July 14, 1980; Tract=15.01;
      0530; MPD;   Victim   and   two   friends   were
      standing next to V's car in front of a bar. O
      drove up in another car and parked next to V's
      car.   V   and   O then involved in an argument. At
      one point V came over to O's car and O thought V
      had a weapon and shot the V. V had alcohol level
      of .15.

      Offender=Black Male, 24; (Washington, James); at
      large

275   Victim=Black Female, 22; ("Jane Doe"); July 14,
      1980; Tract=14.00; 0800; MPD;   Victim was found
      shot in the head lying in the bushes between a
      fence and a building. V had her dress up above
      her waist and $35 clutched in her hand. She may
      have been a prostitute but her identity has not
      been determined and thus thre is no way to check
      on her past. Thus she is a "Jane Doe."

      Offender=Unknown

276   Victim=Black   Male,   29;   July   15,   1980;
      Tract=106.01; 0555; PSD;   Victim was a drug
      dealer and had record for robbery. The O was his
      body guard who evidently decided to assasinate his
      boss in a drug rip-off. V was shot and thrown
      from a pick-up truck (passing motorist saw the
      truck flee and the V floundering by the roadside).

      Offender=Black   Male,   27;   (King,   Marshall);
      (80-14805); Charged with Murder I; Judge 17; first
      jury trial was hung; Second jury trial O found not
      guilty.
      Offender=Black Male, 29; (Bryant, Larry); Charged
      with Murder I and accessory after the fact (this O
      was passenger in the pick-up truck); Judge 17;
      Charges dismissed;

276

277 Victim=Black Male, 32; July 16, 1980; Tract=18.01;
     2315; MPD;   Victim was involved in a fist fight
     with the O when another person handed the O a
     knife and then O stabbed the V to death. V had
     alcohol level of .32.

     Offender=Black Male, 24; (Sanders, Willie
     Charles); (80-13385); Charged with Murder II, pled
     to Murder II; Judge 09; Sentenced to 5 years
     probation with condition that O spend one year in
     county jail (adjudication withheld).

280 Victim=Black Male, 18; July 20, 1980; Tract=72.00;
     0400; MPD;   Victim and O were in an argument in
     a bar but then went outside of bar. Patrons heard
     several shots coming from outside and then V
     stumbled through the bar door and collapsed. It
     appears that both V and O had guns while in the
     bar and that they went outside and shoot-out
     ensued.

     Offender=Black Male, 26;   no charges filed;
     Justifiable homicide Prosecutor could not disprove
     O's account (that V pulled gun first) and thus
     case is non-prosecutable.

286 Victim=Black Male, 39; July 22, 1980; Tract=1600;
     PSD;   Victim and his wife were separated and a
     divorce was in the process. V had moved in with
     another woman. On this date V had just gotten off
     work when his wife shot him as he was walking
     across the parking lot.

     Offender=Black Female, 46; (Freeney, Lydia)
     (80-13397); Charged with Murder I & use o
     firearm; pled to manslaughter & use of firearm
     Judge 05; Sentenced to two concurrent five yea
     prison terms (with recommendation for ear.
     release).

287 Victim=Black Male, 26;
288 Victim=Black Male, 26; July 25, 1980; Tract=26.00;
1235; MPD;   The two victims entered a pawn shop
and attempted to pawn a bad stereo which store
employee refused to accept.   One V then jumped
over the counter, armed with a revolver, and both
victims were shot by the co-owner of the store.

Offender=Anglo Male, 30;   No   charges   filed;
justifiable homicide

291 Victim=Black Male, 45; July 25, 1980; Tract=9.02;
2045; PSD;   Victim became involved in verbal
altercation with the O at a gas station where O &
V and 4 other B/M's were gambling. O shot V and
one other B/M (in leg).

Offender=Black Male, 33;   (Wims, Roosevelt);
(80-14016); Charged with Murder II, attempted
Murder II, shooting into occupied building, use of
firearm; Judge 10; Charges dismissed.   V had
reputation of always carrying gun when gambling.
O had argument with V and left. When O came back
V had gun in his lap under a towel. O drew a gun
and shot the V.   All witnesses claimed it was
self-defense and state saw no way to prove
otherwise.

292 Victim=Black Male, 49; July 27, 1980; Tract=15.01;
0305; MPD;   Victim had been involved in a dice
game earlier in the evening at which time he
became involved in an altercation with another B/M
(the O).   O claimed that he had been
cheated/robbed.   O called police and said that V
had robbed him (police put O in their car and they
cruised around looking for the V but did not find
him).   Then later O saw the V and some friends on
a street corner. The O went up to the V and said,
"I want my money." When the V refused the O shot
the V. V had alcohol level of .26.

Offender=Black   Male,   39;   (Akins,   Jimmy);
(80-13704); Charged with Murder II & use of
firearm; jury trial; Judge 18; not guilty. Jury
learned that O earlier in day had been robbed by
the V. Also two witnesses had disappeared and
only remaining witness was facing a rape charge
and not very credible.

294   Victim=Black Male, 58; July 17, 1980; Tract=37.01;
      1120; MPD;   Victim found lying in a vacant lot
      near a labor pool (V was a laborer, did odd jobs).
      V had been beaten by a blunt instrument. Motive
      and offender are unknown. Police suspect it may
      have been a robbery.

      Offender=Unknown

295   Victim=Black   Male,   37;   July   28,   1980;
      Tract=113.00;   2120;   PSD;   Victim and   a B/F
      became involved in a verbal   altercation.   The V
      went to his residence and returned with a machete
      and struck the O with the instrument.   O then shot
      the V.

      Offender=Black Female, 52; No charges   filed,
      Justifiable homicide

296   Victim=Black Male, 33; July 29, 1980; Tract=4.06;
      0745;   PSD;   Victim and his wife were involved
      in an argument during which V said, "You'll have
      to kill me to get rid of me." V had thrown a
      shovel at her (they were in front yard and on
      porch of their home). V then went to his car and
      got what wife thought to be a gun. O then got a
      gun and fired once. When V continued in pursuit
      of O she fired again killing V.

      Offender=Black Female, 30; No charges   filed;
      Justifiable homicide

306   Victim=Black Male, 45; Aug 2, 1980; Tract=4.06;
      0045;   PSD;   Victim was in the process of
      commiting an armed robbery of a market when he was
      shot numerous times by the proprietor.   V had
      traces of three different drugs in his body.

      Offender=Black Male; No charges filed; Justifiable
      homicide

307   Victim=Black Female, 24; Aug 2, 1980; Tract=31.00;
      2319; MPD;   Victim and the O had been living
      together for some time. They got into an argument
      when O became angry at V for going to a bar by
      herself. O went to get her and upon their return
      they argued and V decided to move out and began
      packing. O then shot her several times. V had
      alcohol level of .14.

      Offender=Black Male, 29; (Davis, Joe); (80-14216);
      Charged with Murder II and use of firearm; jury
      trial; Judge 14; not guilty.

309   Victim=Black Female, 55; Aug 4, 1980; Tract=18.01;
      0905; PSD;   Victim was sitting on the trunk of
      a parked vehicle in the parking lot of her apt.
      complex with several others when a vehicle
      occupied by about five Black Males drove past and
      fired several shots into the crowd, killing the V.
      Police believe the shooting to be a feud between
      two groups of Jamaicans (a drug "war" among
      Rastafarians) and the V got caught in the
      crossfire. A Witness came forward and identified
      the O as the shooter. O fled but arrested in NY
      on a double homicide (which he beat) and was
      extradicted to Miami. By then the W had left town
      and no other evidence against O. Speedy trial
      limit up before W could be located again.

      Offender=Black Male, 25; (Thompson, John Henry);
      (81-28140);   Charged with Murder I & use of
      firearm; Judge 07; Charges dismissed since W could
      not be located before Speedy Trial time limit.

313   Victim=Black Male, 21; Aug 7, 1980; Tract=10.04;
      0655; PSD;   V was a Jamaican whose body was
      found lying in the parking lot of a truck service.
      Police believe the V was involved in sale of drugs
      and that the killing was some type of drug
      rip-off.

      Offender=Unknown

317 Victim=Black Male, 27; Aug. 9, 1980; Tract=18.01;
0240; PSD;   V was escorting 2 B/F's home from a
bar when 3 B/M's attempted to rob them. V was
stabbed to death. V's personal property was
strewn over the scene and front pocket was turned
out. V had alcohol level of .17.

Offender=Three unknown Black Males

320 Victim=Black Male, 50; Aug 10, 1980; Tract=18.03;
2250; PSD;   Victim became involved in domestic
argument with his wife at which time V chased wife
outside of house with a tire iron. Wife (O)
called police. After police left, V chased wife
out of house again, this time with a chair. O
then got a knife and cut the V on the arm. V went
to several neighbors to request that someone take
him to the hospital but all refused. V then
proceeded to drive himself to the hospital (at 70
MPH) and struck a tree. V died of stab wounds.

Offender=Black Female, 36; No charges filed;
Justifiable homicide

321 Victim=Black Male, 21; Aug 11, 1980; Tract=114.00;
2230; PSD;   Victim became involved in verbal
altercation with his girlfriend's sister (the O).
As the argument became more heated the O produced
an 8 inch kitchen knife and stabbed the V.

Offender=Black Female, 22; (Murphy, Eleanor);
(80-14847); Charged with Murder II, agg. battery,
carrying concealed weapon; jury trial; Judge 06;
guilty on Murder II, agg. battery & carrying
concealed weapon; Sentenced to 20 years in prison
(and concurrent terms of 10 and 1 on other
counts).

324 Victim=Black Male, 30; Aug 13, 1980; Tract=37.02;
1800; MPD;   Victim was stabbed during the
burglary of his hotel room by a man who lived in
an adjacent room. V was attempting to steal his
TV. V had alcohol level of .19.

Offender=Black Male, 39; No Charges filed;
justifiable homicide

325   Victim=Black Male, 32; Aug 14, 1980;   Tract=2.06;
      1913; PSD;   Victim was at a bar (had alcohol
      level of .01) when he became involved in an
      argument with another patron of the bar. When a
      third patron and an employee also became involved
      the V made verbal threats to the employee who then
      shot the V.

      Offender=Black Male, 46; (Samuels, Franklin);
      (80-15028); Charged with Murder II and use of
      firearm; pled to manslaughter; Judge 10; Sentenced
      to 5 years in prison.

327   Victim=Black Male, 22; Aug 15, 1980; Tract=18.03;
      1700; PSD;   V and another B/M were attempting
      to break into a vehicle in front of a pool hall
      (vehicle was owned by owner of pool hall). Owner
      went outside but was ushered back into the pool
      hall by the V and the other B/M, who had a
      shotgun. Upon entering the pool hall several
      armed employees shot the V. The other B/M (one
      who had the shotgun) was arrested and charged with
      felony murder in the death of his companion. The
      store employees who shot the V were not charged.
      V had alcohol level of .14.

      Offender=Black Male, 18; (Taylor, Jeffrey);
      (80-15093); Charged with Murder II & robbery; pled
      to Murder II; Judge 01; Sentenced as youthful
      offender to 4 years in prison to be followed by 2
      years on probation.

329   Victim=Black Male, 37; Aug 16, 1980; Tract=4.03;
      0200; PSD;   V was an alcoholic and was 80%
      disabled from the military (had mental problems).
      V was involved in domestic dispute with his
      girlfriend (who was a nurse). V had a record of
      beating the O (the girlfriend) and on this date
      had begun to beat her (was on top of her beating
      her). O cut V in chest area (with a knife he had
      forced her to carry for her own protection) to get
      him off of her. However, the cut hit a main
      artery and blood poured out. V then would not let
      O (a nurse) give him first aid and he bled to
      death.

      Offender=Black Female, 47; No charges filed;
      Justifiable homicide

330   Victim=Black Male, 23; Aug 19, 1980; Tract=14.00;
       0015; MPD;   Victim and a friend were parked on
       a dead-end street near a junkyard. The owner of
       junkyard approached them and asked them what they
       were doing. According to the friend of V owner
       then shot the V. According to the O the V had a
       tire iron and was raising it when he fired (from
       25 feet away).

       Offender=Black   Male,   52;   (West,   Lewis);
       (80-15321); Charged with Murder II, attempted
       Murder II, use of firearm; Judge 13; Charges
       dismissed

334   Victim=Black Male, 60; Aug 23, 1980; Tract=10.02;
       2135; PSD;   V was a small-time numbers and drug
       dealer. It appears that two B/M's ripped him off
       and killed him (in a burned out warehouse).   One
       of the suspected O's was later killed by a drug
       dealer who wanted to keep him quiet about this
       murder.

       Offender=Unknown but probably two Black Males, not
       enough evidence to charge

338   Victim=Black   Female,   36;   Aug.   24,   1980;
       Tract=10.04;   9999; PSD;   V was found dead
       (strangled) near a market and behind a dumpster
       next to a warehouse. V was partially disrobed and
       had been raped. V had alcohol level of .26. Body
       was found 6 hours after the killing. There were
       no witnesses and no suspects.

       Offender=Unknown Male

345   Victim=Black Male, 21; Aug 28, 1980; Tract=105.00;
       1230; PSD;   Victim got involved in a fight with
       subject at a bar (V had alcohol level of .14) and
       was stabbed.

       Offender=Black Male, 22; (Henry, Elton L.);
       (80-16086); Charged with Murder II and possession
       of weapon in an offense; pled to manslaughter;
       Judge 10; Sentenced to 7 years in prison.

350   Victim=Black   Female,   27;   Aug   31,   1980;
Tract=14.00; 0700; MPD;   V was a prostitute and
got involved in an argument with a Black Male (the
O) over $60.   The O stabbed her with a broken soda
bottle.

Offender=Black   Male,   20;   (Latulas,   Mack);
(80-16424); Charged with manslaughter; Judge 20;
jury trial; guilty of manslaughter; sentenced   to
15 years in prison.

355   Victim=Black   Male,   28;   Aug.   1980   (found);
Tract=10.04;   9999;   PSD;   V   was   found   in
advanced stage of decomposition in a   weeded   lot.
V   was   known   to   be   a   bisexual   or   homosexual
"hustler" who would pick up members of either   sex
at   a local bar to sell sexual favors.   V was also
a drug user and is known to have been a small-time
dealer at times.   Police believe V   either   killed
by   a   "john"   or as part of a drug deal that went
sour.

Offender=Unknown

360   Victim=Black Male, 32; Sept 5, 1980;   Tract=34.00;
0120;   MPD;   V was involved in a dispute with a
B/M over   a   woman   (who   was   also   present).   V
threatened   the   B/M   (the   O)   with   a bottle but
others broke up this altercation.   V   then   walked
away.   O followed and told the woman to get out of
the way and then O shot the V.

Offender=Black   Male,   36; . (Lewis,   Charles);
(80-16587); Charged with Murder I and use of
firearm; pled to Murder II and   use   of   firearm;
Judge 10; Sentenced   to   two   concurrent 10 year
prison terms with provision that after 8 years the
sentence be suspended for remaining 2   years,   not
eligible for parole for 3 years.

361 Victim=Black Male, 24; Sept 5, 1980; Tract=20.02;
     2030; MPD;   V and the O were acquaintances and
     got involved in an altercation that developed into
     a fist fight. V pulled a gun but O took it away
     from V and pistol whipped him with his own gun.
     The fight was broken up by others who were
     present. However, the O again picked up the gun
     and then shot the V.

     Offender=Black Male, 30; (Johnson, Ronald);
     (80-16609); Charged with Murder II & use of
     firearm; jury trial; Judge 06; guilty of Murder II
     and use of firearm; Sentenced to 30 years in
     prison.

365 Victim=Black Male, 60; Sept 7, 1980; Tract=17.02;
     1230; PSD;   V and his wife were asleep when
     they heard their dogs barking. V got up to
     investigate and went into the yard. V was then
     shot by unknown persons. V was a fence and it may
     be that he was killed in some dispute over stolen
     goods. Police have no firm motive or suspects.

     Offender=Unknown

372 Victim=Black Male, 28; Sept 11, 1980; Tract=31.00;
     MPD;   V and the O became involved in a verbal
     altercation over a dog. Then the argument "got
     personal" and O told V to get off his porch. V
     then walked away but came back a few minutes later
     and while V was standing on the sidewalk an
     argument broke out again. O took a shotgun from
     inside his house, opened the screen door, and shot
     the V (while he was still on sidewalk). V had
     alcohol level of .08.

     Offender=Black Male, 36; (Smith, John Henry);
     (80-17063); Charged with Murder II, use of firearm
     & possession of short barreled shotgun; pled to
     Murder II & possession of short barreled shotgun;
     Judge 07; Sentenced to two concurrent 5 year
     prison terms & not eligible for parole until 3
     years.

381   Victim=Black Male, 35; Sept 19, 1980; Tract=20.01; 2050; MPD;   V owned an auto repair shop and had bought some drugs but didn't pay. O kept asking for his money. On this date O asked for his money but V told him to get out (this was at the auto shop). O left but came back (with a gun) and crawled under a car (where V was working) and shot the V in the head as he was working on a car.

Offender=Unknown Black Male (Jamaican); Police only know his nickname

384   Victim=Black Male, 17; Sept 20, 1980; Tract=30.02; 1213; PSD;   V was involved in verbal argument with a B/F prostitute. V was advised by prostitute's pimp (the O) to leave or get shot. V pulled a gun from his pants and fired at the O, hitting O in the leg. O then shot and killed the V.

Offender=Black Male, 26; No charges filed; Justifiable homicide

385   Victim=Black Male, 56; Sept 20, 1980; Tract=34.00; 0515; MPD;   V and the O were both winos (V often slept in street or in back yard of houses). On this date O hit the V on head with liquor bottle after V hit O with a stick that had a nail in it. V then went "home" to back yard of a neighbor and told them that he had been hit on the head (he had laceration of head). V refused to go for treatment. The next morning V was found dead (from the laceration) on the steps to back door of witness' house. V had alcohol level of .05.

Offender=Black Male, 29; No charges filed; Justifiable homicide

386   Victim=Black Male, 57; Sept 20, 1980; Tract=15.02; 0615; PSD;   V left his house at 6:00 AM to buy gasoline to mow his yard. A neighbor saw V coming around the corner saying, "I've been stabbed." It appears that V may have been robbed as a number of such robberies had been occurring in early morning hours by juveniles in that area.

Offender=unknown

387   Victim=Black   Male,   26;   Sept.   18,   1980;
       Tract=23.00; 1215; MPD;   V accused his wife of
       having an affair with another B/M (the O) and took
       his wife over to the residence of the O to
       confront them together with this accusation. An
       argument ensued and O stabbed the V (the husband).
       V died 2 days later.

       Offender=Black Male, 25; (Brown, Ira); (80-17633);
       Charged with Murder II, agg. battery & unlawful
       possession of weapon; pled to Murder II, Judge 06;
       Sentenced to 10 years in prison to be followed by
       2 years of probation.

388   Victim=Black Male, 24; Sept 20, 1980; Tract=3.01;
       2345; PSD;   V was a Jamaican who was involved
       in drug trade. He had served as the middleman in
       a drug sale for 3 buyers from Los Angeles. The
       three buyers (2 B/M's and 1 B/F) sent the female
       with the V to the sale but she was robbed. The 2
       B/M's figured they had been set up by the V (he
       was   not   robbed) and decided to "take him for a
       ride." The female was sent back to the hotel and
       the two B/M's took the V out and shot him. The 3
       then flew back to L.A. State charged one B/M with
       felony murder (third degree) but has only the
       female O as a witness against him and she has been
       missing for eighteen months.   The O was also a
       Jamaican.

       Offender=Black Male,   31;   (Wright,   Winston);
       (81-23735); charged with third degree (felony)
       murder; Pending as of July 13, 1982.

389   Victim=Black Male, 39; Sept 19, 1980; Tract=83.01;
       1830; PSD;   Victim was harrassing the O in a
       verbal manner and threatening him. O told him to
       stop but when he didn't O picked up a wooden 2 by
       4 and beat V to death with it. Since V was a big
       guy and O was little and since V had threatened
       the O the prosecutor ruled that the case was one
       of self-defense (or at least non-prosecutable).

       Offender=Black Male,   45;   No   charges   filed;
       justifiable homicide

390 Victim=Black Male, 15; Sept 22, 1980; Tract=99.03; 1745; PSD;   V was in a discount store when security guard (the O) observed the V in act of shoplifting. The O grabbed the V, there was a struggle, and V ran out of the store with O in pursuit. O ordered V to stop & when V did not stop, O shot V in the back, killing the V. O was from Nigeria.

Offender=Black Male, 19; (Akpavie, Ogbedober); (80-17996); Charged with manslaughter; Judge O2; O is at large

391 Victim=Black Male, 17; Sept 23, 1980; Tract=19.01; 1215; MPD;   Victim and a friend were at a fast food chicken restaurant when two unknown B/M's pulled up in a vehicle. Driver (O) asked V for a cigarette (which V refused to give to O) and O pulled a gun and shot the V.

Offender=Black Male, 24; (Bannister, Keith); (80-19660); Charged with Murder I, attempted Murder I, & use of firearm; pled to Murder II, attempted Murder I and use of firearm; Judge 17; Sentenced to two concurrent life terms (ineligible for parole for 3 years).

392 Victim=Black Male, 26; Sept 23, 1980; Tract=4.03; 0620; PSD;   V was involved in a drug transaction. V and a friend got into a vehicle occupied by two other unknown B/M's. The V tested some cocaine & decided not to buy it. He and his friend exited the vehicle. Then the driver got into an argument with V and shot him. Prosecutor chose not to prosecute since the O claimed the V pulled a gun first and there were no witnesses to testify that this was not the case.

Offender=Black Male, 22; No charges filed; Justifiable homicide

393   Victim=Black Male, 55; Sept. 4, 1980; Tract=72.00;
1805; MPD;   V and another B/M (O) got involved
in a verbal altercation over a lawn mower. V
pulled his own gun and first hit the O with the
gun and then shot at the O. O then pulled his own
gun (which he said he carried for his own
protection since he had a physical handicap--he
was victim of polio) and shot and killed the V.

Offender=Black Male, 25; No charges filed;
justifiable homicide

401   Victim=Black Male, 53; Sept 19, 1980; Tract=17.01;
2130; PSD;   V was a drunk who usually hung out
in front of the grocery store where this homicide
occurred. In the parking area by the store there
was an altercation between the O and the 3 other
B/M's over a beer. The V approached the O and the
3 others walking with a table leg which he used as
a cane. The O took away the cane and hit the V
over the head with it (V and O did not know each
other previously). V had alcohol level of only
.02.

Offender=Black Male, 54; (Harper, Wm.);
(80-018251); Charged with Murder II; jury trial;
Judge 07; guilty of Murder II; Sentenced to 5
years in prison. Conviction overturned (Feb.,
1982) by appellate court due to inflammatory
comments to jury by prosecution. Prosecutor said,
"All he did was kill a wino and he is
sorry,....And so is the victim's wife and three
children. They are sorry too."

402   Victim=Black Male, 19; Sept 24, 1980; Tract=13.00;
2125; MPD;   V was robbing an Anglo Male, 66,
when the latter produced a revolver from his hip
pocket and shot and killed the V.

Offender=Anglo Male, 66; No charges filed;
justifiable homicide

406 Victim=Black Male, 33; Sept 25, 1980;   Tract=4.03;
     2115; PSD;   Victim was attempting to break into
     his wife's home (V had restraining order against
     his visiting or bothering his ex-wife). The
     ex-wife (O) shot the V.

     Offender=Black Female, 34; No charges filed;
     justifiable homicide

407 Victim=Black Male, 25; Sept 26, 1980;   Tract=4.08;
     2325; PSD;   V was having a drink in a bar when
     he was approached by an unknown B/M who shot V
     from behind. V was involved in the drug trade and
     police believe the O killed the V in some type of
     dispute involving drugs, probably involving
     Jamaicans.

     Offender=Unknown Black Male

410 Victim=Black Male, 57; Sept 27, 1980; Tract=19.02;
     1300; MPD;   V and his wife were involved in a
     verbal altercation (V had alcohol level of .28).
     The O claims that the V had threatened to throw
     boiling water on her. At one point the O got the
     V's fishing knife and stabbed the V several times
     (in stomach, back and chest).

     Offender=Black Female, 42; (Dell, Sally);
     (80-18418); Charged with Murder II; pled to
     manslaughter; Judge 05; Sentenced to 10 years of
     probation with condition that she spend 11 months
     in county jail & complete alcoholic rehab.
     program. O has 10 children.

428 Victim=Black Male, 45; Oct 11, 1980; Tract=17.02;
     1630; PSD;   O was from Tenn. had made friends
     with the V and his wife (they were neighbors).
     The V and O got involved in an argument (V had
     alcohol level of .32) and at one point V beat O
     with belt. O then got a kitchen knife and stabbed
     the V.

     Offender=Black Female, 40; (Rogers, Martha); Judge
     01; O was arrested but prosecutor dropped charges
     because it   was   believed   that   she   acted   in
     self-defense (or they could not prove otherwise).
     During initial investigation it was found that
     state's main witness had concealed evidence which
     showed   O had acted in self-defense after V
     attacked her with a belt buckle (this was evidence
     withheld). State decided O acted in self-defense
     and dropped charges.

429 Victim=Black Male, 1; Oct 12, 1980; Tract=83.03;
     1015; PSD;   Victim's father was told by his two
     other   children that their mother was killing the
     baby. At that time the father went into the
     bedroom and observed his wife standing over the V
     and stating that she had just killed the devil's
     son.   The   woman   was a Haitian and believed in a
     type of voodoo religion. O married at 16 and had
     three other children.

     Offender=Black Female, 21; (Parks, Patricia);
     (80-19634); Charged with Murder II; Prosecution
     pending since O has been judged to be incompetent
     to stand trial (she was first ruled incompetent,
     then competent, then incompetent again).

432 Victim=Black Male, 52; Oct 15, 1980; Tract=18.01;
     1915; PSD;   V was sitting at home when his
     common-law wife came home to get a pack of
     cigarettes. She (the O) is a security guard and
     was in uniform and armed. The V and the O became
     involved in a physical altercation. O claims that
     she was struck by the V and that she then pulled
     her gun and fired at him, killing him.

     Offender=Black Female, 42; (Price, Lilian);
     (80-22781); Charged with Murder II; Judge 20; Jury
     trial; not guilty.

434   Victim=Black Male, 25; Oct 17, 1980; Tract=95.02; 1920; PSD;   V and the O (an attendant at a gas station) became involved in physical altercation at a gas station over amount of money owed (46 cents). Attendant shot the V. V had alcohol level of .30.

Offender=Iranian Male, 25; (Firdaush, Irani K.); (80-20102); Charged with Murder II and use of firearm; jury trial; Judge O2; guilty of manslaughter and use of firearm; Sentenced to two concurrent 5 year prison terms.

435   Victim=Black Female, 20; Oct 18, 1980; Tract=13.00; MPD;   V was a prostitute who was found strangled to death (with electric cord from a lamp) at a "hooker's hotel." The O was a B/M who was a "john" and evidently, after a dispute, strangled her in the room. V had alcohol level of .09 and benzo in body.

Offender=Black Male, 20; (Green, James); (80-21461); Charged with Murder II; pled to manslaughter; Judge 22; Sentenced to 5 year prison term followed by 5 years probation.

440   Victim=Black Male, ??; ("John Doe"); Oct 13, 1980; Tract=14.00; 2240; MPD;   This V is a "John Doe" (identity unknown) who was confronted by 3 B/M's and was shot to death. The 3 fled on bicycles. The motive is unknown (may have been robbery attempt or result of some prior dispute) partly because the identity of the body is not known thus police cannot find out anything about past behvior, acquaintances, etc. V was found dead on the street.

Offender=Three Unknown Black Males

442   Victim=Black Male, 29; Oct 20, 1980;   Tract=15.01;
      2300; MPD;   V went to a residence to buy drugs.
      Later he went back and asked for his money back.
      V found gun in the house and went for it but O
      beat him to the draw and shot the V.

      Offender=Black Male, 22;   (Hall,   James   L.);
      (81-189); Charged with Murder II and use of
      firearm; Judge 17; Charges dismissed

445   Victim=Black Male, 58; Oct 24, 1980;   Tract=18.02;
      1400; MPD;   V was shot by his wife after he had
      grabbed her, taken her inside the house and
      started to beat her. She got a gun and shot him.

      Offender=Black Female, 38; No charges   filed;
      Justifiable homicide

446   Victim=Black Male, 28; Oct 24, 1980; Tract=108.00;
      1920; PSD;   V and the O went drinking together
      to S. Dade then returned to V's apt. complex. V
      accused O of stealing a gun of his and said he
      would kill O if he did not return the gun. V
      later came back with another gun in his hand and O
      ran to his apt. and got a gun. O was trying to
      avoid the V but V cornered him and shot at O (but
      gun misfired). O then shot back and killed the V.
      V had alcohol level of .07 plus benzo in body.

      Offender=Black Male, 25;   No   charges   filed;
      Justifiable homicide

447   Victim=Black Male, 20; Oct 24, 1980; Tract=90.01;
      2000; PSD;   V and the two offenders were all
      associates in armed robbery. On this date one O
      was angry about a gun he had bought from the V and
      the two O's took V to west Dade and shot him.

      Offender=Black Male, 18;   (Crompton,   Sidney);
      (80-20608); Charged with Murder I, kidnapping, use
      of   firearm and unlawful possession of short
      barreled shotgun; jury trial; Judge 18; guilty of
      Murder   II (at a second trial after earlier
      mistrial on this charge), false imprisonment, use
      of firearm and unlawful poss. (all at first
      trial); Sentenced to life and concurrent 25 and 5
      year prison terms (this O was the shooter).
      Offender=Black Male, 31; (Young, Ronald); Charged
      with Murder I, kidnapping; jury trial; Judge 18;
      not guilty of Murder II but guilty of false
      imprisonment;   Sentenced to 5 years probation
      (adjudication withheld) with special condition
      that O complete 500 hours of community service.
      Jury evidently felt this O was not guilty of
      felony murder since he was just at wrong place at
      wrong time. Second O was witness against first O
      at his second trial.

448   Victim=Black Male, 51; Oct 25, 1980; Tract=113.00;
      9999; PSD;   O was involved in an argument with
      another B/M (not the V) outside of a bar. The V
      was sitting nearby and approached the two and got
      involved in the argument (at this point the first
      B/M walked away). The V was pointing his finger
      at the O, O then punched the V and V fell to the
      pavement hitting his head on the rim of an auto
      tire.   This injury was complicated by an old
      injury and the V subsequently died. Also, the V
      had alcohol level of .13. Prosecutor considered
      this to be a case of excusable homicide.

      Offender=Black Male, 30;   No   charges   filed,
      excusable homicide

449   Victim=Black Male, 46; Oct 26, 1980; Tract=34.00;
1210; MPD; V and his girlfriend were involved
in an argument. The V began to beat the O during
the argument but eventually V decided to leave and
as he was leaving the O (girlfriend) stabbed him
in the back with a diving knife. V had alcohol
level of .10.

Offender=Black Female, 18; (McGill, Maggie);
(80-20677); Charged with Murder II; Judge 13;
Charges dismissed (the O was a juvenile, bound
over to adult court, charges dismissed). State
investigated and found that V went for knife but O
got it first. V then lunged at O and was impaled
with knife. Motion to dismiss granted.

452   Victim=Black Male, 31; Oct 25, 1980; Tract=4.03;
1800; PSD; V had been visiting his
ex-girlfriend when an argument broke out between V
and ex-girlfriend's brother. After this dispute
was quelled, V left the apt. But as the O left
the apt. the V reappeared and another argument
ensued. At one point O stabbed the V. Police
know the identity of the O but prosecutor says
there is insufficient evidence to charge.

Offender=Black Male, 33; identity known but
insufficient evidence

454   Victim=Black Male, 75; Oct 28, 1980; Tract=19.02;
1430; MPD; The victim was found shot to death
at his home. Nothing was stolen so it does not
appear to be a burglary or robbery.

Offender=Unknown

456 Victim=Black Male, 32; Nov 2, 1980; Tract=28.00;
1300; MPD;   V and another B/M were walking on
the sidewalk when they were confronted by a third
B/M (the O) who argued with the companion of the V
(these two had fought earlier in the day). The O
was shouting obscenities at the companion when he
pulled out a gun and began firing. The shots hit
the V rather than his companion and the V died.

Offender=Black   Male,   35;   (Gibson,   Esau);
(80-23362); Charged with Murder I and use of
firearm; Charges were dismissed

457 Victim=Black Male, 22; Nov 2, 1980; Tract=18.03;
0045; PSD;   The V was a Jamaican and was shot
to death in front of his residence. Police
believe that the V was killed in a war among
Rastafarians over the sale of drugs. Two
Rastafarians are suspects in the killing.

Offender=Unknown,   probably   two   Black   Males
(Jamaicans, Rastafarians)

458 Victim=Black Male, 28;
459 Victim=Black Male, 27; Nov 2, 1980; Tract=4.06;
2200; PSD;   The two victims and a third B/M
attempted to rob a drive-in food store. One
robber got out to buy some milk while a second
robber produced a gun and told the clerk it was a
robbery. The clerk pulled a gun, killed two of
the robbers and wounded the third. The surviving
robber was charged with felony murder in the death
of his two companions. The clerk was not charged.

Offender=Black   Male,   24;   (Anderson,   Randall);
(80-21292); Charged with Murder II & robbery;
Judge 10; Judge suppressed the confession and with
no other evidence (of 3rd robber's intent to
commit robbery) the state dropped the charges.

460   Victim=Black Male, 20; Nov 4, 1980; Tract=37.01;
       0600; MPD;   Two Anglo Males, both juveniles,
       picked up a B/M (which later turnd out to be a
       male in "drag") prostitute and "she" took them to
       an old hotel in a Black section of town.   After
       the two juveniles had paid for and received oral
       sex they returned to their car and found it had
       been vandalized. They then saw a B/M (the V)
       walking away with a radio that was taken from
       their car. One juvenile attempted to get his
       radio back but a group of Blacks approached and
       threatened him. The V and the juvenile got into
       struggle over the radio. The other juvenile (the
       O) got into the car and backed up rapidly to
       rescue hwas buddy who he felt is in danger from
       the V and the "mob." The car hit the V pinning him
       against a column & he was killed. The other
       juvenile jumped into the car and they fled. Two
       cars with Black occupants chased the juvenile's
       car but did not catch them. Police later found
       the car and arrested the driver (no charges were
       filed against the 2nd juvenile). The V had a long
       record of arrests for various offenses. Both
       juveniles were from wealthy families. Though the
       death was classified as a homicide by the Medical
       Examiner it is not considered to be a murder or
       manslaughter by the police or prosecutor.

       Offender=Anglo Male, 16; Charged in juvenile court
       with leaving the scene of an accident and failure
       to stop and render aid; Judge 32; O adjudicated as
       a delinquent and placed on probation with
       condition that he complete 40 hours of community
       service and driver's license be suspended.

461   Victim=Black Male, 36; Oct 27, 1980; Tract=68.00;
       1600; MPD   Victim was found floating in a 55
       gallon drum in Biscayne Bay. V had been chained
       and shot. Police believe V was killed in a
       dispute over drug trade and that he was killed by
       a Latin Male (who has since been killed by police)
       who had committed a number of other drug related
       murders in Dade.

       Offender=Latin Male; Offender now dead.

465 Victim=Black Male, 43; Nov 7, 1980; Tract=74.00;
2045; PSD;   V   and his two brothers were
involved in a game of checkers and had been
drinking for some time (V had alcohol level of
.12). An argument ensued and V ran from the
scene. His two brothers chased and caught him and
stabbed him to death.

Offender=Black Male, 47; (Sawyer, Hubert);
(80-21605); Charged with Murder I and agg.
battery; Judge 36; pled to manslaughter; Sentenced
to 2 years in prison.
Offender=Black Male, 42; (Sawyer, Charles);
Charged with Murder I and agg. battery; Judge 22;
Pled to Murder II; Sentenced to 10 years in
prison.

467 Victim=Black Male, 48; Nov 8, 1980; Tract=14.00;
0920; MPD;   V and his girlfriend had been
arguing at his apt. when the girlfriend (O) shot
the V. V had alcohol level of .38.

Offender=Black Female, 44; (Beaver, Cleo);
(80-21680); Charged with Murder II & use of
firearm; Judge 20; Judged to be incompetent to
stand trial, committed to DHRS, then ruled
competent; pled to Murder II; Sentenced to
probation with special condition that O serve one
year in county jail and complete alcoholic rehab.
program.

477 Victim=Black Male, 42; Nov 14, 1980; Tract=15.02;
1955; PSD;   V was shot while driving his
vehicle, lost control and crashed. Police could
not find out where shot came from and have no idea
as to motive or suspect. V had alcohol level of
.13 plus benzo in body.

Offender=Unknown

481   Victim=Black Male, 60; Nov 3, 1980; Tract=83.03; 2030; PSD;   V was drinking wine with 3 other B/M's and a B/F prostitute. All were arguing over various things. V was beaten to death by someone in the room but no one admits to seeing anything (all said they left before he was beaten). All 3 males had arrest record for murder and the female for agg. assault. The 3 males were all in 50-65 age range and the female was just under 30. V's alcohol level not tested since he didn't die until 10 days later.

Offender=Unknown Black (either one of 3 B/M's or a B/F)

482   Victim=Black Male, 24; Nov 15, 1980; Tract=83.03; 0325; PSD;   V got involved in altercation with his mother's boyfriend at V's residence. The boyfriend (0) then shot the V.

Offender=Black Male, 29; (Dorsey, Willie); (80-22103); Charged with Murder II & use of firearm; Judge 17; jury trial; not guilty. At trial 0 claimed V had attacked him first with garden hoe. Police did find V next to a hoe but Medical Examiner stated at trial V died from 2 gunshot wounds in back. Jury evidently felt it was self-defense. Judge dismissed the firearm charge.

484   Victim=Black Male, 35; Nov 15, 1980; Tract=104.00; 2000; PSD;   Victim became involved in an argument with the 0 (0 is V's wife's uncle) over an old debt. V was armed with two handguns and when 0 sees one gun he goes and gets his own gun and at gunpoint takes one gun from the V. Then the V went for his second gun and 0 shot V.

Offender=Black Male, 53; (Polite, Isiah); (80-22139); Charged with Murder II, use of firearm; jury trial; Judge 10; not guilty on both counts. Testimony at trial indicated 0 grabbed gun from V and tried to persuade him to leave. V went for another gun and 0 shot him. Jury evidently felt shooting was justifiable. One picture shown at trial showed V clutching a revolver.

488   Victim=Black Male, 73; Oct 5, 1980; Tract=17.02;
      9999; PSD;   The O and another B/M had an
      altercation during which the O cut the other B/M
      with a butcher knife. The V had been the person
      that called the police which resulted in O going
      to jail for a brief time. When O got out of jail
      he went to same apt. and found the other B/M and
      the V there. At that point the O said to the V,
      "you called the police but you won't do that
      anymore." O then picked up the V and threw him off
      a balcony 17 feet to the ground. The V died of
      these injuries and pneumonia which he developed in
      the hospital.

      Offender=Black Male, 30; (Davis, Robert E.);
      (80-22915); Charged with Murder II and agg.
      battery; Judge 37; jury trial; guilty on Murder II
      and agg. battery; Sentenced to 30 years in prison
      (15 for each count).

490   Victim=Black Male, 1; Nov 13, 1980; Tract=30.01;
      1430; MPD;   Victim was left with a baby sitter
      by his mother. Baby (V) was hit with blunt object
      and at first babysitter (a friend of V's mother)
      blamed a two-year old playmate. However, police
      believe now that babysitter did it. Also another
      child had been injured and died while in her care
      a few months earlier.

      Offender=Black Female, 28; Identity known but not
      enough evidence to charge

492 Victim=Black Male, 44; Nov 17, 1980; Tract=37.02;
     0245; MPD;   This V was killed due to mistaken
     identity and inability to understand Spanish.
     Earlier in the day a Latin Male (the O) had been
     in a fight with another B/M (not the V).   Later
     the O saw the V sitting in a downtown park and
     thought this was the B/M he had fought with
     earlier in the day.   O walked up to the V and
     pointed at his eye (which had been injured in the
     fight) and spoke in Spanish. The V shrugged to
     indicate he didn't understand (but which O
     probably interpreted as a lack of concern for the
     injury). The O then shot the V.

     Offender=Latin Male, 23;   (Velasquez, Jorge);
     (80-22849); Charged with Murder I, attempted
     Murder I, use of firearm, unlawful poss. of
     firearm by convicted felon; pled to Murder II,
     att. Murder I, use of firearm & unlawful poss. of
     firearm by felon; Judge 13; Sentenced to life in
     prison.

495 Victim=Black Male, 22; Nov 18, 1980; Tract=23.00;
     2030; MPD;   A neighbor heard someone saying,
     "Please don't shoot," and heard gunshots.   V was
     found shot in alleyway between the house & car.
     Police believe the killing resulted from a robbery
     attempt but are not sure of the motive and have no
     suspects.

     Offender=Unknown

499 Victim=Black Male, 25; Nov 24, 1980; Tract=10.02;
     2320; PSD;   V had broken into a residence and
     stabbed one of the occupants (who did not die).
     Police were next door investigating a previous
     break-in committed by the V when they heard the
     screams for help and ran next door and shot the V.

     Offender=Metro Police Officer; No charges filed;
     Justifiable homicide.

502   Victim=Black Male, 45; Nov 23, 1980; Tract=34.00;
1320; MPD;   V and a witness were standing on a
sidewalk when a vehicle occupied by a B/F and two
B/M's approached.   The two males in the car were
heard by the witness to say two or three times to
the female, "Is this the guy?" The two males then
attempted (at gunpoint) to force the V (who had
been identified by the female) into their car.
When the V refused he was shot to death.   Police
believe this may have been a case of mistaken
identity.

Offender=Two Unknown Black Males

504   Victim=Black Male, 35;
573   Victim=Black Female, approximately 25;   ("Jane
Doe');   Nov.   12,   1980;   Tract=114.00; 9999;
PSD;   V found shot to death on a roadway in far
south Dade.   The two V's came to Miami from
Detroit to buy heroin. The sellers, 2 L/M's and
L/F decided to rip-off the V's for the $29,000
they had with them instead of making the sale.
O's handcuffed the 2 V's and took them to far
southeast Dade.   Male V taken from car (left
female V with female O in car) and killed him.
They came back & debated whether they should kill
the female (while she begged for her life).   The
female O gave order For her to be killed and so
she was killed. Later the wife of one of the O's
came forward (after numerous beatings by her
husband) and told whole story to police (she was
with the O's when killings took place). She is
now in protective custody.

Offender=Latin   Male,   29;   (Cuevas,   Carlos);
(82-15219); Charged with Murder I (2 counts) and
robbery; Judge 37; Pending.
Offender=Latin   Male,   45;   (Navarro, Emilio);
Charged with Murder I (2 counts) and robbery;
Judge 37; Pending.
Offender=Latin Female, 26; (Cuevas, Sonia); O
(sister of other O) is at large

506   Victim=Black Male, 28; Nov 24, 1980;   Tract=23.00;
      1154;   MPD;   V was last seen on his way to eat
      at a local restaurant. Apparently as he returned
      towards his place of work, he went into an open
      field and was shot. V had alcohol level of .13.
      Police have no idea as to motive or suspects.

      Offender=Unknown

511   Victim=Black Male, 17; Nov 27, 1980;   Tract=27.01;
      0208;   MPD;   V was an armed robber and he and
      another robber/friend followed two homosexuals,
      also Black Males, and tried to rob them with a
      gun.   One of the two intended v's had a knife and
      stabbed the V (robber). The identity of the two
      intended robbery victims (one being the O) is not
      known but police believe that the homicide would
      be listed as a justifiable if they could talk with
      the O.

      Offender=Unknown   Black   Male   but   probably
      justifible

513   Victim=Black Male, 16; Nov 27, 1980;   Tract=14.00;
      2100; MPD;   The V and a friend were standing in
      front of a residence when an old Cuban man walked
      by and V made an obscene comment to him. The V &
      his friend then tried to rob the old man but in
      this attempt a struggle ensued and the old man
      shot and killed the V. This case would probably
      be listed as justifiable if the O could be found
      and interviewed.

      Offender=Unknown Latin Male, approximately 60.

516 Victim=Black Female, 13; Nov 28, 1980; Tract=83.03; 1500; PSD; V was alone at home when someone tried to break into her home. She called 911 and reported the attempted break-in in progress but the operator thought the call was a juvenile disturbance and a non-emergency and thus police did not come for almost an hour. By that time the intruder had broken in, sexually assaulted the young girl and killed (strangled and stabbed) her. The intruder/killer was a juvenile who lived in the neighborhood.

Offender=Black Male, 17; (Mainor, Gerard); (80-23965); Charged with Murder I, sexual battery, buglary; jury trial; Judge 01; guilty of Murder I, sexual battery & burglary; Sentenced to life for Murder I, life for the burglary and 15 years for the sexual assault, all to run consecutively.

517 Victim=Black Male, 20; Nov 29, 1980; Tract=44.00; 1935; MPD; V was involved in a domino game with the offenders when an argument ensued, then a fight, then a second fight. At this point the O's stabbed the V. V and both O's are Haitians (Black Males).

Offender=Black Male, 43; (Smith, Jimmy); (80-23393); Charged with Murder II, Judge 02; Charges dismissed
Offender=Black Male, 28; (Destilien, Destine); Charged with Murder II, Judge 02; Charges dismissed. No witnesses actually saw crime so charges dismissed.

518   Victim=Black   Female,   33;   Nov   29,   1980;
Tract=14.00; 1700; MPD;   V and the O were both
married (to others) but were lovers. On this date
the V and the O were in an argument when a
struggle ensued and the V cut the O with a knife.
Then both calmed down and agreed to leave.   They
separated and both went to their cars. But then
the O used his car to block the path of V's car
and (with   a   gun   he took from his glove
compartment) then shot into the car wounding the
V. The V then got out of her car and attempted to
grab O's gun but he threw her to ground and then
straddled her and shot her twice more as she lay
on ground.   O then kicked her in face several
times.

Offender=Black Male, 47; (Symonnete, Jonathan);
(80-23122); Charged with Murder II; O first ruled
incompetent and spent 4 months in mental hospital
but then ruled competent; Judge 17; pled to
manslaughter; Sentenced to 10 years on probation
and   adjudication withheld.   State believed V
partially responsible as she attacked O first; O
had no prior record; O was mentally unstable; O
had already been in jail 3 months awaiting trial.

519   Victim=Black   Female,   44;   Oct   25,   1980;
Tract=15.02; 2000; PSD;   The V and the O (her
common-law husband) had lived together for 3
years. V had been charged 6 days before with agg.
battery on the O for assaulting him with knife.
On this date both had been drinking all day and V
began to accuse the O of having an affair with
another woman. The O stabbed the V with a knife
in the neck.   V was taken to hospital where she
died 6 days later due to complications arising
from other medical problems which V had (history
of seizures).

Offender=Black Male, 43; (Frazier, John Wesley);
(80-21117); Charged with Murder II; Judge 01;
Charges dismissed

305

520   Victim=Black   Female,   26;   Nov   30,   1980;
      Tract=17.02;   9999;   PSD;   V   was found shot to
      death   inside   a   garbage   dumpster   by   a   person
      dumping   trash.   The   V   is   known   to   have been
      associating with people who   were   into   the   drug
      trade   but   it   is   not known if she was involved.
      Police believe this killing was drug   related   due
      to   pattern   of   killing (multiple shots and being
      dumped) and fact that   cocaine   and   "ludes"   were
      found in V's body.

      Offender=Unknown

526   Victim=Black   Female,   24;   Dec.   2,   1980;
      Tract=36.01;   1310;   MPD;   V was living with one
      boyfriend (the   father   of   her   child)   and   also
      frequently   visiting   (for sex and drugs) a second
      boyfriend.   She   was   found   dead   in   second
      boyfriend's   apt.   Police gave polygraph exams to
      both boyfriends and both   passed   thus   they   were
      unable   to charge anyone.   Police think one of the
      two boyfriends committed the murder.

      Offender=Unknown, probably one of two Black Males

527   Victim=Black   Female,   65;   Dec 1   or   2,   1980;
      Tract=10.01;   9999;   PSD;   V   was found shot to
      death in her home.   Police believe she was   killed
      by   an   old   boyfriend who would periodially visit
      her to shake her down.   They evidently got into   a
      dispute and he shot her.

      Offender=Black Male, 33; identity   known   but   not
      enough evidence to charge

530   Victim=Black Female, 19; Dec 4, 1980; Tract=55.02;
      2150;   MPD;   V and the O were   lovers   and   were
      involved   in   a domestic argument at a motel.   The
      boyfriend shot and killed the V and then shot   and
      killed himself (suicide).   V had 4 different drugs
      in her body.

      Offender=Black   Male,   44;   (Bowen,   Carlton);   No
      charges filed, O committed suicide.

532 Victim=Black Male, 29; Dec 6, 1980; Tract=71.00;
     0310; MPD;   V and another B/M attempted to rob
     three A/M juveniles as they were entering a movie
     theatre.   One of the Anglo juveniles pulled out a
     knife and stabbed the victim/robber in the back.
     The two robbers then fled and the juveniles filed
     a robbery report with the police. Police later
     found the victim/robber dead near the theatre
     where he had collapsed. V had alcohol level of
     .17.   V was escapee from a state prison where he
     was serving 25 years for robbery.

     Offender=Anglo Male, 17; No charges filed;
     Justifiable homicide

533 Victim=Black Male, 17; Dec 6, 1980; Tract=18.03;
     1615; PSD;   V and O had argued earlier on the
     same day as the fatal incident. Later that day, V
     left a pool room and got into another argument
     with the O. At some point the O stabbed the V. V
     had alcohol level of .08.

     Offender=Black   Male,   20;   (Adell,   Walter);
     (80-23851); Charged with Murder II; Judge 02; O
     was on probation for robbery and in the probation
     violation hearing the court found that O had
     stabbed the V in a justifiable homicide and thus
     the prosecutor had failed to satisfy the
     conscience of the court that O had violated his
     probation. The charges against the O were dropped
     (for prosecution of a new crime) at this time.

534 Victim=Black Male, 48; Dec 7, 1980; Tract=34.00;
     0335; MPD;   The V and the O (both had extensive
     prior criminal records) were in an argument at a
     bar when the O said something offensive to the V
     and his girlfriend. V then threw the O out of the
     bar.   O waited outside the bar until V and his
     girlfriend left and "ambushed" them about 3 blocks
     from the bar. O shot the V. V had alcohol level
     of .12.

     Offender=Black   Male,   36;   (Nixon,   Edward);
     (80-23967); Charged with Murder I and use of
     firearm; pled to Murder II and use of firearm;
     Judge 10; Sentenced to 9 years in prison with 3
     year mandatory for firearm.

307

536 Victim=Black Male, 27; Dec 6, 1980; Tract=4.03;
     9999; PSD;   V and the O's (two brothers) were
     members of a band. The V and another B/M went to
     pick up their band members and upon arrival the V
     and members of the band began to argue. Two of
     the members (the O's) entered their residence and
     returned with knives. The O's then stabbed the V,
     who was in the van at this time. They then
     dragged him out of the van and continued to stab
     him.

     Offender=Black Male, 25; (Streeter, Murrell Lee);
     (80-23702); Charged with Murder II, attempted
     Murder II, unlawful poss. of weapon; Jury trial;
     Judge 05; guilty of Murder III, unlawful poss. of
     weapon; Sentenced to 30 years in prison (and terms
     of 15, 5 and 5, all to run concurrently with 30
     year term).

     Offender=Black Male, 21; (Streeter, Alexander);
     charged with attempted Murder II, use of firearm;
     pled to attempted Murder II, use of firearm; Judge
     05; Sentenced to 10 years & 5 years concurrently.

537 Victim=Black Male, 40; Nov 16, 1980; Tract=15.02;
     1830; PSD;   V and O were acquaintances.
     Earlier that evening the V had slapped the O's
     girlfriend and O went to confront V about this
     incident. V pulled a knife but the O took the
     knife from him and stabbed him with his own knife.
     V died 3 weeks later.

     Offender=Black Male, 41; No charges filed;
     Justifiable homicide.

538   Victim=Black   Female,   47;   Dec   12,   1980;
Tract=105.00;   0900;   PSD;   0   went   to   the
residence of his ex-wife (V) to talk her into
moving back in with him. He went to her bedroom
to talk with her and during this argument pulled
out a revolver (which he carried in a shoulder
holster) and shot and killed her. 0 then called
911 for police to respond and turned himself in.

Offender=Black   Male,   27;   (Bennett,   Owen);
(80-24228); Charged with Murder I and use of
firearm; jury trial; Judge 08; guilty of Murder II
and use of firearm; Sentenced to life in prison
(suspended entry of firearm sentence).

539   Victim=Black Male, 27; Dec. 12, 1980; Tract=20.02;
1235; MPD;   V and another Black (Haitian) Male
were walking when approached by four B/M's who
asked them for money (a robbery). The V and his
companion did not understand English so they
backed off. Two of the B/M's then pulled guns and
started shooting. The V was killed.

Offender=Two Unknown Black Males

545   Victim=Black Male, 21; Dec. 1, 1980; Tract=14.00;
1900; MPD;   V was found lying on the couch of
his apt. with a gunshot wound to his head. There
were no signs of forced entry or damage in the
apt. Police have no idea as to motive or suspect.

Offender=Unknown

546   Victim=Black Male, 76; Dec 15, 1980; Tract=14.00;
1350; MPD;   V was sitting on a chair near his
apt. when a young B/M approached and asked the V
for money. When the V said that he had no money
the 0 stabbed the V.

Offender=Unknown Black Male juvenile

550   Victim=Black Male, 38; Dec. 16, 1980; Tract=72.00;
      1435; MPD;   V and two B/M's were standing in a
      parking lot by a bar. An argument ensued and one
      B/M handed the other a revolver.   The other B/M
      then shot the V.   Police believe the argument was
      over drugs.

      Offender=Black   Male,   18;   (Higgs,   Anthony);
      (80-24646); Charged with Murder II and use of
      firearm; Judge 19; Charges dismissed. Case based
      on statement of O and one witness. W then changed
      her testimony (probably after threats by O) and
      claimed police made her testify falsely.   Only
      other evidence was the statement of O but it was
      inconsistent with medical examiner's testimony.

553   Victim=Black Male, 23; Dec 19, 1980; Tract=4.06;
      1300; PSD;   V was shot to death while a clerk
      at a convenience store in an armed robbery. The O
      confessed (O was driver) and implicated two other
      B/M's, the lookout and the triggerman.   The
      robbery netted $150.

      Offender=Black   Male,   22;   (Foust,   Lazell);
      (81-9536); Charged with Murder I and robbery;
      Judge 36; Pending.
      Offender=Black Male, 24; (Hampton, Rufus); Charged
      with Murder I and robbery; Judge 36; Pending.
      Offender=Black Male, 26; (White, Wendall); Charged
      with Murder I and robbery; Judge 36; Pending.

554   Victim=Black Male, 23; Dec 19, 1980; Tract=4.03;
      1642; PSD;   V and the O were acquaintances and
      became involved in an altercation in the street.
      V pulled a gun but in a struggle O took gun from
      the V and shot him to death. O then fled.

      Offender=Black   Male,   36;   No   charges   filed;
      Justifiable homicide.

560   Victim=Black Male, 43; Dec 23, 1980;   Tract=19.02;
      0355;   MPD;   V and a L/F were living together
      and he (the V) had a history of beating her.   On
      this occasion he started to beat her again and she
      got a gun and shot him. V had alcohol level of
      .10.

      Offender=Latin Female, 31; No Charges filed;
      Justifiable homicide

561   Victim=Black Male, 19; Dec 25, 1980;   Tract=19.02;
      0010; MPD;   V was standing on a sidewalk when a
      car pulled alongside him and occupant(s) began
      firing at him, killing him. The V was known to
      have frequently robbed people, especially drug
      dealers (and even friends), and often said that he
      expected to be killed. The occupants of the car
      are thought to be two Black Males.

      Offender=Two Unknown Black Males

571   Victim=Black Female, 32; Sept 29-Oct 2, 1980;
      Tract=100.01; 9999; PSD;   V was found shot to
      death in her home (had alcohol level of .18).
      Police suspect her boyfriend (a B/M pimp, 37)
      killed her. The V and O lived together and O
      often free-based cocaine and when on drugs became
      paranoid and often "freaked out." He believed
      police had a "bug" in their apt. and appears to
      have ransacked the house looking for the bug
      (while stoned) and got into argument with V over
      this "search." He probably shot her during this
      argument.

      Offender=Black Male, 37; (Cobbs, Jimmy); identity
      known but not enough evidence to charge.

002   Victim=Latin Female, 46; Jan 1, 1980; Tract=17.03; 0100; PSD;   The V became involved in a domestic argument with her boyfriend. He stabbed her and then tried to commit suicide (but suffered only superficial knife wounds). Neighbor found the V expired in bed next to her boyfriend.

Offender=Latin Male, 54; (Garay, Guillermo); (80-55); Charged with Murder II, prosecution pending since offender found incompetent to stand trial; Judge 01

006   Victim=Latin Male, 38;
007   Victim=Latin Male, 33;
008   Victim=Latin Male, 29; Jan 8, 1980; Tract=????; 0200; PSD;   A passerby enroute to work saw car on I-95 parked and on fire. Witness stopped and extinguished fire. Closer investigation revealed four dead bodies (see case no. 005 in Anglo list for 4th victim) and all were wrapped in blankets. Two were in the trunk, one in rear seat and one in front seat. Police report that the quadruple murder involved a drug rip-off. The four were stabbed and beaten at a residence and taken to this location. Three Anglo males were arrested and charged with Murder I; kidnapping and robbery.

Offender=see information on three offenders at case no. 005 in Anglo list

011   Victim=Latin Male, 27; Jan 12, 1980; Tract=63.02; 0300; MPD;   V set up drug deal between group of 5 or 6 Blacks. The Blacks took the money and fled, then the Latins shot the V in anger after the rip-off and then took V to hospital where he died.

Offender=Latin Male, 45; not enough evidence to charge

013   Victim=Latin Male, 62; Jan 14, 1980; Tract=36.02;
0400; MPD;   V had stabbed a girl, the O chased
him and caught him in parking lot and shot him. V
had alcohol level of .21.

Offender=Latin Male, 42; (Rodriguez, Nemesio M.);
(80-1217);   Charged with Murder II; pled to
manslaughter; Judge 07; Sentenced to 3 years

015   Victim=Latin Male, 28; Jan 17, 1980; Tract=24.00;
1800; MPD;   V had entered a drug store with
intent to rob. He had a screw driver wrapped in a
sweater. During the attempted robbery, the store
owner shot the victim/robber in chest with a
revolver.

Offender=Latin Male, 40;   No   charges   filed;
Justifiable homicide

019   Victim=Latin Female, 20;
020   Victim=Latin Male, 40; Jan 20, 1980; Tract=4.06;
1330; PSD   A neighbor heard 5-6 muffled shots
coming from inside of the residence of the male
victim and then saw two Latin Males run from the
house. The V's were then discovered dead inside
the house. Both V's were Columbian aliens,
arriving in 1979. Murder was probably drug
related as evidence found suggesting that the
female victim was working for male V in
transporting drugs from Miami to NY.

Offender=Two Unknown Latin Males

021   Victim=Latin Male, 23; Jan 21, 1980; Tract=66.00;
2350; MPD;   V became involved in argument with
an acquaintance over a girlfriend. He was later
found shot lying on the sidewalk shortly after
leaving a bar.

Offender=Latin Male, 25; (Vargas, Frank); offender
known but at large

314

026 Victim=Latin Male, 30; Jan 25, 1980; Tract=27.01;
    0710; MPD;   V was Columbian and was at home in
    bed when a Columbian male (the O) knocked at the
    door. V and guest (O) got into argument and V
    told O to leave. O pulled a gun and shot the V.
    The dispute appears to have been drug related.

    Offender=Latin Male, 38; (Ruiz, Wilton); offender
    known but at large

029 Victim=Latin Male, 20; Jan 26, 1980; Tract=34.00;
    0930; MPD;   V was Venezuelean. With other
    Venzueleans V went to Black area to buy drugs and
    contacted Black street dealers. During the buy
    the driver became afraid and so pulled out a bee
    bee gun to scare the sellers. One of the Black
    dealers pulled out a real gun and shot the V who
    was a passenger in the car. The other people in
    the car (the Venezueleans) went back to Venezuela
    and thus there is not enough evidence without them
    to identify/charge any of the drug dealers.

    Offender=Three unknown Black Males, probably
    juveniles

030 Victim=Latin Male, 22; Jan 27, 1980; Tract=24.00;
    1435; MPD;   V and the O were neighbors. V had
    a fight with his neighbor during which he struck
    the O with a concrete block on the arm. V then
    went to O's house to apologize but O asked him to
    leave.   V then pushed open the screen door and O
    went and got his shotgun and told V not to come
    any closer or he would shoot him. V moved toward
    O who was in kitchen. O fired one shot striking
    the V in the head.

    Offender=Latin Male, 62; No charges filed against
    the O as homicide was considered justifiable.

031   Victim=Latin Male, 56; Jan 27, 1980; Tract=24.00;
       2315; MPD;   V had been playing pool at a bar
       and left the bar. 20 minutes later barmaid found
       him lying dead on the ground (on sidewalk). No
       witnesses to the shooting but there had been an
       argument earlier in the bar with a Latin Male over
       a $5 bet on a pool game.

       Offender=Unknown, probably a Latin Male

033   Victim=Latin Male, 53; Feb. 1, 1980; Tract=24.00;
       1300; MPD;   V was last seen alive at a bar
       about 8:00 PM. He left bar heavily intoxicated
       (alcohol level of .37). The next morning he was
       found dead (strangled) in rear yard of abandoned
       rooming house.   V was an alcoholic and lived on
       the streets. The V had been seen the night before
       with a Puerto Rican Male, a drinking buddy, and he
       is suspect.

       Offender=Unknown, perhaps the Puerto Rican male

036   Victim=Latin Male, 28; Feb 1 or 2, 1980;
       Tract=82.04; 9999; PSD;   V (a Columbian) ripped
       off the O's (two L/M's) in a drug deal for two
       kilos of cocaine. Offenders chased V and shot
       him.

       Offender=Two Latin Males; offenders known but not
       enough evidence to charge

042   Victim=Latin Male, 45; Feb 6, 1980; Tract=22.02;
       0500; MPD;   V was a drug dealer (with extensive
       arrest record). He was evidently killed in a
       dispute over drugs. He was found dead on side of
       a roadway and had been shot nearby and dumped
       there.

       Offender=Unknown

044 Victim=Latin Male, 19; Feb 8, 1980; Tract=115.00;
     2215; PSD;   V and the O (a Latin Male) had been
     in a continuing argument for a month over a debt.
     Three days before the V threatened the O with a
     handgun and was arrested for agg. assault. On
     this occasion the V was outside the O's trailor
     and threatened to burn it down (he also had a
     gun). The O turned out the lights in the trailor,
     got his rifle and shot the V thru the window. V
     was found expired, clutching a semi-automtic
     handgun.

     Offender=Latin Male, 26; No charges filed;
     Justifiable homicide

045 Victim=Latin Female, 37;
055 Victim=Latin Female, 47; Feb 9, 1980; Tract=53.02;
     1630; MPD;   The O, a 23 year old Latin Male,
     was in love with the 37 year old Latin Female but
     she considered him a nuisance. O often came into
     the restaurant where she was a waitress. On this
     occasion the O's "girlfriend" and a female friend
     (the second victim) were coming out of her apt.
     when the O approached them and shot them both
     (without saying a word). O emptied the 5 shot
     revolver and put one additional bullet in the gun
     and then shot himself in the head. The
     "girlfriend" died that day while her friend was on
     the critical list for 10 days and then died.

     Offender=Latin Male, 23; (Delgado, Miguel); No
     charges, O committed suicide

046 Victim=Latin Male, 49; Feb 10, 1980; Tract=65.00;
     2025; MPD;   V apparently killed by his wife
     during a domestic argument/fight. V was bitten,
     stabbed and shot.

     Offender=Latin Female, 45; (Rosell,); No charges
     filed, not enough evidence

047   Victim=Latin Male, 39; Feb 12, 1980;   Tract=53.02;
       0225;   MPD;   V   had   reputation   for   being
       argumentative and had a   long   arrest   record   for
       robbery/mugging (he was released from prison a
       week before). V was found by a cab   driver   lying
       in   the   doorway   of   a   bar with multiple gunshot
       wounds. The bar was closed (it was 2:00 AM) but
       beer   and other drinks were on the bar (appears it
       was closed after the shooting). No one admits to
       seeing anything though appears several patrons
       were present at the time of the killing.   Probably
       a bar argument.

       Offender=Unknown, probably a Latin Male present in
       the bar

051   Victim=Latin Male, 19; Feb 14, 1980;   Tract=70.01;
       1510;   MPD;   V was shot during an argument over
       a parking space. V was visiting his parents when
       argument   broke   out   over a parking space between
       two Latin Males and the V and his family.   One   of
       the two O's produced a revolver and threatened the
       family.   The   other   O began yelling, "Shoot him,
       shoot him," and then put his hand on the gun   the
       other O was holding. The gun discharged striking
       the V. The V's brother was also wounded by the O
       holding   the   gun   and   that O also fired at V's
       mother but missed.

       Offender=Latin   Male,   54;   (Dominicis,   Carlos);
       (80-2507); Charged with attempted Murder II and
       use of firearm; jury trial; Judge 07; not guilty;
       (this O was not the shooter). Jury evidently felt
       that   there was no culpable negligence on this O's
       part   since   he   "only"   yelled   "shoot him" and
       grabbed the gun.
       Offender=Latin Male, 49; (Tauler, Mario); Charged
       with   attempted Murder II and use of firearm; jury
       trial; Judge 07; guilty of manslaughter, agg.
       assault and use of firearm; Sentenced to 20 years
       in   prison (15 for manslaughter with 5 more
       consecutive years for assault). This O was the
       shooter.

056   Victim=Latin Male, 39; Feb 20, 1980; Tract=113.00; 0300; PSD;   V had arrived in Miami the day before from Immokolee, Fl, and apparently registered in a transit house in Homestead. The bldg. was set on fire and all escaped the fire but the V. Fire was evidently set by a Latin Male who had recently been evicted from the house and was angry about the eviction. This is case of felony murder.

Offender=Latin Male, 24; (Lopez, Juan Manuel); Offender is known but at large

063   Victim=Latin Male, 64; Feb 23, 1980; Tract=7.01; 1430; HPD;   V was stabbed by his son-in-law when the latter went to the home of the V and his (the O's) estranged wife to wait for her. After the wife arrived she was also stabbed (as was the mother-in-law). The O then attempted suicide. All these events took place in front of the O's two young daughters.

Offender=Latin Male, 47; (Martinez, Roberto); (80-3051); Charged with Murder II, attempted Murder I and attempted Murder II; Jury trial; Judge 24; guilty on all counts; Sentenced to life in prison.

064 Victim=Latin Male, 26; Feb. 24, 1980; Tract=51.00;
     0530; MPD;   V was innocent bystander who was
     killed in a shoot-out in a dispute over drugs
     between two gangs. The V had earlier danced with
     a girl who was associated with a member of one
     gang so the members of the other gang (all
     Columbians) thought he was a member of the other
     gang and V shot in shootings that followed.

     Offender=Latin (Columbian) Male, 39; (Losado,
     Luis);
     Offender=Latin (Columbian) Male, 23; (Israel,
     Rafael);
     Offender=Latin (Columbian) Male, 30; (Maldonaldo,
     Camelo);
     Offender=Latin (Columbian) Male, 19; (Rondon,
     Camelo); (80-30578); All four charged with Murder
     II and use of firearm but charges against all were
     dismissed by Judge 13 since the prosecution could
     not tie guns to specific shooters and witnesses
     afraid to testify. The police got a description
     of van used by gunmen and spotted a similar van
     and chased it. Firearms were thrown out of the
     van from window during the chase. However, the
     only Witness denied any of the occupants were the
     shooters;   no fingerprints on guns matched
     occupants; ballistics came up with "maybe" on one
     gun; no eyewitnesses.

066 Victim=Latin Male, 19; Feb 25, 1980; Tract=53.01;
     2030; MPD;   V was involved in a argument over a
     tape deck with several other L/M's, several shots
     were fired by unknown offenders. The V was struck
     once in the chest.

     Offender=Two Unknown Latin Males

068 Victim=Latin Male, 25; Feb 29, 1980; Tract=89.02;
     0015; PSD;   V was Columbian who was involved in
     drug trade. V and a female were leaving a shopping
     center cafeteria when they were shot by unknown
     persons in the parking lot. It is unknown whether
     the O's were also Columbians but police believe
     the killing was drug related.

     Offender=Unknown

073 Victim=Latin Female, 37; Mar 3, 1980; Tract=90.02;
    1700; PSD;   V worked at a shopping mall and
    found dead in her car in the parking lot of the
    mall by her mother who was concerned that she had
    not returned home. V shot with a revolver with a
    silencer (4 or 5 shots). Apparently she was
    running from someone, jumped into the car and was
    shot while trying to flee. Motive and offender
    unknown though police believe it may have been a
    domestic in that she was going thru a divorce and
    there was a lot of bad feelings.

    Offender=Unknown

074 Victim=Latin Male, 48; Mar 4, 1980; Tract=27.01;
    2100; MPD;   V was a drug dealer. He was ripped
    off for drugs and money. It is likely that he was
    killed by at least two L/M's but only one charged
    since his fingerprints found at scene.

    Offender=Latin Male, 29; (Pedrera, Jorge);
    (80-5405); Charged with Murder I, burglary,
    robbery, grand theft, escape, kidnapping, agg.
    battery, & use of firearm; jury trial; Judge 01;
    guilty of Murder II; Sentenced to life in prison.

079 Victim=Latin Male, 50; Mar 10, 1980; Tract=85.01;
    1350; PSD;   V and his wife had been having
    domestic problems for some time. On this date the
    V returned home after being away for two days and
    an argument began (probably over another woman).
    At one point wife went to bedroom and returned
    with a handgun and shot the V several times.

    Offender=Latin Female, 45; (Leal, Haydee);
    (80-3986); Charged with Murder II, use of firearm;
    0 pled to manslaughter; Judge 04; Sentenced to 5
    years probation with special condition she serve 1
    year in county jail with work furlough recommended
    (adjudication withheld). Sentence later modified
    to allow 0 to serve her 1 year during daytime and
    she was released to go home each night (there was
    no one else to care for her children).

082   Victim=Latin Male, 48; Mar 12, 1980; Tract=115.00;
       9999; PSD;   V arrived in May of 1979 from Cuba
       where he was political prisoner for 12 years
       (released a few months before immigrating). V's
       body found by farm worker in advanced stage of
       decomposition. Two shotgun shells found nearby.
       V's pants were pulled down to thigh. Motive and O
       unknown.

       Offender=Unknown

084   Victim=Latin Male, 22; Mar 15, 1980;   Tract=13.00;
       0613;   MPD;   V was in federal prison (for
       conspiracy to sell drugs, cocaine) for 3 years and
       living in a halfway house in NY while working.
       After work one day he few to Miami, left his
       things in airport locker. V found dead on the
       street in Miami. He may have been in town to
       collect a debt or to sell drugs. Probably drug
       related.

       Offender=Unknown

089   Victim=Latin Male, 44; Mar 17, 1980;   Tract=55.02;
       2220;   MPD;   V was co-owner of a bar and was
       tending bar. Two L/M's and a L/F were siting
       nearby. The V's wife was a former girlfriend of
       one of the L/M's (the O). The O demanded a drink
       from the bartender (the V). V refused to serve
       the O. O took out a gun and shot the V once
       between the eyes while saying, "Yes, you will."
       The two males and the female then fled.

       Offender=Latin Male, 49;   (Garcia,   Napoleon);
       (80-4571); Charged with Murder II and use of
       firearm; Jury trial; Judge 10; guilty on both
       counts and sentenced to 30 years in prison.

103 Victim=Latin Male, 41; Mar 28, 1980; Tract=77.02;
     1655; PSD;   The V was a Columbian who had
     arrived in Florida only one week before. V was
     involved in drug traffic and was killed (shot) in
     a dispute over selling of drugs. O was caught
     before he could take the drugs and money (which he
     stole in this killing/robbery) and flee. O was
     tied to the crime partly by teeth marks on the
     body (V was killed in brutal fashion).

     Offender=Latin Male, 44; (Arranga, Carlos);
     (80-5372); Charged with Murder I, use of firearm;
     jury trial; Judge 35; guilty of murder I, use of
     firearm; Sentenced to death penalty.

106 Victim=Latin Female, 21; Mar 31, 1980 (found);
     Tract=115.00; 9999; PSD;   V was member (or
     associated with) motorcycle gang in Broward
     County. She was found dead in a canal with her
     head and both feet cut off (she was identified by
     a tatoo on one hand). Earlier she had been a
     witness to a homicide in Broward (related to
     motorcycle gang). Two males were arrested and
     "taking the rap" for a third. It is thought that
     the third male killed her to eliminate her as a
     witness (afraid she might implicate him). Her
     testimony was only way he could be tied to the
     case.

     Offender=One or more members of the motorcycle
     gang; not enough evidence to charge

107 Victim=Latin Male, 25; Ap 1, 1980 (found);
     Tract=101.03; 9999; PSD;   V found dead under
     300 lbs. of coral rock and foliage along a dirt
     road next to a lake. V's car found in
     Jacksonville where 4 persons arrested. One of the
     four was charged with this murder (and suspected
     in 2 other murders). Appears that the V and O had
     been involved in a drug deal. V called O and said
     he had one gram of TCP he would sell for $90. O
     was not willing to pay this price (he suggested
     $75) and so told another he would rip-off the V
     (he also later told others he killed the V).

     Offender=Latin Male, 21; (Hoyas, Alex);
     (80-10216); at large for several months, now
     arrested; Pending as of July 13, 1982.

108   Victim=Latin Male, 42; Ap 1, 1980; Tract=101.01;
1600; PSD;   V and the offenders were involved
in selling drugs. On this date V found in bedroom
with his pocket turned out and a broken knife in
his chest (he was also handcuffed). He had also
been shot. $2,000 was found in a bureau drawer
and 3 bales of marijuana were in the house.
Appears to have been some dispute over drugs.

Offender=Two Unknown Latin Males

109   Victim=Latin Female, 43; Ap 5, 1980; Tract=22.01;
1156;   MPD;   V was from Nicaragua and was
involved with her husband in ongoing domestic
dispute.   Husband felt that the wife showed more
attention to the kids than to him. He got a
revolver and shot his wife twice (he also fired at
and struck his son).

Offender=Latin   Male,   49;   (Rivera,   Ramon);
(80-5942); Charged with Murder I, attempted Murder
I, agg. assault and use of firearm; pled to Murder
II; Judge 14; Sentenced to 15 years in prison.

110   Victim=Latin Male, 32; Ap 6, 1980; Tract=54.02;
2315; MPD;   V was involved in an argument with
his girlfriend (a Latin) in a bar. The girlfriend
left the bar with two female friends. The 3 women
discussed the longstanding dispute between the V
and the girlfriend and one of the females (the O)
said she would "get that bastard for you." The 3
went back to the bar and O stood in doorway and
fired 10 shots at the V (4 hit the V while 1 hit a
barmaid in the leg).

Offender=Latin Female, 32; (Valero, Margarita);
(80-6060); Charged with Murder I, attempted Murder
I & use of firearm; jury trial; Judge 07; guilty
on all counts; Sentenced to two concurrent life
terms.

112 Victim=Latin Male, 24;
113 Victim=Latin Male, 23; Ap 7, 1980; Tract=7.01;
0005; HPD;   The two victims were in a bar when
three L/M's entered (robbery) and ordered patrons
against the wall. When one patron resisted shots
were fired and the two victims were killed (3
other patrons were also shot but not killed).

Offender=Three Unknown Latin Males

115 Victim=Latin Male, 25; Ap 8, 1980; Tract=43.00;
0640; MBPD;   V had been drinking (alcohol level
of .12) and got into argument with the O (an
acquaintance) near his residence. V ran from
assailant who chased him into the lobby of his
residence and shot him twice.

Offender=Unknown Latin Male

117 Victim=Latin Male, 19; Ap 11, 1980; Tract=84.04;
2300; PSD;   The V and offenders were all
Columbians. The V and his brother had robbed
other Columbian drug dealers and the V's brother
had been killed a month earlier in retaliation for
this activity. V was in a car with those
suspected of killing his brother. This car &
another car were travelling together when first
car (with V inside) stopped and other car stopped
behind it. V tried to exit the first car when
another passenger in that car exited and shot the
V. The V found dead as both cars fled.
Apparently a dispute over drugs or argument over
death of V's brother.

Offender=Unknown Latin (Columbian) Males, perhaps
6-8.

119   Victim=Latin Female, 20; Ap 13, 1980; Tract=39.02;
       1800; MBPD;   Two Latin couples regularly went
       out together.   On this occasion the O was angry
       because his wife wanted to go out with V and
       another woman. For some unknown reason the O shot
       the V (he often fired a gun in the apt. and
       threatened people). The V was wearing lot of
       expensive jewelry as her husband was wealthy
       businessman from Venezuela. O then committed
       suicide.

       Offender=Latin Male, 26; (Rueda, Jose); No charges
       filed, O committed suicide

125   Victim=Latin Male, 30; Ap 21, 1980; Tract=115.00;
       9999;   PSD;   V was Columbian who had past
       criminal record for theft and immigration
       violations in N.J. Three days before his death V
       was involved in a cocaine deal with a Columbian.
       Police believe that the murder was drug related.
       The body was found on the side of the road.

       Offender=Unknown, possibly Columbian Males

127   Victim=Latin Male, 32; Ap 22 or 23, 1980;
       Tract=6.06; 9999; HPD;   V was Columbian and was
       one of a gang of 5 who abducted the wife of a
       wealthy Columbian drug dealer. The gang got the
       ransom money but then one by one they were all
       killed or fled the country (evidently the
       Columbian drug dealer put out a contract on all of
       them). Case no. 364 was another member of the
       gang who was killed in 1980.

       Offender=Unknown Latin (Columbian) Males

128 Victim=Black Latin Male, 23; Ap 23, 1980;
Tract=10.01; 9999; PSD; V and another Black
Latin Male, 31, were in process of burglarizing an
apt. when owner woke up and confronted them with a
gun and ordered them to freeze. The V kept moving
toward the owner and was shot. The other burglar
was thus charged with felony murder (the death of
his companion).

Offender=Black Latin Male, 31; (Nunez, Miguel B.);
Charged with Murder II (felony murder), and
burglary; pled to Murder II and burglary; Judge
13; Sentenced to four years on probation with
condition he serve 5 months in county jail (which
he already had done at time of sentencing, thus
given time served plus probation). No charges
were filed against the homeowner.

133 Victim=Latin Male, 21; Ap 30, 1980; Tract=30.01;
0245; MPD; V and another Latin Male were
attempting to rob a Black Male. There was a
struggle for the gun and the B/M was shot but then
took the gun away from the V and emptied the gun
into the V. The B/M then went to the hospital and
told police he had been shot during an attempted
robbery by two L/M's (he had the gun with him).
This story appears to be true thus the surviving
robber was charged with felony murder.

Offender=Latin Male, 23; (Sosa, Jorge); (80-7612);
Charged with Murder II, attempted robbery, agg.
battery and use of firearm; Judge 13; Charges were
eventually dismissed. No charges were filed
against the B/M. O claimed he was only riding in
car when V decided to rob a pedestrian (thus he
would not have had intent for underlying felony in
felony murder). Judge 13 ruled there was no
evidence to establish his participation in robbery
and dismissed charges.

134   Victim=Latin Male, 50; May 2, 1980; Tract=5.03;
       1524; PSD;   V was from Venezuela and owned a
       mini warehouse which served as a processing place
       for cocaine. On this occasion V was at his place
       of business when shots were heard and V was found
       shot to death. Police belive V was shot by other
       South American drug dealers.

       Offender=Unknown Latin Males

140   Victim=Latin Male, 29; May 6, 1980; Tract=24.00;
       2320;   MPD;   V's   brother   is   extremely
       intelligent but somewhat crazy and was obsessed
       with V's kids and thought his brother was a poor
       father. Police believe that the brother killed
       the V's wife in 1979 and then the V in 1980
       because he wanted the kids. However, there is not
       enough evidence to charge the brother.

       Offender=Latin Male, 30.

142   Victim=Latin Male, 22; May 7, 1980; Tract=107.01;
       9999; PSD;   V was having an ongoing dispute
       with a Latin Male for several months prior to this
       episode. On this date V was at his residence and
       O came to see him. V then left residence and O
       left shortly thereafter. The O and another L/M
       stopped their car to talk with the V a short
       distance from the residence. A struggle ensued
       and V was shot. The two L/M's and another car
       occupied by 2 L/M's was also at the scene and both
       cars fled.

       Offender=Latin Male, 25; No charges filed,
       prosecutor believed case was non-prosecutable

143 Victim=Latin Male, 47; May 7, 1980; Tract=100.05;
     2300; PSD;   V and his girlfriend were riding in
     V's car when they began to argue. V had a history
     of threatening and assaulting her (there were
     several past police reports of this nature).
     Since the V had a gun on this occasion, the
     girlfriend (the O) felt threatened. She then took
     a revolver from the glove compartment and shot the
     V several times.

     Offender=Latin Female, 35; No charges filed;
     Justifiable homicide

144 Victim=Latin Male, 22; May 8, 1980; Tract=48.00;
     1250;   PSD;   V was Columbian and had just
     arrived in Miami from Bogota with his wife and 2
     others. They had just cleared customs at the
     airport when they were confronted at the sliding
     glass doors by an unidentified L/M who fired 4
     shots at the V. O then fled on a motorcycle with
     another L/M who was driving the "getaway bike."
     Police believe the murder was a "hit" by other
     drug dealers as police believe the V was involved
     in the drug trade.

     Offender=Two Unknown Latin Males, probably
     Columbians

329

146   Victim=Latin Male, 17; May 10, 1980; Tract=34.00;
       2220; MPD;   V and a friend drove to an area
       known as the "Candy Strip" (place where drugs were
       openly sold like candy) to buy marijuana. After
       buying the drug the buyers tried to leave without
       paying. The sellers, all B/M's were angered and
       one B/M jumped into the car and (2 blocks away)
       shot the V. The 3 other B/M's (who were charged)
       followed in another car.

       Offender=Black Male, 25; (Starling, Dwight);
       (80-8653); Charged with Murder I, attempted Murder
       I and use of firearm; pled to manslaughter & use
       of firearm; Judge 28; Sentenced to 7 years in
       prison (this O was the shooter).
       Offender=Black Male, 21; (Harden, M.); Charged
       with manslaughter; Judge 28; Charges dismissed
       Offender=Black Male, 15; (Minnis, Frank); Charged
       with manslaughter; Judge 28; Charges dismissed
       Offender=Black Male, 19; (Stanley, Karl); Charged
       with manslaughter; Judge 28; Charges dismissed.
       State dropped case against the second and fourth
       offenders since Judge 28 felt they were only
       attempting to aid a friend and didn't participate
       in the shooting. The third O was given immunity
       for testimony against the first O. The two Latin
       V's admitted they tried to rip-off the dealers.

149   Victim=Latin Male, 40; May 11, 1980, (found);
       Tract=27.01; 1820; MPD;   V's body was found
       severely decomposed at water's edge on Venetian
       Causeway. The motive is unknown but may have been
       a robbery as the O was found with V's car.

       Offender=Latin (Mariel Refugee) Male, 26; not
       enough evidence to charge

154   Victim=Latin Male, 26; May 12, 1980; Tract=21.00;
       1950; MPD;   V found dead in hotel room with
       bullet in head. Another L/M, 23, was also in the
       room at the time of shooting but claims to have
       been in bathroom when he heard shot and says V was
       either playing with the gun and accidently shot
       shot himself or committed suicide. However,
       police says there was no psychological profile
       indicating suicide (and angle of wound would seem
       to preclude suicide) and V was very familiar with
       firearms and is not likely to have shot himself
       accidently. Both V and O were involved in drug
       trade and police believe the L/M or someone else
       shot the V, perhaps in dispute over drugs or just
       simply a "personal" argument.

       Offender=Latin Male, 23; Identity known but not
       enough evidence to charge

156   Victim=Latin Male, 39; May 13, 1980; Tract=49.00;
       1815; MPD;   V was Columbian who was shot in
       parking lot of public park as he stood near his
       car.   The O's (several L/M's) approached him on a
       motorcycle and in a car. "Hit" man many have been
       a Venezuelean who is known to have killed numerous
       others.   The hit may have been ordered in
       retaliation for the V being involved in a gang
       that kidnapped for ransom the wife of another drug
       dealer.

       Offender=Unknown Latin Males

157   Victim=Latin   Female,   42;   May   13,   1980;
       Tract=42.00; 2240; MBPD;   V and her husband
       (the O) argued over husband's allegations that the
       wife was having an affair with the landlord.   The
       O bought a gun two days before and threatened to
       kill her if she continued the affair.   On this
       occasion an argument began and V tried to flee. O
       shot her (in their home) and as the children were
       coming into the house he shot himself (and died).

       Offender=Latin Male, 44; (Sosa, Carmelo);   No
       charges filed; O committed suicide

159   Victim=Latin Male, 22; May 15, 1980;   Tract=91.00;
       1625;   PSD;   V   and   another   person   were
       burglarizing a residence when they were   surprised
       by the owner of the house. Both V and an unknown
       person ran from the house as owner fired shots and
       struck the V.

       Offender=Latin Male,   44;   No   charges   filed;
       Justifiable homicide

171   Victim=Latin Male, 67; May 17, 1980;   Tract=10.04;
       2200;   PSD;   During   the   May   riots   the V was
       driving his car when it was   stoned   by   a   crowd.
       The car was overturned and 30-40 Blacks approached
       his car and beat on the car with sticks and rocks.
       The   V   was   trapped   in the car and was jabbed at
       with sticks and rocks. The car was   then   set   on
       fire. V died due to stab wounds and burns.

       Offender=Black Male,   21;   (Pickett,   Ivory   Lee);
       (81-21021); charged with Murder I and arson; Judge
       02;   jury   trial;   guilty   of Murder II and arson;
       Sentenced to life plus (consecutive) 30 years.
       Offender=Black Male,   20;   (Ferguson,   Jaspar);
       Charged with Murder I and arson; Judge 02; pled to
       Murder   II   &   arson;   Sentenced   to   20   years in
       prison.

187   Victim=Latin Male, 70; May 23, 1980;   Tract=36.01;
       1200; MPD;   V was homosexual and police believe
       he   was   stabbed   by   a   male   lover (there was no
       forced entry and the V was found nude).

       Offender=Unknown Male, perhaps an Anglo Male, 55.

191   Victim=Latin Male, 32; May 17, 1980; Tract=54.02;
      1955; MPD;   V was a Mariel Refugee and was a
      "mental case." V was in and out of mental
      facilities since his arrival in the U.S. The V
      (during the May riots, but not riot related) was
      brought to mental health clinic from a refugee
      center where he was diagnosed as paranoid
      schizophrenic. He ran from the clinic but then
      returned an hour later and pulled razor and
      threatened the staff. He then left. Police were
      called and saw the V running down alley holding
      razor to his throat. The officer tried to talk to
      him but then V started moving toward them with the
      razor. The police officer then shot the V (V died
      3 weeks later). V was first Mariel Refugee to be
      a homicide V.

      Offender=Miami Police Officer, Latin Male, 35; No
      charges filed; Justifiable homicide

192   Victim=Latin Male, 22; May 28, 1980; Tract=49.00;
      2345; MPD;   V became involved in verbal
      argument with a L/F over a parking space. V and a
      friend leaned into the car to take O's car keys
      from ignition. O carried a gun for self-defense
      and had it in her hand. V grabbed for the gun and
      it went off killing the V. Judge 10 felt that the
      state had no evidence of culpable negligence and
      granted motion to dismiss.

      Offender=Latin Female, 43;   (Duran, Alicia);
      (80-9721); Charged with Murder II; Charge
      dismissed since Judge 10 ruled that there was no
      evidence of culpable negligence.

195   Victim=Latin Male, 37; May 29, 1980; Tract=36.02;
      1900; MPD;   V was at a friend's house when he
      became involved in an argument with an
      acquaintance (the O). O pulled out a gun and shot
      the V.   V had alcohol level of .33 and benzo in
      body.

      Offender=Latin Male, 38; (Castillo, Rojello);
      (80-9827); Charged with Murder II and use of
      firearm; jury trial; Judge 02; guilty on both
      counts; Sentenced to 20 years in prison.

197   Victim=Latin   Female,   21;   May   30,   1980;
      Tract=48.00; 9999; PSD;   V was a prostitute and
      involved in drug trade. She was found dead at a
      construction site by several workers (a tin foil
      packet of narcotics was found near her body).
      Police believe she was either killed by a male
      client (she had a reputation of ripping off
      "Johns") or was killed by associate in drug
      business. V had alcohol level of .12 and benzo in
      body.

      Offender=Unknown

202   Victim=Latin Male, 26;
203   Victim=Latin   Female,   24;   June   3,   1980;
      Tract=61.02;   9999;   PSD;   This   couple   (the
      female was Columbian, the Male was Cuban) and
      their baby checked into a $110 a night room in an
      exclusive hotel. They were later found shot to
      death in the room (the baby was not harmed). It
      appears that this was a drug ripoff as the two
      victims were involved in drug trade. Also $49,000
      in cash found at scene.   It appears that the
      killers stole cocaine valued up to five million
      dollars. The male V had alcohol level of .08 plus
      three other drugs in his body. The female had a
      trace of alcohol and another drug in her body.

      Offender=Unknown but police believe that   the
      offender(s) included a Latin Male who is wanted
      for several kidnappings and murders.

212   Victim=Latin   Female,   29;   June   7,   1980;
      Tract=70.02; 2030; MPD;   V was stabbed by her
      husband during a domestic argument (he then hid
      knife on roof). She bled to death in her bed and
      was found the next morning by her son.

      Offender=Latin   Male,   36;   (Ortiz   Pablo);
      (80-10475); Charged with Murder II, pled to Murder
      II; Judge 10; Sentenced to 19 years in prison.

                              354

218   Victim=Latin Male, 30; June 13, 1980; Tract=56.00; 1230; MPD;   V was involved in drugs with O's brother. The O, an off-duty Miami police officer went to their apt. and argument ensued. O claims that the V pulled a gun on him and he fired in self-defense. O's brother refused to give a statement.

Offender=Anglo Male, 26; identity known but not enough evidence to charge.

219   Victim=Latin Male, 47; June 14, 1980; Tract=108.00; 2315; PSD;   V was involved in an altercation in front of a convenience store with another L/M over the V's common-law wife. O struck the V over the head with a baseball bat (V died the next day).

Offender=Latin Male, 62; (Reves, Evaristo); (80-10933); Charged with Murder II; Jury trial; Judge O1; not guilty

225   Victim=Latin Male, 50; June 19, 1980; Tract=4.01; 0610; PSD;   V owned a market and was shot as he was walking across the street from the parking lot to his place of business. Police believe that he was killed in retaliation for the killing of a member of the O's gang (of drug dealers). Two of the V's employees sold cocaine and were part of the other gang.

Offender=Unknown Latin Males

233 Victim=Latin Male, 48; June 22, 1980; Tract=37.02;
2300; MPD;   V and the O lived in the same apt.
building. The O was 73 years old but had a
younger girlfriend and the V made some comments to
the girl. Later that night when O was in bed the
V knocked on the door and got into argument with
O. O then took a knife out and stabbed the V as
he stood in the doorway. V walked away but found
dead short time later on the sidewalk (a trail of
blood led to door of O). V had alcohol level of
.22.

Offender=Latin Male, 73; (Mora, Evaristo, P.);
(80-11787); Charged with Murder II; pled to
manslaughter; Judge 23; Sentenced to 10 years of
probation (adjudication withheld).

236 Victim=Latin Male, 40; June 23, 1980; Tract=58.01;
2200; MPD;   V was drinking in a bar when an
argument broke out among 3 or 4 Columbians.
Police don't believe the V was involved in the
argument but someone in the group of Columbians
started to shoot and the other patrons in the bar
started shooting & V was caught in the middle (V
had revolver in his pocket but never pulled or
fired it). One other patron was wounded. Poice
found 54 bullet holes in the walls of the bar. V
had alcohol level of 17.

Offender=Unknown Latin Male, probably one of four
Columbian Males who began the shooting.

238 Victim=Latin Male, 32; June 24, 1980; Tract=26.00;
2210; MPD;   V along with a L/F and a Black
Latin Male attempted to rip-off another L/M for
$180 in a drug (qualude) deal. During the
struggle between the robbery victim and the B/L/M
the shotgun being used in the robbery discharged
and struck the V (one of the robbers). Thus the
B/L/M was charged with felony murder in death of
his fellow robber.

Offender=Black Latin Male, 24; (Bultron, Juan);
(80-12127); Charged with Murder III, grand theft
and use of firearm; bench trial; Judge 07; not
guilty, a directed verdict of acquittal. V was
alleged co-conspirator in a drug rip-off and a
shotgun went off accidently killing V so O charged

with felony murder. However, no testimony proved
O actually participated in robbery or fight with
buyer thus no intent for underlying felony proven.

239   Victim=Latin   Female,   48;   June   24,   1980;
      Tract=44.00;   2310;   BPD;   V   was   shot   by her
      boyfriend. She had moved out on him (they had been
      living together) & he angry about this. He caught
      her on way home from work and shot her down in the
      street. Then police officer approached (O still
      had gun in his hand) and O pointed gun at officer.
      Officer   fired   at O but his gun misfired.   O then
      put the gun to his head and shot himself.

      Offender=Latin   Male,   55;   (Dulfo,   Manuel);   No
      charges filed, O committed suicide.

247   Victim=Black   Latin   Male,   33;   June   28,   1980;
      Tract=8.02;   1203;   HPD;   V and another L/M (both
      Mariel   Refugees)   got   into   an argument with the
      owner of a bar and were asked to leave.   The   two
      patrons   did   leave but owner went and got his gun
      and opened door of bar and shot the V as he sat in
      the car. The owner admitted   that   they   did   not
      have a gun in the bar but believed they would get
      one in the car so he shot first.

      Offender=Latin   Male,   33;   (Diaz,   Francisco);
      (80-11794);   Charged   with   Murder   II;   Charges
      dismissed by Judge O7 as he ruled   that   precedent
      existed   that   don't have to be in fear of life at
      moment if threat made earlier. State   also   having
      trouble getting witnesses in the bar to testify.

249   Victim=Latin Male, 30; ("John Doe'); June 29, 1980
      (found); Tract=101.12; 9999; PSD;   V found in a
      field in advanced stage of decomposition.   Police
      have no idea as to motive or offender.

      Offender=Unknown

251   Victim=Latin Female, 27; June 30, 1980; Tract=103.00; 9999; PSD; V was killed by her ex-husband. He told others he could not bear to live without her and was also angry that she had filed rape charges against him. On this date, he picked her up from work and shot her several times (while in the vehicle). He then shot himself (fatally) once in the head.

Offender=Latin Male, 37; (Hernandez, Jose); No charges filed, O committed suicide

258   Victim=Latin Male, 39; July 5, 1980; Tract=36.02; 0515; MPD; V was a Mariel Refugee and with another Latin Male was burglarizing a bar. They were discovered by a security guard (also a Mariel Refugee) who shot the V/burglar.

Offender=Latin Male, 44; No charges filed; ruled justifiable (other burglar not caught so he not charged with felony murder in death of fellow burglar).

263   Victim=Latin Male, 29; July 7, 1980; Tract=30.01; 2009; MPD; O (a Mariel Refugee) and another male argued at a pool hall. The other male then went outside and sat on a bench. O left and got a gun and returned and pointed gun at the male. V (also a Mariel Refugee) tried to intervene by pushing the other male aside but O fired one shot and hit the V.

Offender=Latin Male, 24; (Bacallo, Roberto); (80-13365); Charged with Murder I and use of firearm; Judge 11; charges dismissed. Only witness was 13 year old who said he saw B/M shoot V. He gave description of B/M. However, this description did not match that of the O who was arrested on another tip. Also the W changed his story. W said he suffered from epileptic seizures and had metal plate in his head and also had a bad memory. Motion to dismiss granted by Judge 11.

264 Victim=Latin Male, 30; July 7, 1980; Tract=70.02;
    0100; MPD; V was in his car with another L/M
    when they stopped at an intersection. Another
    vehicle drove by and shot into the car killing the
    V. The O and the V had argued earlier (V was a
    Mariel Refugee).

    Offender=Latin Male, 32; (Dubal, Leslie);
    (80-12491); Charged with attempted Murder II (2
    counts) and use of firearm; Judge 07; Charges
    dismissed. The only witness claimed V was shot by
    someone in moving car but ballistics showed that
    fatal shot came from 3-4 feet away. Also one week
    before trial witness was arrested for armed
    robbery and refused to testify in this case. No
    deal sought for his testimony since the physical
    evidence did not support his testimony. Also it
    later appeared W ducked after one shot and thus
    didn't see fatal shot.

271 Victim=Latin Male, 55; July 13, 1980; Tract=20.01;
    0513; MPD; V was sitting on a bus bench at
    5:30 AM (was going to work) when a B/M on a Moped
    approached him from the front and another B/M came
    up behind him on foot. B/M on motorcycle told V
    to give them his money and V gave them $2. O (on
    motorcycle) looked at the money then at the V (but
    said nothing) and shot the V.

    Offender=Black Male, 19; (Ragans, Amos);
    (80-12721); Charged with Murder I, robbery, use of
    firearm; Judge 14; pled to Murder II and robbery;
    Sentenced to two concurrent life terms. This O
    was the shooter.
    Offender=Black Male, 19; (Nesbitt, Earl); charged
    with Murder II, robbery; Judge 10; charges
    dismissed. The second O agreed to testify against
    first O and this testimony was vital since the
    only other witness could not identify the first O
    at bond hearing.

273 Victim=Latin Male, 23; July 19, 1980 (found);
    Tract=101.02; 9999; PSD; V (A Columbian) was
    found dead in advanced stage of decomposition in
    field by two men dumping trash. Police believe
    the V was killed in dispute over drugs.

    Offender=Unknown

278   Victim=Latin Male, 22; July 19, 1980; Tract=73.00;
       0320; MPD;   V and another male were in rear
       seat of a car in a church parking lot when a B/M
       approached and saw the two men in the car engaged
       in a homosexual act. The B/M (O) called them a
       name and fired once into the car hitting the V.

       Offender=Unknown Black Male

281   Victim=Latin Male, 38;July 20, 1980; Tract=9.01;
       1045; PSD;   V was at home when three L/M's
       entered his residence, tied him up and shot him.
       The O's (all Mariel Refugees) found out that the V
       (who was a drug dealer) kept a lot of money in his
       home and decided to rob him. They carried off
       around a million dollars but left $800,000 in
       small bills which they could not carry. The
       father of this V (who was also a drug dealer) to
       avenge his son's death searched for the 3 O's and
       found one the next day. He offered this O a "deal
       he could not refuse", his life and money to lead
       him to the other two O's. The other O's were then
       killed in retaliation (these are victims in cases
       284 & 285).

       Offender=Latin Male, 27; killed the next day
       Offender=Latin Male, 50; killed the next day
       Offender=Latin Male; This O (the informant) is at
       large

282   Victim=Latin Male, 47; July 20, 1980; Tract=55.01;
       2200; MPD;   V was in feud with the O and agreed
       to meet the O at location of assault. When V
       arrived O shot him with shotgun. V walked 200 ft.
       and collapsed.

       Offender=Latin Male, 38; (Nodal, Rigobato);
       (80-13309); Charged with Murder II and use of
       firearm; jury trial; Judge 02; not guilty

283   Victim=Latin Male, 44; July 21, 1980; Tract=9.01; 1625; PSD;   V was "squeaky clean" pharmacist who became involved in verbal argument with two B/M's. One of the B/M's pulled a gun, V grabbed for the gun and B/M shot the V. O's escaped on a motorcycle. Motive is unknown, does not appear to be robbery and V not involved in anything illegal.

Offender=Unknown Black Male

284   Victim=Latin Male, 27;
285   Victim=Latin Male, 50; July 21, 1980; Tract=101.02; 1730; PSD;   These two victims (both Mariel Refugees) killed in retaliation for the murder the day before of a drug dealer (see details at case 281).

Offender=Unknown Latin Males

289   Victim=Latin Male, 72; July 25, 1980 (found); Tract=91.00; 9999; PSD;   V was old Cuban man who always frequented a Cuban coffee shop that was now frequented by several Mariel Refugees and/or drug dealers. He was angry that his hangout was deteriorating and complained out loud for all in the ' coffee shop to hear. Police believe one or more of the Mariel Refugees and/or drug dealers abducted him and killed him. His body was found floating in a canal in advanced stage of decomposition.

Offender=Unknown, probably one or more Latin Males

290   Victim=Latin Male, 32; July 25, 1980; Tract=37.01; 9999; MPD;   V and O were involved in an altercation in front of a bar. O stabbed V. V and O were acquaintances.

Offender=Latin Male, 45; (Rosa, Pedro Juan); (80-13610); Charged with Murder II; jury trial; Judge 12; guilty as charged; Sentenced to 60 years, judge retaind jurisdiction for first 20 years (O cannot be paroled without permision of judge for 20 years).

293 Victim=Black Latin Male, 49; July 28, 1980;
    Tract=49.00; 0500; MPD; V had thrown a party
    at his residence that lasted until early morning
    hours. At some point there was evidently a
    dispute between the V and an unknown male over a
    girl, V was shot by O. Everyone had been drinking
    (V had alcohol level of .20).

    Offender=Unknown Latin Male

297 Victim=Black Latin Male, 43; July 29, 1980;
    Tract=100.08; 1940; PSD; V was known to be in
    drug trade. On this occasion he arrived home with
    a female and they were confronted by three B/M's
    (Rastafarians from Jamaica). The V was then shot
    and killed. Police believe the killing involved a
    drug rip-off.

    Offender=Three Unknown Black Males (Rastafarians)

299 Victim=Black Latin Male, 23; July 31, 1980;
    Tract=50.00; 0700; MPD; V found lying on a
    median strip of the road by a passing motorist.
    Police believe he had been involved in an argument
    over money owed with an unknown offender.

    Offender=Unknown

301 Victim=Latin Male, 32;
302 Victim=Latin Female, 38; July 31, 1980;
    Tract=52.00; 2200; MPD; The female V was
    divorced from her husband but they lived in the
    same house and had separate bedrooms. The female
    V met the male V (a Mariel Refugee) at another
    house and as they were leaving the house (already
    in a car) the ex-husband approached and shot them
    both. Appears to have been a jealousy triangle.

    Offender=Latin Male, 40; (Gross, Gustavo);
    identity known but at large

342

304   Victim=Black Latin Male, 23;   Aug 2, 1980;
      Tract=34.00; 1218; MPD;   V became involved in a
      verbal argument with the offender who accused the
      V of making homosexual advancements toward her
      boyfriend. The O (a B/F) then stabbed the victim.

      Offender=Black Female, 22;   (Brinson, Vera Mae);
      (80-14174); Charged with Murder II; jury trial;
      Judge 02; guilty; Sentenced to 20 years in prison.
      The O had an extensive prior record.

305   Victim=Latin Male, 41; Aug 2, 1980;   Tract=113.00;
      0039; MPD;   V was in a bar and became involved
      in an altercation with one or two L/M's.   Both V
      and the two L/M's were Mariel Refugees. At some
      point the L/M's shot the V.

      Offender=Unknown Latin Male

312   Victim=Latin Male, 47; Aug 5, 1980;   Tract=57.02;
      2355; MPD;   V was a "mule" for drug dealer. It
      appears that a drug deal went sour and V was
      stabbed to death. A large amount of cocaine was
      found on the scene.

      Offender=Unknown

314   Victim=Latin Female, 44; Aug 8, 1980; Tract=88.01;
      1100; PSD;   V and her husband were involved in
      a minor traffic accident which then led to a
      verbal altercation between the V's husband and
      several L/M's who were in the other car. The V
      was shot during the altercation.

      Offender=Latin Male; (Castillo, Jose M.); identity
      known and a warrant has been issued but O is at
      large (O arrested and convicted in 1984 after end
      of data collection)

315 Victim=Black Latin Male, 32; Aug 9, 1980; Tract=36.02; 0215; MPD; V was refugee from Dominican Republic and was in a bar where he got into argument with a Mariel Refugee over buying drinks for women. The Mariel Refugee then shot and stabbed the V. V had alcohol level of .14 and was living on streets and in an abandoned laundry.

Offender=Latin Male, 27; (Lopez, Jorge L.); (80-14786); Charged with Murder II and use of firearm; O first declared incompetent, then competent (7 months later); bench trial; Judge 01; Acquitted by reason of insanity. O also had history of suicide attempts.

316 Victim=Latin Male, 55; Aug 8, 1980; Tract=30.02; 2045; MPD; V was in a bar when two L/M's came in and pulled a gun out of a pouch and said, "We've killed before and we will kill again," (which was true as they had killed another man earlier). One of them then shot the V as he was coming out of the bathroom (they apparently did not know him and thus there appears to be no motive). Only one of the two men was captured. The V was a Mariel Refugee.

Offender=Latin Male, 29; (Parado, Carlos); (80-14662); Charged with Murder II and 2 counts agg. battery; jury trial; Judge 15; guilty on all counts; Sentenced to 99 years plus 15 plus 15 (3 consecutive terms) for the 3 counts.

318 Victim=Latin Male, 35; Aug 10; 1980; Tract=114.00; 0900; PSD; V was Columbian who had arrived only 2 days before. He was found dead in a field (shot to death). Police believe this was a Columbian "Cocaine Cowboy" hit.

Offender=Unknown, probably two Latin (Columbian) Males

323   Victim=Latin Male, 19; Aug 12, 1980; Tract=113.00;
        2230; PSD;   V was in a car with 3 other   L/M's.
        They stopped to purchase drugs (marijuana). Two
        B/M's approached the car and gave them an   envelop
        (with drugs) and the L/M's attempted to flee
        without paying. V was shot by one of   the   B/M's.
        V had alcohol level of .16.

        Offender=Black Male, 23; (Bradley, Vernon Daniel);
        (80-15536); Charged with Murder II and use of
        firearm; Judge 10; Charges dismissed. Three other
        L/M's unable to identify shooter but testimony
        from others present led to arrest of this O.   The
        3 who originally said this O was the shooter could
        not be found at several trial dates so these
        charges nolle prossed.

326   Victim=Latin   Female,   23;   Aug   15,   1980;
        Tract=91.00; 0100; PSD;   The V was found dead
        in a field on the side of a roadway.   The   motive
        and offender is unknown but it is known that the V
        was into the drug scene (use not sale) and often
        attended discos late at night. Her alcohol   level
        was .13 and had methaqualudes in body.

        Offender=Unknown

328   Victim=Latin Male, 38; Aug. 16, 1980; Tract=99999;
        1215; MPD;   V was sitting at restaurant counter
        and 3 L/M's were sitting at a nearby table. The V
        and the 3 L/M's recognized each other (there
        appears to have been a prior dispute over drugs).
        The 3 L/M's got up to leave and as they went by
        the V (who had his back to them) the last L/M shot
        the V in the back of the head (as V sat on stool).
        The 3 L/M's fled.

        Offender=Unknown Latin Males

331   Victim=Latin Male, 37; Aug 20, 1980 (found);
        Tract=101.12; 9999; PSD;   V was involved in
        drug trade and smuggling of weapons. Police
        believe his death was over a drug dispute. V's
        body was found in a canal with hands tied behind
        his back and his feet bound.

        Offender=Unknown

336 Victim=Latin Male, 33; Aug. 25, 1980; Tract=5.02;
1845; HPD;   V was a Columbian who had been the
victim of an attempted homicide 3 weeks earlier.
On this occasion V was shot multiple times in apt.
complex parking lot. Police believe the murder to
involve a drug dispute and believe that the
offenders are Columbians.

Offender=Unknown Latin (Columbian) Males

342 Victim=Latin   Female,   21;   Aug   27,   1980;
Tract=37.01; 0300; MPD;   V was driving an auto,
accompanied by a Latin Male friend when an unknown
B/M approached her side of the car window &
attempted to grab her gold chain. V evaded him
but B/M then shot the V.

Offender=Unknown Black Male

343 Victim=Latin Male, 27; Aug 22, 1980; Tract=58.02;
0850; MPD;   Offender, a Mariel Refugee, and his
wife had separated. She was dating another man,
husband (O) was jealous and went to her house,
called the other man out of the house and shot him
(didn't even argue or talk, just shot him when he
came out of house). The V was also a Mariel
Refugee.

Offender=Latin Male, 46; (Echevarria, Andres);
(80-15540); Charged with Murder II and use of
firearm; Pending

344 Victim=Latin Male, 33; Aug. 27, 1980; Tract=28.00;
1845; MPD;   V was patron in a bar when an
unknown B/M entered the bar and attempted to rob
the bartender. The V attempted to take the gun
from the robber and was shot.

Offender=Unknown Black Male

351   Victim=Latin Male, 31; Aug 31, 1980; Tract=102.00; 1145; PSD;   V was owner of several taxi cabs. He had apparently fired an employee two weeks earlier because the employee had stolen property and cash. The former employee (the O) on this date drove to V's residence and shot the V.

Offender=Anglo Male, 39; (Staas, Evert); (80-16229); Charged with Murder II and use of firearm; jury trial; Judge 01; guilty on both counts; Sentenced to life in prison.

352   Victim=Latin Female, 46;
353   Victim=Latin Female, 29; Aug. 31, 1980 (found); Tract=76.04; 9999; PSD;   The two victims were killed in a drug dispute. They were found dead in advanced stage of decomposition. The gun used to kill them was found in home of another person who has since been murdered in a drug dispute. The gun was also used in another double killing that was drug related. Police believe a Columbian drug gang is responsible for this double killing.

Offender=Unknown, probably Latin (Columbian) Males

354   Victim=Latin Male, 24; Sept 1, 1980; Tract=17.01; 1202; PSD;   The V and the O were both Mariel Refugees. The V came to O's trailor to wake him up and O got upset. He came out into the street with a rifle and shot the V after they argued. V had alcohol level of .29.

Offender=Latin Male, 42; (Costa, Gonalo Montegudo); identity known and warrant issued but at large

357   Victim=Latin Male, 30;
358   Victim=Latin   Male,   30;   Sept.   4,   1980;
      Tract=101.03;   1340; PSD;   V (a Mariel Refugee)
      was killed along with another L/M in a dispute
      over money owed due to transportation of relatives
      during the Mariel boatlit. These two victims and
      another L/M (also a refugee) worked at an
      Industrial Park where the shooting occurred. The
      3 L/M's drove to the location and approached the
      owner at which time a gunfight ensued. Two of the
      three L/M's were killed by the owner. Police
      believe the three were trying to extort money from
      the owner and thus the surviving L/M was charged
      with felony murder. The owner was not charged.

      Offender=Latin Male (Mariel Refugee), 58; (Nava,
      Domingo); (80-16550); Charged with Murder II,
      attempted robbery, extortion, attempted Murder I
      and use of firearm; Judge 06; Charges dismissed.
      The O was only surviver of 3 O's but original
      Victim in this case who shot the 2 other O's
      testified that this O was not armed and never
      threatened him or tried to extort money. Since
      the other witnesses were dead the state dropped
      charges.

362   Victim=Latin Male, 55; Sept 6, 1980; Tract=6.03;
      1035; HPD;   V was in a vehicle when he was shot
      by three unknown L/M's in a car which pulled
      alongside his car. Police believe the killing
      involved a dispute over V's political activities
      in South America.

      Offender=Unknown Latin Males

364   Victim=Latin Male, 19; Sept. 7, 1980; Tract=26.00;
      0120; MPD;   V was Columbian who was shot as he
      stood in a vacant lot talking to two Columbian
      males who were in a truck. A package of cocaine
      was found nearby and V had a gun in his pants.
      Police believe V was killed in a drug trade
      dispute.

      Offender=Unknown Latin (Columbian) Males

371   Victim=Latin Male, 36; Sept 11, 1980; Tract=62.00;
       0930; PSD;   The V (a Mariel Refugee)   was
       involved in an argument with another L/M. at a
       bar. The O left the bar and got a shotgun and
       shot the V as he left the bar. V had alcohol
       level of .15 and amphetamines in body. O was also
       a Mariel Refugee.

       Offender=Latin Male, 28; Identity known but not
       enough evidence to charge

373   Victim=Latin Male, 2; Sept 12, 1980; Tract=8.01;
       1300; HPD;   V had been repeatedly battered and
       taken to local hospitals. On the day of the fatal
       assault the neighbors heard screams and strap
       hitting the child and later the child was found
       dead. Police believe that the child was beaten
       and killed by the Mother's boyfriend (who was from
       Costa Rica).   The Mother (was was from Puerto
       Rico) worked for a county organization that was
       involved in fighting child abuse. Both the mother
       and the boyfriend left Florida shortly after the
       death and are at large.

       Offender=Latin Male; identity known but at large

349

375　Victim=Latin Male, 17; Sept. 14, 1980; Tract=5.02;
2200; PSD;　　V and six other Mariel Refugees
from a Refugee Center were in the process of
burglarizing a home when the owner of the home
discovered the V in the kitchen and shot him.
Four of the surviving burglars were charged with
felony murder in the death of their companion
burglar.

Offender=Latin Male, 21; (Reyes, Alberto);
(80-17393); Charged with Murder II and burglary;
Judge 20; Jury trial; not guilty (even though the
3 juvenile O's testified against him at the
trial).
Offender=Latin Male, 17; Charged in Juvenile Court
with Murder II and burglary; pled to Murder II and
burglary; Judge 30; Sentenced to training school
Offender=Latin Male, 17; Charged in Juvenile Court
with Murder II and burglary; pled to Murder II and
burglary; Judge 30; Sentenced to training school
Offender=Latin Male, 16; Charged in Juvenile Court
with Murder II and burglary; pled to Murder II and
burglary; Judge 30; Sentenced to training school.
All 3 spent less than a year in training school

376　Victim=Black Latin Male, 30; Sept. 15, 1980;
Tract=58.01; 0622; MPD;　　The V was a Mariel
Refugee who was cut on the arm during a bar fight
and bled to death (he was found lying beside his
car and there was a trail of blood leading to the
bar). V had alcohol level of .12.

Offender=Unknown

377　Victim=Latin Male, 46; Sept. 6, 1980; Tract=20.02;
0340; MPD;　　The V got involved in an argument
with an acquaintance in a grocery store when he
ran. The O chased him (first in his car, then on
foot). The O finally cornered the V, beat him
with a tire iron, and drove off. The V died of
these injuries. O is thought to be a Haitian
Male.

Offender=Unknown Black (Haitian) Male

379   Victim=Latin   Male,   23;   Sept.   16,   1980;
       Tract=13.00; 1145; MPD;   V became involved in
       argument at a bar. A gunfight erupted among a
       number of Latin Males. The V's brother (who was
       in bar with V) shot at O as he fled after killing
       the V. Several other persons were wounded during
       the shooting. V had alcohol level of .12.

       Offender=Latin Male, 32; identity known but not
       enough evidence to charge.

380   Victim=Latin   Male,   27;   Sept.   17,   1980;
       Tract=34.00; 0330; MPD;   V was Mariel Refugee
       who lived in "Tent City" (the   temporary refugee
       camp   in downtown Miami set up for boatlift
       refugees). V involved in argument in a bar which
       spilled over into the street. He was shot by
       unknown Latin Male. V had alcohol level of .18.

       Offender=Unknown Latin Male

382   Victim=Black Latin Male, 39;
383   Victim=Latin   Male,   59;   Sept.   18,   1980;
       Tract=101.12; 0100; PSD;   The two V's were
       found dead in a Lincoln Continental.   Both were
       involved in the drug trade. The older V was from
       L.A. and came here two weeks prior on drug deal.
       The younger V was also from L.A. but had apt. in
       Miami and was driver and "go-fer" for the older
       drug dealer, V. Appears that the two were ripped
       off for their drugs (not their money) before they
       could leave.

       Offender=Unknown

394   Victim=Latin Male, 30; Sept 6, 1980; Tract=47.03;
       1000; PSD;   The V was Columbian who had checked
       into a motel with another person. He was found
       the next morning by the maid shot to death.
       Police believe the killing was drug related.

       Offender=Unknown

396 Victim=Black Latin Male, 24; Sept. 13, 1980; Tract=52.00; 0125; MPD; V and the O, a L/M, had argued earlier in the day. V had cut O's girl two weeks earlier in an altercation. Earlier on date of this killing, O had shot at V and missed. V then went to O's house and broke a number of windows. O angry about all these events. O was riding on a "jitney" (small autobus) when he saw the V waiting on the sidewalk for the same jitney. O fired two shots from the jitney and killed the V.

Offender=Latin Male, 23; (Romero, Pedro); (80-19310); identity known and warrant issued but O is at large

397 Victim=Latin Male, 28; Sept. 14, 1980; Tract=11.01; 1950; MPD; V and 3 other L/M's were exiting their vehicle at an apt. complex when they became involved in verbal confrontation with 3-4 Black Puerto Rican Males. There had been a dispute over the Puerto Ricans moving into the complex and also arguments over a woman. One night before the V and another had broken out windows and shot into an apt. belonging to the other "gang." First a friend of the V was shot by one B/L/M and the V took him to the hospital. When he returned the V was grabbed by the same group and also shot. The V died but the first shooting victim (his friend) did not.

Offender=Black Latin Male, 23; (Romero, Pedro); (80-19309); charged with Murder I, attempted Murder I and use of firearm; Case Pending since O has fled and is at large.

399 Victim=Latin Male; Sept 16, 1980; Tract=64.00; 1745; MPD; V was a Mariel Refugee who became involved in an argument with two L/M's on the sidewalk in front of 200 domino players. V was stabbed and appears to be no witness (who will talk) even though the killing occurred in public view. V was known as a "mental case" and had alcohol level of .13.

Offender=Unknown Black Latin Male (Mariel Refugee), approximately 35; identity of offender unknown

400　Victim=Latin Male, 25; Sept. 21, 1980; Tract=27.02; 0200; MPD;　V was at bar when five Mariel Refugees came in and started argument with the barmaid. V told them to leave her alone, an argument ensued, and one of the Refugees shot the V. The Refugees tried to flee to NY by plane but were arrested at airport.

Offender=Latin Male, 35; (Quevedo, Christabal); (80-17869); Charged with Murder II and use of firearm; jury trial; Judge 04; convicted of agg. assault; Sentenced to 5 years in prison (with 3 year mandatory minimum for use of firearm). Offender=Latin Male, 36; (Quevedo, Pedro); Charged with Murder II and use of firearm; jury trial; Judge 04; convicted on both counts; Sentenced to life (this O was the shooter).

403　Victim=Latin Male, 23; Sept 25, 1980; Tract=60.01; 0100; PSD;　V and his estranged wife were having domestic problems. The wife (the O) called V on phone and asked to talk with him, she then drove to his house. When he came out to the front yard to meet her she shot him.

Offender=Latin Female, 19; (Corral, Aymee Camejo); (80-18266); Charged with Murder I and use of firearm; jury trial; Judge 19; Convicted of Murder II and use of firearm; Sentenced to 3 years in prison (with mandatory minimum of 3 years before parole eligibility for use of firearm).

404　Victim=Latin Male, 32; Sept. 25, 1980; Tract=16.02; 0119; HPD;　The V and another L/M (both Mariel Refugees) were in process of robbing a convenience store. The other robber shot the V one time. The bullet travelled thru the clerk's shoulder and struck the first robber (the V) in the chest. The shooter was charged with felony murder.

Offender=Latin Male, 30; (Morales-Morejon, Leonelo); (80-18200); Charged with Murder I, attempted Murder I, robbery, and use of firearm; pled to Murder II, attempted murder I, robbery and use of firearm; Judge 01; Sentenced to three concurrent life terms.

405   Victim=Black Latin Male, 26; Sept 25, 1980; Tract=13.00; 1140; MPD; The V and several other L/M's were at a bar (known for drug trade). V went into bathroom with 2 or 3 L/M's then several shots were heard and V found shot to death. Police believe he was robbed but that original dispute was over drugs.

Offender=Unknown Latin Males

408   Victim=Latin Male, 20;
409   Victim=Latin Male, 26; Sept 27, 1980; Tract=13.00; 1045; MPD; The two V's were in a bar known for drug trade (see case 405) when an argument broke out that resulted in a shootout. An unknown L/M shot both V's.

Offender=Unknown Latin Male

411   Victim=Latin Male, 31; Sept 28, 1980; Tract=36.02; 0020; MPD; The V and another L/M were robbed and shot while at a bar. One of the robbers shot the V twice in the head while an accomplice took a gold chain from the V and went thru his pockets.

Offender=Unknown Latin Males, thought to be Mariel Refugees

412   Victim=Black Latin Male, 32; Sept 29, 1980; Tract=53.02; 0050; MPD; The V was a Mariel Refugee who was in a bar with two other Latin Males. (Earlier the V had been chasing and shooting at a woman). A friend of the woman came into the bar and recognized the V as the man who had been shooting at his (woman) friend. The O then started firing and killed the V and wounded another bar patron.

Offender=Latin Male, 24; (Colon, Juan R.); identity known but O at large

354

413 Victim=Latin Male, 50; Sept 29, 1980; Tract=2.01; 1320; PSD; V and another L/M set up an appointment with the O at an apt. (to buy or sell drugs). The O and a B/M ripped off the V and his partner. There was then a gun battle, the V was killed.

Offender=Two Unknown Black Males

416 Victim=Latin Male, 16; Oct 1, 1980; Tract=90.02; 1900; PSD; V and a friend (another L/M) went to the friend's girlfriend's house where friend got into altercation with girlfriend's stepfather who told them he didn't want them coming to the house anymore. O got a gun and shot both youths (the friend did not die). O claimed he only wanted to scare them away.

Offender=Latin Male, 36; (Aldondo, Eloy); (80-18820); Charged with Murder II, attempted Murder II, use of firearm; pled to Murder II, attempted Murder II, use of firearm; Judge 22; Sentenced to life and 30 years (concurrent) on first two counts and sentence suspended on use of firearm.

417 Victim=Latin Male, 33; Oct 3, 1980; Tract=52.00; 1945; MPD; The V was found stabbed under a tree and staggered to middle of street where he died. There appears to have been an argument earlier over money with the O. O was "somewhat crazy" and into a type of voodoo religion that is popular in Cuba. Police found drawings in O's apt. of the V under a tree, dead, thus killing was some type of ritual. V was retarded.

Offender=Latin Male, 41; (Rodriguez, Juan); (80-20108); Charged with Murder I; Judge 36; ruled incompetent, then (after 15 months) competent; Jury trial in July, 1982; not guilty.

419   Victim=Latin Male, 28; Oct 6, 1980; Tract=48.00;
      0205; PSD;   V became involved in a fight with
      his girlfriend inside of a restaurant. The owner
      told them to leave but the fight broke out again.
      When the owner attempted to break up the fight the
      V picked up a coke cylinder and threw it at the
      owner. When the V attempted to then thow a second
      object at the owner the latter shot the V. V had
      alcohol level of .10.

      Offender=Latin Male, 52;   No   charges   filed;
      Justifiable homicide

420   Victim=Black Latin Male, 32; Oct 6, 1980;
      Tract=101.08; 0230; PSD;   V began to date the
      girlfriend of the O. The O became jealous and
      shot the V. The murder was possibly drug-related
      as the O and V were discussing a drug deal shortly
      before the shooting. The V was a Mariel refugee
      while the O arrived in Dade from S. America two
      years earlier. V had alcohol level of .10.

      Offender=Latin Male, 20;   (Doxon, Allan);
      (80-19087); Charged with Murder I and use of
      firearm; jury trial; Judge 22; Convicted of Murder
      II and use of firearm; Sentenced to two concurrent
      life terms.

421   Victim=Latin Female, 34; Oct 7, 1980; Tract=52.00;
      1030; MPD;   V was found strangled in bed. V
      was involved in a lot of illegal activity (drug
      trade, stolen property) and had numerous
      boyfriends. Police believe some of this activity
      was the cause of her death. Motive and offender
      unknown.

      Offender=Unknown

423   Victim=Black Latin Male, 41; Oct 7, 1980; Tract=43.00; 0207; MBPD; V and the O were both Mariel Refugees. They were in a bar drinking (the V had alcohol level of .30). V asked O to buy him a drink, O refused, argument began. O then chased V out of the bar and caught him. O stabbed V twice with butcher knife (which O was carrying), V got up and O stabbed him 4 more times. V got up and again and ran but was caught and stabbed again (17 stab wounds in all). V was into selling drugs and dispute may have partly involved drugs. A passerby (with a gun) then chased O and caught him and had him spread-eagled on the ground when police arrived.

Offender=Black Latin Male, 25; (Ramirez, Lazaria Luis); (80-19135); Charged with Murder I; Jury trial; Judge 20; Convicted of Murder II; Sentenced to life in prison.

424 Victim=Latin Male, 51; Oct 11, 1980; Tract=21.00;
2105; MPD;   V and his common-law wife were
taking a walk when they were approached by 3 B/M's
who first asked for directions but then the first
O got out of the car and attempted to snatch chain
from neck of the V. V resisted and O pulled a gun
and shot him. The three O's then fled. The 3 O's
had been cruising looking for robbery victim. Two
weeks after this murder the first O and another
B/M killed a fellow robber (see case no.   447 in
Black List) and first O got life at 2nd trial. In
2nd trial co-defendant agreed to testify against
first O and told of first O's involvement in this
murder. This tip led to 2nd O (who was also in
prison) & he confessed. 2nd and 3rd O's
implicated first O. (The wife of Robbery victim
in this case was poor witness and thus state
relied on 2nd and 3rd O's stories.)

Offender=Black Male, 21; (Crompton, Sidney);
(81-24912); charged with Murder I and robbery;
Judge 37; Pending as of July 13, 1982.
Offender=Black Male, 21; (Mathis, Robert); charged
with Murder I & robbery; Judge 37; Pled to Murder
II; Sentenced to 15 years in prison.
Offender=Black Male, 19; (Porter,Gerald); charged
with Murder I and robbery; Judge 37; jury trial;
guilty of robbery only; Sentenced to 5 years in
prison. Jury may have felt that this O
participated in robbery but had no intent to kill
(though if they believed he was guilty of robbery
he should have been guilty of felony murder).

427 Victim=Latin Male, 31;
439 Victim=Black Latin Male, 21; Oct 11, 1980;
Tract=54.02; 1630; MPD;   The two V's attempted
(with guns) to rob a retail store but were shot
and killed by one of the two store employees (both
V's were Mariel Refugees).

Offender=Latin Male, 31; No charges filed;
Justifiable homicide

431   Victim=Latin Male, 52; Oct 14, 1980; Tract=90.01;
      1700; PSD;   V was killed in his bedroom by
      unknown person(s). Police believe the killing was
      drug related as V was involved in drug trade.   V
      was Columbian.

      Offender=Unknown

433   Victim=Latin Male, 34; Oct 17, 1980; Tract=49.00;
      1800; MPD;   V was Columbian and was confined to
      a wheelchair (as result of being shot in drug
      dispute in Columbia) and was attempting to get
      into his vehicle when he was shot numerous times
      by unknown occupants in a van. Police believe the
      killers were Columbians and that killing is drug
      related.

      Offender=Unknown Latin Males, probably Columbians

441   Victim=Latin   Female,   23;   Oct   19,   1980;
      Tract=24.00; 2200; MPD;   V and her husband had
      been having domestic problems for some time.
      Husband (the O) had been out of town and when he
      returned he found the V at home on the couch with
      another L/M. The husband then shot and killed his
      wife and then shot himself. Both V and O were
      Mariel Refugees.

      Offender=Latin Male, 28; (Balbuena, Antonio); No
      charges filed; O committed suicide

443 Victim=Latin Male, 42; Oct 22, 1980; Tract=49.00;
     1420; MPD;   The O believed that the V was
     having an affair with his wife. (O had been
     thrown out of the house by his wife 2 weeks
     earlier so they were not living together). The O
     planned to kill his wife so he went to her house
     (was let in by their son) and told the son to go
     to the restaurant and get his mother. But as the
     son left he heard gunshots and O fled the house.
     It appears that the O had shot the V (who was
     having the affair with his wife) prematurely as he
     planned to wait for wife's return and kill both
     the V and his wife.

     Offender=Latin Male, 37; (Hernandez, Roberto);
     (81-510); Charged with Murder I and use of
     firearm; Warrant hs been issued but O is at large.

450 Victim=Latin Male, 44; Oct 25-26, 1980 (found);
     Tract=101.09; 9999; PSD;   V found shot to death
     by a jogger in a field (V's hands were tied behind
     his back).   Police believe the killing was drug
     related. V had alcohol level of .18.

     Offender=Unknown

451 Victim=Latin Male, 25; Oct 27, 1980; Tract=5.02;
     0100; PSD;   V met the O, O's sister and another
     girl in bar (the two girls had heard of V
     previously but not met before this occasion).   V
     went with the three to a small airport where they
     engaged in drug use (smoked marijuana). For no
     apparent reason the O started beating V with a
     club and then started stabbing V with a knife (V
     was stabbed 13 times). The O did not even give a
     motive in his confession as he just said he didn't
     know why he did it. V had alcohol level of .17.

     Offender=Anglo Male,   25;   (Gray,   Duane);
     (80-21252); Charged with Murder I and robbery;
     pled to Murder II; Judge 02; Sentenced to life in
     prison.

469   Victim=Latin Male, 28; Nov 8, 1980; Tract=44.00;
       2035; MBPD;   V was in apt. with several other
       L/M's (all Mariel Refugees) when another Refugee
       entered the apt. and shot the victim 4-5 times.
       3 of the L/M's tried to take the V to a hospital
       in a car but got lost trying to find the hospital
       and left his body (he had died) on the street near
       MPD headquarters. The motive is unknown.

       Offender=Latin Male (Mariel Refugee), 25; identity
       known but not enough evidence to charge

470   Victim=Latin Female, 20;
480   Victim=Latin Male, 21; Nov 8, 1980; Tract=101.09;
       0020; PSD;   The two V's were both Columbians
       and were found shot at their home. The Male had
       his hands tied behind his back and feet tied while
       the right ear of the female had been cut off.
       Police believe that this killing was drug related.
       They believe that the two offenders were Columbian
       males who had been involved in several other
       "hits." One of the two suspected O's has since
       been convicted in another case (and received the
       death penalty) while the other is uncaught.

       Offender=Unknown, probably two Columbian Males.

471   Victim=Black Latin Male, 27; Nov 9, 1980;
       Tract=90.01; 2300; PSD;   The V and the O were
       both Mariel Refugees, were acquainted and
       frequented the same bar. They lived near each
       other and on this date V went home and found O
       going through his room (he lived in a home in
       exchange for maintenance). V punched the O and O
       left.   V told the family he lived with about the
       incident and that he feared the O because he was a
       "nut." Later that night the family heard the O
       outside their house making wierd sounds. The next
       morning the V was found dead (strangled) in his
       room.

       Offender=Black Latin Male, 24; (Quilla, Emilio);
       (80-21699); Charged with Murder I; prosecution
       pending since O found incompetent to stand trial
       and committed to forensic hospital; After 15
       months ruled competent; Pending;

472   Victim=Latin Male, 22; Nov 1, 1980; Tract=54.02;
0045; MPD;   The V and another L/M robbed the O
outside of a bar and fled. Later when the O left
the bar he was again attacked by the same two men
as he got into his car. The O reached into his
glove apt., got his gun, and shot one of the two
robbers. V had alcohol level of .15. All three
persons involved (the two robbers and the C) were
Mariel Refugees.

Offender=Latin Male, 59; No   charges   filed;
Justifiable homicide

473   Victim=Latin Male, 22; Sept 17, 1980; Tract=66.00;
0130; MPD;   The V was a Mariel Refugee who
lived in "Tent City" (the temporary camp in
downtown Miami set up after boatlift). He was
last seen by his roommate at midnight. When the
roommate returned at 1:30 AM he found the V on his
cot shot to death. The motive and offender are
not known

Offender=Unknown

474   Victim=Latin Male, 28; Nov 11, 1980; Tract=5.03;
1010; PSD;   V and his wife had been having
domestic problems. The wife went to V's place of
business (a body shop) and they became involved in
a struggle. The wife shot the V with a revolver
she had brought with her.

Offender=Latin Female, 34; (Figueroa, Lilith);
(80-21871); Charged with Murder II and use of
firearm; pled to manslaughter; Judge 10; Sentenced
to 7 years in prison.

476   Victim=Latin Male, 57; Oct 8, 1980; Tract=63.01;
       2135; MPD;   V (who lived 5 weeks) stated that
       he was shot thru the window while he was in his
       living room.   Police believe the killing was the
       result of a domestic argument.

       Offender=Unknown

479   Victim=Latin   Female,   41;   Nov   15,   1980;
       Tract=79.02;   0200; PSD;   V was shot by her
       husband during a domestic argument. V's alcohol
       level of .15.

       Offender=Latin Male, 42;   (Pulido,   Gilberto);
       (80-22118); Charged with Murder I and use of
       firearm; Judge 20; charges dismissed. The only
       witness to the shooting was present at bond
       hearing but upon advice from his attorney pled the
       5th amendment.   Then this witness disappeared.
       State got material witness bond but W could not be
       found before expiration of speedy trial rule.

483   Victim=Latin Male, 25; Nov 15, 1980; Tract=110.00;
       0135; PSD;   The V and the O (both Mariel
       Refugees and acquaintances) were in a parking lot
       drinking and an argument developed.   O pulled a
       gun and shot the V.

       Offender=Latin Male,   38;   (Cabrera,   Rafael);
       (80-22282); charged with Murder II and use of
       firearm; Judge 37; O ruled incompetent to stand
       trial; Pending;

486 Victim=Latin Male, 26;

505 Victim=Black Latin Male, 34; Nov 17, 1980; Tract=59.02; 0115; PSD; The two V's were Mariel Refugees and were attending a religious (the "voodoo" religion popular in Cuba) meeting. An argument broke out between the owner of the residence where ceremonies taking place and the two victims. At one point the V's tried to take a necklace from the owner (the O). The O drew a gun and shot both. He then went to his car to reload and came back and shot them both again. V's had alcohol level of .16 and .21.

Offender=Latin Male, 28; (Hernandez, Ramiro); (80-22245); Charged with 2 counts of Murder II and use of firearm; pled to 2 counts of manslaughter and use of firearm; Judge 08; Sentenced to 10 years in prison.

491 Victim=Latin Female, 24; Nov 17, 1980; Tract=48.00; 0600; PSD; The V was dating a big drug dealer. She had been given cocaine to sell but kept back part of money received and this angered her drug dealer/boyfriend so he had two of his men "hit" her. She was shot while driving her car. After being shot she stopped her car, got out and was assisted by unknown witness. The hit men then made a U-turn and came back. One O got out of his car and shot the V several more times. The O's were involved in several murders, the first is now under death penalty (which was eventually overturned by Fl Supreme Court, see case no. 524 & 525) for another murder and the second is at large. The V was a Columbian and police believe her two killers are also Columbians.

Offender=Latin Male (Columbian), 22; (Jaramillo, Anibal); (80-24457); Charged with Murder I and use of firearm; jury trial; Judge 09; found not guilty even though this O's prints found at scene.
Offender=Latin Male (Columbian); identity known but not enough evidence to charge

494   Victim=Latin Male, 45; Nov 18, 1980; Tract=76.04;
      1750; PSD;   V was involved with the drug trade
      and part of a gang of Cubans that was selling
      drugs. It appears that some Columbians wanted to
      take over the gang's business (to cut out the
      middle-man) and sell the drugs on the street that
      they smuggled in.   Thus this V was "hit" to
      eliminate him. V was shot as he changed a sign in
      front of his restaurant. The Columbian hit men
      who are suspected have been involved in several
      murders.

      Offender=Unknown, but police believe two Columbian
      Males are the O's but there is not enough evidence
      to charge.

496   Victim=Latin Male, 37; Nov 19, 1980; Tract=64.00;
      1800; MPD;   The   V became involved in   an
      argument with another Latin Male at a Latin Night
      club over a bill. O pulled a gun and shot the V
      (V had alcohol level of .13).

      Offender=Latin Male, 37;   (Tacoronte,   Felix);
      (80-23404); Charged with Murder I and use of
      firearm; jury trial; Judge 04; convicted of Murder
      II and use of firearm; Sentenced to life in
      prison.

497   Victim=Latin Male, 41; Nov 20, 1980; Tract=37.02;
      2020; PSD;   The V owned a service station and
      was found dead (shot) at the station.   Police
      believe there may have been a robbery or theft as
      he had been working on a car (changing tires) and
      the car was gone as was the cash (owner's gun was
      also missing though he was known to be armed).

      Offender=Unknown

498 Victim=Latin Male, 27; Nov 23, 1980; Tract=107.01;
2100; PSD;   The V and the O lived at a labor
camp (the V was a Mexican and O was Mexican or
Puerto Rican) and had a longstanding feud. O went
and got gun (after argument) and came back and
shot the V. V had alcohol level of .26.

Offender=Latin   Male,   26;   (Barrera,   Jose);
(80-022755); Charged with Murder I and use of
firearm; pled to manslaughter & use of firearm;
Judge 01; Sentenced to 5 years on each count
(concurrent). Though convicted of use of firearm
record indicates that the 3 year mandatory minimum
was not imposed.

500 Victim=Latin Male, 61; Nov 24, 1980; Tract=37.01;
1900; MBPD;   V was taxi driver who picked up a
fare at bus terminal.   Later police were
dispatched to a fight and upon their arrival they
found the driver shot in his cab and cab crashed
into wall. The driver had been robbed. At first
appeared there were no witnesses but then polie
found another cab driver who had seen a B/M get
into cab and 2 B/F's (prostitutes) saw the actual
fight and crash of the cab and O fleeing. One
B/F agreed to cooperate and gave leads that led to
arrest of this O. She picked out his picture from
mug shots at police HQ. Case relies upon this
witness.

Offender=Black   Male,   19;   (Bastion,   Glenn);
(82-10181); Charged with Murder I, robbery and use
of firearm; Judge 38; Pending as of July 13, 1982.

501 Victim=Latin   Female,   28;   (Nov   24,   1980);
Tract=57.02;   2250;   MPD;   The   V   and   her
boyfriend had been living together.   They began
arguing on this particular evening and during the
argument the boyfriend shot the V.

Offender=Latin Male, 30; (?????, Pedro); identity
known but at large

507   Victim=Latin Male, 21;
508   Victim=Latin Male, 26; Nov 25, 1980; Tract=115.00;
      9999; PSD;   Victims were both Colubians and
      involved in the drug trade. They were found in a
      field and had been shot, dragged and then rolled
      over (with a car). Police believe they were
      killed by other Columbians in a drug dispute.

      Offender=Unknown Latin Males, probably Columbians

509   Victim=Latin   Female,   53;   Nov   23,   1980;
      Tract=93.03; 9999; HPD;   The V was robbed and
      killed at her home. She had been doing business
      with two Mariel Refugees by selling jewelry to
      them. They evidently decided to rob her. She was
      later found dead by her husband, with her feet and
      hands bound.

      Offender=Latin   Male,   18;   (Palazio,Raul);
      (80-22896); Charged with Murder I and robbery;
      pled to Murder II and robbery; Judge 09; Sentenced
      to two concurrent life terms.
      Offender=Latin Male; identity known but not enough
      evidence to charge

510   Latin Male, 25; Nov 25, 1980; Tract=47.01; 2255;
      PSD;   The V had broken up recently with his
      girlfriend. He went to meet with the men who had
      been responsible for the break-up (to confront
      them about "lies" they had told). The V got into
      car with 3 of the men, witnesses saw a struggle
      inside the car and heard gunshots. The V had been
      shot. The V and the three offenders were all
      Mariel Refugees.

      Offender=Three Unknown Latin Males, approximately
      25, all Mariel Refugees.

515   Victim=Latin Male, 42; Nov 15, 1980; Tract=101.08;
      0100; PSD;   The V and the two O's were all
      Mariel Refugees.   The V was hired to live on a
      construction site (as guard) and wanted to quit.
      He went to home of his employer to quit and the
      two O's were there. When V left and went to a
      restaurant the two O's followed to talk him out of
      quitting.   The 3 got into a car and drove to
      remote area of west Dade. One of the O's then
      lured V out of car and shot him and threw him in
      canal.

      Offender=Latin Male, 41; (Campanioni, Carlos);
      (80-22397); Charged with Murder I and use of
      firearm; pled to Murder II; Judge 27; Sentenced to
      life in prison.
      Offender=Latin Male, 41; (Palli, Angel); Charged
      with Murder I, use of firearm, and accessory after
      the fact (this O did not shoot the V and was not
      aware of intent of other O but he did help throw
      body into canal); pled to accessory after fact;
      Judge 05; Sentenced to one year in prison.

522   Victim=Black Latin Male, 22;   Nov 6, 1980;
      Tract=34.00;   1820; MPD;   V was walking when an
      unknown Black Male made him walk into an alley,
      robbed him at gunpoint of $150 and then shot him.

      Offender=Unknown Black Male

523   Victim=Latin Male, 29; Nov 29, 1980; Tract=53.02;
      1830; MPD;   V forced his way into an apt.
      building where he entered the apt. manager's room
      at knife point and demanded money. A struggle
      ensued and the V was finally stabbed by the apt.
      manager with the V's knife. The V was a Mariel
      Refugee and had alcohol level of .16 and
      amphetamines in body.

      Offender=Latin Male; No charges filed; Justifiable
      homicide

524 Victim=Latin Male, 36;

525 Victim=Latin Female, 47; Nov. 30, 1980; Tract=101.12; 1900; PSD; The two V's were Columbians who were found in their residence bound and gagged and shot. A witness had seen two L/M's with guns approach the house about the time V's were killed. Police believe the two were victims of a "hit" by a Columbian drug ring. O was tied to crime by fingerprints on a butcher knife, bag & rope found by the bodies. The V's were shot 3 times each with a silencer equipped machine gun.

Offender=Latin Male, 22; (Jaramillo, Anibal); (80-24540 & 80-24457); Charged with 2 counts of Murder I and use of firearm; Jury trial; Judge 14; guilty; Sentenced to death (this is the O police believe was hit man in several Columbian murders). In July of 1982 the Fl Supreme Court reversed this conviction and set O free from death row. O had claimed he was at residence the night before the killing and left his fingerprints while cleaning out garage. Court ruled that prosecution failed to overcome this "reasonable explanation" as required by state law. Cout ruled there was insufficient evidence to convict and thus set O free and did not remand to new trial.

528 Victim=Latin Male, 53; Dec 3, 1980; Tract=20.01; 2310; MPD; V was a fence who was killed after a dispute over a gun he had previously sold to the O. The O regularly sold stolen goods to the V. The V was shot as he was standing at rear of his car examining a piece of jewelry (for possible buy). V had alcohol level of .13.

Offender=Two Unknown Black Males

529 Victim=Latin Female, 45; Dec 4, 1980; Tract=9.01; 1745; PSD; V was shot as she opened front door of her residence. O then fled the scene. Police believe the murder was drug related as the O had been making a number of calls to Columbia.

Offender=Unknown

540 Victim=Latin Male, 42;
541 Victim=Latin Female, 45;
542 Victim=Latin Female, 45;
543 Victim=Latin Male 30; Dec. 13, 1980; Tract=49.00;
     1030; MPD;   The four victims were found shot to
     death in their residence. Several weapons and
     drugs were found in the house. All four victims
     had benzo in their body. Police believe the
     killings were drug related.

     Offender=Unknown

547 Victim=Black Latin Male, 24; Dec 16, 1980;
     Tract=101.03; 1030; PSD;   The V was a Mariel
     Refugee who was shot and killed by three other
     Mariel Refugees on a dirt road near a nursery.
     Police believe the killing involved a dispute over
     the drug trade.

     Offender=Three unknown Latin Males, approximately
     25.

548 Victim=Latin Male, 22; Dec 8, 1980; Tract=36.02;
     1830; MPD;   V was a Mariel Refugee who was shot
     while walking on the street. Police do not know
     motive, however, the V had stolen a car and it is
     possible the O was retaliating for that theft. V
     had alcohol level of .20.

     Offender=Unknown

549 Victim=Black Latin Male, 28; Dec 11, 1980;
     Tract=36.02; 1950; MPD;   V was Mariel Refugee
     and was found shot to death in a parking lot. He
     had been in a bar a short time earlier. The
     Police have no idea as to motive unless it
     involved an argument in the bar.

551 Victim=Black Latin Male, 24; Dec 16, 1980;
     Tract=101.08; 2130; PSD;   V was Mariel Refugee
     who was shot to death at a constrution site. The
     police believe that V was killed by other Mariel
     Refugees in dispute over proceeds from a burglary
     (which they committed together).

     Offender=Unknown Latin Male, approximately 25.

552 Victim=Latin Female, 45; Dec 18, 1980; Tract=6.01;
     0050; HPD;   The V and her boyfriend   were
     involved in a domestic argument. The boyfriend
     (the O) got a gun, she (the V) ran to front lawn
     of their residence, O followed her and shot her.
     O was Mariel Refugee.

     Offender=Latin Male, 31;   (Botello,   Armando);
     (80-24738); Charged with Murder II and use of
     firearm; pled to Murder II & use of firearm; Judge
     05; Sentenced to 15 years in prison (with 3 year
     mandatory minimum for firearm).

555 Victim=Black Latin Male, 36; Dec. 19,   1980;
     Tract=29.00; 2325; MPD;   V was Mariel Refugee
     who attempted to rob the owner of a hotel/bar.   A
     friend of the bar owner saw what was happening and
     shot and killed the V/robber. V had alcohol level
     of .14.

     Offender=Latin Male, 47;   No   charges   filed;
     Justifiable homicide

557 Victim=Black Latin Male, 44; Dec. 20,   1980;
     Tract=52.00; 2315; MPD;   The V got into an
     argument with two Mariel Refugees at a coffee
     shop/gas station.   V called them Marielitos and
     they both drew guns and shot the V.

     Offender=Latin Male,   25;   (Barbon,   Rolando);
     (80-25093); Charged with Murder II, use   of
     firearm, and carrying concealed weapon;   jury
     trial; Judge 06; guilty on all counts; Sentenced
     to 30 years on the murder and 5 (to   run
     concurrent) on carrying concealed weapon.
     Offender=Latin Male, 20;   (Arocha,   Salvador);
     Charged with Murder II, use of firearm and
     carrying concealed weapon; jury trial; Judge 06;
     guilty on all counts; Sentenced to 30 years on the
     murder and 5 (to run concurrent) on carrying
     concealed weapon.
     (In both cases Judge 06 suspended entry of
     sentence on use of firearm thus avoiding 3 year
     mandatory minimum.)

558   Victim=Latin Male, 36; Dec. 21, 1980; Tract=60.01; 1910; PSD; V and other relatives were entertaining guests in their home when an argument (perhaps over "insult" about wife of one O) broke out between V and two of his guests (the O's both Mariel Refugees). Gunfight erupted and it appears V and the two O's (who were brothers) all had guns. It was a "wild west" shootout with 4-5 persons wounded including one O and wife and son of V. V had alcohol level of .17.

Offender=Latin Male, 36; (Martinez, Alfonso); (80-25153); identity known but at large (this O did most of shooting and his weapon was same calibre used to kill V).

Offender=Latin Male, 25; (Martinez, Angel); Charged with 3 counts of attempted Murder I, one count of Murder I and use of firearm; Charges dismissed; Judge 01. This O surrendered but his story was that V was first to pull a gun. Police did determine that family had hidden a gun owned and used by the V and lied to police. Thus family's story was contradictory and false at points. State could not disprove that V did not fire first and couldn't tie weapons of O's to V's body. If the first O is found that case will also likely be dropped. Judge 01. All the physical evidence indicated first O killed V and gun carried by second O was not cause of any injury. Five guns were in the house at time of gunfight so first O could have used self-defense and thus there would be no felony murder.

562   Victim=Black Latin Male, 27;
572   Victim=Latin Male, 39; Dec. 25, 1980; Tract=113.00; 2100; MPD; The O and the two V's (all three were Mariel Refugees) were arguing in a cafe. One V challenged the O to a fight. They all 3 went outside and the O shot the other 2. V's had alcohol levels of .19 and .00.

Offender=Latin Male, 25; O killed in a 1981 homicide. Police closed this case since O now dead.

563   Victim=Latin   Female,   31;   Dec.   26,   1980;
      Tract=88.01;   1215;   PSD;   V was in process of
      walking to her front door when she was   confronted
      by her estranged husband. An argument ensued and
      he began stabbing her with a knife.

      Offender=Latin Male; (Noda, Glodaldo); (80-25240);
      Charged with Murder II; pled to Murder II; Judge
      19; Sentenced to 15 years in prison

564   Victim=Latin Male, 45; Dec 27, 1980; Tract=24.00;
      0300; MPD;   The V owned a bar and became
      involved in an argument with his   girlfriend (the
      0) over a barmaid she wanted fired (due to
      jealousy). 0 had lived with the V since her
      release from prison and at time of murder she was
      already wanted for kidnapping. 0 shot V.

      Offender=Latin Female,   26;   (Castillo,   Daisy);
      (80-25328);Charged   with   Murder   II;   Judge   04;
      Charges dismissed

565   Victim=Latin Male, 44; Dec 27, 1980; Tract=64.00;
      1745;   MPD;   V   was   shot   outside   door   of
      restaurant/bar where he had just dined. V shot by
      L/M (his dinner companion) as they had argued
      during the   meal and after walking outside 0 shot
      V.

      Offender=Latin Male, 45; identity   known   but   not
      enough evidence to charge

566   Victim=Latin Male, 37; Dec 28, 1980; Tract=28.00;
      0015; MPD;   The   V and the 0 were both roomers
      in "fleabag" hotel. The 0 was a B/M and did not
      speak or understand Spanish. The V provoked the
      0, pulled a knife on him and backed him into a
      corner (other Latins present tried to calm the V
      to no avail). At this point the 0 (a soft-spoken
      and quiet man) pulled out a gun and fired a
      warning shot. When the V kept coming the 0 fired
      again and killed the V.

      Offender=Black Male,   22;   No   charges   filed;
      Justifiable homicide

567 Victim=Latin Male, 30; Dec 26, 1980; Tract=8.02; 1840; HPD; The V and the O were both Mariel Refugees and acquaintances. They had longstanding feud from Cuba. V and O had been in dispute for 2 days and threats were made by both. It appears O decided to "get" V before the V could do the same. So he went to his house and without saying a word shot the V in front of two witnesses, then fled.

Offender=Latin Male, 32; (Ballester, Eligio); (80-25395); charged with Murder I, burglary and use of firearm; pled to Murder II; Judge 02; Sentenced to 7 years in prison. State agreed to plea after almost lost case when only 2 witnesses (Mariel Refugees) "split". Witnesses found in Orlando and brought to Miami by force just before speedy trial period up. When O learned this he pled.

570 Victim=Latin Male, 32; Dec 26, 1980; Tract=42.00; 1719; MBPD; The V was shot by an off-duty police officer after the officer witnessed a fight between the V and a security guard. The V drew a gun during the fight with the other man and then turned when officer arrived and pointed gun at the officer. The officer shot the V.

Offender=Police Officer (Latin Male), 23; No charges filed; Justifiable homicide

574 Victim=Latin Male, 33; Sept. 12, 1980; Tract=101.10; 2210; HPD; V was at girlfriend's apt. and playing with a gun when he apparently shot himself. The V & girlfriend and others present were Columbian and took V to hospital. They all appeared to be in drug trade. Medical Examiner conducted investigation and decided this was a homicide. However, police believe it was a suicide and thus did reclassify it as homicide but list it as unsolved.

Offender=Unknown, perhaps a suicide

ABOUT THE AUTHOR

William Wilbanks received a Ph.D. in Criminal
Justice from the State University of New York at
Albany in 1975. He has taught in the graduate
programs at Sam Houston State University, State
University of New York at Albany and Florida
International University. He currently is an
associate professor of Criminal Justice at Florida
International University in Miami, Florida. His
primary reseach areas are homicide (several of his
published articles are listed in the reference
list of this volume), the elderly offender, the
female offender and race and crime. He may be
contacted at the following address:

Dr. William Wilbanks
Department of Criminal Justice
Florida Interntional University
Bay Vista Campus, AC-I-284
N. Miami, Florida 33181
(305) 595-6102